International and Development Education

Series Editors
W. James Jacob
Collaborative Brain Trust
American Fork, UT, USA

Deane E. Neubauer
East-West Center
Asia Pacific Higher Education Research
Honolulu, HI, USA

The *International and Development Education Series* focuses on the complementary areas of comparative, international, and development education. Books emphasize a number of topics ranging from key higher education issues, trends, and reforms to examinations of national education systems, social theories, and development education initiatives. Local, national, regional, and global volumes (single authored and edited collections) constitute the breadth of the series and offer potential contributors a great deal of latitude based on interests and cutting-edge research. The series is supported by a strong network of international scholars and development professionals who serve on the International and Development Education Advisory Board and participate in the selection and review process for manuscript development.

Series Editors
W. James Jacob, *Vice President of Innovation and International, Collaborative Brain Trust, and Fulbright Specialist, World Learning and U.S. Department of State*

Deane E. Neubauer, *Professor Emeritus, University of Hawai'i at Mānoa, and Adjunct Senior Fellow, East-West Center*

International Editorial Advisory Board
Clementina Acedo, *Webster University, Switzerland*
Philip G. Altbach, *Boston University, USA*
N'Dri Thérèse Assié-Lumumba, *Cornell University, USA*
Dennis Banda, *University of Zambia*
Carlos E. Blanco, *Universidad Central de Venezuela*
Sheng Yao Cheng, *National Chung Cheng University, Taiwan*
Evelyn Coxon, *University of Auckland, New Zealand*
Edith Gnanadass, *University of Memphis, USA*
Wendy Griswold, *University of Memphis, USA*
Ruth Hayhoe, *University of Toronto, Canada*
Yuto Kitamura, *University of Tokyo, Japan*
Jing Liu, *Tohoku University, Japan*
Wanhua Ma, *Peking University, China*
Ka Ho Mok, *Lingnan University, China*
Christine Musselin, *Sciences Po, France*
Yusuf K. Nsubuga, *Ministry of Education and Sports, Uganda*
Namgi Park, *Gwangju National University of Education, Republic of Korea*
Val D. Rust, *University of California, Los Angeles, USA*
Suparno, *State University of Malang, Indonesia*
Xi Wang, *University of Pittsburgh, USA*
John C. Weidman, *University of Pittsburgh, USA*
Weiyan Xiong, *Lingnan University, China*
Sung-Sang Yoo, *Seoul National University, Republic of Korea*
Husam Zaman, *UNESCO/Regional Center for Quality and Excellence in Education, Saudi Arabia*

Collaborative Brain Trust 45 W South Temple, #307, Salt Lake City, UT 84010, USA

Asian Pacific Higher Education Research Partnership East-West Center 1601 East-West Road, Honolulu, HI 96848, USA

More information about this series at
http://www.palgrave.com/gp/series/14849

Phan Le Ha • Asiyah Kumpoh
Keith Wood • Rosmawijah Jawawi
Hardimah Said
Editors

Globalisation, Education, and Reform in Brunei Darussalam

palgrave
macmillan

Editors
Phan Le Ha
Sultan Hassanal Bolkiah Institute
of Education
Universiti Brunei Darussalam
Bandar Seri Begawan, Brunei

University of Hawai'i at Mānoa
Honolulu, HI, USA

Keith Wood
Sultan Hassanal Bolkiah Institute
of Education
Universiti Brunei Darussalam
Bandar Seri Begawan, Brunei

Hardimah Said
Sultan Hassanal Bolkiah Institute
of Education
Universiti Brunei Darussalam
Bandar Seri Begawan, Brunei

Asiyah Kumpoh
Faculty of Arts and Social Sciences
Universiti Brunei Darussalam
Bandar Seri Begawan, Brunei

Rosmawijah Jawawi
Sultan Hassanal Bolkiah Institute
of Education
Universiti Brunei Darussalam
Bandar Seri Begawan, Brunei

International and Development Education
ISBN 978-3-030-77118-8   ISBN 978-3-030-77119-5 (eBook)
https://doi.org/10.1007/978-3-030-77119-5

© The Editor(s) (if applicable) and The Author(s), under exclusive licence to Springer Nature Switzerland AG 2021
This work is subject to copyright. All rights are solely and exclusively licensed by the Publisher, whether the whole or part of the material is concerned, specifically the rights of translation, reprinting, reuse of illustrations, recitation, broadcasting, reproduction on microfilms or in any other physical way, and transmission or information storage and retrieval, electronic adaptation, computer software, or by similar or dissimilar methodology now known or hereafter developed.
The use of general descriptive names, registered names, trademarks, service marks, etc. in this publication does not imply, even in the absence of a specific statement, that such names are exempt from the relevant protective laws and regulations and therefore free for general use.
The publisher, the authors and the editors are safe to assume that the advice and information in this book are believed to be true and accurate at the date of publication. Neither the publisher nor the authors or the editors give a warranty, expressed or implied, with respect to the material contained herein or for any errors or omissions that may have been made. The publisher remains neutral with regard to jurisdictional claims in published maps and institutional affiliations.

Cover illustration: © MirageC / Moment / gettyimages

This Palgrave Macmillan imprint is published by the registered company Springer Nature Switzerland AG.
The registered company address is: Gewerbestrasse 11, 6330 Cham, Switzerland

Preface and Acknowledgements

Moving to Brunei from the University of Hawai'i at Mānoa in the second half of 2018 to take up an appointment as Senior Professor in the *Sultan Hassanal Bolkiah Institute of Education* (SHBIE) at Universiti Brunei Darussalam (UBD), I found myself excited, energised as well as challenged by so many things I know so little about in this country, in its education system and the workplace. As a scholar researching, writing and teaching in international and global education more broadly, I would not allow myself to remain uninformed and indifferent to the very place that just became my new home and my new base.

While I proactively looked for readings, websites and newspapers that could help me gain some knowledge about Brunei, I soon realised that the best teachers would be my own colleagues, students, educational institutions and schools in Brunei. I attended as many seminars on campus as possible to learn about various research projects colleagues here were conducting. I sat in classes delivered by other colleagues to educate myself about different programmes and modules. I also helped other colleagues in giving advice and feedback to their students' projects. I walked to different units on campus to learn about different offices, their functions and the ways in which they normally operate. I am thankful to every colleague and every student who had their arms and hearts open to me in my first days, weeks and months in Brunei, and until today.

I eagerly attended the convocation at UBD on 16 August 2018, less than a month after my arrival. I saw with my own eyes so many young graduates appreciating their education. I was moved by the joy and happy tears from those graduates' parents and family members. I was again reminded of the fact that the first university in Brunei was only established in 1985, and this means that many of those graduates were among the first generation in their families that went to college. I was curious about the traditional costumes worn by most Bruneians that day. And I was speechless with surprise when His Majesty the Sultan graced the convocation with his presence. It was so impressive to see that the Sultan, the head of state, not only attended the convocation, but that he also gave an inspirational speech and hand delivered the degrees to each and every graduate that morning. This would not happen in most other countries and societies. I found myself filled with gratitude, appreciation, blessings and humility. I could see that education held an extremely special position in Bruneian society and among its communities. And during the convocation the special place of education unfolded naturally, generously and genuinely through smiles, laughter, tears, hugs, photos and quiet moments of reflections. I am grateful for this experience.

As I became a little more knowledgeable about Brunei and its education system and practice, and about my university UBD and my own faculty SHBIE, in October 2018 I initiated a series of workshops and seminars with my colleagues in SHBIE on research writing and project development. Through these seminars, I then learnt more about my colleagues' educational journeys, their research interests and their aspirations as scholars and teacher educators. They were all interested in doing research and writing on different aspects of the education system and teacher education in Brunei. And I found myself conceiving ideas for an edited book on Brunei's education so as to introduce and showcase a wide range of research work from my colleagues in SHBIE. I was thrilled to receive so much enthusiasm from my SHBIE colleagues as I shared with them the book ideas I had in mind. The starting point of this book was as simple and honest as this. As the ideas for the book were consolidated, I invited Prof Keith Wood and Dr. Hardimah Said in SHBIE to join me as co-editors. Prof Wood and Dr. Said specifically provided assistance to the chapters included in Part 2 of the book, which focuses on teacher education, curriculum and classroom practice. I thank Prof Wood and Dr. Said for their collegiality and continuous support throughout the book project.

And to my genuine surprise, the scope of the book kept expanding as I got to know more colleagues in other units within the university, and as I interacted more with students through my teaching of both undergraduate and graduate courses. In particular, the expansion and enrichment of the scope and contents of the book also resulted from the establishment of the *International and Comparative Education Research Group* (ICE) which I initiated in early 2019 at UBD. Through this research initiative, colleagues and graduate students from across the university and other institutions nationally and internationally have come together to build a mutual intellectual home in international and comparative education in its broadest sense. As I was exposed and introduced to more research areas and expertise from other colleagues and graduate students, I was able to see a larger picture for the book project. The book was no longer confined to teacher education, classroom pedagogy and curriculum development as initially conceptualised. Instead, I saw it spanning across disciplines and featuring interdisciplinary and multidisciplinary dialogues among scholars and researchers in education, languages and linguistics, sociology, anthropology, history, Islamic studies, creative industries and policy studies, as everyone would have something to say about education and its relations with globalisation and policy reforms. I saw these dialogues firmly anchored in the very dynamic and unique conditions of Brunei, which I strongly felt the need to explore, examine, understand and communicate with the world.

And to enable this aspiration to fruition, I invited Dr. Azmi Mohamad, an inspiring scholar of Contemporary Islamic Thought, who was then a lecturer at Universiti Brunei Darussalam (UBD), to join the book project as another co-editor. Dr. Azmi Mohamad played a key role in co-developing the project and made significant contributions to the diversification of authors and contents of the ten chapters in Part 1 and Part 3 of the book, which pay particular attention to the multiple roles that *Melayu Islam Beraja* (MIB) or *Malay Islamic Monarchy*—Brunei's national philosophy—play in the Bruneian society and across its education system. As the book was progressing well in every way, Dr. Azmi Mohamad was recruited by the Ministry of Foreign Affairs, and his new appointment and departure from the University in August 2020 meant that he would no longer be able to continue with the book as co-editor, author and co-author. While he had to formally withdraw from the book, he still kindly helped several contributing authors with their respective chapters as much as he could before he officially commenced his new appointment. I am forever indebted to Dr. Azmi Mohamad for his generosity, intellectual depth and sophistication, and his dedication to the whole book project. This book is not possible without his contribution and co-leading role, at least for all the time he was part of it.

When Dr. Azmi Mohamad left, I felt strongly that the book project would need another co-editor who would be able to continue Dr. Azmi Mohamad's role. And Dr. Asiyah Kumpoh in the *Faculty of Arts and Social Sciences* was very kind to accept my invitation to step up, and together with me she took charge of the chapters in Part 1 and Part 3. Dr. Kumpoh demonstrated the highest sense of commitment and worked extremely diligently with me and the authors to ensure all their chapters were completed and delivered in good shape. Dr. Kumpoh never said no, was always very modest and always strived her best to contribute and share the editorial responsibilities. I cannot thank Dr. Asiyah Kumpoh enough for the role she has played in this book project. Alongside Dr. Asiyah Kumpoh was Dr. Rosmawijah Jawawi who joined the editor team a little later. Despite her extremely busy schedules as Dean of *Sultan Hassanal Bolkiah Institute of Education* at UBD, who also works closely with the Ministry of Education, Dr. Jawawi was able to contribute to the book project via her extensive knowledge about, and her established expertise and experience in the education system, teacher education and educational policy reforms in Brunei for the past decades, and via her first-hand capacities in various leadership roles.

I would also like to highlight the steady and strong contributions from the *International and Comparative Education Research Group* (ICE) at UBD for its whole seminar series on 'COVID-19, Society and Education' that later formed the final part of the book with four chapters (Part 4). The contributing authors of these chapters had to work on their writing under a much tighter timeline and with much less available resources because of the novelty of the topic. Nonetheless, they showed an admirable commitment and were able to deliver their chapters with high flying colours.

This book, all in all, has been the result of collective efforts and hard work from all the co-editors and all the contributing authors. I would also like to thank Dr. Nur Raihan Mohamad, lecturer in the Faculty of Arts and Social Sciences at UBD, and Dr. Najib Noorashid, research assistant in the International and Comparative Education Research Group, for their help with copy editing. Their thoroughness and attention to detail helped tremendously in giving all the chapters a clean and smart look. Going through a huge list of references and checking religious terms for accuracy and consistency throughout the chapters was in and of itself a demanding job. I am greatly appreciative of their work and their willingness to work under a tight timeline and across two languages, English and Malay.

The project has also received continuous support and encouragement from the university, particularly UBD Vice Chancellor Datin Dr. Anita Abdul Aziz, UBD Special Academic Advisor Chair Professor Dr. Tong Chee Kiong, and UBD Assistant Vice Chancellor and Vice President (Research) Dr. Abby Tan. Many other colleagues at UBD have expressed much enthusiasm about the book and conveyed their congratulations to the book editors and contributing authors. I feel very honoured and humbled by everyone's good wishes and eagerness about the publication of the book. It does feel special that this collection is truly the first book in English on Brunei's education system and its dynamic relations with globalisation and policy reform.

Seeing the entire manuscript coming together in this solid form has moved me to tears. The two-year journey has come to fruition. Through this journey, I have made many friends, been enriched and nourished by the kindness, humility and care given to me by so many individuals. I am most grateful for the trust that all of us have built among one another as we have progressed with this book. I believe we all hold it dear in our hearts. Thank you to Brunei, Universiti Brunei Darussalam, and colleagues and students for all what you have done for me and my being here for the past over two years!

Bandar Seri Begawan　　　　　　　　　　　　　　　　　　　　　　Phan Le Ha
Brunei Darussalam
3 January 2021

Praise for *Globalization, Education, and Reform in Brunei Darussalam*

"This book is a thoughtful and timely contribution to scholarly literature showcasing the transformative agenda of current day education in Brunei. The relatively new Bruneian higher education system has come a long way since the mid-80s and is undergoing a sustained period of massive reform. In reflecting this, the studies showcased in the book provide examples of Bruneian's strong commitment to quality education.

The carefully selected chapters of the book encompass a wide scope of multidisciplinary studies, from teacher education and curricular reform—including its internationalisation—to pedagogical practices that promote truly inclusive education and cater for the needs of ethnic minorities in the mainstream formal education, and from the role of state actors and policy makers in education to contemporary themes that explore the complexities inherent in education during the current global pandemic. Of particular note is an entire section dedicated to *Melayu Islam Beraja*, the quintessential philosophy behind Brunei's education that makes it unique and exemplary at the same time.

All these chapters are sensitively written and consider the historical situatedness of the changing ideologies and policy priorities in contemporary Brunei, and the role of education in nation building in the backdrop of globalisation and the internationalisation of education.

The book has a robust international outlook, thanks to the editors' inclusive, culturally and ideologically sensitive approach to diversity. Together the carefully selected chapters open new avenues and possibilities for future scholarship and offer opportunities for scholars to bring Brunei into the forefront of international debates on education."

—Raqib Chowdhury, *Senior Lecturer, Faculty of Education, Monash University, Australia*

"This is a welcomed edition that provides a comprehensive investigation into the Brunei education system in a critical and evidence-rich manner. The editors and authors not only marshal in-depth insights into the intricate workings of education reforms, teacher education and pedagogical approaches in general, but also furnish timely accounts of how the COVID-19 pandemic has impacted the Brunei education landscape and the actions that educators have put in place. The issues discussed are not only relevant to Brunei and Southeast Asia, but also speak to

broader issues of education inequalities brought along by globalisation. As such, this edited volume provides an invaluable resource for scholars of international and comparative education studies, teacher education, migration and sociology of education research fields to develop a deep understanding of education in Southeast Asia and beyond."
—Cora Lingling Xu, *Assistant Professor, Education, Durham University, UK*

"This book provides a fascinating account of the dynamics of globalisation, nation-building, education and reform in Brunei Darussalam. The book responds to the need for a comprehensive account of Brunei's remarkable success in reforming its education system along the lines of its national philosophy, Malayu Islam Beraja (MIB), first officially proclaimed when the country achieved independence from Great Britain in 1984. The twenty chapters in the book, written by specialists on different aspects of Brunei's education system, are organised around the four overlapping themes of history and culture, curriculum and pedagogy, teacher training, and education and society.

There has been no previous scholarly publication on the scale of this book about the education system in Brunei Darussalam. As well as throwing light on the system, the book provides a case study of how an education system built on Islamic thought can successfully negotiate contemporary social issues and the need to prepare students for global engagement."
—Martin Hayden, *Emeritus Professor, Higher Education, Southern Cross University, Australia*

Contents

1 **Contextualising Globalisation, Education and Reform in Brunei Darussalam**   1
Phan Le Ha, Asiyah Kumpoh, Keith Wood, Rosmawijah Jawawi, and Hardimah Said

Part I   Contextualising Brunei and Its Education System: History, Ideology and Major Reforms   19

2 **History and Development of the Brunei Education System**   21
Norhazlin Muhammad and Mohamad Iskandar Petra

3 **Malay, Muslim and Monarchy: An Introduction to Brunei Darussalam and Its National Identity**   45
Salbrina Sharbawi and Shaikh Abdul Mabud

4 ***Melayu Islam Beraja* in the *Titahs* of His Majesty the Sultan of Brunei (2011–2020): The Leader's Transformative Vision and Aspirations**   67
Muzhafar Marsidi

5 MIB and Islamic Education in Brunei Darussalam: An Overview 85
Norhazlin Muhammad and Mohammad Hilmy Baihaqy

Part II Curriculum and Pedagogical Issues, Teachers' Knowledge and Beliefs, and New Developments 105

6 From Pedagogical Beliefs to Implementation: The Development of Pre-Service Teachers' Technology, Pedagogy and Content Knowledge for Student-Centred Learning 107
Sallimah Mohd. Salleh, Juraidah Musa, Marlizayati Johari, and Noraisikin Sabani

7 Beginning Teachers' Use of a Constructivist Teaching Approach to Improve their Students' Understanding of Science Through Classroom Discussion 133
Hardimah Said

8 The Development and Growth of Inclusive Education in Brunei Darussalam 151
Siti Norhedayah Abdul Latif, Rohani Matzin, and Aurelia Escoto-Kemp

9 Using Role-Play to Teach Minority Ethnic Languages: A Case Study at Universiti Brunei Darussalam 177
Norazmie Yusof and Yabit Alas

10 Standardised Testing and Students' Wellbeing: A Global or Local Problem? 197
Siti Norhedayah Abdul Latif

Part III	MIB in Teacher Training, Curriculum, Classroom Practice, and Society	217
11	Training MIB Among Teachers in Brunei's Religious Teachers University College Nazirul Mubin Ahad and Mohammad Hilmy Baihaqy	219
12	Internalisation Strategies of the Malay Islamic Monarchy Philosophy in Year 7 Curriculum in Brunei Darussalam Abu Bakar Madin, Rozaiman Makmun, Suraya Tarasat, Noradinah Jaidi, Sri Kartika A. Rahman, and Najib Noorashid	235
13	Malay Language and MIB Teacher Educators' Perceptions of the Year 7 MIB Curriculum Abu Bakar Madin, Rozaiman Makmun, Suraya Tarasat, Noradinah Jaidi, Sri Kartika A. Rahman, and Najib Noorashid	261
14	The Integration of Quranic Spiritual Knowledge in Brunei Darussalam's Science Education Curriculum Mohammad Hilmy Baihaqy	285
15	MIB Beyond the Classroom: Local Influencers and Their Impact on the Public Understanding of the State Philosophy Nazirul Mubin Ahad	305
Part IV	COVID-19, Society and Education	323
16	COVID-19: Educational Practices and Responses in Brunei Darussalam Masitah Shahrill, Najib Noorashid, and Chester Keasberry	325
17	Higher Education Institutions in the New Semester: Moving Beyond 'Pandemic' Pedagogy Najib Noorashid, Phan Le Ha, Yabit Alas, and Varissa Yabit	355

18	**Digidemic and Students' Hysteresis During Online Learning**	377
	Meredian Alam and Chang-Yau Hoon	
19	**Student Experiences During COVID-19: Towards Humanistic Internationalisation**	393
	Chester Keasberry, Phan Le Ha, Mohammod Moninoor Roshid, and Muhammad Adil Iqbal	
20	**Wrap Up to Move Forward**	415
	Phan Le Ha, Asiyah Kumpoh, and Keith Wood	

| Glossary | 431 |
| Index | 435 |

Notes on Contributors

Nazirul Mubin Ahad Ph.D., is a religious and motivational speaker in Brunei, weekly speaker for '*Klinik Minda*' in Radio Televisyen Brunei. During his six years of more than 400 places of preaching, He saw the opportunity of *da'wah* towards the society through the media by any means of writing or lecture. He holds a PhD in Islamic Studies from Universiti Brunei Darussalam. He was also awarded a Master's Degree from Jordan University and the top student in Islamic University of Sultan Sharif Ali, and a Bachelor degree from the International Islamic University Malaysia. He is actively involved in presenting in seminars and writing articles, and he is currently an academic staff and the Assistant Director of Publication Centre in Seri Begawan Religious Teachers University College (KUPU SB), a member of PPPQ MABIMS (The Unofficial Meetings of Religious Ministers in Brunei, Indonesia, Malaysia, and Singapore), as well as Brunei Youth Leaders for the Commonwealth Meetings.

Meredian Alam Ph.D., is Assistant Professor of Sociology at Faculty of Arts and Social Sciences, Universiti Brunei Darussalam (UBD). He was formerly involved in Australian Research Council Discovery Project 'Fostering pro-environment consciousness and practice: environmentalism, environmentality and environmental education in Indonesia' from 2014 to 2019. His key interest in the area of international comparative education specifically situates in the current trend of global environmental education that has become a space for contemporary youth cultures and cultural capital modalities. He received a Research Higher Degree Award (Distinction) from the University of Newcastle, NSW, Australia.

Yabit Alas Ph.D., was the Head of the Malay Language and Linguistics (2006–2008), Director of the Language Centre (2009–2010), Director of the Continuing Education Centre (2011), Dean of the Faculty of Arts and Social Sciences (2012–2013), Director of the Continuing Education Centre (2013–2016) and Director of the Language Centre since 2016. His expertise is on Comparative Linguistics, specifically on the Austronesian Languages. His area of research is mostly on the Dusunic Languages spoken in the north Borneo. He is actively researching on Malay languages, especially Standard Malay and its relevance to globalisation. He set up and became the first director of the Borneo Studies Network (BSN) (2014–2016), whose interest is to enhance research on Borneo.

Mohammad Hilmy Baihaqy Ph.D., is a lecturer at Faculty of Islamic Development Management, Sultan Sharif Ali Islamic University (UNISSA), Brunei Darussalam. Previously he worked at Seri Begawan Religious Teachers University College (KUPU SB) for five years and served as a Deputy Dean at the Faculty of Education, KUPU SB. He specialises in the philosophy of Islam and science education. At the age of 28, he had successfully obtained his PhD from Universiti Brunei Darussalam (UBD). In 2019, he was a research visiting fellow at Temple University, Philadelphia, and George Washington University, DC.

Aurelia Escoto-Kemp is a Registered Educational Psychologist at Special Education Unit, Ministry of Education in Brunei Darussalam. She completed her training as an Educational Psychologist at the University of Otago, New Zealand. She holds a Bachelor of Arts (BA) degree in Psychology, a Master of Arts (MA) degree in Psychology, a Master of Education (MEd) degree in Educational Psychology and a Postgraduate Diploma in Educational Psychology. She is a member of the New Zealand Psychologist Board (NZPB), the New Zealand Psychological Society (NZPS), NZPS' Institute of Educational and Developmental Psychology and the Allied Health Professions Council of Brunei Darussalam. She is currently undertaking a Doctor of Philosophy (PhD) degree in Education at Universiti Brunei Darussalam.

Chang-Yau Hoon Ph.D., is the Director of Centre for Advance Research (CARe) and Associate Professor of Anthropology at the Institute of Asian Studies, Universiti Brunei Darussalam. He is also an Adjunct Research Fellow at the University of Western Australia, Chair of Academic Advisory Board of Brunei Research Centre, College of ASEAN Studies, Guanxi

University for Nationalities (China), and fellow at the King Abdullah International Centre for Interreligious and Intercultural Dialogue (Austria). Prior to this, he was Assistant Professor of Asian Studies and Sing Lun Fellow at Singapore Management University (SMU), where he was awarded the SMU Teaching Excellence Award in 2012 and SMU Research Excellence Award in 2014. He is an active researcher specialising on the Chinese diaspora, identity politics, multiculturalism, and religious and cultural diversity in contemporary Southeast Asia.

Muhammad Adil Iqbal is a PhD Candidate in Sultan Omar Ali Saifuddien Centre for Islamic Studies, Universiti Brunei Darussalam (UBD). He is a recipient of UBD Graduate Scholarship and is pursuing PhD in Islamic Civilisation and Contemporary Issues. He has earned Master's Degree in Defence and Strategic Studies from Quaid-i-Azam University (Islamabad), Political Science from University of the Punjab (Lahore) and Master of Philosophy in International Relations from Preston University (Islamabad). He has previously served at the Senate of Pakistan, Ministry of Foreign Affairs Islamabad, United States Agency for International Development (USAID) and British Council. He is an avid reader and occasionally writes for various national dailies of Pakistan. He is one of the associate editors for the *Journal of Islamic Governance*, Institute of Policy Studies, UBD. He is also the President of the UBD International Students Club (UBDISC), UBD, since 2019.

Noradinah Jaidi is Lecturer in Malay Language Education and Literacy at the Sultan Hassanal Bolkiah Institute of Education, Universiti Brunei Darussalam. She earned her Master's Degree in Education from University of Wales Institute, Cardiff, UK, and a Bachelor's Degree in Primary Education from UBD. She has researched and published journals on Malay language pedagogies and values in education.

Rosmawijah Jawawi Ph.D., is a senior assistant professor and the current Dean at the Sultan Hassanal Bolkiah Institute of Education, Universiti Brunei Darussalam (UBD). She received a Bachelor of Education from UBD, a Master of Education from the University of Leeds and a Doctor of Philosophy from the Institute of Education, University of London. Her research interests are teacher education, innovative pedagogies, assessment for learning, citizenship education, humanities and social sciences education. Her research collaboration projects include the Twenty-First Century Learning Design with Stanford Research Institute International

(SRI International), Comparative Study on ASEANNESS and Citizenship Education in Ten Countries with Oita University, Japan, and Systems Approach for Better Education Results (SABER) with the World Bank. She was involved with Virtual University for Small States Countries (VUSSC), Commonwealth of Learning for the curriculum design of Master of Educational Leadership in Singapore and Postgraduate Diploma in Education in Samoa. In 2018, she was appointed as the Acting Director for UBD-FPT Global Centre in Da Nang, Vietnam.

Marlizayati Johari Ph.D., is a lecturer at the Sultan Hassanal Bolkiah Institute of Education (SHBIE), Universiti Brunei Darussalam (UBD). She has been a member of the faculty since 2008. She joined SHBIE in 2008 as a Tutor, where she worked alongside Senior Lecturers teaching physics content modules and method of teaching in science education. Her research interests are in the areas of teaching and learning in science education, representation in science education and teacher education specifically in physics education.

Chester Keasberry Ph.D., is a lecturer in the Design and Creative Industries programme at the Faculty of Arts and Social Sciences, Universiti Brunei Darussalam (UBD). His academic pursuits have included learning design and technology, linguistics, communication and comparative education, and these journeys have brought him far afield, from the UK, to Australia, and even to Honolulu, Hawaii in the United States. His research interests include communication and media studies, the usage of social media in education, and the design of technology and learning.

Asiyah Kumpoh Ph.D., is an assistant professor at Faculty of Arts and Social Sciences, Universiti Brunei Darussalam (UBD). She received BA in History from UBD and MA in Asian Studies from Australian National University. In 2012, she was awarded her PhD from University of Leicester. She teaches Brunei history, research methodology, and philosophy and theories in historical studies. Her current research and publications focus on conversion narratives, the Brunei Dusuns, and the historical evolution of religion, culture and ethnic identity in Brunei Darussalam and Southeast Asia. She has served as the Vice-President (Brunei Darussalam) and the council member for the Malaysian Branch of the Royal Asiatic Society since 2017.

Siti Norhedayah Abdul Latif Ph.D., is a lecturer at the Sultan Hassanal Bolkiah Institute of Education, University Brunei Darussalam (UBD).

She obtained her PhD (Education) from Edinburgh University. Her other qualifications are in Master of Education (Psychology), University of Manchester, and BA in Education (UBD). Her areas of specialisation are in educational psychology, developmental psychology and assessment. She currently teaches at UBD and supervises PhD, Master of Education (by coursework and research) and Master of Teaching for Initial Teacher Training Programme. Her research areas are in the fields of teaching and learning, educational and developmental psychology, well-being of adolescents, mental health and assessment. She recently participated in a number of national research grants from the Ministry of Health such as a project for World Health Organization for Adolescents Friendly Health Services and Ministry of Education on Students' Wellbeing project. She is also invited to review manuscript for international journals such as *Journal of Personality and Individual Differences*.

Phan Le Ha Ph.D, is a senior professor at Sultan Hassanal Bolkiah Institute of Education, Universiti Brunei Darussalam (UBD) and head of the International and Comparative Education Research Group (ICE) at UBD. Prior to this, she was tenured full professor in the Department of Educational Foundations, College of Education, University of Hawai'i at Mānoa (UHM), where she maintains her affiliation, and senior lecturer at the Faculty of Education, Monash University, Melbourne, Australia. She has taught and written extensively on English language education, identity-language-culture-pedagogy, global/international/transnational higher education, international development, and education, educational mobilities, and sociology of knowledge. Her research work has covered many contexts in Southeast Asia, East Asia, the Asia-Pacific and the Gulf regions.

Shaikh Abdul Mabud Ph.D., is Associate Professor of Islamic Spirituality, Ethics and Education at the Sultan Omar 'Ali Saifuddien Centre for Islamic Studies, Universiti Brunei Darussalam (UBD). He is also the honorary Director General of the Islamic Academy in Cambridge, UK, where he has been based since 1983. Previously he taught at the University of Rajshahi, Bangladesh, and the University of Utah, Salt Lake City, United States. His main academic interests are in the area of education, religion and Islamic philosophy. He is the editor of Cambridge-based educational journal, *Muslim Education Quarterly*, which deals with the problems of Muslim education in various countries of the world.

Abu Bakar Madin (Abu Bakar Hj Madin), Ph.D., is Lecturer in Humanities and Social Sciences Education at the Sultan Hassanal Bolkiah Institute of Education, Universiti Brunei Darussalam (UBD). He obtained his PhD from the International Islamic University Malaysia (IIUM), a Master's Degree in Curriculum Studies from The University of Hull, UK, and a Bachelor's Degree in Primary Education from UBD. He has researched and published book chapters and journals on Pedagogy of Teaching Malay Islamic Monarchy Education, Malay Language, Values Education and History Education.

Rozaiman Makmun (Hj Rozaiman Makmun), Ph.D., is Assistant Professor of Malay Language and Literature at the Sultan Hassanal Bolkiah Institute of Education, Universiti Brunei Darussalam (UBD). He holds a PhD in Malay Literature Education from the Universiti Kebangsaan Malaysia (UKM), a Master's Degree in Malay Language Education from Universiti Malaya, Kuala Lumpur, and a First Class Bachelor's Degree in Secondary Education from UBD. He has researched and published books and journals on Malay Islamic Monarchy, Malay Language, Values Education and Malay Literature Education.

Muzhafar Marsidi (Ahmad Muzhafar Haji Marsidi), Ph.D., is a graduate researcher in the field of youth governance and Islamic ethics from the Sultan Omar 'Ali Saifuddien Centre for Islamic Studies, Universiti Brunei Darussalam (UBD). He obtained a Bachelor's Degree in Islamic Theology from the University of Jordan. Additionally, as a member of an Ash-Shaliheen Mosque youth committee, Brunei Darussalam, he actively participates in youth development programmes for the whole nation.

Rohani Matzin Ph.D., is a senior assistant professor at the Sultan Hassanal Bolkiah Institute of Education, University of Brunei Darussalam (UBD). She obtained her PhD (Psychology) from Curtin University of Technology, Perth, Australia. Her other qualifications are in BA Primary Education (UBD) and Master of Education (Educational Psychology), University of Sheffield, England. Her areas of specialisation are in Educational Psychology, Curriculum Design and Development, History Education, Sociology Education and Secondary Social Studies Education. She currently teaches at UBD and supervises a number of PhD, Master by Education by Coursework and by Research, and Master of Teaching students. She participated in research project activities involving research grants from the Ministry of Education and UBD. She has published in

Scopus-indexed journals and peer-reviewed journals. She also reviewed entries in local journals such *Brunei Darussalam Journal of Special Education* and *Journal of Applied Research in Education*, and in international journals such as *Journal of Education and Training* and *Journal of Global Research in Education and Social Science*.

Norhazlin Muhammad Ph.D., is an assistant professor at Sultan Hassanal Bolkiah Institute of Education, Universiti Brunei Darusaalam (UBD). She obtained her B Ed. Islamic Studies honours degree from UBD. In 2000, she joined UBD as an academic staff. She then pursued her study and obtained her M Ed in Islamic Education from International Islamic University Malaysia and PhD in Islamic Studies from the University of Birmingham, UK, in 2009. She was affiliated to the Sultan Omar Áli Saifuddien Centre for Islamic Studies, UBD, from 2012 to 2020 and held administrative posts as Deputy Director and Director of the centre. She was a Visiting Research Fellow at the Oxford Centre for Islamic Studies, University of Oxford, UK; and Visiting Researcher at the Prince Alwaleed bin Talal Centre for Muslim-Christian Understanding, Georgetown University, Washington DC, United States.

Juraidah Musa Ph.D., is a lecturer at Sultan Hassanal Bolkiah Institute of Education (SHBIE), Universiti Brunei Darussalam (UBD), since 2007. She obtained her degree in education from SHBIE, UBD, and Master of education Technology at University of Leeds, UK. She completed her PhD at Kings College London with a title of 'Enhancing Digital Literacy Skills While Playing Casual Games: Young People in Brunei as a Case Study'. She teaches technology in education modules such as Teacher, Pedagogy and Content Knowledge (TPACK), Digital Innovation and Learning. Her interests lie in the area of digital technologies in education.

Najib Noorashid Ph.D., graduated with Bachelor's Degree (Hons.) in Secondary Education (2011) and Masters in Sociolinguistics (2012) from Universiti Brunei Darussalam (UBD) and University of Essex, UK, respectively, and completed his Ph.D. in Applied Linguistics (UBD) in 2019. He previously worked as news journalist for Local News (2007) and news editor/director (2014–2015) for both Malay and English (World News) national broadcasting at Radio Televisyen Brunei. His research interests include multidisciplinary research of sociolinguistics, media studies, literary studies and education, and have since published in Palgrave Macmillan, Springer, Elsevier and *IJAL*, and will be published in Cambridge University Press, among others. He had worked as Adjunct Professor of English

Language at Seri Begawan Religious Teachers University College and has been working as a research assistant for several research projects in UBD and is currently an external reviewer and editor for manuscripts at Brunei's Dewan Bahasa dan Pustaka.

Mohamad Iskandar Petra Ph.D., obtained his BEng Honours degree and Master in Control Engineering from the University of Glasgow. In 2000, he joined Universiti Brunei Darussalam (UBD) as an academic staff. He then pursued his study and obtained his PhD in Biomedical Engineering from Aston University, Birmingham, UK. Since then, he has been actively researching on multi-disciplinary areas including smart sensors to Internet of Things (IOT) and advanced materials to energy. To date he has published over 50 technical papers, and most are Scopus-indexed. He has six patents granted and one is filed.

Sri Kartika A. Rahman is Lecturer in Malay Language and *Jawi* Education at the Sultan Hassanal Bolkiah Institute of Education, Universiti Brunei Darussalam (UBD). She earned her Master's Degree in Language Learning and Education from University of York, UK, and Bachelor's Degree in Primary education from UBD. She has researched and published books and journals on Malay language pedagogies, *Jawi* education and Values in education.

Mohammod Moninoor Roshid Ph.D., is Associate Professor of English Language Education and the Head of the Department of Language Education in the Institute of Education and Research (IER), University of Dhaka, Bangladesh. He completed his PhD at Monash University, Australia. He has several publications on English as a business lingua franca, materials development, discourse analysis, and graduates' employment published by Sage, Sense, Springer, Routledge, Multilingual Matters and Cambridge Scholars. His recent co-edited volumes are: *Engaging in educational research: Revisiting policy and practice in Bangladesh* (2018) by Springer, Singapore, and *The Routledge Handbook of English Language Education in Bangladesh* (2021).

Noraisikin Sabani Ph.D., is a lecturer and research coordinator for the Faculty of Humanities in Curtin Malaysia. Her research interest revolves around interdisciplinary areas of educational technology, Islamic pedagogy and comparative education, particularly concerning youths and their varying socio-cultural backgrounds. In her free time, she loves spending time with her nephews and nieces, and enjoys reading tremendously.

Hardimah Said Ph.D., is Lecturer in Physics and Science Education at Sultan Hassanal Bolkiah Institute of Education, Universiti Brunei Darussalam (UBD) over the last 14 years. She graduated from UBD with a degree in Bachelor of Science Education, major in Physics and minor in Mathematics. She was awarded her Master's Degree of Art in Science Education at the University of Leeds, UK. Her thesis on students' and teachers' understanding of physics concepts particularly focusing on the topic Newton's third law has been published as a chapter in the book *Successful Science Education Practices* edited by her PhD supervisor at the University of Melbourne, Australia. Her current interest is in the exploration of science and physics teachers' development in the dynamics of their personal and professional identity formation processes.

Sallimah Mohd. Salleh Ph.D., is a senior assistant professor at the Sultan Hassanal Bolkiah Institute of Education, Universiti Brunei Darussalam (UBD). She has 30 years of experience in teacher education. She pursued her graduate study and obtained her PhD in Education from the University of Southern Queensland, Australia, in 2005. She wrote her PhD dissertation on Factors influencing Bruneian Secondary Teachers' Use of ICT in education. Currently, her research interests are on teachers' professional development for twenty-first-century teaching and learning, innovative teaching and learning, and teachers' pedagogical beliefs.

Masitah Shahrill Ph.D., is a senior assistant professor and teacher educator at the Sultan Hassanal Bolkiah Institute of Education (SHBIE), Universiti Brunei Darussalam (UBD). She was appointed as a lecturer in UBD in August 2001 and pursued her graduate studies in Mathematics Education at the University of Melbourne, Melbourne, Australia. Her previous administrative appointments included the Programme Leader in Initial Teacher Preparation at SHBIE and the Director of Studies for the Office of Assistant Vice Chancellor of Academic Affairs, UBD. Her research interests lie in teacher education, mathematics education, higher education, teaching and learning, assessment and classroom research.

Salbrina Sharbawi Ph.D., is Senior Assistant Professor of Linguistics at the Faculty of Arts and Social Sciences of Universiti Brunei Darussalam (UBD). In addition to investigating the pronunciation of the English variety spoken in Brunei, her research also includes investigations on the evolving status of English in the country and the effects the development has on Brunei's language landscape and socio-cultural practices.

Suraya Tarasat Ph.D., is Senior Assistant Professor of Malay Language and Literacy Education at Sultan Hassanal Bolkiah Institute of Education, Universiti Brunei Darussalam (UBD). She received her D.Phil in Education from University of Southern Queensland, Australia. She holds a B.Ed (Hons.) from UBD and an MA from Malaysia National University. Her research interest includes classroom interaction and talk, assessment, teacher education, curriculum design, development and pedagogy, history education, values in education as well as students' learning strategies.

Keith Wood Ph.D., is Professor of Education at the Sultan Hassanal Bolkiah Institute of Education, Universiti Brunei Darussalam (UBD). He is also the Editor-in-Chief of the *International Journal for Lesson and Learning Studies* and an Executive Committee Member of the World Association of Lesson Studies. His recent publication: Wood, K. and Sithamparam, S. (2020) *Changing Teaching, Changing Teachers: Twenty-First Century Teaching and Learning Through Lesson and Learning Study*, London and New York: Routledge.

Varissa Yabit received her BHSc in Biomedical Sciences from Universiti Brunei Darussalam (UBD) (2018) and MSc in Clinical Pharmacology from University of Aberdeen (2019). During her time in UBD, she conducted an anti-bacterial and pharmacological research on a traditional plant (*Melastoma malabathricum*) that was commonly found in Brunei. She also had the opportunity to do her internship in the Department of Pharmacology at Kagawa University (2016) and the Department of Parasitology at Universiti Putra Malaysia (2017). Whilst her research interests are in the medicinal and herbal actions of various traditional plants in Brunei Darussalam, she has also developed an interest in the study on comparative education focusing on internationalisation, social mobility and higher education in Brunei Darussalam and beyond. She researched on the effects of COVID-19 on education during her term as a research assistant at the International and Comparative Education (ICE), UBD.

Norazmie Yusof joined the Language Centre, Universiti Brunei Darussalam (UBD) in 2014. He currently teaches Brunei Ethnic Language (Dusun Language), Malay for Beginners and Basic Practical Malay. Apart from teaching, he was selected as the Co-Investigator for Community Engagement in Education (CEiE) Project 1 for Early Childhood Education in Sultan Hassanal Bolkiah Institute of Education, UBD (completed in 2017). He was an assistant researcher in UBD for numerous projects in 2013 and 2014. Since 2014, he has been active in writing, presenting and publishing research papers locally and internationally. His research interest is in pedagogy, Brunei ethnic languages and drama in education. He graduated with BA in Education (2010) from UBD and MA in Education (2012) from University of Warwick, UK. He recently completed his PhD in Linguistics at Universiti Malaysia Sabah (2020).

Abbreviations

21CTL	21st Century Teaching and Learning
ACCIE	ASEAN Co-operative Conference on Inclusive Education
AMIC	Active Mathematics in the Classroom project
APB	Academy of Brunei Studies
APTJSO	ASEAN Plus Three Junior Science Odyssey
ASEBA	Achenbach System of Empirically Based Assessment
BCP	Business Continuity Plan
BDQF	Brunei Darussalam Qualification Framework
BMTC	Brunei Malay Teachers College
BRC	Brunei Research Council
BTTC	Brunei Teachers Training Center
CARe	UBD's Centre for Advanced Research
CDD	Curriculum Development Department
CEFR	The Common European Framework of Reference for Languages
CK	Content Knowledge
CoE	Centre of Excellence
CoRT	Cognitive Research Trust
COVID-19	Coronavirus Disease 2019
CPD	Continuous Development Programme
CSPS	Centre of Strategic and Policy Studies
CUP	Conceptual Understanding Procedure
DBPB	Dewan Bahasa dan Pustaka Brunei or Brunei's National Language and Literature Bureau
DICE	Drama Improves Key Competences in Education
digidemic	digital pandemic
DPL	Designated Priority Levels
DY	Discovery Year

ECE	Early Childhood Education
EFA	Education for All
ESSA	Educational Stress Scale of Adolescents
GenNEXT	Generation Next (University Curriculum)
GHID	Global Halal Industry Development Division
GITC	Global IT Challenge Competitions
HBL	Home-Based Learning
HE	Higher Education
HEI	Higher Education Institution
HLP	Home-Learning Packs
IaH	Internationalisation at Home
IAU	International Association of Universities
IBTE	Institute of Brunei Technical Education
ICE	International and Comparative Education Research Group
ICT	Info-Communication Technology
IEP	Individual Education Programme
IHE	internationalisation of higher education
IRK	Islamic Religious Knowledge
ISE	Inclusive Special Education
ISPM	Inter-agency Student Progress Meeting
ITB	Institut Teknologi Brunei or Institute of Technology Brunei
ITP	Initial Teacher Preparation
IVF	In vitro fertilisation
JAPEM	Jabatan Pembangunan Masyarakat or Department of Community Development
KAFA	Counselling and Religious Understanding Unit
KUPU SB	*Kolej Universiti Perguruan Ugama Seri Begawan*
LAD	Language Acquisition Device
LATs	Learning Assistant Teachers
LC	Language Centre
LEAPS	Learning Programme Styles
LS	Lesson Study
MIB	*Melayu Islam Beraja* or Malay Islamic Monarchy
MMI	Multiple-Mini-Interviews
MoE	Ministry of Education
MoRA	The Ministry of Religious Affairs
NGO	non-governmental organisation
OECD	Organisation for Economic Co-operation and Development
PAI	*Pelajaran Al-Quran dan Pengetahuan Agama Islam* or Learning Al-Quran and Islamic Revealed Knowledge
PCK	Pedagogical Content Knowledge
PISA	Programme for International Student Assessment

PK	Pedagogical Knowledge
PMB	*Peperiksaan Menengah Bawah* or Lower Secondary Examination
PRB	*Partai Rakyat Brunei* or Brunei People's Party
QAA	Quality Assurance Agency
RE	Religious Education
RELA	Reading and Language Acquisition project
RTB	Radio Televisyen Brunei or Radio Television Brunei
S2S	Steps to Success
SAS	Studying At School
SBA	School-Based Assessment
SBT	School-Based Team
SBTC	The Seri Begawan Teachers College
SENA	Special Education Needs Assistant Teachers
SEU	Special Education Unit
SHBIE	Sultan Hassanal Bolkiah Institute of Education
SMJA	Sultan Muhammad Jamalul Alam
SMS	Short Message Service
SOASCIS	Sultan Omar Áli Saifuddien Centre for Islamic Studies
SOP	Standard Operating Procedure
SPA	Student Progress Assessment
SPCO	Syariah Penal Code Order
SPE	Student Progress Examination
SPN21	*Sistem Pendidikan Negara Abad ke-21* or National Education System for the 21st Century
TC	teacher candidate
TCK	Technological Content Knowledge
TK	Technological Knowledge
TPACK	Technology, Pedagogy and Content Knowledge
TPK	Technological Pedagogical Knowledge
TTE	Teacher Training Education
UBD	Universiti Brunei Darussalam
UNESCO	United Nations Educational, Scientific and Cultural Organization
UNISSA	Universiti Islam Sultan Sharif Ali
UTB	Universiti Teknologi Brunei or University of Technology Brunei
Vtech	Primary Education, Secondary Education, and Vocational and Technology Education
WALS	World Association of Lesson Studies
WSID	Whole School ICT Development
YSR	Youth Self Report

List of Figures

Fig. 1.1	21CTL Rubric for Collaboration (SRI, 2013)	9
Fig. 6.1	Technological, pedagogical and content knowledge	112
Fig. 6.2	Example of the teachers' use of the TPACK framework and knowledge dimension: (D) declarative, (P) procedural, (Sc) schematic and (St) strategic	119
Fig. 6.3	Example of teacher C's lesson plan for the declarative knowledge dimension	120
Fig. 6.4	Students using laptops and mobile phones to search for information on the Internet	121
Fig. 6.5	Lesson plan for the procedural knowledge dimension	122
Fig. 6.6	TPACK framework of procedural knowledge dimension lesson activities	122
Fig. 6.7	Students searching for cupcake recipes	123
Fig. 6.8	Lesson plan for the schematic knowledge dimension	124
Fig. 6.9	Students watching a YouTube video on baking cupcakes	125
Fig. 6.10	Lesson plan for strategic knowledge dimensions	126
Fig. 6.11	Collaborative interdisciplinary teaching for bake sale project	127
Fig. 6.12	Students' bake sale	128
Fig. 7.1	A example of a CUP worksheet	136
Fig. 7.2	A CUP worksheet designed by a teacher candidate	137
Fig. 7.3	Stage One individual answers	139
Fig. 7.4	Stage Two group answer	139
Fig. 7.5	The CUP worksheet by a teacher candidate	145
Fig. 8.1	The alignment of the Strategic Plan 2018–2022 to Wawasan 2035 and international declarations (Escoto-Kemp & Matzin, 2019)	159

Fig. 9.1	Krashen input hypothesis (2009, p. 16)	180
Fig. 9.2	The students during discussion	186
Fig. 9.3	The students during role-play	186
Fig. 9.4	Pre- and post-oral test	187
Fig. 10.1	Bar chart of highest percentage on items of Youth Self Report	207
Fig. 13.1	The core values of MIB (Brunei Curriculum Development Department, 2010, p. 10)	266
Fig. 14.1	Chapter 1 from the Year 7 secondary science textbook	292
Fig. 16.1	De-escalation stages of school operation amid COVID-19 (Ministry of Education, 2020, p. 2)	332
Fig. 19.1	Top host destination, 2019. (Source: A quick look at global mobility trends: Project Atlas, 2019, UNESCO, 2019)	396

List of Tables

Table 1.1	21CTL outcomes for teachers (21CTL 3 months follow-up questionnaire, n = 106)	10
Table 5.1	Number of schools, teachers and students in religious schools from 1956 to 1968 (Muhammad, 2014, p. 129)	86
Table 6.1	TPACK framework for the pedagogy, technology and content knowledge module	110
Table 6.2	Changes in Teacher A's practice after TPACK	115
Table 8.1	The impact of national policies and international declarations on Brunei's inclusive education system (1979–2018)	155
Table 8.2	Summary of SEU initiatives to implement and uphold inclusive education practices in mainstream schools between 1994 and 2019	162
Table 9.1	Research design	184
Table 9.2	Paired sample t-test of experiment group	188
Table 9.3	Paired sample t-test of control group	189
Table 9.4	Students' perception on teaching technique	189
Table 9.5	Students' perception on their confidence and understanding	190
Table 10.1	PISA snapshot on Brunei students' exposure to bullying	199
Table 10.2	A summary of concerns adolescents have in schools	207
Table 12.1	Content analysis of year 7 MIB textbook	240
Table 14.1	Summary of chapters and verses in the Year 7 secondary science textbook	300
Table 16.1	The number of schools in each cluster	328
Table 16.2	The government and private higher education institutions in Brunei	337

Table 16.3	Summary of teaching, learning and assessment approaches during the pandemic (Taken and adapted from Shahrill & Hardaker, in press)	339
Table 17.1	Public HEIs in Brunei Darussalam	357

CHAPTER 1

Contextualising Globalisation, Education and Reform in Brunei Darussalam

Phan Le Ha, Asiyah Kumpoh, Keith Wood, Rosmawijah Jawawi, and Hardimah Said

1.1 Setting the Scene

Writing about a single country's education is never easy, as you may wonder why there is a need to do so, particularly when such a country is so small like Brunei Darussalam (henceforth Brunei)—an Islamic monarchy located on the island of Borneo and with a population of less than half a million people. Many people do not even know where it is on the world map. But we will prove you wrong. Working on this book has taken us

---

Phan, L. H. (✉)
Sultan Hassanal Bolkiah Institute of Education, Universiti Brunei Darussalam, Bandar Seri Begawan, Brunei

University of Hawai'i at Mānoa, Honolulu, HI, USA
e-mail: leha.phan@ubd.edu.bn; halephan@hawaii.edu

A. Kumpoh
Faculty of Arts and Social Sciences, Universiti Brunei Darussalam, Bandar Seri Begawan, Brunei
e-mail: asiyah.kumpoh@ubd.edu.bn

© The Author(s), under exclusive license to Springer Nature Switzerland AG 2021
Phan, L. H. et al. (eds.), *Globalisation, Education, and Reform in Brunei Darussalam*, International and Development Education, https://doi.org/10.1007/978-3-030-77119-5_1

from one surprise to another; and this very spirit has kept us focused, determined and energised. Brunei's internationally-praised responses to the ongoing impacts of the COVID-19 pandemic, which has had a tremendous impact on societies and education globally, has also offered us new angles to approach education, policy, leadership and social aspirations.

This book is the first-ever book dedicated to the examination of the education system, schooling, teacher education and the relationships of Brunei's national philosophy *Melayu Islam Beraja* (MIB) or *Malay Islamic Monarchy*, its education and society in the context of globalisation and policy reform. These very areas deserve thorough and comprehensive discussion as well as in-depth intellectual engagement. Indeed, the existing literature on education in Brunei, in general, is rather limited. Apart from a small number of scattered book chapters, journal articles, reports and conference papers published on various aspects of Brunei's education (see e.g. Bradshaw & Mundia, 2006; Goh, 2014; Ismail et al., 2015; Kani et al., 2014; Mundia, 2010, 2012; Matzin et al., 2015; Seng, 2009; Sercombe, 2014; Shahrill et al., 2014; Wood et al., 2017; Wood et al., 2018), there has not been a single scholarly book that places Brunei's education and its dynamic and evolution on the centre stage. Likewise, within the rather modest published literature, discipline-based teacher education and classroom teaching have been the main focus, while other important aspects of the education system and their interactions with the society at large are under-examined. This book is, hence, a refreshing and much-needed reference as Brunei Darussalam is gaining more visibility in Southeast Asia, Asia, the Asia-Pacific region and in the world map.

As shall be discussed in greater detail throughout the book, over the past three decades a series of major education reforms have been witnessed in Brunei Darussalam: the introduction of bilingual education *(Sistem Pendidikan Dwibahasa)* in 1985; the introduction of a noble/moral values core curriculum at all levels of the education system, *Melayu Islam Beraja (MIB)*, in 1991; the introduction of a national curriculum for the twenty-first century, *Sistem Pendidikan Negara Abad 21 (SPN21)*, in

---

K. Wood • R. Jawawi • H. Said
Sultan Hassanal Bolkiah Institute of Education, Universiti Brunei Darussalam, Bandar Seri Begawan, Brunei
e-mail: keith.wood@ubd.edu.bn; rosmawijah.jawawi@ubd.edu.bn; hardimah.said@ubd.edu.bn

2008; the reform of teacher education in 2009 to ensure that all teachers enter the profession with a *Master's Degree in Teaching (MTeach)*; and entry to the OECD *Programme for International Student Assessment (PISA) in* 2018. New aspects of education, since the 1990s, have also been gradually introduced into the teacher education curriculum such as early childhood education, inclusive education and counselling. Brunei's increasing attention to STEM education and to how PISA might enhance the country's global rankings and its education performance have also been driving the country's educational reforms. The current vision for the education system (*Wawasan Brunei 2035* or Brunei Vision 2035) is intended to secure the nation's share of new opportunities and to rise to the challenges of participation in the global economy. Brunei Vision 2035 identifies education as one of its essential pillars for advancement, nation building, and for equipping young Bruneians with knowledge, skills and attributes required to be successful globally.

The above-mentioned policy reforms and transformations as well as aspirations for change in Brunei can be seen as organic transformations from within the sultanate, and as responses and manifestations of globalisation and changes taking place regionally and internationally. When globalisation as a process started remains arguable among scholars, however, globalisation 'came into use as a term during the 1990s' (Parr et al., 2013, p. 19). The term captures and reflects the world's noticeably increasing interconnectedness and convergences that can be seen in almost every aspect of life and at every corner globally (Appadurai, 1996; Friedman, 2005; Phan, 2017; Rizvi & Lingard, 2010; Stromquist & Monkman, 2014). In this very context, the borrowing and transfer of policies, ideas, discourses, practices, knowledge(s) and aspirations across borders has been on the rise and increasingly shaping many discussions about global, regional and local issues including compulsory education, gender empowerment, development, innovation, migration and climate change, among others. In the sphere of education, the promotion of, for instance, PISA and STEM by major international organisations and governments have both been driving and shaping global education, leading to endless introduction of educational reforms at varied levels (see e.g. Lingard & Lewis, 2017; Sellar & Lingard, 2018).

Global discourses and practices such as those mentioned above have tremendous impacts on national education systems as well as their teacher education and classroom practices. As Parr et al. (2013, p. 21) show, under these conditions 'teachers have to change, to reimagine themselves as educators in a globalising world, often having to unlearn their most fundamental assumptions about teaching, identity and educational work'. This unlearning process has come with many complications, raising scepticisms and debates surrounding the appropriateness of the 'global' in 'local' contexts. This process has also brought to the fore a sense of crisis among policy makers, educators, parents and students, who can recognise how 'local' values and practices are constantly challenged and dominated by multiple sets of desirable global values and norms. While globalisation has enabled many good changes, it has evidently caused many dilemmas, scepticism, tensions and burdens for national education systems and their teachers and students as well as society at large. Although there are similarities in how national education systems have responded to, accommodated to, and resisted globalisation, different national contexts have also showed their different approaches and unique stances towards this force (cf. Symaco, 2013; Harman et al., 2010; Hawkins et al., 2018; Neubauer & Collins, 2015; Neubauer et al., 2019; Phan & Doan, 2020; Sercombe & Tupas, 2014; Tsui, 2020, among others). In the process, national and local education systems, to varied extent, take into account their traditions, cultural values and religions as well as state ideologies in their attempts and consideration to change and transform. In the midst of all these complexities and mixed responses, obtaining more insights into and understanding of national and local educational contexts and their most affected populations is essential.

Taking into careful consideration all the above factors and realities, never before has the need to develop a book-length volume dedicated fully to education in Brunei been this urgent. This book, hence, is the first attempt to respond to this urgent need and gap in the existing literature and scholarship. It is also the first book dedicated fully to examining education, society and reform in Brunei Darussalam in tandem with global developments and the mobilities of reform policies and practices. These very areas deserve thorough and comprehensive understandings as well as rigorous engagement. Together with providing a historical understanding of what has been in place in the country's education, it also offers in-depth discussions based on policy analyses and empirical data. It tells Brunei's story of educational reform and change in its own language, narratives, accounts and unique standpoints. All of us editors and contributing authors are collectively convinced that the book will be a much-looked-for contribution to knowledge and scholarship on education studies in general and in international and comparative education studies in particular.

The book is inter/multi-disciplinary in nature, with scholarly work developed from various disciplines and informed by a wide range of methodological approaches. Many contributing chapters draw on significant historical and textual sources in three languages, namely Arabic, English and Malay. The book consists of four interactive parts, each of which focuses on a specific theme and builds on from one another, as we shall soon show in more detail.

In what follows, we are not going to discuss what each chapter included in the book is about, as the final chapter (Chap. 20) will take up this important task as a way to wrap up and open avenues for further work. Rather, as shall be seen below, we focus more on the key topics, issues and questions that each part of the book collectively addresses and examines.

1.2 Wawasan 2035, SPN21, MIB and Education in Brunei: An Initial Look

Part I, '*Contextualising Brunei and Its Education System: History, Ideology and Major Reforms*', features four chapters which collectively emphasise the history and development of Brunei education, both religious and non-religious education, as well as the transformative changes which have become more evident after the country gained independence in 1984. The discussion revolves around MIB and its philosophical foundations which have been responsible in shaping the development of the education system. MIB was promulgated as the national ideology of Brunei in 1984, concomitantly to the country's declaration of independence. Its direct relationship with Brunei's independence automatically defines its role in nation building and the country's national identity. Evidently, since its promulgation in 1984, MIB has essentially become the 'homogenisation agent of the country' and embodies the Bruneian identity (Kumpoh et al., 2017, p. 17). Although the components of MIB cannot stand on their own independently (Ibrahim, 2003, p. 111), collectively they demonstrate a remarkable political, social and cultural strength as they transform to become interlocking principles and a robust source of national solidarity, loyalty and respect. By the turn of the twenty-first century, there had been an increasing incorporation of MIB in national policies and government planning.

The centrality of Brunei's national philosophy, Melayu Islam Beraja (MIB), to the country's development and planning is evident in policies and strategies that have been implemented by the government since the

1990s. The most recent and pivotal of these policies and strategies are Brunei Vision 2035 and SPN21, both of which pursue excellence in knowledge and moral character based on the teaching of the MIB. Linked to these is teacher education, a programme that promotes teachers' proficiency and competence for improving students' learning in the context of Brunei, for producing a well-rounded generation who can preserve the country's national philosophy. This means that the MIB is both a means and a goal for Brunei's national development.

At the same time, considering the educational environment which is becoming increasingly competitive and globally exposed and affected, it is also pertinent to pay attention to the training of teachers and the professional development of teachers as teachers are required to align their expertise and experience to the changing functions and needs of the education system. In Brunei, the main institute for teacher training is Sultan Hassanal Bolkiah Institute of Education (SHBIE) at the Universiti Brunei Darussalam (UBD). SHBIE was first established as a teacher training centre, and in 1959 it was upgraded into Sultan Hassanal Bolkiah Teachers College. In 1987, it was then named as the Sultan Hassanal Bolkiah Institute of Education. In 1988, it was merged with the national university, UBD, which was established in 1985. Until 2008, SHBIE offered undergraduate teacher education programmes including certificates in education, diplomas in education, bachelor's degrees in education and the postgraduate certificate in education.

The main purpose for the establishment of SHBIE has been to provide and develop professionals as primary, secondary and technical school teachers, and educational administrators. SHBIE is guided by the belief that the professional education of teachers is an ongoing process. It begins with the initial teacher training and continues throughout the teachers' careers through their participation in upgrading and in-service courses. In defining 'quality teacher', SHBIE refers to Brunei Darussalam Qualification Framework (BDQF) where a quality teacher is defined as an educator who possesses the knowledge and competency at the master's level of BDQF, equivalent to Level 7 of Quality Assurance Agency for Higher Education (QAA for HE). In addition to using BDQF and QAA for HE as a reference for the definition of quality teachers, SHBIE also refers to several departments in the Ministry of Education so that beginning teachers acquire the expected criteria as quality teachers.

In its efforts to further raise teachers' quality and professionalism, SHBIE was transformed into a graduate school of education in 2009. This is a clear transformative milestone in the development of SHBIE as one of the leading providers of teacher training in Asia. Concomitantly, the Institute launched the Master of Teaching programme (MTeach), an innovative overhaul of the nation's teacher education, for three main reasons. First, it was a necessity to have teachers with in-depth knowledge of content and skills in their taught subjects. Second, it was necessary to improve the quality of teaching for an effective education system by having rigorous admission requirement for initial teacher preparation. Third, the successful implementation of the SPN21 curriculum vastly depends on highly qualified teachers. These reasons undoubtedly demonstrated SHBIE's commitment to providing quality Initial Teacher Education (ITE) as teacher education contributes to the economic, social and global development as well as the development of the twenty-first-century competencies in line with the SPN21. After a decade, MTeach has become the flagship for the Initial Teacher Education programme of the Institute, bolstering SHBIE's vision to develop itself into a First-Class Graduate School of Education with a distinctive national and international identity.

To further cement its standing as the only teaching institute in the Southeast Asian region that offers initial teacher preparation only at the graduate level, SHBIE also offers other master's degree programmes such as Master of Education and Master in Counselling. In the Master of Education programme, SHBIE offers several specialisations, among them are Islamic Education, Malay Language and Literature Education, Special Needs Education, Early Childhood Education, Mathematics Education, Science Education and MIB Education. Alongside its PhD programme, SHBIE also offers a field of doctoral specialisation. Such programmes not only ensure a continuous professional development of teachers but also build and retain a high-quality teacher workforce which is critical to fulfil the demands and expectations of the increasingly challenging educational environment. These transformations in SHBIE have also been taking place alongside its continued endorsement and upholding of the national philosophy—MIB.

MIB has been placed centrally in the development and progress of Brunei's national education system. It is present in the formulation of strategies and policies of educational institutions at all levels, and permeates all aspects of the society in general and of education in particular. While the connection between the MIB philosophy and government policies and strategies is nationally acknowledged, much of what is understood from it appears to be abstract, tacit and under-researched. Little to no research has been carried out to explore, on the one hand, how the MIB as a whole or in its tripartite parts has given shape and meaning to the above-mentioned twenty-first-century innovations, and, on the other hand, how MIB has been used in those innovations to promote its own teaching. This book, collectively, sheds some light on this critical observation and scholarly gap, as shall be further elaborated in the subsequent parts and throughout the book.

1.3 Curriculum and Pedagogical Issues: Teachers' Knowledge and Beliefs, and New Developments

Part II, '*Curriculum and Pedagogical Issues: Teachers' Knowledge and Beliefs, and New Developments*', focuses in particular on all-level efforts to improve teaching and learning in Brunei's education system. SHBIE at UBD has been playing an important role in these efforts. Let us now discuss several specific endeavours and developments that we consider key in the improvement of teaching and learning. As we discuss them, we also show areas that invite further examination and reflection.

Take, for example, in 2013, a four-year UBD/Ministry of Education research-practice partnership focused on Twenty-First Century Teaching and Learning (21CTL) which was initiated with the support of a major grant from the Brunei Research Council (BRC) with the intention to cultivate teachers' engagement with SPN21. This teacher development project working with consultant SRI International engaged 150 teachers in the development of approaches to teaching that could support the aims of the new national curriculum. Rubrics originated by SRI focused teachers' attention on the skills of collaboration, interdisciplinary knowledge construction, self-regulated learning, real-world problem solving and innovation, and skilled communication.

Teachers engaged in cycles of Lesson Study (LS) action research with SHBIE, UBD, academics in the role of facilitators. Lesson Study was introduced to Brunei Darussalam more than a decade ago, when the country hosted the World Association of Lesson Studies (WALS) international conference, with the intention of developing teachers' pedagogical content knowledge (PCK). Noting that educational objectives are insufficient in themselves to inform teachers of what is to be learnt by students, LS supports collaborating groups of teachers in the adoption of a second-order perspective to reveal the *critical* aspects of the object of learning for their students, that is, what the students need to learn to achieve the

1. The students are not required to work together in pairs or groups.
2. The students do work together BUT they do not have shared responsibility.
3. The students do have shared responsibility BUT they are not required to make decisions together about the content, process or product of their work.
4. The students do have shared responsibility and they do make substantive decisions together about the content, process or product of their work BUT their work is not interdependent
5. The students do have shared responsibility and they do make substantive decisions together about the content, process or product of their work and their work is interdependent

Fig. 1.1 21CTL Rubric for Collaboration (SRI, 2013)

intended outcome. With this insight, the teachers proceed to the design of learning situations. Following an action research model, the teachers collect evidence of the effect of their design and, if necessary, re-design for subsequent cycles until their students achieve an intended object of learning. The outcomes in focus in our project were the five twenty-first-century skills listed above, each informed by a rubric detailing increasing levels of outcome (see Fig. 1.1). The LS process supports the development of teachers' pedagogical content knowledge as they gain insights into the different ways that students discern and work with different objects of learning, and they gain insights into how they as teachers might work with those objects of learning to enable the students to achieve powerful learning outcomes (Wood et al., 2017).

The results of teachers' participation in 21CTL are indicated in Table 1.1 with reference to active collaboration, deeper learning, learners' self-regulation, real-world problem solving and deeper subject matter understanding.

In an exit interview, the teachers were asked if they would continue to teach using the new approach to teaching and learning. It was made clear to us that the extant configuration of the curriculum and assessment would not support the 21CTL approach to teaching and learning. The following extract using pseudonyms from such an interview is illustrative of the tension experienced by teachers.

Interviewer: Have you noticed any changes in the students' learning due to the changes that you made to the learning activity?
Nadiah: Students are more confident now, they talk to me more. At first … before this they were so serious, they didn't want to talk. They were just quiet. They're friendlier, yeah, they

Table 1.1 21CTL outcomes for teachers (21CTL 3 months follow-up questionnaire, $n = 106$)

To what extent do you agree with the following statements about the results of your participation in 21CTL?	Strongly disagree/disagree (%)	Strongly agree/agree (%)
A. I have better practical understanding of twenty-first century teaching and learning because of 21CTL	4.7	95.3
B. 21CTL gives me practical ideas I can use in my classroom.	2.8	97.2
C. I have better understanding of how to promote deeper learning through the use of ICT	8.5	91.5
D. I have better understanding of how to guide students to self-regulate their learning.	13.2	86.8
E. I have a better understanding of how to give students real-world problem solving experiences in my classroom.	21.7	78.3
F. I have a better understanding of how to foster more active collaboration among students	5.7	94.3
G. I have a better understanding of how to help students build deeper subject matter understanding	14.2	85.8
H. I have more productive ways to discuss teaching and learning with my colleagues	12.3	87.7

	talk to me more. They ask questions, even the shy ones are now talking … I think it's because of the independence we gave them to decide. The chance to decide what they wanted to do. Some even presented so I think that gave them a bit more confidence.
Interviewer:	Do you think you will continue working on those [21CTL lesson designs]?
Nadiah:	Yeah, I think so …
Siti:	Maybe we can just use it only for a few topics. We can't do it for all.
Interviewer:	Why?
Siti:	Covering the syllabus.
Nadiah:	Yeah, there's too much to teach and the pressure of you know, producing good results for the SPE [public examination].
Interviewer:	So what's the strategy for getting the good results?
Nadiah:	Drilling.

Siti:	Drilling works for every student.
Interviewer:	So what's the difference between drilling and the kind of lesson we've been looking at [with 21CTL design]?
Nadiah:	Yeah, it's different. Drilling is when you are …
Siti:	Focusing on the exam question. Make sure the students understand the question, understand what is asked, how to answer it. What we're doing now [with 21CTL] is we try to make them *understand* the concept.
Interviewer:	That's the difference?
Siti:	Yes. Drilling is for grades.

Currently, Strategic Objective 01 of the Ministry of Education of Brunei Strategic Plan seeks the transformation of the education system towards a performance-driven culture based on 'a comprehensive human resource competency framework that defines the required competencies to deliver intended results' (Ministry of Education, 2018). Reflecting on the effectiveness of such frameworks to measure teaching competencies, Day (2019) reminds us that good teaching is more than achieving a set of competencies and meeting standards:

> teachers need to be able to "read" and understand the classroom, school, pupil and policy contexts in which they work, to exercise "considered" judgements and to manage the emotional cauldrons of classroom lives. They also need to be motivated and committed (to their subjects, their students, their colleagues) and they need to have capacities for hope, academic optimism and resilience which encompass but go beyond baseline standards and competences. (p. 3)

Almost without exception, the teachers who participated in the 21CTL, research-practice partnership, professional development programme endorsed the relevance of 21CTL but expressed their concerns about the time available to them to teach twenty-first-century skills and the competing need to cover the syllabus. This is a reminder that the development of teachers is not a process that can proceed independently of the cultural script of teaching in schools (Stigler & Hiebert, 1999; Elliott, 2014) which Elliott describes as the 'beliefs and values that are tacitly embodied in the structure of a lesson, its major features, patterns of interaction between teacher and students and between the students themselves, and aspects of the learning process the students engage with'. It is to be hoped that the introduction of a teacher competency framework in Brunei will include the competency of teachers to nurture deep learning, to develop learners' capability for self-regulation, to focus on real-world problem solving, and to achieve deeper subject matter understanding through active collaboration. The challenge is to develop an appraisal system that supports teachers in their endeavours to achieve good grades for their students through conceptual understanding rather than drilling.

As discussed earlier, the Master of Teaching programme was introduced in Brunei by SHBIE, UBD, more than a decade ago with the aim of developing ethical, learner-centric, needs-driven, research-informed, pedagogically knowledgeable teachers for the twenty-first century achieved through deliberate, reflective, evidence-based practice. The Master of Teaching experience for beginning teachers includes:

- University-based foundation courses in learning theory and teaching design, learning with technology, twenty-first-century skills development, language and assessment.
- University- and school-based collaborative practice supported by clinical specialists, subject specialists and teacher mentors.
- Educational action research through lesson and learning study supported by university specialists to prepare teachers for career-long collaborative professional development to meet the demands of providing effective twenty-first-century education.

The intended outcome is an education professional who has the capability to engage students in active, intellectually challenging learning activities developed from well-articulated and relevant content; who can analyse and use information about students in the design of learning situations related to their individual learning needs, who is able to establish and communicate intended learning outcomes and criteria for assessment and use valid evidence to assess student learning and provide formative feedback; one who engages in reflective practice in a process of continuous development.

While three out of five chapters in Part II refer to developments in the MTeach programme (Salleh et al., Said, and Latif et al.), the other two chapters focus on other pedagogical and educational issues beyond teacher education and the MTeach programme (Yusof & Alas, and Latif). It will be clear to the reader that the activities, initiatives and discussion presented in all the five chapters collectively show continuous efforts on the part of policy, teacher training, professional development, curriculum and classroom teaching in aspiring to accomplish the mission set out by the Ministry of Education, which is to provide a holistic education system through a meaningful curriculum and relevant and up-to-date educational programmes, implemented with attention given to students.

1.4 MIB in Teacher Training, Curriculum, Classroom Practice and Society

Part III of the book specifically focuses on the incorporation of MIB in Brunei's formal education system as well as on how individuals in society internalise and put it in practice in and beyond the sphere of education. As discussed in the previous sections and further explored in this part, MIB is an integral part of the Bruneian society and a major component of the education system from the primary level up to the tertiary level. For example, UBD has a structure where all undergraduate students regardless of majors are required to take a compulsory MIB subject within their 4-year course. There is also a teacher training college in Brunei called Seri Begawan Religious Teachers University College (KUPU SB) that prepares Islamic religious teachers in a programme that has MIB as a compulsory core subject.

The chapters under Part III pay attention to the roles of MIB teachers in classroom teaching and in the educational and moral growth of their students. As such, the chapters explore and discuss the requirements for MIB teachers to fully comprehend MIB as the national ideology, and for them to incorporate their personal experiences in their teaching before they can acquaint their students with the values and principles of MIB. Another major emphasis found in these chapters involves the training of MIB teachers and the classroom practice of MIB teacher educators and curriculum developers who are expected to be well versed in the Islamic components of MIB. They are also expected to be able to ensure that accurate comprehension and appreciation of MIB can be achieved among teacher trainees and students. Likewise, they are expected to demonstrate that effective integration of the Quranic knowledge in the formal education system is evident.

The incorporation of MIB in teacher training and professional development programmes has also come with issues and challenges. For example, as demonstrated in this Part, the current teacher training curriculum emphasises more on the cultural components of the national ideology in a historical context such as traditional food, games, music, costume and wedding ceremony. There is a real need for the MIB courses in the curriculum to link the integral concept of the national ideology to current issues, potentially in the areas of leadership and education. This is not to say that the cultural aspects have a secondary importance to the current issues but as would-be religious/MIB teachers, the students undertaking the teacher training course should be able to demonstrate their competent understanding of the national ideology and their abilities to apply their understanding to the current world. Moreover, obtaining a more well-rounded exposure to MIB values and potentials could result in a much more comprehensive and balanced understanding, which could significantly prevent the student teachers from perceiving MIB as merely traditional and static.

At the same time, the challenges involving the incorporation of MIB in teacher training and professional development programmes also come from many student teachers and in-service teachers themselves as they do not possess an adequate understanding of the value components of MIB. Neither do they demonstrate sufficient competence and comprehension of Islamic knowledge conveyed through the teaching of the Quran and through Quranic verses. These inadequacies have made it difficult for the MIB philosophy and for the religious knowledge to be acquired, appreciated and internalised comprehensively and with sophistication by these students and teachers. Their teaching, accordingly, is affected by their own insufficient knowledge and comprehension.

Alongside MIB, Part III also touches upon the Islamisation of knowledge, particularly of science, as found in science textbooks in Brunei. The integration of Quranic spiritual knowledge in the Year 7 Science curriculum textbook, for instance, is discussed. Indeed, the science curriculum in Brunei's schools is influenced by global movement of Islamisation of knowledge in which spirituality is integrated within the science subjects. There are clearly similar concerns in relation to the national philosophy of MIB expressed in the previous chapters. Everyone, be they in the education sector or not, has an important role in the global movement of Islamisation of knowledge. Teachers and teacher educators must be committed to making Islam a motivating factor in directing their everyday practices and in shaping Brunei's education such as in science and technological development. The alignment of MIB and Islamisation of knowledge with the national education system has contributed to the formation of Brunei's unique identity in the region and globally. Through this unique identity and positioning, Brunei aspires to make meaningful contributions to the contemporary world.

While the MIB subject is prioritised in the school curriculum and is central to any school's vision and direction, and permeates every aspect of life in Brunei, how far MIB is being implemented and practised by individuals beyond schools remains more or less unexplored, as we have argued earlier in this chapter. Hence, what is discussed in Part III (Chap. 15 in particular) regarding social media influencers and MIB is not only refreshing but is also much needed in the overall scholarship on MIB and its relevance to the current world. Social media influencers build their audience through online platforms and inevitably have strong influence on young people as they feel the influencers are much more relatable and form strong connection with their followers. Thus, in reference to the earlier discussion on teacher educators as role models, this new form of *celebrification* tends to offer much more exciting and trendy role models for young people to emulate and copy.

1.5 COVID-19, Society and Education

The book idea had been conceptualised before the outbreak of the COVID-19 pandemic. As the book has been taking into shape, the world has also been more and more affected by the unprecedented impacts of the pandemic. The education system in Brunei, like those in other countries, has been going through massive interruptions as well as has been the experimental ground for new pedagogical and technological interventions throughout 2020 and into the future. Talking about education today is no longer possible without mentioning COVID-19. Thus, it is both necessary and essential to bring COVID-19 into the picture. By the same token, the pandemic has both forced us as well as offered us conditions and materiality to rethink education and to reflect upon the many current policies, conceptualisations and practices that have been driving teaching, learning, research, educational mobilities and the internationalisation of education. The purposes and ethics of globalisation and the role of the nation state in containing the pandemic and in mobilising resources and providing leadership are being re-examined and re-imagined so rigorously and constantly since the outbreak of COVID-19 in early January 2020. The chapters featured under Part IV of this book—'***COVID-19, Society, and Education***'—reflect this spirit.

Specifically, '*COVID-19, Society, and Education*' resembles the theme of a seminar series spearheaded by the International and Comparative Education Research Group (ICE) at Universiti Brunei Darussalam. ICE is under the leadership of Senior Professor Phan Le Ha, who also initiated and has been leading this book project. During the first semester of the 2020–2021 academic year, 10 ICE seminars on this COVID-19 theme were given at the university, resulting in a number of academic and media publications, including four commentaries on varied aspects of the theme co-developed by members of ICE. These commentaries have been published on University World News—a global outlet for higher education updates, debates and engagement (cf. Iqbal & Phan, 2020; Keasberry et al., 2020; Noorashid et al., 2020; and Phan & Phung, 2020). They have been developed much further into the four chapters included in this final part of the book. These four chapters altogether offer a detailed coverage of and discuss the ongoing impacts of the COVID-19 pandemic on Brunei's education and society, which other national and educational contexts could relate to and learn from. These chapters also generate new scholarship and provide the foundation for new research that could benefit from interdisciplinary approaches and comparative analyses.

All in all, we would like to invite readers to engage with the book as a whole and with every chapter featured in this collection.

References

Appadurai, A. (1996). *Modernity at large: Cultural dimensions of globalization.* University of Minnesota Press.
Bradshaw, L., & Mundia, L. (2006). Attitudes and concerns about inclusive education: Bruneian inservice and preservice teachers. *International Journal of Special Education, 21*(1), 35–41.
Day, C. (2019). What is teaching about? Professionalism and the limitations of standards and competences. *European Journal of Education, 00,* 1–4.
Elliott, J. (2014). Lesson study, learning theory, and the cultural script of teaching. *International Journal for Lesson and Learning Studies, 3*(3).
Friedman, T. L. (2005). *The world is flat: A brief history of the twenty-first century.* Farrar, Straus and Giroux.
Goh, A. Y. S. (2014). Insights form a Bourdieusian lens: The relationship between college-based and workplace learning in becoming a vocational-technical education teacher in Brunei. *Journal of Workplace Learning, 26*(1), 22–38.
Harman, G., Hayden, M., & Pham, T. N. (Eds.). (2010). *Reforming higher education in Vietnam: Changes and priorities.* Springer.

Hawkins, J. N., Yamada, A., Yamada, R., & Jacob, W. J. (2018). *New directions of STEM research and learning in the world ranking movement: A comparative perspective*. Palgrave Macmillan.

Ibrahim, H. A. L. (2003). *Melayu Islam Beraja: Pengantar Huraian*. Universiti Brunei Darussalam.

Iqbal, M. A., & Phan, L. H. (2020, April 18). Care for international students brings greater commitment. *University World News*.

Ismail, S. F. Z., Shahrill, M., & Mundia, L. (2015). Factors contributing to effective mathematics teaching in secondary schools in Brunei Darussalam. *Procedia—Social and Behavioral Sciences, 186*, 474–481. https://doi.org/10.1016/j.sbspro.2015.04.169

Kani, N. H. A., Nor, N. M., Shahrill, M., & Halim, R. A. (2014). Investigating the leadership practices among mathematics teachers: The immersion programme. *International Journal of Contemporary Educational Research, 1*(2), 113–121.

Keasberry, C., Phan, L. H., Hoon, C. Y., Alam, M., Alas, Y., & Noorashid, N. (2020, December 5). Facing the mental health challenges of COVID-19 in HE. *University World News*.

Kumpoh, A. A., Wahsalfelah, S. N., & Hj-Othman, N. A. (2017). Socio-cultural dynamics in Bruneian society. In *Comparative studies in ASEAN cultures and societies* (pp. 1–44). Semadhma Publishing House.

Lingard, B., & Lewis, S. (2017). Placing PISA and PISA for schools in two federalisms, Australia and the USA. *Critical Studies in Education, 58*(3), 266–279. https://doi.org/10.1080/17508487.2017.1316295

Matzin, R., Jawawi, R., Jaidin, J. H., Shahrill, M., & Mahadi, M. (2015). Brunei lower secondary students' engagement in school and beliefs about the self under the ongoing SPN21 curriculum reforms: Implications for educational and counseling interventions. *Journal of Sustainable Development, 8*(6), 133–145. https://doi.org/10.5539/jsd.v8n6p133

Ministry of Education. (2018). *Strategic Plan 2018–2022*. Brunei Strategic Enterprise Performance and Delivery Unit (SEPaDU) Ministry of Education.

Mundia, L. (2010). Implementation of SPN21 curriculum in Brunei Darussalam: A review of selected implications on school assessment reforms. *International Education Studies, 3*(2), 119–129.

Mundia, L. (2012). The assessment of math learning difficulties in a primary grade-4 child with high support needs: Mixed methods approach. *International Electronic Journal of Elementary Education, 4*(2), 347–366.

Neubauer, D., & Collins, C. (2015). *Redefining Asia Pacific higher education in contexts of globalization: Private markets and the public good*. Palgrave Macmillan.

Neubauer, D., Mok, K. H., & Edwards, S. (2019). *Contesting globalization and internationalization of higher education*. Palgrave Macmillan.

Noorashid, N., Phan, L. H., Alas, Y., & Yabit, V. M. (2020, October 10). Beyond the pandemic, integrating online learning. *University World News*.

Parr, G. B., Faine, M., Phan, L. H., & Seddon, T. L. (2013). Globalisation and its challenges for history teaching. *Agora: History Teachers' Associations of Victoria, Collingwood Victoria Australia, 48*(2), 19–26.

Phan, L. H. (2017). *Transnational education crossing 'Asia' and 'the west': Adjusted desire, transformative mediocrity, and neo-colonial disguise*. Routledge.

Phan, L. H., & Doan, B. N. (Eds.). (2020). *Higher education in market-oriented socialist Vietnam: New players, discourses and practices*. Palgrave Macmillan.

Phan, L. H., & Phung, T. (2020, August 29). COVID-19 opportunities for internationalisation at home. *University World News*.

Rizvi, F., & Lingard, B. (2010). *Globalizing education policy*. Routledge.

Sellar, S., & Lingard, B. (2018). International large-scale assessments, affective worlds and policy impacts in education. *International Journal of Qualitative Studies in Education, 31*(5), 367–381. https://doi.org/10.1080/09518398.2018.1449982

Seng, P. L. (2009). Ethnicity and educational policies in Malaysia and Brunei Darussalam. *SA-eDUC JOURNAL, 6*(2), 146–157.

Sercombe, P. (2014). Brunei Darussalam: Issues of language, identity and education. In P. Sercombe & R. Tupas (Eds.), *Language, education and nation-building: Assimilation and shift in Southeast Asia* (pp. 22–44). Palgrave Macmillan. https://doi.org/10.1057/9781137455536_2

Sercombe, P., & Tupas, R. (Eds.). (2014). *Language, education and nation building: Assimilation and shift in Southeast Asia*. Palgrave Macmillan.

Shahrill, M., Abdullah, N. A., Yusof, J., & Suhaili, A. S. (2014). *Informing the Practice of Teaching Mathematics in Upper Primary Classes*. Proceedings of the International Conference on Education in Mathematics, Science & Technology (ICEMST 2014) (pp. 168–172). Necmettin Erbakan University.

SRI International. (2013). *21 CLD learning activity rubrics*. Microsoft Partners in Learning.

Stigler, J. W., & Hiebert, J. (1999). *The teaching gap*. The Free Press.

Stromquist, N. P., & Monkman, K. (Eds.). (2014). *Globalization and education: Integration and contestation across cultures* (2nd ed.). Roman and Littlefield.

Symaco, L. P. (Ed.). (2013). *Education in South-East Asia*. Bloomsbury.

Tsui, A. (Ed.). (2020). *English language teaching and teacher education in East Asia: Global challenges and local responses*. Cambridge University Press.

Wood, K., Jaidin, J. H., Jawawi, R., Perera, J. S. H. Q., Salleh, S. M., Shahrill, M., & Sithamparam, S. (2017). How and what teachers learn from collaborative professional development. *International Journal for Lesson and Learning Studies, 6*(2), 151–168.

Wood, K., Jaidin, J. H., Jawawi, R., Perera, Q., Salleh, S., Shahrill, M., & Sithamparam, S. (2018). Lesson study in Brunei Darussalam: Changing the paradigm for teaching and learning. In K. J. Kennedy & J. C. K. Lee (Eds.), *Routledge international handbook of schools and schooling in Asia*. Routledge.

PART I

Contextualising Brunei and Its Education System: History, Ideology and Major Reforms

CHAPTER 2

History and Development of the Brunei Education System

Norhazlin Muhammad and Mohamad Iskandar Petra

2.1 Introduction

Education is an important component in achieving a nation's aspirations. Each country has a unique system of education. Apart from maintaining the state's national values, the quality of education should indeed be put at the highest priority in fulfilling and updating the needs of developing global skills and progressive knowledge. Brunei Darussalam, also known as Brunei, the Abode of Peace, has its own history of the development of its education system. Brunei has undergone changes in its education system due to influencing elements from Hindu Buddhism and Islam as well as influences from Brunei's time as a British Protectorate. Brunei has

---

Muhammad, N., & Petra, M. I. (2021). History and development of the Brunei education system. In Phan, L. H., A. Kumpoh, K. Wood, R. Jawawi, & H. Said (Eds.), *Globalisation, education, and reform in Brunei Darussalam* (pp. 21–44). Palgrave Macmillan.

N. Muhammad (✉) • M. I. Petra
Universiti Brunei Darussalam, Bandar Seri Begawan, Brunei
e-mail: norhazlin.muhammad@ubd.edu.bn; iskandar.petra@ubd.edu.bn

© The Author(s), under exclusive license to Springer Nature Switzerland AG 2021
Phan, L. H. et al. (eds.), *Globalisation, Education, and Reform in Brunei Darussalam*, International and Development Education, https://doi.org/10.1007/978-3-030-77119-5_2

transitioned from being a Malay Hindu Buddhist Kingdom to the current Malay Islamic Monarchy state.

In view of these influences, Brunei Darussalam currently has its own unique system of education and the state's current Sultan, His Majesty Sultan Haji Hassanal Bolkiah Mu'izzaddien Waddaulah ibni Al-Marhum Sultan Haji Omar 'Ali Saifuddien Sa'adul Khairi Waddien, the Sultan and Yang Di-Pertuan of Brunei Darussalam, has placed great emphasis on the quality of education without neglecting national values. This was highlighted in His Majesty's *titah* (command):

> In view of the illuminating influence of education on one's life, it should, therefore, be upheld as a matter of national importance that needs to be fulfilled. This can be done by, among others, providing a national curriculum with the objective of developing a lifelong learning culture, thereby producing knowledgeable Bruneians at all age levels. In other words, the national education should provide dynamic, forward looking educational programmes to yield the knowledge and skills required by industries and services without ignoring values. (Excerpt from His Majesty's *titah* during the 13th Teachers' Day Celebration, 23rd September 2003; See Ministry of Education, 2013, p. 1)

His Majesty's *titah* highlights the importance of implementing national standard curriculum to fulfil the national aspiration, maintain national identity and values, and develop knowledgeable Bruneians who are equipped with skills required by industries and services without neglecting the necessity of lifelong learning education. In this chapter, we will discuss the history and development of the Brunei education system before and during the British Protectorate, and its development after independence.

2.2 The Educational System of Brunei Before 1888

In the early life of human beings, education was delivered informally. The delivery of knowledge was for the survival of individuals and groups of people. The purpose of education was to ensure the inheritance of religion and culture were preserved and passed on to the next generation. In the case of Brunei Darussalam, there is a lack of literature in regards to education before the coming of Islam. The earliest writings on the intellectual activities in Brunei were based on a report by a Chinese translator named

Magat. In 1578, he wrote a report to the Governor of Spain, Le Sanda, as reported by Cesar Adib Majul (1973), in *Muslims in the Philippines*:

> *likewise in other books they say that the Borneons have always desired to make Moros of the Christian—the thing that he also heard declared by the Catip (Arabic Khatib, for preacher) whom the said Borneon Mohama. This said catip and others with like expressions preach the said doctrine of Mohama, so that the said native observe it.* (p. 89)

Majul states that *catip* is an Arabic preacher and in Brunei, it refers to an official of a mosque who is a rank below an *Imam* (Majul, 1973). According to Mahmud Saedon (2003, see Mail & Asbol, 2017), a controversial issue among international researchers is when exactly Islam first came to Brunei. Local researchers claim that Islam was introduced in Brunei as early as the tenth century (Mail & Asbol, 2017).

In his book, *Catatan Sejarah Perwira-Perwira dan Pembesar-Pembesar Brunei II*, Pehin Orang Kaya Amar Diraja Dato Seri Utama (Dr) Awang Haji Jamil Al-Sufri (2000) notes that Brunei was a vassal state of the Majapahit Empire during the early reign of Awang Alak Betatar (see Serudin, 2000, p. 3) who was the first Sultan of Brunei. His conversion to Islam led to its acceptance in 1368 CE. He later changed his name to Sultan Muhammad Shah (Al-Sufri, 2000). The Majapahit Empire weakened after the death of Hayam Worok (1350–1389 AD) and it was then that the Sultan proclaimed Brunei as a sovereign Independent State. This led historians to conclude that Brunei was an independent and sovereign Malay Sultanate ruled by a Muslim ruler named Sultan Muhammad (1363–1402 AD) (Serudin, 2000). According to Pehin Orang Kaya Amar Diraja Dato Seri Utama (Dr) Awang Haji Jamil Al-Sufri (2000), the spread of Islam in Brunei originated much earlier than the conversion of Awang Alak Betatar because geographically, Brunei is situated at a strategic location on the sea-trade route between western Asia and China, and was used as a refuelling port of call for Muslim merchants who also disseminated Islamic teachings in the area (Al-Sufri, 2000).

The Brunei Annual Report 1963 recorded that with the coming of Islam, intellectual activity was conducted at private houses and the palace. During this period, education was conducted in an informal way. The Ministry of Religious Affairs (MoRA) (1996) states that the role of a palace as a place for the teaching of Islamic education became prevalent in the sixteenth century and this was witnessed by the Christian missionaries themselves who arrived in Brunei with the Spanish army troop (Mail & Asbol, 2017). Sweeney's (1998) view is that that before the building of mosques, religious education (RE) was conducted in a *balai* (community hall). In his view, the term *balai* is known to be much older and existed in Brunei much earlier than the mosque and the difference between *balai* and *surau* is not clear. The terms were used interchangeably for religious centres below the level of the mosque (Mansurnoor, 1992). Sultan Sharif Ali, the third Sultan of Brunei who ruled from 1425 AD to 1432 AD, built the first mosque in Brunei due to the increased number of Muslim converts. Apart from being a place for prayer, the mosque was also used for religious activities and the teaching of Islamic education. The informal teaching of Islamic education at mosques in Brunei is still in practice today under the supervision of the MORA.

The literature shows that the educational system during this period was implemented in a traditional and informal way conducted in private and instructor houses, *surau, balai,* mosques and palaces. There was no standardised national curriculum and most of the curriculum content was on Islamic education.

2.3 The Educational System of Brunei Under the British Protectorate (1888–1984 AD)

Brunei was a protectorate of the British Resident from 1888 to 1984 and the residential system of administration was imposed in 1906. It was then in 1912 that the first formal system was established, as reported by the Department of State Secretariat (1973) in the Report of the Education Commission Brunei 1972:

> *Formal education in Brunei began in 1912 with the opening of a small vernacular school in Brunei Town. Records show that there were 53 boys on the roll.* (p. 40)

Unfortunately, the aim of education during this period was merely to remove illiteracy among the Bruneian people and only targeted to develop low-level potentialities such as practical skills for labourers, carpenters, fishermen, policemen, government clerks and so on (Jumat, 1989, pp. 113, 118). In the *Brunei Annual Report 1918*, Cator (1919, p. 4) reports:

These do not aim at providing a high standard of education. They do, however provide the children with elementary training and also teach them discipline, punctuality and personal cleanliness, qualities in which their parents are markedly lacking.

Dato Marsal bin Maun (1957) stated in *Hiboran* magazine that although Brunei had its own aims of education, the state did not have any education policy (see Jumat, 1989, p. 150).

In 1914, Douglas reported that

there is a small Malay vernacular school in Brunei town with about 30 boys attending. Hitherto it has been held in the mosque, but in October was removed to the building formerly used as the monopolies office. (1915, p. 5)

The above report shows that the first formal school was held in a mosque. It shows that the role of the mosque in Brunei was not only a place for prayers or religious rituals but it also acted as a centre for the teaching and learning of Islamic education. When the first government Malay vernacular school was opened in 1912, the statistics showed that there were only 53 boys attending the school. The number had fallen in 1914 to 30 boys only. The school's attendance progress was considered unsatisfactory. However, records showed that the attendance had risen from 42 to 123 people in 1921 (Allen, 1922).

In regards to girls' education, it was reported that there were no girls attending government schools from 1912 to 1929. This was due to parents' reluctance to send their daughters to co-educational schools and that girls tend to get married at a young age. Traditionally, girls get married between the average age of 15 to 17 mostly through the process of arranged marriages (Chuchu, 1990). The first girls' school was opened in 1930. Unfortunately, there was only one female teacher who later became ill and the school was shut down as the government was unable to find a replacement teacher (Upex, 2006). It was reopened in 1932 with an enrolment of only 13 students; but two years later the school was again closed. It can be concluded that the progress of girls' schooling was much slower than that of boys' schools (Jibah, 1983).

In 1916, the Chinese community successfully established the first Chinese medium school. This was an effect of the tremendous political and social change in China that led to the educational development among the Chinese community in Brunei (Chuchu, 1990). The opening of the school was for the benefit of Chinese shopkeepers' children as Cator reported in the *Annual Report on the State of Brunei for the year 1916* (Cator, 1917, p. 6). By 1939, there were five Chinese schools in the state with a total of 261 boys and 180 girls (Chuchu, 1990).

A private English school was opened in 1933 by the British Petroleum Company (now known as the Brunei Shell Petroleum Company Sendirian Berhad) organised under the Anglican mission. By the end of 1939, there were four English private schools with a total of 188 pupils (Chuchu, 1990). These were Brunei's first co-educational schools and their medium of instruction was in English. The discovery of oil in 1929 led to the opening of these schools. There was an increase in the number of foreign labourers who worked at oil industries in the state and the schools provided for these labourers' children (Upex, 2006).

Despite this, the Malay vernacular school still had poor attendance. The British Resident took initiative by introducing the School Attendance Enactment of 1929, which enforced that Malay boys aged seven to fourteen living within two miles of a school attend the Malay vernacular school that was provided by the government. Parents had to pay 50 cents to $1.00 or more, depending on how many times they disobeyed this law (Jibah, 1983). The enactment was effective, and attendance increased from 198 students in 1928 to 672 by the end of 1929. In 1939, the School Attendance Enactment was re-enacted and this time it was further implemented in the Kuala Belait district area. Through this enactment, offenders had to pay $5.00 or be sentenced to 14 days of imprisonment.

In 1942, Brunei was occupied by the Japanese. As a result of this occupancy, oil fields were closed down, many schools were demolished and some were changed to Japanese medium schools and the British retreated from the country (Jibah, 1983, p. 7). According to Mohamad Noor, the Japanese occupation (1941–1945) led to a decline in interest among Bruneian parents to send their children to schools (Chuchu, 1990). Three years later, the Japanese were successfully expelled from Brunei by the British. The British Resident returned to Brunei and governed the country through the British military administration.

The 1946 Annual Report on Education of Brunei stated that after the war, the government tried to rebuild new schools and to reopen schools that had been closed (Peel, 1948). Some schools were in poor condition and were housed in temporary *Kajang* (palm-leaf screen) houses (Chuchu, 1990). The primary concern of the British was also to re-establish the administrative machinery, rehabilitate the country, and reopen the Seria oil fields. Education after the Second World War was still geared towards eradicating basic illiteracy and also towards practical pursuits, such as handicrafts, gardening and physical training. The main aim of education was the transmission of Malay culture and the maintenance of Malay social cohesion. Despite these challenges, the government's attendance records showed a statistical increase in the number of students going to school (Chuchu, 1990).

According to Ahmad Jumat (1989), the Japanese war tragedy initiated a new paradigm of thinking within the mindset of Bruneian society. The sense of nationalism led them to reinvent their national identity. They saw education as an important element in realising the future identity of the country. To achieve the outlook of the people, the Department of Education was established in 1951 to specifically supervise Malay and English government schools (Jumat, 1989).

After the Japanese war, there was a rapid increase in student enrolment as a result of the shifts in the outlook of the people and the exploitation and exportation of the state's oil, which financed the education. Following this progress, the government successfully set up the first primary English school in 1952 and a secondary English school in 1953 under the supervision of the MoE (Ministry of Education, 2004a, p. xxviii). As a result, parents were more confident in sending their children to government schools. The confidence might have resulted from the establishment of formal government religious schools on 16 September 1956 by command of His Late Majesty Al-Marhum Sultan Haji Omar Ali Saifuddien III. Seven schools were opened in four different towns (Mohd Daud, 2004). These schools were located in the same buildings as the Malay and English schools (Rahman, 1998, p. 10).

The opening of these religious schools was in response to the report made by two officers; Haji Othman bin Haji Mat Saad, an inspector (officer) of the Johore religious school and Haji Ismail bin Omar Abdul Aziz, a judge from Sagamat (see Chap. 5). In the early stages, most of the teachers and office administrators were hired from Johore State. These religious lessons were conducted during the afternoon, separately from the normal public Malay and English teaching. The curriculum followed only the existing curriculum and system of education used in Johore religious schools during the time. The same textbooks were also used (Mohd Daud, 2004).

According to Jumat (1989), the educational system during this period was a result of gradual growth and evolution. Lack of firm educational policy before the 1959 constitution resulted in the emergence of three different systems of education in the state; the specifications of which were that the Malay medium vernacular schools were only for Malays and were run by the Department of Education, Chinese medium schools were only for the Chinese and were privately run by the Chinese community, and the English medium schools were for English children and middle-class Malay and Chinese people, and were privately run by the British Petroleum company under the organisation of the Anglican mission (Jumat, 1989, pp. 112–113).

Apart from these three types of schools, the state also provided religious schools for Muslims in other racial and class groups, monitored by the Department of Religious Affairs and Communities Welfare within its own system of education.

2.4 The Educational System of Brunei During the Pre-independence Period (1959–1983)

Finally, Brunei signed the 1959 constitution in which it was granted internal self-government of the country; the post of the British Resident was abolished and a high commissioner was appointed to advise the sultan and his government. The posts of *Menteri Besar* (chief minister) and state secretary were created and held by local Muslims; the Governor of Sarawak ceased acting as high commissioner for Brunei. The constitution also provided for the establishment of two important councils, the Privy Council and Legislative Council of which the Executive Authority was of most importance as it was to be presided over by the Sultan, with the Director of Education being a member of this Executive Authority (see Jumat, 1989, p. 132).

As stated in the 1959 constitution that

> His Majesty the Sultan and Yang Di-Pertuan may appoint from among citizens of Brunei Darussalam any number of Ministers and Deputy Ministers who shall be responsible solely to His Majesty the Sultan and Yang Di-Pertuan for the exercise of executive authority and who shall assist and advise His Majesty the Sultan and Yang Di-Pertuan in the discharge of His Majesty the Sultan and Yang Di-Pertuan's executive authority. (See Attorney General Chambers, 2020, p. 17)

According to Jumat (1989), the proclamation of the 1959 Constitution initiated a new era for Brunei Darussalam in all fields including education. Pengiran Mustapha (1979), in *Educational Policy in Brunei with Special Reference to the National Language*, states:

> A new form of Government materialized from the 1959 Agreement whereby Brunei became a self-governing sovereign state. This emergent nation at this stage was more concerned to lay the foundations of a national education policy. A major turning point was to establish a system of education that could meet the needs of the nation. (See Jumat, 1989, p. 132)

In 1959, two experts from Malaya were invited to the state to advise the government concerning the general policy and principles that should be followed in education. The two experts, Aminuddin Baki and Paul Chang, were both from the Central Advisory Committee in Malaysia (Upex, 2006). They spent two weeks in Brunei then submitted their recommendations in the *Aminuddin Baki/Paul Chang Report*. The experts recommended that Malay should be the language of instruction in all schools. The report also mentioned that different racial groups of children need to be fostered towards the common loyalty of a national education system and policies. Therefore, Brunei should be provided with an education policy that should be implemented for all racial groups of children. In short, this report initiated a demand to formulate a national education system. The recommendations of this report were accepted by the government and became the National Education Policy of 1962. Although it was adopted, it was never implemented (Jumat, 1989).

According to Ahmad Jumat (1989), there were many reasons why this report was not implemented. Firstly, the report was insufficient; Baki and Chang only spent two weeks in the state and used the *Malayan Tun Razak* report as the source of their recommendations. Secondly, there was a political dispute between the *Partai Rakyat Brunei* (PRB) or Brunei People's Party and the Sultan's government after the report was adopted; on the night of 8 December 1962, there was a rebellion by the PRB. The government managed to defeat them with the help of the British troops in Hong Kong. As a result, the educational changes recommended by the experts were left out. Another reason was the confidentiality of the report, which even compared to the present time has never been released to education officers, professional teachers and researchers. Although the 1959 report was not successful, it created the initial base of 'national' schools in Brunei Darussalam (Jumat, 1989, pp. 154–158).

With the collapse of the PRB and the failure to actualise the *1959 Education Report*, the government sought to launch the first Five Year Development plan (1962–1967). The plan was designed to strengthen and improve the economic, social and cultural life of the Bruneian people (see Jumat, 1989). The initiatives under this plan included the establishment of the first Malay medium secondary school to improve the quality of education in Brunei in 1966 (Ministry of Education, 1987). Then in 1969, the Brunei Youth Council organised a historic seminar on education, which emphasised the need and importance of having a national education policy. His Highness the Sultan and Yang Di-Pertuan appointed an education commission in May 1970 to highlight to the community that the system and development of education was an important tenet for assessing the socio-economic progress of the country (Jumat, 1989).

The government also made an effort towards modifying the former 1959 report on education by constructing a 1972 report, which later became the government's education policy, known as the Brunei Education Commission of 1972. Unfortunately, the policy was not fully implemented until the time of Brunei's independence in 1984 (Jumat, 1989).

The 1972 commission reads as follows:

I. To make Malay the main medium of instruction in National Primary and Secondary schools as soon as possible in line with the requirement of the constitution;
II. to raise the standard of the usage of English in the primary and Secondary schools in this country;
III. to place more emphasis on religious tuition (Islam) in line with the requirements of the constitution;
IV. to provide a continuous education for all Brunei children for a period of 9 years; 6 years in the Primary schools and 3 years in the Lower Secondary schools;
V. to ensure, by the provision of syllabuses of common content that the standard education is complementary in all schools;
VI. to provide all Brunei children with every possible opportunity to make themselves useful in the development of the country in order to meet the needs of the country would be fulfilled by Brunei people themselves; and

VII. to promote by means of the above, a national identity upon which a sense of loyalty to Brunei rests, as wheel as generating the necessary efficiency and flexibility in the Education System to meet the development needs of the country. (Cited from Report of the Education Commission Brunei for the Year 1972, 1973, pp. 8, 9)

Under the 1972 education policy, all Bruneian children must be given equal opportunities in education and a common national should be adopted by all schools in Brunei. As a result, both male and female children are obligated to attend schools and all Chinese and English language medium mission schools adopted the common government's national syllabus and public examinations in 1974.

The Malay language is the country's main language in national schools, while not neglecting the importance of the English language as the world's lingua franca in education. Both languages are equally important for the socio-economic development of the country. Apart from the emphasis on Malay and English languages in the educational system, Islamic elements in vernacular school must also be upgraded and through this, hopefully, the Bruneians will project their own national identity (Jumat, 1989).

On 1 July 1965, the government introduced the teaching of Islamic Religious Knowledge (IRK) as a subject included in the Malay and English government school curriculum, as well as Islamic education in religious schools. The teaching of the subject started with Sultan Muhammad Jamalul Alam (SMJA) then was slowly implemented in all schools in Brunei (see Rahman, 1998). According to Pg. Abd Rahman, the teaching of IRK in Malay and English government schools was to give an option to some parents who were not able to send their children to religious schools (Rahman, 1998).

The following year, on 11 March 1966, an Arabic secondary school for boys (Hassanal Bolkiah Boys School) opened with the enrolment of 50 students. The opening of this school was in response to a proposal by His Majesty Sultan Omar 'Ali Saifuddien on 15 January 1956 regarding the effectiveness of Islamic education in Brunei. This school was located temporarily at the Madrasah Department of the Ministry of Religious Affairs building. According to Abdul Aziz bin Juned (1968), the first Arabic girls' school, Raja Isteri Pengiran Anak Damit Religious Arabic Secondary School opened in 1967 with an intake of 61 female students. The two Arabic schools had to share the same building because the new buildings for the studies were not yet ready (see Rahman, 1998).

Thus far, there were three systems in the formal school sector for the teaching of Islamic knowledge. The Islamic studies taught in Arabic and religious schools were under the supervision of the MoRA, while the teaching of the IRK subject in primary and secondary public schools was under the MoE. In this time, system of education in Brunei was in three media of instruction: Malay, English and Arabic (Ministry of Education, 1988).

2.5 The Educational System of Brunei After Independence (1984)

The 1st of January 1984 marked a historical achievement for the people of Brunei Darussalam. During the proclamation His Majesty Sultan Haji Hassanal Bolkiah declared that Brunei will be

> *forever a sovereign, democratic and independent "Malay Islamic Monarchy" based upon the teachings of Islam according to the Ahl Al-Sunnah Wa Al-Jemā'ah and based upon the principle of liberty, trust and justice and ever seeking the guidance and blessing of Allah (Whom praise be and Whose name be exalted) the peace and security, welfare and happiness of the people of Brunei Darussalam.* (Ministry of Education, 1989, p. 6)

His Majesty declared that the Malay Islamic Monarchy philosophy would be the cornerstone of the state's social, political and cultural stability. It is hoped that every aspect, including education, should fulfil the state's aspiration.

In the first year of independence, the education system remained the same (Educational Report Annual Report for the Year 1981–1984, p. 153). Immediately after, the MoE took a step towards changes in the education system following the national aspirations and former national objectives outlined in the 1972 educational report. A new system of education known as '*Sistem Pendidikan Dwi Bahasa*' (the Bilingual Education System) was introduced in April 1984 to accomplish these objectives (Ministry of Education, 1988). This new system is a means of 'ensuring the sovereignty of the Malay language, while at the same time recognizing the importance of the English language' (Ministry of Education, 1987, p. 33). It was fully implemented in all government schools in 1985 and in non-government schools in 1992 (Ministry of Education, 2004b).

In this system, Malay remained as the state's national language without neglecting the importance of English as the world's academic lingua franca. A high degree of proficiency in both languages should be achieved. Being proficient in the English language has enabled students to enter higher overseas institutions, where the medium of instruction is in English. Subjects that are substantially dependent on the English language at a higher level of education were taught in English, while those that were not dependent on English were taught in Malay. This system, which is free and compulsory, gave equal opportunity to study both languages. According to Jumat (1989) both Brunei and Singapore have recognised English as one of their educational media because both countries saw English as a language of international communication, commerce, trade, economics and banking. Concepts of the national philosophy (Malay Islamic Monarchy) are implemented in the school curriculum in support of the localisation of curriculum materials that are: introduction of a civics subject in primary schools, introduction of an MIB subject in lower secondary schools, and learning the *Jawi* script in the Malay language curriculum (Ministry of Education, 1989).

The Bilingual System implemented in all vernacular schools in Brunei was under the supervision of the MoE while the religious and Arabic Schools remain under MoRA. After independence, the development of Islamic education became more progressive. In 1993, the Tahfiz Al-Quran Sultan Haji Hassanal Bolkiah institute was established by His Majesty Sultan of Brunei under the MoE. The vision of this institute is to produce *ḥuffāẓ* (persons who memorise the Quran) without neglecting other academic fields. This institute has successfully produced *ḥuffāẓ* and at the same time specialised in different academic fields. By 2004, this institute had successfully produced 43 *ḥuffāẓ*. The students managed to further their studies in local and overseas institutions in the area of Engineering and Islamic studies; *Shar'iyyāt*, Revealed Knowledge, and the Quran and *Qirā'āt* (Ministry of Education, 2004c). On 2 January 2003, His Majesty Sultan Haji Hassanal Bolkiah consented on the transferring of the supervision of this institute from MoE to Yayasan Sultan Haji Hassanal Bolkiah and it was later transferred to MoRA integrated with the programmes at *Pusat Pengajian dan Penyebaran* Al-Quran MABIMS (Centre for MABIMS Al-Quran Studies and Dissemination) on 1 January 2006 (Kementerian Hal Ehwal Ugama, 2020).

Ahmad Jumat (1989) views that there is a lack of integration in the educational system as there is a divide between religious and non-religious schools. He is concerned that the dual approach to education has created the 'two worlds' problem in a child's mind; a religious world and a scientific one, with each held in isolation from the other (Jumat, 1989). This matter was discussed by *Allahyarham* Dato Paduka Seri Setia Prof. Dr Haji Awang Mahmud Saedon in his paper *School Curriculum Following Islamic Perspective* (1998). He argued that this dualism in the system has resulted in the categorisation of knowledge into religious and non-religious in the mindset of the people. The impact is that people tend to have a misconception that religious knowledge has no connection or relationship with the world and environment, and also has nothing to do with the development of science and technology.

This problem was discussed during the educational convention in 1998 with the theme *School Curriculum Towards the Twenty-First Century*. As a result, the placement of three sections from the Islamic Studies Department and the Ministry of Religious Affairs: the Inspectorate Section, Examination Section and Curriculum Section were under the jurisdiction of the department concerned in the MoE, effective from 1 March 2001. This was followed by the placement of other sections: administrative and scholarship under the administration of the MoE. The merger was fully implemented in January 2002 with the transfer of the Department of Islamic Studies and all the religious schools under its jurisdiction to the MoE. The purpose of this merger was to solve the problem in terms of control and management. Both religious schools and general schools share the same building, facilities, and come under the single management of MoE. Furthermore, on 14 February 2002, the MoE organised the 'Whole Day Schooling Pilot Scheme' called '*Skim Rintis Pendidikan Sepadu*' (Pilot Scheme on Integrated Education) which integrated 37 public schools and religious schools under one management under the MoE (see Chap. 5 for an overview of Islamic education in Brunei).

The MoE has conducted several projects in schools; one of the most important ones is the '*Pelajaran Al-Quran dan Pengetahuan Agama Islam*' (PAI) (Learning Quran and Islamic Revealed Knowledge) as a subject in the public schools that replaced the IRK. The PAI project had been conducted in 1994 in nine schools in the state. The aim was to make Bruneian children capable of reading the Quran. The curriculum of this subject was later integrated into the new religious education curriculum in the year 2004 (Ministry of Education, 1999, 2004c).

2.6 The Educational System of Brunei After 20 Years of Independence

Two years after the successful implementation of the 'Whole Day Schooling Pilot Scheme', the MoE introduced the new 'Integrated Education System' on 3 January 2004, which ensures that students acquire all aspects of the development of education: physical, emotional, spiritual, intellectual and social. This system also aimed to prevent the dualism of education as the focus shifts to an integrated education, which is

> to integrate the religion and general education or in other words, integration of revealed knowledge (as the foundation) with acquired knowledge. In these ways, the education is targeted at producing a balanced individual who not only emphasizes intellectual aspects but also has strong faith, is pious and is of good character, so as to balance the life of the present world and the hereafter. (Skim Rintis Sistem Pendidikan Bersepadu, 2004c, p. 5)

In this system, religious schools are integrated into the public school system. The contents of the three curricula—the Religious Schools curriculum, single religious education subjects taught in public schools (IRK) and PAI—are integrated into one curricular component: Religious Education (RE) (Ministry of Education, 2004a, p. 7). Unfortunately, the Integrated Education System was discontinued in December 2005. Brunei then resumed its former Bilingual System and Religious School System. Not long after, there was a reshuffling of the cabinet which resulted in the return of the administration of religious education to the MoRA.

Fieldwork research was conducted in 2008 among 114 school teachers on six general primary schools in the Brunei District and the findings showed that there had been opposition and complaints regarding the system. The survey findings demonstrate that there are five main issues and challenges concerning the implementation of the Integrated Education System. The first is the lack of knowledge on the issue of dualism in education among teachers; the second is misunderstanding and incorrect perceptions regarding the aims and curriculum structure of the system; the third is the lack of infrastructure and facilities; the fourth is the working culture and attitudes among teachers; and the fifth is an insufficient acknowledgement of the implementation of the system (Muhammad et al., 2013).

The MoE reviewed the education system and developed improvement plans and refocused its attention to general, technical and higher education. A review committee was formed and they recommended that the new education system should be aligned with the MoE Strategic Plan. Thus, the National Education System for the 21st Century or 'Sistem Pendidikan Negara Abad ke-21' (SPN21) was formed and officially launched in January 2009. SPN21 is used as a platform to realise the Ministry of Education Strategic Plan 2007–2011 and the 2012–2017 Plan, and to act as a driving force in achieving the goals of the national vision known as *Wawasan* (Vision) Brunei 2035. This alignment with *Wawasan* Brunei 2035 also affirms the Ministry's continuous commitment towards quality education for the nation (Ministry of Education, 2013). This includes developing critical skills in mathematics, science, languages and ICT; entrepreneurial skills and lifelong learning; and study skills and values education. It sets out the foundation policy for learning and assessment in schools to bring it in line with twenty-first-century demands and needs. There is also an emphasis on the inculcation of spiritual, moral, social, cultural attitudes and values, as well as physical development (Ministry of Education, 2013). Generally, the SPN21 aims to produce students with highly skilled learning performance, who are creative and have critical and analytical ways of thinking, good communication skills, able to work collaboratively with peers as well as to develop good moral values (Ministry of Education, 2009, p. 10).

In SPN21, a common curriculum is implemented at primary levels (Year 1 to Year 6) and secondary levels (Years 7 and 8) with eight various combinations of subjects. The assessment system in SPN21 has changed from an exam-oriented assessment towards student-centred learning. Previously, Year 9 students sat for the Lower Secondary Examination or *Peperiksaan Menengah Bawah* (PMB), but this was stopped in 2010 and replaced with the Student Progress Assessment (SPA). SPA marks are taken from both the School-Based Assessment (SBA) and the Student Progress Examination (SPE). At the end of Year 8, students have to undertake SPE, for which the core subjects' examinations are organised by the Department of Examination and other subjects are organised by a special committee. Students' marks obtained from SPE will be added to their SBA marks given by their teachers, and the overall marks will be carried forward to Year 9 (Ministry of Education, 2009). The SBA applies across all subjects whereas teachers are urged to vary the ways in which they evaluate students' work. SPN21 demands a shift from traditional types of student assessments towards SBA, such as mind mapping, projects, inquiry, students' self-assessment, peer assessment and others (Ministry of Education, 2009).

Another change in SPN21 is that IRK is taught as a single subject. One way to maintain and strengthen the delivery of religious knowledge to Muslim children is with the commencement of *Perintah Pendidikan Ugama Wajib 2012* (Order 2012 of Compulsory Religious Education) where all Muslim students are obligated to attend religious school starting on 1 January 2013 (Attorney General's Chambers, 2020). Also, *Jawi* writing and Arabic language components are included in the IRK subject curriculum (Ministry of Religious Affairs, 2015).

In terms of higher institution, there are currently four universities in Brunei Darussalam namely; Universiti Brunei Darussalam (UBD), Universiti Teknologi Brunei (UTB), Universiti Islam Sultan Sharif Ali (UNISSA) and *Kolej Universiti Perguruan Ugama Seri Begawan (KUPU SB)*. UBD, UTB and UNISSA are under the purview of the MoE, whereas *KUPU SB is under the MoRA*.

UBD was established in 1985 and regarded as the premier university in the country. *The mission of UBD* is to 'empower future-ready leaders through innovative education and enterprising research, driven by national aspirations and guided by the values of Malay Islamic Monarchy (MIB)' (Ministry of Education, 2020). UBD is guided by its five core values; people, expertise, aptitude, relevance and leadership (Ministry of Education, 2020). There are nine academic faculties, seven research institutes and one support centre. UBD is a comprehensive university offering vast disciplines including Islamic studies, Business, Arts, Science, Health Sciences, Asian Studies, Policy Studies, Education, Biodiversity and Engineering (Universiti Brunei Darussalam, 2020). In 2009, UBD introduced the GenNEXT Programme (Universiti Brunei Darussalam, 2020), which is

> An education framework designed for students to excel according to their individual learning styles. Broad-based and transdisciplinary, it provides the flexibility and adaptability necessary to ensure that students are able to fully explore their potential in a hands-on and accountable manner, while also providing thorough and rigorous training across disciplines. The GenNEXT degree ensures that students emerge from UBD with a high-quality education that is catered to their individual needs, as well as the needs of a constantly changing world environment.

In 2011, UBD introduced the Discovery Year (DY) programme as part of the GenNEXT Programme where students are required to leave the university for one year to either study abroad, participate in student exchange programmes, internship or volunteer in community outreach programmes. This is to promote real-world experiential and design-centric learning, while giving undergraduates the opportunity to gain community based or international experience outside of the UBD campus. UBD also provides Lifelong Learning which seeks to produce holistic and well-rounded generation leaders who are guided by three principles; innovation and entrepreneurship, industry-relevant skills, and a passion for lifelong learning. This is in line with the university motto *Ke Arah Kesempurnaan Insan* (Towards Human Excellence) (Universiti Brunei Darussalam, 2020a).

In 2020, UBD climbed 22 places in the QS world rankings for university under 50 years old. In the Times Higher Education ranking, UBD placed 78th in the world in the young university category. In the last three years, UBD has filed over 40 patents through its Innovation and Enterprise Office, eight of which have been granted both in Brunei and internationally. Research at UBD continues to be driven by national relevance, with emphasis on innovative and entrepreneurial initiatives and frameworks. Such initiatives are made possible through UBD's active networks and engagement with industry players to ensure its research and teachings are relevant to the needs of the market (Universiti Brunei Darussalam, 2020b).

UNISSA was established on 1 January 2007 as the second university through the commencement of His Majesty Sultan Hassanal Bolkiah's *titah* at UBD's 16th (2004) and 17th (2005) convocation. The overall aim of the new university is to become a centre for the spread of Islam in the region. The vision of UNISSA is 'to produce righteous and capable leaders who contribute to the development of the Ummah through academic excellence, research and community services' and its mission is 'to become an Islamic Higher Education Hub in Asia' (Universiti Islam Sultan Sharif Ali, 2020). To date, UNISSA has five faculties, including Faculty of *Usuluddin*, Faculty of *Shariah* and Law, Faculty of Arabic Language, Faculty of Islamic Economics and Finance and Faculty of Islamic Development Management. UNISSA also has centres, including the Centre for Promotion Knowledge and Language, Centre for Graduate Studies, *Mazhab Shafii* Research Centre, Centre for Research and Publication, Centre of International and Public Relations, *Halalan Thayyiban* Research Centre, Centre of Leadership and Lifelong Learning, and Technology and Multimedia Centre (Universiti Islam Sultan Sharif Ali, 2020).

Another established institution in the field of Islamic education is Kolej Universiti Perguruan Ugama Seri Begawan (Seri Begawan Religious Teacher University College). KUPU SB is a university college that produces trained religious teachers to fulfil the national needs and open their door to international students. KUPU SB was established on the 20 January 2007 with the commencement of His Majesty the Sultan dan Yang DiPertuan Negara Brunei Darussalam in conjunction with the new *Hijrah* (Muslim calendar) year 1428. His Majesty granted his consent to upgrade the existing KUPU SB to become a university. Currently, the university college has three faculties: The Faculty of *Usuluddin*; Faculty of *Syariah*; and the Faculty of Education, and eight centres: Centre of Core Knowledge, Language Centre, Centre of Post Graduate and Research, Research Centre of *Ahl as-Sunnah Wa al-Jama'ah* Understanding, Research Centre of *Fiqh al-Usrah,* Research Centre of Jawi and Kitab Turath, Centre of Multimedia and Technology, and Publications Centre (Kolej Universiti Perguruan Ugama Seri Begawan, 2020).

The fourth university is Universiti Teknologi Brunei. UTB was set up in January 1986 as Institut Teknologi Brunei (ITB), with the primary objective of catering for a range of interests in technical and commercial education. Its establishment was supported by Leeds Polytechnic, United Kingdom (now known as Leeds Metropolitan University) which indicates UTB's early aspiration to become a local institution that strives for international recognition. His Majesty the Sultan and Yang Di-Pertuan of Brunei Darussalam consented to upgrade the institution to a university in his decree at the Teacher's Day Celebration on 18 October 2008. The name of the University was changed from Institut Teknologi Brunei to Universiti Teknologi Brunei on 1 March 2016. Academic programmes at undergraduate and graduate levels are being offered by the Faculty of Engineering, School of Computing and Informatics and the UTB School of Business. There are now 20 undergraduate degree, 5 Taught Masters, and also Masters by Research and PhD programmes on offer. The Faculty of Engineering comprises four programme areas: Civil Engineering, Electrical and Electronic Engineering, Mechanical Engineering, and Petroleum and Chemical Engineering. The School of Computing and Informatics consists of three programme areas: Creative Computing, Computer Information Systems and Computer Network Security. Meanwhile, the UTB School of Business has three programme areas:

Economics, Accounting and Management. The Centre for Communication, Teaching and Learning supports the faculty and schools in terms of students' language proficiencies and soft skills development (Universiti Teknologi Brunei, 2020).

Apart from government's schools and higher institutions, there are a number of private learning schools and institutions in Brunei Darussalam. These private learning schools and institutions are implementing either their own education system or curriculum or following the national education system designed structure.

2.7 Conclusion

The present education system in Brunei Darussalam is structured and designed in accordance to the nation's identity and state philosophy of MIB and it aims to produce students with twenty-first-century skills and to achieve quality education for the nation. Islamic teaching and values place great importance in a nation's education and the *Perintah Pendidikan Ugama Wajib 2012* (Order 2012 of Compulsory Religious Education) made it mandatory for all Muslim students to attend religious school. At the same time, the Islamic elements and practices are embedded across the curriculum. The current structure of education makes it compulsory for all children in Brunei to attend public school and for Muslim children to attend both public and religious schools. The public schools are under the supervision of the MoE whereas the religious schools are under the MoRA, which also caters to the Arabic Schools and Tahfiz Al-Quran Sultan Haji Hassanal Bolkiah Institute. The dualism in the state's current educational system started when the first formal school was established by the British Resident in 1912. It continued when Brunei implemented the Bilingual System in 1984 and followed it with an effort to solve this problem by the implementation of Integrated Education System, but unfortunately this effort was short-lived.

Immediately after the Integrated Education System was discontinued, SPN21 was implemented in stages. This educational system still portrays dualist characteristics but the government of Brunei Darussalam has undertaken initiatives to bridge the gap such as through the inculcation of verses of Quran in the science textbook so that students do not perceive that religious knowledge is compartmentalised with the knowledge of sciences but both are rather interrelated. The suggestions for the future are to revise the curriculum so that there is no overlapping content between public school and religious school, specifically curriculum content related to Islamic Knowledge. The overlapping content should also be avoided in the public school as well so that the school hours can be shortened rather than having students attend long hours of schooling from morning until late afternoon. Through the revision of the curriculum, the learning and teaching outcomes will be more efficient and other important components can be included.

The strength of SPN21 is that it continues the legacy of maintaining Malay as the national language, preserving MIB as national identity while still realising the importance of the usage of the English language particularly in their eligibility to pursue further studies abroad. SPN21 also emphasises on the implementation of student-centred learning among the students as a way to develop the twenty-first-century skills. However, the challenge now is to monitor the reliability on the usage of the technology. Therefore, teachers must ensure that their students will gather their information from reliable resources from the Internet and if it is related to the Islamic teaching, the information must not contradict the teaching of *Ahl as-Sunnah Wa al-Jama'ah* The safety of the students is also a concern. The schools must ensure and monitor their students so that they will not be victims of hackers, cyber-bullying and other types of cybercrimes. Another improvement in SPN21 is that public schools and religious schools provide the learning of *Jawi* writing as a way to preserve the Malay heritage. The teaching of Arabic language is also included in both schools' curriculum. These improvements ensure students will be able to read the Quran and understand Arabic words.

To conclude, although the current national education system in Brunei Darussalam is still compartmentalised, it provides a holistic education to fulfil the national, societal, religious and economic needs. It portrays the unique identity of the modern Bruneian people blended with religion, customs and culture without neglecting the importance of helping students in mastering twenty-first-century skills.

References

Allen, L. A. (1922). *Report on the state of Brunei for the year 1921*. Federated Malay States Government Printing Office.

Al-Sufri, M. J. (2000). *Tarsilah (Chronicles) Brunei: The early history of Brunei up to 1432 AD*. Pusat Sejarah Brunei.

Attorney General Chambers. (2020). *Constitutional matters I—Constitution of Brunei Darussalam (B.L.R.O 2/2011)*. Retrieved from Constitution I (13.11.2010).fm (agc.gov.bn)

Attorney General's Chambers. (2020). Government Gazette Part II 2012. http://www.agc.gov.bn/Lists/gazetteII/NewDispForm.aspx?ID=81

Cator, G. E. (1917). *Report on the state of Brunei for the year 1916*. Federated Malay States Government Printing Office.

Cator, G. E. (1919). *Report on the state of Brunei for the year 1918*. Federated Malay States Government Printing Office.

Chuchu, M. N. (1990). The development of education in Brunei Darussalam. *Jurnal Pendidikan*, 1(Year 1), 37–64.

Department of State Secretariat. (1973). *Report of the education commission Brunei 1972*. Jabatan Setia Usaha Kerajaan.

Douglas, F. W. (1915). *Annual report on the state of Brunei for the year 1914*. Singapore Government Printing Office.

Jibah, M. (1983). Perkembangan Persekolahan Melayu di Brunei Dalam Pentadbiran Sistem Residen (1906–1959) (The development of Malay schools in Brunei Darussalam during the administration of resedential system). *Brunei Museum Journal*, 5(3), 1–26.

Jumat, A. (1989). *A chronological study of the development of education in Brunei Darussalam from 1906 to 1984: With special reference to education policies and their implementation*. PhD thesis, California Coast University.

Kementerian Hal Ehwal Ugama. (2020). *Institut Tahfiz Al-Quran Sultan Haji Hassanal Bolkiah*. http://www.kheu.gov.bn/SitePages/Institut%20Tahfiz%20Al-Quran%20Sultan%20Haji%20Hassanal%20Bolkiah.aspx

Kolej Universiti Perguruan Ugama Seri Begawan. (2020). *Latar Belakang*. http://www.kupu-sb.edu.bn/SitePages/Latar%20Belakang.aspx

Mail, H., & Asbol, A. (2017). *Pensejarahan Brunei Islam dan Evolusi Sosial*. Pusat Sejarah Brunei.

Majul, C. A. (1973). *Muslims in the Philippines*. The Asian Center by the University of the Philippines Press.

Mansurnoor, I. A. (1992). Intellectual tradition in a Malay world: Ulama and education in Brunei. *Jurnal Pendidikan*, 3(Year 3), 34–60.

Ministry of Education. (1987). *Education in Brunei Darussalam (an outline) 1986*. Public Relations Section, Permanent Secretary's Office, Ministry of Education.

Ministry of Education. (1988). *Educational annual report for the year 1981–1984*. Jabatan Perkembangan Kurikulum.

Ministry of Education. (1989). *Education in Brunei Darussalam* (Revised Edition). Public Relations Section, Permanent Secretary's Office, Ministry of Education.

Ministry of Education. (1999). *Laporan Konvensyen Pendidikan: Kurikulum Sekolah Abad Ke-21* (Convention report on education: School curriculum for the 21st century). Ministry of Education.

Ministry of Education. (2004a). *Integrated education*. Unpublished manuscript, Ministry of Education, Brunei Darussalam.

Ministry of Education. (2004b). *Pencapaian dan Penilaian 20 Tahun Pendidikan (1984–2003) dan Perancangan 20 tahun Akan Datang (2004–2024)* (Achievement and evaluation in 20 years of education (1984–2003) and future 20 years planning (2004–2024). Ministry of Education.

Ministry of Education. (2004c). *Skim Rintis Sistem Pendidikan Sepadu* (Pilot scheme on the integrated education system). Unpublished manuscript, Ministry of Education, Brunei Darussalam.

Ministry of Education. (2009). *Sistem Pendidikan Negara Abad ke-21 (SPN21)*. Ministry of Education.

Ministry of Education. (2013). *The national education system for the 21st century (SPN21)*. Ministry of Education.

Ministry of Education. (2020). *Higher education*. http://moe.gov.bn/SitePages/Higher%20Education.aspx

Ministry of Religious Affairs. (1996). *Pendidikan Ugama di Negara Brunei Darussalam* (Religious education in Brunei Darussalam). Jabatan Percetakan Kerajaan, Kementrian Undang-Undang.

Ministry of Religious Affairs. (2015). *Sukatan Pelajaran dan Panduan Mata Pelajaran Asas Pengetahuan Ugama Islam Tahun 1–3 Sekolah-Sekolah Rendah Negara Brunei Darussalam* (Syllabus and guidelines for core subject Islamic revealed knowledge year 1–3 at primary schools in Brunei Darussalam). Jabatan Pengajian Islam.

Mohd Daud, A. H. (2004) *Perkembangan Persekolahan Agama di Negara Brunei Darussalam dari Tahun 1956–1984* (The development of religious schools in Brunei Darussalam from 1956–1984), Dewan Bahasa dan Pustaka Brunei.

Muhammad, N. B. P. H., Bakar, D. O., & Mustafa, B. (2013). Implementation of the 'integrated education system' in Brunei Darussalam: Issues and challenges. *Journal of Middle Eastern and Islamic Studies (in Asia)*, 7(4), 97–120. https://www.tandfonline.com/doi/pdf/10.1080/19370679.2013.12023234

Peel, W. J. (1948). *Brunei annual report on the social and economic progress of the people of Brunei for the year 1946*. British Resident.

Rahman, P. A. P. H. M. (1998). *Perkembangan Pelajaran Agama di Negara Brunei Draussalam Dalam Zaman Pemerintahan Sultan Omar' Ali Saifuddien 1950–1967* (The development of religious schools in Brunei Darussalam from 1956–1984). *Jurnal Pendidikan*. Bil. 6, 7–46.

Saedon, M. (1998). Kurikulum Sekolah Mengikut Perspektif Islam: Bentuk dan Kandungannya (School curriculum following Islamic perspective: It's structure and content). In *Laporan Konvensyen Pendidikan: Kurikulum Sekolah Abad*

Ke-21 (Education convention report: School curriculum towards the 21st century) (pp. 37–50). Jabatan Perkembangan Kurikulum.

Serudin, M. Z. (2000). *Brunei an Islamic nation: Islamic background*. Ministry of Religious Affairs.

Sweeney, P. L. (Ed.). (1998). Silsilah Raja-Raja Berunai (Chronicles of the Berunai Sultans). In *Papers relating to Brunei* (pp. 46–127). MBRAS Reprints.

Universiti Brunei Darussalam. (2020a). *Quick facts*. https://ubd.edu.bn/about/quick-facts/

Universiti Brunei Darussalam. (2020b). *Organisation*. https://ubd.edu.bn/about/organisation/ubd-history.html

Universiti Islam Sultan Sharif Ali. (2020). *About us*. https://www.unissa.edu.bn/about-us/

Universiti Teknologi Brunei. (2020). *Past & present*. http://www.utb.edu.bn/university/past-present/

Upex, S. G. (2006). The history of education in Brunei, 1911–1980s. In *Fifty years of teacher education in Brunei Darussalam: A special commemorative publication 1956–2006* (pp. 7–21). University Brunei Darussalam.

CHAPTER 3

Malay, Muslim and Monarchy: An Introduction to Brunei Darussalam and Its National Identity

Salbrina Sharbawi and Shaikh Abdul Mabud

3.1 Introduction

Within the Malay-Muslim majority country of Brunei, national sentiments about life, thought and identity revolve predominantly around the national philosophy, officially and constitutionally known as *Melayu Islam Beraja* (Malay-Islam-Monarchy; henceforth MIB). This philosophy is traditionally described as a coherent amalgamation of three distinct but interrelated fundamentals of life upheld by the Malays in Brunei since the time of the proclamation of its independence. This philosophy serves as a moral and

---

Salbrina, S., & Mabud, S. A. (2021). Malay, Muslim and Monarchy: An introduction to Brunei Darussalam and its national identity. In Phan, L. H., A. Kumpoh, K. Wood, R. Jawawi, & H. Said (Eds.), *Globalisation, education, and reform in Brunei Darussalam* (pp. 45–66). Palgrave Macmillan.

S. Sharbawi (✉) • S. A. Mabud
Universiti Brunei Darussalam, Bandar Seri Begawan, Brunei
e-mail: salbrina.sharbawi@ubd.edu.bn; shaikh.mabud@ubd.edu.bn

ethical framework for all aspects and levels of domestic governance in the country. To ensure the preservation and practice of MIB, the Government of Brunei has invested tremendous efforts in educating its people on the values and virtues of this philosophy, including its introduction as a compulsory subject in the national curriculum at all stages of education. This chapter provides a theoretical insight into the meaning of the MIB philosophy, the impact that it has had on the country's national development, education systems, beliefs, values and customs. Additionally, this chapter introduces key themes, concerns and issues that readers will encounter in the ensuing chapters relating to the successes and challenges involved in preserving the MIB philosophy amid rapid modernisation of education in the country.

The philosophy of MIB was officially proclaimed by His Majesty the Sultan of Brunei on the day of independence on 1 January 1984:

> *Brunei Darussalam, with the permission and the grace of Allah subhanahu wa ta'ala will continue to remain as a Malay Islamic Monarchy State which is an independent, sovereign and democratic state, based on the teaching of Islam according to the ahlus sunnah wal jama'ah.* (His Majesty Sultan Haji Hassanal Bolkiah Mu'izzaddin Waddaulah, 1 January 1984)

It was proclaimed that this Malay-majority and Muslim-majority Southeast Asian country would forever be a nation of Malay-Islam-Monarchy (*Himpunan Titah*, 2018). This proclamation is said to have finally marked the official acknowledgement of MIB as a state philosophy and the collective identity of the country. His Majesty's historic independence speech highlighting MIB as Brunei's national ideology was further reinforced in his *titah* (royal decree) during the *Majlis Ilmu* (Knowledge Convention) held in conjunction with his 64th birthday:

> Brunei Darussalam's history is imbued with a valuable legacy—*Melayu Islam Beraja* (MIB). This is not a choice, but a blessing from Allah *subhanahu wa ta'ala*. As a blessing, it is, therefore, invaluable; more valuable than something that is a product of our own hands. (His Majesty Sultan Haji Hassanal Bolkiah Mu'izzaddin Waddaulah, 26 July 2010)

Local scholars and historians believe that the essence of MIB had existed and had been practised by the people of Brunei long before 1984, dating back to the conversion of the first Sultan of Brunei, Sultan

Muhammad Shah (born Awang Alak Betatar), into Islam in 1368 (Haji Awang Asbol et al., 2019). Indeed, archaeological artefacts have indicated its manifestations in Brunei, back when it was still known as *Po-ni*, some 600 years ago (Muhammad Hadi, 2017a). However, from 1368 until 1984, Brunei went through upheavals of triumphs and trials, which included a Golden Age (1485–1578) that saw the country blossom into a big empire and then, a 12-year civil war (1661–1673) that sent it spiralling into disunity. Springing from 600 years of turbulent history, the consolidation of MIB in 1984, therefore, came with a powerful emotional plea for unity and collectivity as a means for preserving the Bruneian identity (Haji Duraman, 2002).

MIB consists of three fundamental elements: *Melayu* (Malay), Islam and *Beraja* (Monarchy). 'Malay' encompasses the Malay people, language and culture. 'Islam' refers to the teachings, values and laws of the Islamic religion. 'Monarchy' characterises the monarchical system of administration and governance in Brunei. Each element has a significant historical backstory that has shaped national sentiments and inspired the people of Brunei to describe MIB as not just a national philosophy or a state ideology, but also a way of life. These backstories will be elaborated upon in the following section.

The understanding of MIB in Brunei is represented by a large, but uniform body of literature. Scores of historians, scholars, educators and government spokespeople have contributed to defining and contextualising its meaning and reconstructing its historical roots for the purpose of presenting it to the wider Bruneian audience. Given the venerated status of MIB and the fact that it is traditionally approached with respect and caution, there is little to no variation or disagreement in local scholarship as to what this national philosophy means for Brunei and its people. From school textbooks and scholarly publications to seminars and media talks, MIB is defined in the same way it is conceptualised by the Government of Brunei. Occasionally, local Malay scholars may disagree with each other's reconstruction of events within the Brunei history (i.e. dates, names, locations and sequence of events), but these minor disagreements do not diminish the influence and solidity of MIB.

The philosophy and values of MIB are taught and learned through various means, including top-down approaches by the government (e.g. policies, laws and regulations), formal education and cultural conditioning. Multiple government agencies in Brunei are authorised to promote, disseminate and implement the teachings of this philosophy: the Prime

Minister's Department, the *Adat* and *Istiadat* (Customs and Traditions) Department, the *Dewan Bahasa dan Pustaka* (Language and Literature Bureau), the Ministry of Religious Affairs, the Radio and Television Department, the Information Department and the Ministry of Education. Through the Ministry of Education, for example, MIB is one of the core subjects taught from the first year of primary education, and features consistently as a compulsory subject until Year 11, that is, the final year of secondary education. Additionally, elements of MIB are also prominently showcased in other core subjects such as *Pengetahuan Ugama Islam* (Islamic Religious Knowledge) and *Bahasa Melayu* (Malay Language) and taught through extracurricular activities. MIB is also taught as an academic subject at the tertiary level. In Universiti Brunei Darussalam (UBD), Brunei's first and premier university, MIB and Islam are both compulsory modules for undergraduate students and university requirements for graduation. A special section has been set up in the institution's library, aptly named the 'MIB Corner', where collections on publications and multimedia pertaining to MIB can be found.

Also based in the university is the *Majlis Tertinggi Kebangsaan MIB*, or the MIB Supreme Council, which saw its first conceptualisation in 1986 as *Jawatankuasa Konsep MIB* (the MIB Concept Committee). The change of the name to MIB Supreme Council was realised in 1990, the same year that its Secretariat, *Akademi Pengajian Brunei* (Academy of Brunei Studies, or APB) was established as a new faculty in UBD. Responsible for MIB-knowledge systematising and dissemination, the Supreme Council and the Secretariat began publishing materials on MIB in 1994 (Müller, 2018), in an effort to inform and educate the community about the ideals of MIB (Siti Norkhalbi, 2016).

MIB education is also reinforced by cultural and environmental realities in Brunei. As a Malay-dominated country with a population of approximately 459,500 (Department of Economic Planning and Statistics, 2019), Brunei is conspicuously Malay in institutional infrastructure, social ambience and cultural mentality. Through cultural conditioning and formal education, the people of Brunei are socialised into the Malay way of life—the Malay language, the Malay beliefs, morals and values, the Malay customs and the Malay historico-cultural knowledge are all embedded into the MIB identity. Physical symbols and markers of MIB are also visible and prevalent in the society. These include the Malay-Bruneian cultural and national dress codes, the many billboards and banners placed around the capital emphasising the importance of the Malay language, and the ubiquitous *Jawi* writings on signboards of shops, businesses and public facilities.

The influence of MIB on governance and policymaking in Brunei is perhaps unquestionable. National ideals and aspirations such as Brunei Vision 2035 and *Negara Zikir* (God-conscious nation) are all founded on the tenets of the country's national philosophy, which incorporates the Quranic concept of *Baldatun Tayyibatun wa Rabbun Ghafur* (a peaceful country worthy of God's mercy; Quran 34:15). Government discourses and practices regarding national development and planning, no matter how diverse and complex, never fail to be interlaced with the teachings of MIB.

It is perhaps clear to the readers now that there is a need to understand MIB and its inextricable link with the national and cultural aspirations and ideals of the Brunei government and its people. Considering this book's focus on education, this chapter offers a theoretical discussion on the foundational elements of MIB and the ways in which it shapes the country's philosophy of knowledge and education. To relate to the rest of the chapters in this book, this chapter provides an overarching frame that explains why and how MIB must always be the pillar upon which every state decision and action involving the people of Brunei and the governance of the country is predicated.

3.2 Melayu Islam Beraja: Deconstructing Its Elements

> MIB is our value system. Wherever we are, MIB should always be with us. Do not treat it with disregard. Disregarding MIB equates to disregarding our value system. (His Majesty Sultan Haji Hassanal Bolkiah Mu'izzaddin Waddaulah, 13 December 2015)

The above *titah*, which highlights MIB as an intrinsic element of 'Bruneianness', was delivered during the annual *Junjung Ziarah* (meet-and-greet) with Bruneian students in the United Kingdom and Ireland. Proclaimed to 'embody the core elements of true Bruneian identity' (Noor Azam, 2005, pp. 11–12), MIB is described as having five purposes:

1. It provides a unity of understanding regarding basic views of life, national lifestyle and a nation;

2. It serves as a source of reference and an ideal platform to build a harmonious community through the administrative system, the economy and effective development;
3. It serves as the foundation for all activities that affects the interest of the nation, such as religion, language, culture, socio-economics, governance and systems of development;
4. It embodies the norms and a Bruneian way of life; and
5. It serves as the basis and main guidelines for personal development, character and a Malay identity and the Bruneian way of life. (Mohd Zain, 1996, p. 49)

One of the key underpinnings of the MIB is to safeguard the security and welfare of the Bruneians. Policies which had been enacted since the time of the late Begawan Sultan Haji Omar 'Ali Saifuddien Sa'adul Khairi Waddien, were intended to guarantee peace, harmony and prosperity of the people of Brunei and these same ideals continue to be upheld by the current Sultan (Muhammad Hadi, 2017b), beginning with the pledge made in his *titah* almost five decades ago, when he became the Sultan of Brunei:

> With the guidance of Allah the Almighty, as the Sultan, I will continue to work to preserve the good name of Negeri Brunei Darussalam and for the peace, security, welfare and happiness of my subjects. (His Majesty Sultan Haji Hassanal Bolkiah Mu'izzaddin Waddaulah, 5 October 1967)

Through MIB, past traditions and policies are selectively retained, which are then adapted to suit the features of modernisation. The MIB philosophy also functions as a means of uniting the nation. According to Braighlinn (1992), MIB 'seeks to consolidate (after first asserting the ready existence of) a single national identity, born of convergence on a dominant Malay culture and long binding loyal citizenry to an absolute monarch of the same race, with the blessing and divine sanction of Islam' (p. 19). Simply put, cohesion is achieved by instilling shared values amongst the peoples, most notable of which is patriotism. Through the tenets of Malay and Monarchy, the love of, and for the country and the monarch, is injected and nurtured. Through the third limb of the ideology, Islam, unity is realised among the Muslims via oneness in creed, thought and purpose (Haji Ahmad, 2017).

3.2.1 Malay

The Malay component in MIB is a broad term that includes the Malay race, the Malay language and the Malay culture. The latter includes the beliefs, values, norms, rituals and identity markers of the Malay people. As noted by Noorashid (2018, p. 24), 'the essence of being Malay also means that one must respect the teaching of Islam and the Sultanate'. All of these components together make the Malay in MIB an institution and a way of life that reflect and influence the fabric of the whole Bruneian community. This institution becomes a symbol of unity and national identity, which is achieved through the convergence to the dominant Malay culture and defined by 'the attachment of its people to Malay culture, the Muslim religion and loyalty to the monarchy' (Saunders, 1994, p. 187).

3.2.1.1 Malay as a Race

The Constitution of Brunei defines the Malay race as encompassing seven *Puak Jati* or indigenous ethnic tribes: Brunei, Tutong, Kedayan, Belait, Dusun, Murut and Bisaya (Government of Brunei, 1961). Each tribe has its own cultural distinctiveness, such as dialects, rituals and folklores. By this definition, 'Malay' and 'Muslim' are not identical and, in some cases, are not interchangeable; Bisayas and Dusuns, for example, are traditionally Christians, although many have converted to Islam. The Malay component in MIB is, therefore, inclusive because it unites all these differences under the umbrella of 'Malay' for the sake of solidarity while recognising the right of every tribe to be unique. In other words, the seven ethnic tribes are politically viewed as different subgroups of Malay. According to Noor Azam (2005), this is a politically motivated move towards the creation of a single national identity in which ethnic differences are minimised.

Having 'Malay' in the ideology does not mean that only those subsumed under this term are considered Bruneians. In fact, Brunei citizens also comprise Chinese, Ibans and people of other races and religions. The requirement that is expected to be fulfilled of those applying for Bruneian citizenship is proficiency in the Malay language, details of which will be elaborated in the next section.

3.2.1.2 Malay as a Language

Despite the prevalent use of English—and, to a lesser extent, Arabic—only the Malay language is given official recognition in Brunei. Section 82(1) of the Constitution of Negara Brunei Darussalam states, 'the official language of the state shall be the Malay language and shall be in such script as may by written law be provided' (Government of Brunei, 1959). Historically, the Malay language was pivotal in uniting the leaders and the people of Brunei when foreign powers were substantially involved in the country and subsequently in securing the survival of the country and its identity (Haji Duraman, 2002). As mentioned, behind the national plea for preserving the Malay language, there is a strong historical memory that is interwoven with collective memories of war and suffering and with cultural and national pride. In a *titah* in conjunction with his 44th birthday celebration, His Majesty the Sultan stated:

> From the three words: 'Malay-Islamic-Monarchy', positive values for the perseverance of our nation are imbued; which from the word 'Malay', would be the language. Nobody could deny that *Bahasa Melayu* (the Malay language) is our only effective tool of unity. Without it (the Malay language), we would not be recognised as a sovereign race and would not possess an identity. (His Majesty Sultan Haji Hassanal Bolkiah Mu'izzaddin Waddaulah, 1990)

The importance of the Malay language and its preservation is reflected in national sentiments and discourses about the urgent need to remind the people of Brunei, particularly the younger generation, to not be fascinated with foreign cultures at the expense of their own cultural and linguistic heritage. Signboards placed around Bandar Seri Begawan, the capital of Brunei, and on government buildings express these discourses and sentiments clearly: *Utamakan Bahasa Melayu* (Prioritise the Malay Language). While English is recognised as an indispensable language for human development and economic success (e.g. education, technology and international affairs), concerns have been raised about the declining use of the Malay language in daily communication and for official business (e.g. Khartini, 2018; Kon, 2017; *Perkasa Kedaulatan Bahasa Melayu*, 2018). These concerns are valid, given the link between language and identity; so strong is the connection between the two entities that a single feature of language use is sufficient to identify the group that someone is a member of (Tabouret-Keller, 1997). Thus, a decline in the use of Malay would translate to a loss of the Bruneian identity.

The formidable association between the Malay language and the Bruneian identity is evidenced in the Nationality Act of Brunei 1961 which defined the Malay race as follows: 'any person born in Brunei

Darussalam before, on or after the appointed day who is commonly accepted as belonging to one of the following indigenous groups of the Malay race, namely, Belait, Bisayah, Brunei, Dusun, Kedayan, Murut or Tutong' (Government of Brunei, 1961). It is this definition that has been used as the 'hard and fast rule' (Noor Azam, 2005, p. 16) of Bruneian citizenship; in order to qualify as a citizen of Brunei through the process of naturalisation, one must have knowledge of and demonstrate proficiency in the Malay language through an examination dispensed by the Language Board. Another palpable indicator of how closely linked is the notion of 'Bruneianness' with the Malay language is in the field of education: for Bruneians to qualify for the Brunei Government Scholarship, either to study abroad or in local institutes of higher education, they must have obtained at least a credit in the GCE O-level examination in *Bahasa Melayu* (Malay language), in addition to possessing a yellow-coloured identification card (i.e. proof of citizenship) (Ministry of Education, 2020). Indeed, there are Bruneians of Chinese ethnicity who are highly proficient in the Malay language and this matter was showcased during a *Bahasa Melayu* Public Speaking Competition, organised in 2018 by the Hokkien Association in Brunei Darussalam, which saw encouraging participations from the Brunei Chinese community (Muhammad Hadi, 2018).

Another critical aspect of the Malay language is the *Jawi* script, which was once its standard script before the Roman alphabet replaced it. The *Jawi* script was derived from the Arabic language and introduced to the Malay world through the spread of Islam. Most of the alphabets in the *Jawi* script are identical to the letters of the Quran, except for a few that were added in order to accommodate Malay sounds that do not exist in Arabic. For this reason, the *Jawi* script is unambiguously linked to the Islamic religion and the Muslim identity.

In October 2019, the Mufti of Brunei (the grand religious authority) declared in his lecture at *Majlis Ilmu 2019* (2019 Knowledge Convention) that preserving the *Jawi* script is a duty and a noble deed for the people of Brunei, particularly because it is derived from the letters of the Quran. The Islamic and Malay identity of Negara Brunei Darussalam would always be proven through the *Jawi* script's function as the system of writing for the compulsory Islamic religious education, of which the medium of instruction is Malay. In announcing the establishment of the *Jawi* studies centre in 2019, His Majesty the Sultan linked the Malay-Arabic script as being representative of 'the nation's soul and identity' (Rasidah, 2019).

The use of *Jawi* has also been sanctioned by the government as evident in the following official regulations:

> In compliance with the speech delivered by His Majesty Haji Hassanal Bolkiah, Sultan of Brunei, it is hereby declared that all Ministries and Departments should observe and enforce the use of the *Jawi* script in addition to the Roman script on signs on Government buildings and on private businesses, including name signs, letterheads, notice boards, posters, advertisements, banners, names and street signs and so forth. The *Jawi* script must be twice as big as the Roman script and should be placed on top. (Dewan Bahasa dan Pustaka, 2009, p. 19. Translated from Malay by Coluzzi 2012)

Today, the *Jawi* script remains one of the government's tools for administration and management and a visible phenomenon all across the country through billboards, posters, road signs and the media. The close link between the Malay language and the *Jawi* writing with the MIB philosophy was evident during the 2018 Legislative Council meeting when a call was made to employ a 'whole nation approach' for the preservation and promotion of the use of Malay alongside *Jawi* as a means of further strengthening the Bruneian identity (Danial, 2018).

3.2.1.3 Malay as a Culture

Another dimension of 'being Malay' that can be identified in local writings about MIB is the extent to which a Malay person embraces the Malay cultural life and social conduct, which includes dress codes and etiquettes. Haji Duraman (2002) writes, 'the Malays would lose their identity if this trend [of dress codes changing and innovating] is not curtailed'. Although the Malay identity is much more than just dress codes, the author's concern is shared by many proponents of MIB, not least His Majesty the Sultan himself. In his 1990 *titah* during the Prophet Muhammad's (SAW) birthday celebrations, His Majesty declared:

> As Malays, it is our obligation to embrace the Malay codes of conduct and behaviour: politeness, respect towards each other, affection and kindness towards children and empathy towards the weak and the old. Our Brunei Malay culture and mannerism should also be reflected in our clothing, interactions, way of thinking and our actions. We do not emulate the dress code of other people, the way they socialise and the way they think and behave. If these four aspects are more akin to other people's, then Brunei would not

be Brunei. And this is what we do not wish to happen. (His Majesty Sultan Haji Hassanal Bolkiah Mu'izzaddin Waddaulah, 21 July 1990)

His Majesty the Sultan's declaration here speaks to the notion of distinctiveness, of the uniqueness of being Malay or of 'Malayness'. In the local context, this has often been referred to as '*calak* Brunei', or literally 'the Bruneian mould'. Characteristics which embody this definition of 'Malayness' could be divided into two categories: core and cultural (Haji Mohammad, 1989). The former, which is reflective of Islamic principles, includes, among others, notions of loyalty, responsibility, sincerity, honesty, patience, humility and gratitude. Cultural values, on the other hand, are of six components:

1. *Awar galat* (respectful humility)
2. *Menuakan yang tua* (reverence for the elder and elderly)
3. *Menghormati ibu bapa* (respecting parents)
4. *Mentaati raja* (loyalty to the king)
5. *Menjunjung adat* (upholding tradition)
6. *Identiti kebruneian* (Bruneian identity). (Ibid.)

Of the six, *awar galat* is one that is uniquely Bruneian. A local phrase so distinct that the concept does not have a direct equivalence in English. The closest definition that has been offered is 'humble and respectful' (Low & Ang, 2011, p. 295) but even that does not capture its true essence. To be *awar galat* is more than just to be well-mannered; it also means to possess the knowledge of how to appropriately behave in any particular social instances. So pertinent is this concept to the Brunei Malay culture, that it was highlighted in the Sultan's *titah* in 1991, alongside another 'Malayness' value—that of community solidarity:

In this era of uncertainty, our valuable assets are solidarity and goodwill. Only with these values would we be able to live in harmony, be able to nurture the attributes of *awar galat* and be respectful to others in the community. For without these values, if there were discordance and hatred amongst us, nothing good would come out of it except calamity and disturbance. (His Majesty Sultan Haji Hassanal Bolkiah Mu'izzaddin Waddaulah, 9 March 1991)

One of the key takeaways from the Sultan's *titah* above is that the values of Malayness are crucial for unity, peace and harmony. The Malay arm of MIB, therefore, has far-reaching implications—not only does it denote the Malay race, language and culture, it is also a crucial ingredient for social cohesion and stability.

3.3 Islam

> Islam is the ultimate religion, the one which we profess to be the true religion. *Rasulullah* was sent to spread the message of this religion to the whole of mankind. Among the teachings of Islam is to strive towards moral perfection, in line with our knowledge of a hadith by the Prophet *Sallallahu 'Alaihi wa Sallam*, which states that *Rasulullah* was sent to perfect good character. (His Majesty Sultan Haji Hassanal Bolkiah Mu'izzaddin Waddaulah, 1 October 1990)

In Brunei, Islam is more than just a religion in the sense of faith and rituals. It is an institution that covers all aspects of life and governance and serves as a significant form of socio-cultural identity that binds the society together. Whilst religion has, in the present day and time, been more commonly associated with divisiveness and the source of political instability, that is not the case in the small nation of Brunei. As rightfully pointed out by Mansurnoor (2008), '(R)eligious life in Brunei … is characterized by a marked degree of peace and harmony which is indicated by the absence of schismatic tensions' (p. 65).

Although non-Muslims enjoy the freedom to practise their own beliefs, many elements of the Islamic religion are embedded into the fabric of daily life in Brunei. Islamic architecture manifests in the form of pointed domes and curved arches, which are evident not only on mosques but also on non-religious state-owned buildings. For five times a day, the *adhan*, or call to prayer, can be heard from the mosques' minarets. Like in many Muslim countries, Fridays are off-days for the government sector in respect for the Muslim congregational Friday prayers at noon, during which all businesses are required to close. As an expression of faith, Muslim religious recitations preface and conclude official meetings in the government sector and national events and celebrations. During the holy month of Ramadan, when Muslims fast every day from dawn to sunset, entertainment and sports activities are halted and office hours are reduced in consideration of the faithful's need to enhance their spiritual discipline and connection to the Creator through worship and social welfare activities. Through the Islamic component within MIB, Muslim fundamental beliefs drive all motivations and inspirations at the state level for national development. The welfare of the people, for example, is not merely a basic human right from the perspective of the Brunei government; it is primarily a fundamental Islamic requirement placed upon the head of the state and his government.

Muslim thought in Brunei at the state level is shaped by the established thinking within the tradition of the *Shafi'i* sect of Sunni Islam. The Constitution of Brunei defines the religion of Brunei as 'the Islamic Religion according to the Shafi'ite sect of *Ahli Sunnah Waljamaah*' (Government of Brunei, 1959). In addition to ensuring that Islamic teaching within the country does not deviate from the national requirements and standards, the Brunei Government put into place, in 1955, the Religious Council, State Custom and *Kadis* Courts Enactment which consequently led to the establishment of the Islamic Religious Council in 1956, the primary function of which is to offer advice to the Sultan on matters pertaining to the Islamic religion (Mansurnoor, 2008). On the education front, the Islamic religious education, which is under the purview of the Ministry of Religious Affairs, has been made compulsory for the Brunei Muslim population through the Compulsory Islamic Religious Education Act of 2012 (Azlan, 2013). Under this law, all children of Muslim Bruneians are required to attend *Ugama* (i.e. religious) schools for a duration of seven to eight years, thereby ensuring that the teachings of Islam adequately reach young Bruneians (Haji Asbol et al., 2019) (see Chap. 2). It is also in these schools that the *Jawi* script is used exclusively, thus cementing the association between this system of writing with the religion of Islam and the Malay culture.

The promotion of Islam is not left solely for the Ministry of Religious Affairs to oversee. Other ministries and government departments have also been entrusted to play a part in the propagation of Islamic practice, teachings and beliefs. For instance, the halal food industry, one of the country's economic niches, is overseen by the Ministry of Energy via its Global Halal Industry Development Division (GHID) (Ministry of Energy, 2020); the elevation of Brunei as an international Islamic financial hub is one of the priorities of the Ministry of Finance and Economy; whilst the Attorney-General's Chambers (in collaboration with the Ministry of Religious Affairs) is tasked with the implementation of the Islamic system of law and jurisprudence.

As seen from the above accounts, Islam is not simply a religion, but it forms an integral part of the Bruneian life and displays prolifically throughout the Bruneian society. The national goal of the country is to create a *zikr* nation (*Negara Zikr*), which is one 'that upholds Allah (SWT)'s laws, with noble moral values'. *Zikr*, which literally means 'remembrance of Allah' is not only restricted to the personal level but is also reflected in all facets of life. From the architectural designs, to the clothing and drinking and eating practices, this is indeed what the second tenet of the ideology strives to achieve: the inculcation of Islam in every facet of the Bruneian lives, whilst also advocating widespread respect and appreciation for religious differences, which is essential for social solidarity and living in harmony with others.

3.4 Monarchy

> Monarchy also means a Sultanate. Thus, the interpretation of MIB also means that Brunei Darussalam is an Islamic Malay nation that is ruled by a Sultan. This is not from our effort or creation, but it is the Will of Allah. (His Majesty Sultan Haji Hassanal Bolkiah Mu'izzaddin Waddaulah, 1 October 1990)

The third leg of the philosophy, monarchy, has an overarching definition that encompasses more than simply 'governed by a king'. In the context of MIB, the ruler is the Sultan and, as pointed out by the former Deputy and now current Minister of Religious Affairs during the 2006 Aidil Adha sermon, also one of the *ulil amri minkum* (Azlan, 2006):

> But in the context of a nation and government, '*Ulil Amri Minkum*' means the supreme leader of the government and the nation and in the context of Brunei, '*Ulil Amri*' is His Majesty the Sultan and Yang Di-Pertuan of Brunei Darussalam ... Loyalty should be shown continuously as long as the monarch or *'Ulil Amri'* does not breach or disobey Allah the Almighty.

The notion of *ulil amri* and the concept of loyalty in MIB have often been linked to the Quranic verse from Surah An-Nisa, Chapter 4, Verse 59:

> O you who have believed, obey Allah and obey the Messenger and those in authority (*ulil amri*) among you. (*Sahih International*, published by Dar Abul Qasim, Saudi Arabia, 1997)

Outwardly, three types of 'obedience' is being commanded here—of Allah, the Messenger and those in authority. Lexically, *ulil amri* means those in authority who manage and administer. According to Sayyidina Abu Hurairah (RA) this term signifies officials and rulers who hold the reins of government in their hands. Earlier commentators such as Sayyidina Ibn Abbas, Mujahid and Hasan al-Basri hold the view that this term applies to scholars and jurists (*ulama* and *fuqaha*). According to *Tafsir Ibn Kathir* and *Tafsir al-Mazhari*, this expression refers to both these categories, that is, officials and rulers as well as scholars and jurists as the system of command involves all of them (Shafi, 2011, p. 475).

The expectation for the people of Brunei, therefore, is to maintain obedience and loyalty to the Sultan as the Head of State and the Head of Religion, which in reality is obedience to the commands (*ahkam*) of Allah. In addition to being an act of adherence to the teaching of Islam, loyalty to the leader is also indistinguishably linked to the Malay way of life whereby one dimension of 'being Malay', as argued by local scholars and historians, also means possessing loyalty to the person who leads the community. This is also the view of most of the early exegetes of the Quran as discussed in the preceding paragraph. When a leader rules the country in accordance with Islam, being loyal to him is an Islamic commandment: 'it is necessary to follow Muslim jurists in matters relating to jurisprudence, matters which have not been textually specified and to follow rulers and officials in matters relating to administration. This is what "obedience to those in authority" means' (Shafi, 2011, p. 478).

An early account of Malay loyalty was recorded in *Shaer Awang Semaun*, in which an entourage of 90 indigenous people uprooted their lives to be close to their leader, Awang Alak Betatar, who had resettled on the Brunei River (Muhammad Hadi, 2017a) (see Chap. 2). This stark display of affection and loyalty by the people for and towards their leader laid the foundations of the MIB ideology—a relationship of mutual respect in which the leader loved his people and the people loved their leader. This undivided loyalty towards the Sultan is one of the factors for the relative stability of the monarchy and consequently epitomises unity and solidarity of the people of Brunei (Naimah, 2002). The monarch takes care of his subjects from cradle to grave, and, by and large, offers them an affluent secure life.

According to Fadil (1991), the monarchical system is a tradition in the administration of the Malay race. In the thirteenth century, as a result of the rule of the Hindu-Buddhist Majapahit Empire, the concept of divine kingship, *devaraja*, was adopted in the Malay Archipelago. In this concept, the king was viewed as the embodiment of *deva* (God), which is against the Islamic concept of *tawhid* (monotheism). Following the conversion of Awang Alak Betatar to Islam, the Sultanate of Brunei was established and the Islamic law mixed with customs (*adat*) operated in the country. Consequently, the concept of *devaraja* was replaced by that of Sultan, whose unbroken chain continues until today. The monarch (or *raja*) is the power centre and is the highest ruling authority. The experience of more than 600 years of hereditary monarchical system in Brunei with its current 29th descendant gives a clear picture of a peaceful Brunei and continuous blessings bestowed by Allah upon the king and his subjects.

In accordance with the concept of 'leader' in Islam (as exemplified by the Prophet Muhammad (SAW)), the responsibilities of the monarch of Brunei are not confined to political governance. The monarch is simultaneously the King (*raja*), the Sultan and the Official Head of Religion (*ketua ugama rasmi*, Constitution, Article 3(2)) who has devoted himself to promote the peace, security and wellbeing of Bruneian people in a way that has gained him unswerving loyalty of his people. While harmonising the traditions of the Sultanate with the demands of the modern world, he has been guided by the fundamental principles of Islam. As the Sultan dan Yang Di-Pertuan Negara Brunei Darussalam and the Prime Minister, the power vested in him by the Constitution is a trust (*amanah*) which must be executed for the welfare, prosperity and tranquillity of people residing in Negara Brunei Darussalam. This trust must be understood in the context of the Malay adage, *Raja wajib adil, rakyat wajib taat* (the ruler must be just, the people must be loyal) (*Pelita Brunei*, 2017). People of the country enjoy freedom within the boundaries of the law and many people in Brunei believe that the Sultan will 'always have the best interests of his subjects at heart' (Dato Seri Paduka Haji Kifrawi, 2006). Despite the Constitution providing him with the highest executive authority to involve himself in the administration and management of every government agency, he would not necessarily do so, unless he is convinced that the agencies involved have not functioned in accordance with the prescribed laws and regulations.

Now that the three tenets of MIB have been outlined, the next section will provide an overview of how this national ideology helps in the shaping of Brunei's national identity.

3.5 National Identity

The notion of 'national identity' is a deeply debated issue as both the terms 'nation' and 'identity' lend themselves to different interpretations. It can be said that the identity of a collective entity such as a polity is formed by its organising principles, deeply held beliefs, ideals, values, traditions, dispositions and its characteristic ways of thought. In today's multicultural world in which diversity is the oft-cited buzzword, the concept of national identity has been regarded as problematic. It especially becomes a contested debate when people feel that certain aspects of their ways of life are threatened. This often stems from the irrational fear of losing what they consider to be the most valuable or central to their identity. The point that is often missed is that the identity of a nation is never historically fixed but is a subject of constant reorientation due to changes in external circumstances. If the nation fails to adjust itself to changes, it stagnates, but if it changes too quickly, it can overthrow the societal balance, and the society can become disorientated (Parekh, 1995). Although he accepts the role of religion in the formation of national identity, Parekh contradicts himself when he states that '(I)dentity is not something that we *have*, rather it is what we *are;* it is not a *property* but a *mode of being*. To talk of preserving, maintaining, safeguarding or losing one's identity is to use misleading metaphors' (p. 268, emphasis added). The fundamental principles of religion are not so fluid and malleable as Parekh makes it seem. For a believer, they are sacrosanct and must be preserved, maintained and safeguarded.

Parekh, moreover, remarks that *all* the factors making up an identity can be changed by human beings. As religion has been identified as one of the said factors, by stating the above, Parekh is matter-of-factly denying religion its heavenly source. He further asserts that 'by its very nature a community's identity needs to be constantly reconstituted in the light of its inherited resources, present needs and future aspirations', but he disregards the unchangeable and unalterable aspects of human beings—'the immutable and permanent sea of man's real nature' (Nasr, 1968, p. 10.)—and does not discuss the boundaries of such 'reconstitution'. Instead, he stresses that it is misleading to talk about preserving one's identity. It would be unfair if it is not mentioned that in a tug of war between religion and secularism, Parekh concedes that it is difficult to come up with a balanced response (Parekh, 1995, p. 265).

A secular approach to the question of national identity as a panacea for all multicultural problems only exacerbates the moral and spiritual decline that many sections of our society are suffering from today. It should not, however, come as a surprise that religion is an important part of national identity in Brunei. Despite the chorus of criticism and disapproval on associating national identity with religion, it appears that there is a growing tendency to tie the two together. For example, in a study conducted by the Pew Research Center, many countries of Central and Eastern Europe, which were once atheists, now proclaim to have an official state religion (Kishi & Starr, 2017). Across the 18 countries, more than half (66%) of those surveyed claimed that faith (or religion) is important to national identity. Whilst it is agreeable that national identity may not be historically fixed, for any country that professes to be ruled by religion, or whose people want to see religion play a central role in their life, the primary task of the state is, therefore, to maintain the most fundamental elements of their people's faith.

In the last six decades, Bruneians have undergone many changes in their conception of identity. With the delineation of geographical borders by the British all the ethnic groups living within these borders—the Belait, Bisaya, Brunei, Dusun, Kedayan, Murut and the Tutong—were suddenly bound by a new single political entity called the State of Brunei, with the consequent formation of a new socio-political concept, 'Bruneian Malay', both indigenous and non-indigenous. Whereas in Great Britain, distinctions have been made between state identity and national identity (e.g. being British versus being English), in Brunei, scholarly discussions have mostly concerned the contested space between ethnic and national identities. Concerns were raised on what scholars claim to be an apparent blurring of ethnic identities by the state, but these claims appear to have arisen following the critiques interpreting the MIB ideology according to their own moral, political and social lenses. To proponents of MIB, the national ideology acts as a unifier through which a national identity has emerged; one of Bruneian with Malay-based cultural values and norms and which encompasses peoples of different ethnic identities. In this respect, the Brunei national identity could be construed as a nested or complementary identity, as opposed to one that is contradictory. As rightfully pointed out by Abdul Aziz (2013), 'the utility of MIB becomes visible when there is an awareness of the fact that the peace, stability and harmony we enjoy in Brunei today are driven by a responsible government, underpinned by a multi-racial and multi-religious society' (p. 96).

3.6 Conclusion

Melayu Islam Beraja is an ideology that is deeply rooted in history, rich in long-standing traditions that have been central in the shaping of the Bruneian culture, practices and self-identity. It is an ideological concept that upholds the Islamic teachings, principles and values established in the Holy Quran and based on the hadiths of the Prophet (SAW) and serves as the foundation of the entire gamut of human activities, be they spiritual or material, individual or collective, educational or cultural, economic or political, and national or international. MIB caters to the aspirations of the sovereignty, through the preservation, maintenance and embodiment of the Malay identity and culture and the preservation of the monarchical system of governance. MIB is not simply a philosophy for the nation's development; it also forms the basis of national integrity and is integral in the definition of true Bruneian identity. The monarchical system of Brunei, based on the precepts of Islam, has provided the nation with a way life, a framework for Bruneian people to realise their hopes and aspirations and a stability to the country. With its philosophy of tolerance, which allows other cultures to follow their traditions and practise their religion, this system ensures peace and social harmony among people of all faiths living in the country. The nuances of Bruneian way of thinking can be understood only in the light of its long-standing tradition rooted in the philosophy of MIB that has not only forged the national identity but also provided the nation with a vision and direction. This philosophy, however, is neither immutable nor unchangeable as 'what Brunei has always been is not necessarily what Brunei should be' (Abdul Aziz, 2013, p. 97). Just as the national identity is not historically fixed, the philosophy of MIB is also open to interpretation based on the beliefs, values, needs and social circumstances of the people of Brunei, that is, the unique indigenous context. It is not for outsiders (e.g. Müller, 2016, 2018; Black, 2019) to dictate what form MIB should take or even what should replace it, if need be.

References

Abdul Aziz, U. (2013). Melayu Islam Beraja. *Journal of the Malaysian Branch of the Royal Asiatic Society, 86*(2), 93–97.

Azlan, O. (2006, January 12). Deputy minister upholds loyalty to monarch. *Borneo Bulletin*.

Azlan, O. (2013, January 2). Perintah wajib pendidikan agama. *Borneo Bulletin*.

Black, A. (2019). Brunei Darussalam: Small by choice, but great in the eyes of Allah. In T. Angelo & J. Corrin (Eds.), *Small states: A collection of essays* (pp. 81–108). Comparative Law Journal of the Pacific.

Braighlinn, G. (1992). *Ideological innovation under monarchy: Aspects of legitimation activity in contemporary Brunei*. VU University Press.

Coluzzi, P. (2012). The linguistic landscape of Brunei Darussalam: Minority language and the threshold of literacy. *Southeast Asia: A Multidisciplinary Journal, 12*, 1–16.

Danial, N. (2018, March 21). Brunei: Malay language, Jawi writing are treasures that need to be empowered. *Borneo Bulletin*.

Dato Seri Paduka Haji Kifrawi, D.P.H.K. (2006). *Opening of legal year 2006* [Transcript]. www.agc.gov.bn

Department of Economic Planning and Statistics. (2019). *Population*. http://www.deps.gov.bn/SitePages/Population.aspx

Dewan Bahasa dan Pustaka Brunei. (2009). *Utamakanlah Bahasa Melayu*. Dewan Bahasa dan Pustaka Brunei.

Fadil, S. (1991). Pengislaman Dunia Melayu: Transformasi Kemanusiaan dan Revolusi Kebudayaan. *Dalam Dewan Budaya, 12*(11), 36–39.

Government of Brunei. (1959). *Brunei Constitution 1959, Article 82 (1)* [English version]. Government of Brunei.

Government of Brunei. (1961). Undang2 Taraf Kebangsaan Brunei. Undang2 No. 4. In *Surat2 Perlembagaan Negeri Brunei* (pp. 115–135). Kuala Belait: Government Printer (Brunei Nationality Act, No. 4, in Constitutional Letters of the State of Brunei).

Haji Ahmad, E. (2017). *Falsafah Melayu Islam Beraja: Hubungan dengan Modeniti*. Dewan Bahasa dan Pustaka.

Haji Asbol, H. M., Ampuan Haji Brahim, H. T., & Haji Tassim, H. A. B. (2019). History and development of Islamic education in Brunei Darussalam, 1900–1983: From home instruction to the religious primary school. *International Journal of Innovation, Creativity and Change, 5*(2), 1082–1101.

Haji Awang Asbol, H. M., Haji Brahim, H. T., Nani Suryani, H. A. B., Asiyah Az Zahra, H. A. K., & Haji Tassim, H. A. B. (2019). Melayu Islam Beraja. In *The Malay Islamic Monarchy in Negara Brunei Darussalam prior to 1906: A historical study*. Persatuan Sejarah Brunei.

Haji Duraman, T. (2002). *The implementation of Melayu Islam Beraja in Brunei Darussalam's public administration*. Information Department, Prime Minister's Office.

Haji Mohammad, N. (1989, December 16–21). *Kertas Kerja Kursus intensif Konsep MIB* [Paper presentation]. UBD, Brunei.

Himpunan Titah Kebawah Duli Yang Maha Mulia Paduka Seri Baginda Sultan Haji Hassanal Bolkiah Mu'izzaddin Waddaulah, Sultan dan Yang Di-Pertuan

Negara Brunei Darussalam Tahun 2017. (2018). Jabatan Penerangan, Jabatan Perdana Menteri.

Khartini, H. (2018, September 19). Tingkatkan kemahiran Bahasa Melayu pelajar. Pelita Brunei. http://www.pelitabrunei.gov.bn

Kishi, K., & Starr, K. J. (2017, November 3). *Many Central and Eastern Europeans see link between religion and national identity.* Pew Research Centre. https://www.pewresearch.org/fact-tank/2017/11/03/many-central-and-eastern-europeans-see-link-between-religion-and-national-identity/

Kon, J. (2017, August 26). Malay language losing grip. *Borneo Bulletin.*

Low, P. K. C., & Ang, S. L. (2011). Confucius, Confucian values and their applications on marketing—The Brunei perspective. *Journal of Research in International Business Management, 1*(9), 293–303.

Mansurnoor, I. A. (2008). Islam in Brunei Darussalam. Negotiating Islamic revivalism and religious radicalism. *Islamic Studies, 47*(1), 65–97.

Ministry of Education. (2020). *Scholarship section.* Retrieved July 31, 2020, from http://www.moe.gov.bn

Ministry of Energy. (2020). *Developing the local halal industry in Brunei Darussalam.* Retrieved August 1, 2020, from http://memi.gov.bn

Mohd Zain, S. (1996). *Melayu Islam Beraja: Suatu Pendekatan.* Dewan Bahasa dan Pustaka.

Muhammad Hadi, M. M. (2017a, January 25). *MIB, living foundation of every Bruneian.* MTMIB. https://mtmib.moe.gov.bn/mib-living-foundation-of-every-bruneian/

Muhammad Hadi, M. M. (2017b, February 8). *MIB is our policy.* MTMIB. https://mtmib.moe.gov.bn/mib-is-our-policy/

Muhammad Hadi, M. M. (2018, November 5). Negaraku Brunei Darussalam. Media Permata. http://mediapermata.com.bn

Müller, D. M. (2016). Paradoxical normativities in Brunei Darussalam and Malaysia: Islamic law and the ASEAN human rights declaration. *Asian Survey, 56*(3), 415–441.

Müller, D. M. (2018). Hybrid pathways to orthodoxy in Brunei Darussalam: Bureaucratised exorcism, scientisation and the mainstreaming of deviant-declared practices. *Journal of Current Southeast Asian Affair, 1,* 141–183.

Naimah, S. T. (2002). Resilient monarchy: The Sultanate of Brunei and regime legitimacy in an era of democratic nation-states. *New Zealand Journal of Asian Studies, 4*(2), 134–147.

Nasr, S. H. (1968). Man in the universe: Permanence amidst apparent change. *Studies in Comparative Religion, 2*(4), 1–7.

Noor Azam Haji-Othman. (2005). *Changes in the linguistic diversity of Negara Brunei Darussalam: An ecological perspective.* Unpublished doctoral dissertation, University of Leicester, UK.

Noorashid, N. (2018). *A study on attitudes towards the Malay language and its vitality in Brunei, Malaysia, Indonesia and Singapore*. Unpublished doctoral dissertation, Universiti Brunei Darussalam, Brunei.

Parekh, B. (1995). The concept of national identity. *Journal of Ethnic and Migration Studies, 21*(2), 255–268.

Pelita Brunei. (2017, October 7). Raja wajib adil, rakyat wajib taat. http://www.pelitabrunei.gov.bn

Perkasa Kedaulatan Bahasa Melayu. (2018, July 3). *Media Permata*. https://mediapermata.com.bn/perkasa-kedaulatan-bahasa-melayu/

Rasidah, H. A. B. (2019, October 16). Brunei to set up new Jawi centre. *The Scoop*. https://thescoop.co/2019/10/16/brunei-to-set-up-new-jawi-centre/

Saunders, G. (1994). *A history of Brunei*. Oxford University Press.

Shafi, M. (2011). *Ma'ariful Qur'an (Vol. 2)*. Maktaba Darul Ulum.

Siti Norkhalbi, H. W. (2016). Peranan golongan intelektual Brunei dalam konsep Melayu Islam Beraja. In H. M. Haji Asbol, H. A. D. Mohd Yusop, & H. A. Rosli (Eds.), *Brunei Merdeka: Kumpulan artikel sempena memperingati sambutan 30 tahun Hari Kebangsaan Negara Brunei Darussalam* (pp. 183–198). Yayasan Sultan Haji Hassanal Bolkiah.

Tabouret-Keller, A. (1997). Language and identity. In F. Coulmas (Ed.), *The handbook of sociolinguistics* (pp. 315–326). Blackwell Publishing Ltd.

CHAPTER 4

Melayu Islam Beraja in the *Titahs* of His Majesty the Sultan of Brunei (2011–2020): The Leader's Transformative Vision and Aspirations

Muzhafar Marsidi

4.1 Introduction

Brunei is one of the oldest reigning monarchies in the world and the only surviving monarchy in Southeast Asia. Its current ruler, Sultan Haji Hassanal Bolkiah, is the world's second oldest reigning monarch (the first being Queen Elizabeth II of the United Kingdom) and the 29th monarch

---

M. Muzhafar (2021). *Melayu Islam Beraja* in the *Titahs* of His Majesty the Sultan of Brunei (2011–2019): The leader's transformative vision and aspirations. In Phan, L. H., A. Kumpoh, K. Wood, R. Jawawi, & H. Said (Eds.), *Globalisation, education, and reform in Brunei Darussalam* (pp. 67–83). Palgrave MacMillan.

M. Marsidi (✉)
Universiti Brunei Darussalam, Bandar Seri Begawan, Brunei
e-mail: 19M8285@ubd.edu.bn

© The Author(s), under exclusive license to Springer Nature Switzerland AG 2021
Phan, L. H. et al. (eds.), *Globalisation, Education, and Reform in Brunei Darussalam*, International and Development Education, https://doi.org/10.1007/978-3-030-77119-5_4

in the country's history. Since 1363, when Brunei's first ruler, Sultan Muhammad Shah, ascended the throne, the country has been inhabited by a Malay-Muslim-majority population. Correspondingly, its demographic and cultural reality and history have given it an identity that is instantly recognisable in the region and that its current government never ceases to emphasise—Brunei is and will forever be a Malay Muslim Sultanate (Jabatan Penerangan, 2017). In support of the official, constitutionalised identity of Brunei, the government introduced a national philosophy known as *Melayu Islam Beraja* (Malay Islamic Monarchy in English or simply MIB as it is commonly referred to) in the early 1990s, which serves as an overarching framework within which national development and planning take place (see Chaps. 2 and 3). The MIB philosophy is revered nationwide in Brunei and invoked in the country's national policies, strategies and official documents. The country's national vision for the year 2035 (Brunei Vision 2035), for example, was developed particularly with MIB as its backbone. Similarly, the country's National Education System for the 21st Century (acronymically known as SPN21) was designed in line with the values of MIB and to promote MIB as a national philosophy that must be preserved by the younger generation (see Chap. 2). These examples show the centrality of this philosophy to the governance of Brunei.

Most government policies in the country can be traced to the *titahs* (royal decrees) of Sultan Haji Hassanal Bolkiah. The *titah* enjoys a supreme status; in addition to being the words of the monarch, they often contain royal orders and mandates directed at the country's administration while giving credence and legitimacy to any decision, policy or practice introduced by the government. National philosophies and policies such as Brunei Vision 2035, Zikr Nation (the aspiration to be a God-conscious society), and MIB derive much of their authority from these decrees. For example, on 7 February 2018, when the Sultan of Brunei delivered his *titah* during his first meeting with the then newly sworn-in Cabinet of Ministers, the Sultan decreed that MIB was an indispensable philosophy and practice, and that it would be against Bruneian patriotism to question the national philosophy. This *titah* acted as a warning targeted mainly for the ministers and government officials to constantly be trustworthy and focused when performing their tasks, and omit all personal benefits (Prime Minister's Office, n.d.). Taken into consideration that there have been few scandals among the ministries. This was, of course, neither the first nor the only occasion where MIB was invoked by the monarch; he is known to have advocated it since Brunei gained its independence from the United Kingdom in 1984. For several decades now, the Sultan has consistently defined and illustrated MIB in accordance with his evolving vision as the leader of Brunei. Although the essence of MIB is argued to have existed since the fourteenth century (Mail et al., 2019), its modern post-independence form is a product of continuous refining over the decades amid the rapid evolution of modern life and technology.

Readers of this chapter are, no doubt, aware that MIB is the main focus of this book. Every chapter here, thus, attempts to define it in detail, whether conceptually or in relation to specific empirical data. To avoid redundancy, this chapter refrains from describing all the basic details of MIB, which include its official definition, composition, history, role and function. Readers interested in these details may wish to refer to Chaps. 1 and 2, which provide an excellent background to the ensuing chapters. This chapter focuses instead on the construction (and reconstruction) of MIB as a state philosophy in the *titahs* of the Sultan of Brunei. Keeping in mind the continuous refining of MIB throughout these past three to four decades, the author attempt to examine, first, how and in what context this national philosophy has evolved, and, second, how this evolution has affected or has been translated into practice and policy making. Additionally, the authors try to show how MIB and the *titahs* have inextricably influenced and reinforced each other. Overall, the chapter aims to provide a coherent picture of the philosophy as it is understood and portrayed by the Sultan himself, with emphasis on his vision and aspirations.

Third, instead of presenting the discussion in this chapter using a chronological timeline of the *titahs*, the chapter structures it into four major themes: (1) continuity of tradition, (2) preservation and promotion of religion, (3) evolving education and (4) globalisation and youth. A thematic presentation of the discussion allows this chapter to accentuate not only the key contexts in which MIB was invoked in the decrees but also the specific aspects of the philosophy that have particularly been affected by the evolution of time.

4.2 Continuity of Tradition

One of the most salient portrayals of MIB by the Sultan is that of a universal, unchanging tradition and a central constant in the history of Brunei. On 13 December 2015, in his *titah* during his visit to London addressing the Bruneian community in the United Kingdom and Ireland, the Sultan referred to MIB as the value system of Bruneians, and one that they should always commit to regardless of where they are (Prime Minister's Office, n.d.). He then cautioned the community against reformist ideologies or tendencies targeting mainly youths and students, enticing them to dismiss tradition as old-fashioned, describing them as 'poisonous' (Prime Minister's Office, n.d.). Major English dictionaries, such as Merriam-Webster's Collegiate Dictionary and Collins English Dictionary, define a 'value system' as the beliefs, norms, values, goals and attitudes shared by a society. This definition is in line with the national description of MIB as a tradition or a way of life, which is constituted by long-established beliefs, values, norms, ideals and practices endemic to the Malay-Bruneian people (Serudin, 1998).

In this current age of rapid change and unpredictability, describing cultural elements such as values and beliefs as 'unchanging' may cause raised eyebrows, especially when the opposing view seems more popular: Values and beliefs change with time and social conditions (Kim et al., 2003). Despite there having been no studies to understand the value system of Bruneians in reality, MIB is consistently affirmed to have endured centuries of rollercoaster struggles in the country's history and to remain applicable into the twenty-first century (Tuah, 2001). A two-fold explanation can be offered here: First, the national philosophy is premised upon religious elements and nationalistic sentiments that together imbue it with an eternal quality and an unchallengeable authority according to Muslim beliefs. Second, the national philosophy is made up of both defined and flexible components, the former of which serve as its unchanging foundation while the latter allow it to continually evolve alongside national needs and priorities. These elements, sentiments and components have featured both explicitly and implicitly in the *titahs*, as will be shown in the forthcoming discussion.

One good example for the aforementioned explanation is MIB's role as an ethical and moral guide. Its framework for ethics and morals is derived from the two primary sources of Islam—the Quran (the Holy Book in Islam), and the *Sunnah* (the Prophetic way of life). Societal sensibilities in Brunei are largely religious and aligned with what Muslims universally regard as 'right' and 'wrong' (e.g. public display of affection, which is commonplace in many parts of the secular West, is deemed unorthodox and offensive in both the Bruneian culture and Islam). On 15 February 2011, during the *Mawlid* commemoration ceremony (birthday anniversary of Prophet Muhammad *p.b.u.h)*. His Majesty the Sultan emphasised in his *titah* the importance of abiding by religious teachings and the *Sunnah* (Tradition) as a solution for combating the prevalence of social issues in the modern world. In the same year, he reiterated this importance in another *titah*, where he described the Quran and the Sunnah as the foundational sources of Islam and Islamic civilisation, whose teachings must be upheld and observed completely (Prime Minister's Office, n.d.).

Most Muslims believe that Islam requires no fundamental reform, as the Qur'an describes it as 'complete' and 'perfect' (Corpus Quran, n.d.). Although this belief is neither absolute nor uniform across the Muslim global population (some Muslim scholars do propagate reform), questioning Islam's place and relevance in the modern world is a serious taboo throughout the Muslim world. The sacred and unchallengeable status and power of Islam may apply to anything that borrows or makes use of its corpus, as evidenced not least by the Rushdie Affair in the 1980s and 1990s, when the publication of Salman Rushdie's *The Satanic Verses* was met with violent opposition from Muslims who were offended by what they believed in the novel to be blasphemy against the Prophet Muhammad *p.b.u.h* and Islam. In the context of MIB, the role of Islam is too significant to be denied. The religion is, after all, one of its three key constituents (i.e. 'I' for Islam in MIB).

To a lesser extent, cultural norms and expectations peculiar to Bruneians have also influenced their societal sensibilities. In 2019, several local 'influencers' (social media users with a big following) were lambasted and ridiculed online by Bruneian netizens after pictures of them posing on tables with their shoes on in a yet-to-be-launched branch of McDonalds went viral on social media. Most of the criticisms levelled against them revolved around the sentiment that such poses were disrespectful, uncouth and unrepresentative of the Bruneian values of moderation, politeness and gracefulness. In the *Reddit* post where pictures of the poses and the criticisms against them can be found, some Bruneians, however, showed complete indifference to the controversy. This lends to the argument that what Bruneians consider appropriate or offensive may be subjective and relative to individual perception. What makes MIB so intriguing in this case is that the shared cultural understanding of what this national philosophy means and entails can, in some ways, be abstract and tacit. If anything, that is conventional, appealing, appropriate and non-offensive to Bruneians, can be considered as subsumed under the general notion of the Malay way of life, then this notion itself is a flexible and evolving entity. It is tempting to wonder if what is understood as a Malay way of life is constantly changing, even if in subtle ways, with time and generational trends. Some indigenous practices and rituals, such as tribal wedding rituals, may have already been forgotten by the younger generation.

While MIB's role as an ethical and moral guide in Brunei remains unchanged, its ethical and moral codes have evidently evolved. A quick analysis of the national policies and practices that have been enforced over the past few decades would suffice to show that the government has slowly but steadily become conservative in its moral outlook. This evolution towards moral conservatism (or moral perfection, as is often heard in the national news) has largely been met with a reciprocal response from the society itself, not least due to the government's strategy of gradually introducing regulations and directives and phasing out what it considers to be detrimental to the wellbeing of the people. For example, in 2008 Brunei banned smoking in public places, including sidewalks near business premises and within a six-metre radius of smoke-free buildings. Then, in 2013 the Sultan began introducing the Islamic penal code known officially as Syariah Penal Code Order (SPCO 2013) in three stages. Although Brunei is believed by local scholars to have already begun implementing the penal law many centuries ago, the announcement of the Syariah Penal Code Order in this decade shows that moral code is evolving as a deterrent to social issues, including crime. This reality of evolution in Brunei is, of course, in line with the *titahs* of the Sultan. Through his aspiration to develop the country into one of the most successful nations in the world with a strong national identity, the government has made reform after reform to ensure that the country does not lag behind global standards while preserving the fundamentals of MIB. On the delivery of His *titah* during the 2015 University of Brunei Darussalam's convocation ceremony on 9 September 2015, His Majesty expressed gratitude for the achievement of UBD and its students besides reminding them to always be persistent of their Bruneian identity, legacy and integrity with MIB as the core value. He added that advancement and nation development should be parallel with a strong spiritual sense (Prime Minister's Office, n.d.).

The discussion above shows that MIB is both unchanging and evolving. Its foundation—constituted by its philosophy and values as well as Brunei history—remains sacred, resilient and authoritative, while its form—represented by national strategies and efforts—continues to evolve with time and societal changes.

4.3 Preservation and Promotion of Religion

The decrees have always had direct correlation with and impact on national development, often serving as precursors to nationwide implementations of new ideas, strategies and plans. Strictly from 2011 until 2019, the most stirring and effectual *titahs* of the Sultan involved directives for the ministries and their sub-divisions to fine-tune existing policies and regulations or introduce new ones in accordance with contemporary needs and circumstances. As the forthcoming discussion will show, these *titahs* and their ensuing effects on national development demonstrate the Sultan's direct and instrumental participation in matters of governance across various social and political levels and domains. As these *titahs* were closely aligned with MIB and national aspirations such as *Negara Zikir* and *Wawasan 2035*, their most conspicuous effects occurred largely in the education and religion sectors. Perhaps unsurprisingly, education and religion are also the most predominant themes of the *titahs*.

In the religion sector, one of the best examples for showing the true effect of the *titahs* on national development is the Syariah Penal Code Order 2013 or SPCO 2013, which the government put into effect on 3 April 2019, following three phases of implementation that began on 1 May 2014 (Prime Minister's Office, n.d.). These three phases of implementation were referred to as Phase 1 (1 May 2014), Phase 2 (1 January 2019) and Phase 3 (3 April 2019), each focusing on specific types of criminal offences (Prime Minister's Office, n.d.). The enforcement of the SPCO 2013 was heralded and driven by at least eight *titahs* that dated back to 1984, when Brunei gained its independence from the United Kingdom. These *titahs* served as pivotal precursors to the government's efforts in introducing the penal code into the country's existing legal framework and structure. An analysis of these *titahs* is crucial for this section in order to demonstrate the Sultan's central role in motivating and guiding government agencies throughout the long process of getting the SPCO 2013 off the ground.

On 18 March 1984, the Sultan announced that efforts had begun in ensuring that national laws accorded to the teachings of Islam (Prime Minister's Office, n.d.). On 15 July 1996, the Sultan expressed his consent to the establishment of Syariah courts and indicated that they could, at the right time and in the right context in the future, deal with criminal offences in addition to family law (Prime Minister's Office, n.d.). On 15 March 2011, the Sultan opined that the Common Law (which Brunei has adopted since it became a British Protectorate in the early twentieth century) and the Syariah Law could run in tandem (Prime Minister's Office, n.d.). He repeated this vision of a peaceful co-existence of the two laws in his *titahs* on 10 October and 12 October of the same year (Prime Minister's Office, n.d.). On 15 July 2012, he declared his consent to the establishment of Syariah Penal Code Order (Prime Minister's Office, n.d.). Within the following year, many of his *titahs* were interlaced with a call upon the citizens of Brunei to support this Order. On 22 October 2013, he proclaimed that the Syariah Penal Code Order would be enforced in phases beginning from 6 months after the *titah* (Prime Minister's Office, n.d.). Finally, on 30 April 2014, he announced that Phase 1 of the Islamic Penal Code would come into effect the following day (Prime Minister's Office, n.d.). As shown by the *titahs* above, the Sultan's approach in introducing Islamic Criminal Law into the national legal framework was gradual, yet decisive. This long process began with the Sultan easing the idea of Islamic Criminal Law into public consciousness and encouraging the relevant government agencies to commence preparatory work towards its implementation, which spanned more than 30 years since the first Syariah-related *titah* in 1984. Over time, these Syariah-related *titahs* became more concrete and forthright, as did all the legal work and preparations in the background to get it off the ground.

Alongside the Syariah Penal Code Order, the Sultan made or encouraged several important religious initiatives and changes through his *titahs* from 2011 until 2019. On 29 March 2011, in conjunction with the international seminar of *Ahl as-Sunnah Wa al-Jama'ah*, the Sultan announced the establishment of a research centre within a university college for religious teachers to promote and preserve the Sunni understanding of Islam in Brunei and consolidate the Muslim creed against the ongoing effort in the propagation of anti-Sunni belief (Prime Minister's Office, n.d.). Sunni Islam is one of the two major branches of the religion in the world (the other being Shia Islam), and is the official strand of religion in Brunei. On 24 September 2012, during the national celebration of Teacher's Day, he announced the Compulsory Islamic Education Act, which, after coming into effect the following year on 1 January, requires Muslim children in Brunei to attend religious schools in the afternoon in complementarity with the mainstream school in the morning. Until the introduction of this act, Islamic Education had not been compulsory to Muslims in the country for 50 years. This order was announced with the aim to educate children on the basic knowledge of Islam to the extent of realising MIB among future generations (Prime Minister's Office, n.d.). Another monumental change that he introduced in 2012 was the suspension of all businesses and public services on Fridays from 12 PM to 2 PM, in compliance with the Islamic commandment to perform the obligatory Friday worship congregation. He added in his *titah* that this measure could help deter people from loitering around on the streets or in the malls during the sacred time of the Friday prayer, a behaviour he described as tarnishing the image of Brunei and that of the Islamic religion (Prime Minister's Office, n.d.).

4.4 Evolving Education

Another aspect of Brunei's national development is on the education front, the Sultan's *titahs* were skewed towards the tertiary sector than the primary and secondary sectors. Understandably, Higher Education is more critical now than ever before in determining the economic health and future of a country. As technology advances and digital skills become indispensable in the modern workplace, graduates are expected to possess not only academic qualifications and professional skills, but also digital proficiency and financial literacy. Higher Education is where all these skills and competencies are honed and tested. Correspondingly, the *titahs* of the Sultan relating to Higher Education focused largely on twenty-first-century skills, knowledge economy and high-impact research. The decrees of this nature were given at high-profile education-related events such as Teachers' Day, state-run academic conferences and university convocations. There are currently four Higher Education institutions in Brunei: Universiti Brunei Darussalam (UBD), Universiti Teknologi Brunei (UTB), Universiti Islam Sultan Sharif Ali (UNISSA) and Seri Begawan Religious Teachers Universiti College (KUPU SB). Although the *titahs* given at these institutions had common Higher Education themes, they were hardly homogenous. As is widely known in Brunei, the Sultan often contextualises his speeches to different audiences, themes, situations and needs. UTB, UNISSA and KUPU SB are niche institutions with specialised roles, functions and programmes. As their names suggest, UTB is an engineering and technology university, while UNISSA and KUPU SB are Islamic-oriented tertiary 'seminaries'.

As the oldest and premier university in the country, UBD is a full-fledged institution with a big range of disciplines, a strong international reputation, and the means to conduct high-impact research.

Correspondingly, in the first half of this decade, the Sultan consistently stressed the importance of research output and impact in UBD, particularly on social issues of national concern (e.g. crimes, unemployment and obesity). To support this, he consented to the establishment of UBD's Centre for Advanced Research (CARe), whose research areas now include youth and economy, welfare and poverty, and health and aging. All this was parallel to UBD's efforts in boosting its international reputation through research and student mobility. From 2015 until 2019, the Sultan's emphasis appeared to shift from research output and impact to twenty-first-century skills and digital education. He advised that UBD ensure that their programmes were up-to-date with emerging academic, employment and workforce trends and relevant for producing highly skilled, entrepreneurial, job-creating graduates. This shift in emphasis was in line with national concerns about unemployment and the state's aspiration for a diverse economy that would no longer rely on oil exports.

The Sultan's *titahs* addressing UTB in this decade were even more student centric than those aimed at UBD. Ever since the promotion to becoming a university in 2016, the Sultan had supported UTB and its students to take part in entrepreneurship as initiative in expanding the economy due to the spike of unemployment concerns as urged in his *titah* on 7 November 2016, in conjunction with the 25th convocation ceremony of UTB (Prime Minister's Office, n.d.). The following year was seen as the internationalisation of UTB with the urgency of making it a globally recognised university. During the 26th convocation ceremony in 2017, the Sultan applauded the university for its achievement in the technology and innovation sector. Nonetheless, the impact should be measured by the production of excellent human capital helping with the marketability of graduates, both locally and globally, while continue holding onto the principle of MIB (Prime Minister's Office, n.d.). Subsequently, the Sultan's aspirations for UTB students broadened as he urged the university to update existing programmes relevant to the current challenges. In 2019, he advocates students to develop modern technology skills, acquiring a flexible, creative and innovative mindset with the goal of producing employable, job-ready graduates (Prime Minister's Office, n.d.). Alongside these missions, the Sultan repeatedly reminded UTB to cherish Islam and always carry their national identity, MIB. These are proof of his evolving visions while still remaining true to the unchanging identity.

In comparison, the *titahs* addressed to UNISSA and KUPU SB emphasised significantly on moral education, teaching and learning quality than they did on academic research or twenty-first-century skills. Given the specialised roles of these two institutions, the pressure on them is to educate their students in Islamic scripture and tradition and produce graduates for religion-focused careers such as teachers of Islam, *imams* (leaders of Muslim prayers), preachers, experts of Islamic scripture and law, and so on. In some of his *titahs*, the Sultan reminded these two institutions to not lose sight of their true purpose and admitted that some global Higher Education trends, such as the relentless pursuit of university rankings, may not strictly apply to them (Prime Minister's Office, n.d.). Specifically, in the case of UNISSA, notwithstanding one *titah* in 2019 in conjunction with the 9th convocation ceremony, highlighting the importance of academic research from students, as well as lecturers. The *titahs* addressing them in this decade were primarily directives for ensuring the effectiveness and relevance of their curriculum and teaching approaches.

As for KUPU SB, the Sultan instructed and advised its students consistently to hone their expertise in teaching as they are responsible for the development and the uphold of Islam through Islamic schooling. The *titahs* also stressed the importance of preserving the religion-cultural heritage of Brunei, such as the urgency for strengthening *aqidah* (creed) by supporting for the development of *Ahl as-Sunnah Wa al-Jama'ah* Awareness Research Center and *Jawi* script (a writing system used for writing the Malay language using Arabic letters) aimed at them from 2013 (Prime Minister's Office, n.d.). Later in 2019, the Sultan consented for the establishment of the *Jawi* Research Center. The same year His Majesty implemented Islamic History as part of learning curriculum. These efforts are part of the nation development by preserving the roots and identity of Bruneians especially upcoming teachers. Realising that national identity and moral development of a community comes first from family institutions, the Sultan consented for the building of a research centre specifically for the Islamic family law, namely *Feqh Usrah Research Center,* in his *titah* in 2016 (Prime Minister's Office, n.d.). In the same *titah,* concurrently with the 6th convocation ceremony for KUPU SB, His Majesty commented on the mastery of Arabic Language within Arabic school students, and thus urged for the improvement of Arabic speakers within students. They are perceived to be the agents of Islam while simultaneously upholding its teachings (Prime Minister's Office, n.d.). In the following year, the Sultan emphasised Arabic schools to produce more quality students considering that they are the candidates for local Islamic universities including KUPU SB (Prime Minister's Office, n.d.).

It is not a coincidence that these three institutions are relatively new. Therefore, their focus is more on establishing, compared to UBD which is already established. Interestingly, his message to the Islamic Universities is almost the opposite. From 2011 until 2018, the focus is on programmes, education and graduates. In 2019, he suddenly emphasised research. This is evidence that his *titahs* are not generic. He analyses the contexts and issue advices accordingly.

Another focal point in the Sultan's decrees related to national development and education was the government's long-term heavy investment in human capital development through generous scholarship schemes and its expectations of Bruneian students who had been and were sponsored to study at the tertiary level, both at home and abroad. Within the country, the government not only provides free education throughout the whole education system (primary to tertiary), but it also provides students with a monthly stipend to support their studies. For decades now, the government has sponsored its high achieving youths studying in reputable universities in countries such as Germany, Singapore, the United States, Canada, China, Japan, Jordan, the United Kingdom, Ireland, Egypt, Malaysia, Australia and New Zealand. Of these, the last six have always been the traditional study destinations for Bruneians, mainly due to strong cultural and historical ties and familiarity.

From 2011 until 2019, the Sultan gave at least 15 decrees addressing Bruneian students abroad. For the most part, these *titahs* touched on predictable themes that have been discussed earlier in this chapter: The cultural notion of 'Bruneianness' (see Sect. 4.2), the educated youth as an asset (see Sect. 4.4), Islam as the official religion (see Sect. 4.3), and MIB as the national philosophy (see Sect. 4.2). One theme in particular recurred consistently in these *titahs*; with the exception of the year 2012, this decade saw the Sultan unfailingly emphasise the notion of 'patriotism'. This was largely triggered by reports of sponsored Bruneian students dishonouring their scholarship contract by refusing to return to the country. In his *titahs*, the Sultan declared the violation of the government's trust unpatriotic and reminded all Bruneian students abroad, particularly those sponsored by the Brunei government, to remember their responsibility and duty to serve the country. In one *titah*, he stated that Bruneians should honour their promises and duties to the country (Prime Minister's Office, n.d.). He then urged the ministries to be more discriminating in the scholarship selection process in order to select candidates who are patriotic and cognizant of their commitment to the country.

Correspondingly, the ministries reformed the system by introducing the Multiple-Mini-Interviews (MMI) into its scholarship selection process.

4.5 Globalisation and Youth

Similarly, prevalent with the notions of tradition and continuity in the *titahs* is the connection that the Sultan often makes between MIB and two of probably the most researched and discussed topics of the twenty-first century: globalisation and youth. Across many societies and cultures, these two topics have generated diverse discourses, sentiments and questions about generational shift, sociocultural change and cultural identity. In its most generic sense, globalisation is positively correlated with human development and economic growth (Morady et al., 2017), but it is also described as a 'threat' to cultural heritage and identity (Anheier & Isar, 2007). Meanwhile, the youth is recognised universally as an indispensable group in every society and the future of the world (Guterres, 2018), but they are also often associated with identity crisis due to the 'fluidity' of their beliefs (Rapacon, 2019). Brunei is not an exception to these dual perceptions of globalisation and youth; they recur prominently in the national media and scholarship and, more importantly, the *titahs* of the Sultan. In late 2018, the country's Centre of Strategic and Policy Studies (CSPS) undertook a national survey to investigate social issues affecting young people. The findings of this survey pointed to what the Centre described as 'lack of understanding or pride in the Bruneian identity' among the youth (Centre for Strategic and Policy Studies, 2018). However, the Sultan had long expressed concern over cultural attrition.

In 2011, in his 34th *titah* of the year, the Sultan made clear his disappointment in what he observed as the Malay people of Brunei being comfortable prioritising foreign languages over their mother tongue (Prime Minister's Office, n.d.). He explained that the problem was not learning foreign languages per se, but rather side-lining the Malay language in favour of them. The following year, at the 24th convocation ceremony of UBD, the monarch, as the Chancellor, cautioned the university community against the mistake of minimising the importance of the Malay language as they endeavoured to propel UBD to new international heights (Prime Minister's Office, n.d.). He further advised that the University community be grounded in their roots with dignity and self-respect, implicitly warning against shamelessly copying or worshipping foreign cultures and peoples at the expense of their own identity, principles and heritage. Three weeks later, at the country's 7th National Youth Day, the Sultan singled out the youth as susceptible to foreign sociocultural influences through information technology and other forces of globalisation and then urged them to build a strong self-defence foundation from within (Prime Minister's Office, n.d.). It was clear in this *titah* that said foundation was a reference to Islamic teachings. *Titahs* like these validate the discussion and argument made in the preceding tradition: The state has a clear and enduring definition of 'Malayness', and any phenomenon that contradicts this specific definition of 'Malayness' is, by nature, foreign.

Although globalisation is often discussed alongside social issues, His Majesty the Sultan acknowledged it as a double-edged sword for the youths. In his *titah* in 2012 in conjunction with the 7th National Youth Day, he stated that advanced information technology has enabled various agendas of globalisation to materialise, bringing positive or negative impact on various aspects of life concerning to the socio-culture of a country. Having said that, he further suggested that youth should be equipped with strong resilience, thus acting as blockades guarding from bad influences emerging from globalisation. This cautiousness can be seen in many of his forthcoming *titahs* (Prime Minister's Office, n.d.). For example, he consented to the introduction of fibre optic technology to boost Internet speed in 2012, but cautioning the citizens at the same time about the risk of negative consequences from the misuse of this technology (Prime Minister's Office, n.d.). In this same *titah*, in parallel with the monarch's 66th birthday celebration, he advised the whole society to take advantage of this fibre optic technology in a positive way (Prime Minister's Office, n.d.). Additionally, he roped the responsibility of using said technology wisely with MIB, saying that the citizens of Brunei must practise moral values and protect their national identity in accordance with the ideals of the national philosophy (Prime Minister's Office, n.d.).

Indeed, it is not surprising that the youth of Brunei were featured heavily in the *titahs* of the last decade. According to the latest statistics provided by the country's Department of Economic Planning and Statistics, 69.5% of Brunei citizens (230,700 of the total 331,800) are under 40 years of age (Department of Economic Planning and Statistics, 2019). Within this age group, the biggest population is concentrated in the middle: 20–24 years of age, followed closely by the 15–19 age group. Mapping this population now onto Brunei's education system and its levels, individuals between 15 and 24 years of age are high school and university students. This population, known in the broader literature on youth and generational differences as 'Generation Z', grew up with the Internet and mobile technology in a hyper-connected world. This then puts into perspective the national concern over the youth being the most vulnerable to the challenges brought about by globalisation. It should be emphasised however that the *titahs* never described the youth as weak or inclined towards foreign influences. On the contrary, many *titahs* spoke highly of them, describing them as the most creative group in the society as well as the country's asset and its future leaders (Prime Minister's Office, n.d.). In his 28th *titah* in 2011 at the 5th Southeast Asian Youth Al-Quran Reading Competition, he stressed that some fundamental change was needed to turn around the negative association of youths with moral and social issues in the minds of many into 'heroes of virtues' or 'social remedies' (Prime Minister's Office, n.d.).

To further expand on the preceding *titah*, the discussion should now focus on the Sultan's conceptualisation of the ideal Bruneian youth. In this case, three *titahs* stand out in particular: (1) His *titah* at the 7th National Youth Day in 2012, where he used the phrase '*Belia Shumul*' (the complete youth); (2) His *titah* at the 32nd National Day in 2016, where he used the phrase '*Generasi Berwawasan*' (the visionary generation); (3) His *titah* at the 12th National Youth Day in 2017, where he used the phrase '*Belia Berkualiti*' (the quality youth). *Belia Shumul* (the complete youth) refers to a well-rounded youth population equipped with both secular and religious knowledge (Prime Minister's Office, n.d.). Theoretically, *Belia Shumul* are competent in all dimensions of modern life, while rooted in traditional values and observant of religious teachings. *Generasi Berwawasan* (the visionary generation) refers to a generation who view modern challenges not as burdens, but as opportunities to assist in the development of the country. *Generasi Berwawasan* charges into the future resolutely and wisely despite hurdles in their way (Prime Minister's Office, n.d.). *Belia Berkualiti* (the quality youth) is similar to *Belia Shumul* in essence; it refers to a well-rounded youth population who are educated, skilled and morally sound. *Belia Berkualiti* are youths who creatively, proactively and enthusiastically endeavour to develop the country while conscious of and committed to religious teachings, family commitments, societal responsibilities and national duties (Prime Minister's Office, n.d.). These three concepts of the ideal Bruneian youth encapsulate the underpinning aspirations of the MIB—the heritage of the Malay culture, the teachings of the Islamic religion, and loyalty and allegiance to the Sultan.

Youth cover the majority population of Bruneians, thus it is important that they are well equipped with the right foundation in order to strive through this current globalised world, where contradicting foreign cultures are easily spread within the community. His Majesty's aspirations for the national identity of Bruneian youths throughout the aforementioned *titahs* are proof that it is an evolving concept and a continuous cultivation of MIB among youths.

4.6 Conclusion

Over the past decade, these *titahs* corroborate that the Sultan is expeditious to the advancement of modernism, thus allowing his vision and aspirations of the unwavering national philosophy, Malay Islamic Monarchy (MIB), to constantly evolve in response to the status quo. The discussion and examples have shown that His Majesty the Sultan have participated directly and significantly in the governance of the country, including in micro matters within government agencies. This is understandable given that the monarch also holds ministerial positions such as the Prime Minister, Minister of Defence, Minister of Finance and Economy and Minister of Foreign Affairs.

Additionally, he was able to include MIB and his aspirations to the development of Brunei which can be characterised as both constant to its foundation, while also transforming suitable to the current national and global situations. It is clear from the first theme that Bruneians must always commit to MIB as their value system to preserve tradition and culture, and as a way to combat the negative effects of globalisation especially on youths. It is a framework on which national development takes place. However, the Sultan's thinking gives shape and colour to the national philosophy allowing it to develop and continuously refining.

As discussed previously, one of the best examples to show the impact of the *titahs* on Brunei was the *titah* on the implementation of Syariah Penal Code Order 2013 which the Sultan has begun its initial planning for more than 30 years ago in 1984. It is then put into effect by the government in 2019 after multiple introductory phases. Undoubtedly, the Sultan played a huge role in navigating his government and gradually promoting to the public. Another example is His Majesty's *titah* from 2012 to 2017 on youths. Youths are susceptible to foreign cultures as the world enters into a globalised world. Instead of closing the doors to worldwide integration and modern opportunities, the Sultan shared his notion for modern

Bruneian youths: those who are rooted to their national identity and committed to religious teachings, but also aware of the modern challenges and insights favourable to the development of Brunei.

References

Anheier, H. K., & Isar, Y. R. (Eds.). (2007). *Conflicts and Tensions. Cultures and Globalization Series, 1*. SAGE.

Centre for Strategic and Policy Studies. (2018). *Report of the National Youth Survey: 2018*. Retrieved from http://www.csps.org.bn/2018/12/20/calling-all-youths-we-need-your-input-for-the-national-youth-policy/

Corpus Quran. (n.d.). *The Quranic Arabic Corpus*. Retrieved June 25, 2020 from http://corpus.quran.com/translation.jsp?chapter=5&verse=3.

Department of Economic Planning and Statistics. (2019). *Report of the mid-year population estimates: 2019*. Retrieved July 4, 2020 from http://www.deps.gov.bn/DEPD%20Documents%20Library/DOS/POP/2019/Rep_MidYr_2019.pdf.

Guterres, A. (2018). *Remarks to high-level event—"Youth2030"—to launch the UN Youth Strategy and "Generation Unlimited" Partnership*. Retrieved from https://www.un.org/sg/en/content/sg/speeches/2018-09-24/youth2030-remarks-high-level-Event.

Jabatan Penerangan. (2017). *Kumpulan titah Kebawah Duli Yang Maha Mulia Paduka Seri Baginda Sultan Haji Hassanal Bolkiah Mu'izzaddin Waddaulah, Sultan dan Yang Di-Pertuan Negara Brunei Darussalam tahun 1984, 1985, 1986 dan 1987*. Retrieved from http://www.information.gov.bn/Malay%20Publication%20PDF/8487.pdf.

Kim, U., Aasen, H. S., & Ebadi, S. (2003). *Democracy, human rights, and Islam in modern Iran: Psychological, social and cultural perspectives*. Fagbokforlaget.

Mail, A., Tengah, B., Bakar, N. S., Kumpoh, A., & Abu Bakar, T. (2019). *The Malay Islamic Monarchy in Negara Brunei Darussalam prior to 1906: A historical study*. Brunei Historical Society.

Morady, F., Kapucu, H., & Yalcinkaya, O. (2017). *Development and growth: Economic Impacts of globalization*. IJOPEC Publication.

Prime Minister's Office. (n.d.) *Titah View*. Retrieved from http://pmo.gov.bn/PMO%20Pages/Titah-View.aspx.

Rapacon, S. (2019). How Gen Z is Redefining their World through Technology. Retrieved from https://garage.ext.hp.com/us/en/modern-life/generation-z-redefining-the-world.html.

Serudin, Z. (1998). *Melayu Islam Beraja: Suatu pendekatan*. Dewan Bahasa dan Pustaka Brunei.

Tuah, D. (2001). *Membangun negara berdasarkan falsafah Melayu Islam Beraja: Brunei Darussalam*. Institut Perkhidmatan Awam.

CHAPTER 5

MIB and Islamic Education in Brunei Darussalam: An Overview

Norhazlin Muhammad and Mohammad Hilmy Baihaqy

5.1 Introduction

Melayu Islam Beraja (MIB) and Islamic education are compulsory core subjects in the current educational system in Brunei Darussalam, *Sistem Pendidikan Negara Abad ke-21* (The National Education System for the 21st Century, henceforth, SPN21). MIB is taught in primary and secondary schools under the supervision of the Ministry of Education (MoE),

---

Muhammad, N., & Baihaqy, M. H. (2021). MIB and Islamic education in Brunei Darussalam: An overview. In Phan, L. H., A. Kumpoh, K. Wood, R. Jawawi, & H. Said (Eds.), *Globalisation, education, and reform in Brunei Darussalam* (pp. 85–103). Palgrave MacMillan.

N. Muhammad (✉)
Universiti Brunei Darussalam, Bandar Seri Begawan, Brunei
e-mail: norhazlin.muhammad@ubd.edu.bn

M. H. Baihaqy
Universiti Islam Sultan Sharif Ali (UNISSA), Bandar Seri Begawan, Brunei
e-mail: hilmy.yussof@unissa.edu.bn

© The Author(s), under exclusive license to Springer Nature Switzerland AG 2021
Phan, L. H. et al. (eds.), *Globalisation, Education, and Reform in Brunei Darussalam*, International and Development Education, https://doi.org/10.1007/978-3-030-77119-5_5

while Islamic Religious Knowledge (IRK) is taught as a single subject in public schools and the textbooks used are under the supervision of Ministry of Religious Affairs (MoRA). The SPN21 curriculum took effect in January 2009 starting with Year 1 and Year 4 concurrently, and it has also made gradual changes to the secondary level curriculum. The core subjects for Year 1 to Year 11 are MIB, Malay and English language, Mathematics and Science. In addition, it is compulsory for students in Year 1 to Year 9 to learn IRK, while Year 10 and Year 11 students learn *Tarbiyah Islamiah* (Islamic Education) (Ministry of Education, 2013,

Table 5.1 Number of schools, teachers and students in religious schools from 1956 to 1968 (Muhammad, 2014, p. 129)

Years	Total of Schools	Total of Teachers	Total of Students
1956	7	11	347
1957	15	18	779
1958	29	55	1,271
1959	32	67	1,375
1960	37	110	1,606
1961	49	139	3,705
1962	51	138	4,243
1963	51	142	4,263
1964	49	199	4,954
1965	61	199	5,366
1966	63	276	5,656
1967	65	247	6,784
1968	68	266	7,049
1969	75	260	7,922
1970	80	294	7,800
1971	82	350	7,689
1972	83	306	7,851
1973	84	297	8,760
1974	91	277	8,465
1975	91	276	9,814
1976	96	304	10,494
1977	98	340	11,146
1978	101	450	12,069
1979	101	450	13,802
1980	103	517	13,813
1981	105	562	13,809
1982	100	582	14,013
1983	106	604	14,911

p. 28). Religious and Arabic schools are under the MoRA and they offer other Islamic education subjects for students from level 1 to level 6 (Ministry of Religious Affairs, 2020g). Further details on the history and the development of the educational system can be found in Chap. 2. This chapter will elaborate more on the overview of MIB and Islamic Education in Brunei Darussalam.

5.2 The Development of MIB Education in Brunei Darussalam

MIB is the state philosophy of Brunei Darussalam based on Bruneian customs and their way of life, and the core belief which is Islam. Thus, the inclusion of IRK as a subject in the national educational curriculum is an indirect way for the government to uphold and instil the MIB philosophy among students. In addition, MIB is a compulsory subject at all levels of education (see Chap. 2); it is also offered at the technical educational level, such as at the Insitute of Brunei Technical Education (IBTE) and Politeknik Brunei, to strengthen the preservation of MIB in Bruneian communities.

It is understood that the real meaning of MIB was first revealed on 1 January 1984. However, its understanding among the people was not robust enough (Othman, 2013) and an accurate explanation was required from local experts. Thus, a comprehensive book on MIB was published in 1998 as one of the main resources for readers, especially students at higher learning institutions who wish to enhance their understanding of MIB. This book is entitled *The Malay Islamic Monarchy: A Closer Understanding* written by the former Minister of Religious Affairs, Pehin Jawatan Luar Pekerma Raja Dato Seri Utama (Dr) Ustaz Awang Haji Md Zain bin Hj Serudin. It was first published in the Malay language by the Language and Literature Bureau, also known as '*Dewan Bahasa dan Pustaka*' (DBP) and later translated to English in 2013, and became a project developed and published by the National Supreme Council of the Malay Islamic Monarchy. Before 2013, there were no comprehensive MIB books in English. The book consists of six chapters containing comprehensive information on fundamentals and branches of Islam as a way of life (*al-Din*) and the evolution of its full absorption into the lives of the Brunei Malays. In addition, the book tries to amplify general knowledge and understanding of the three elements of the national philosophy: Malay, Islam and Monarchy (Othman, 2013).

The Academy of Brunei Studies (APB) in Universiti Brunei Darussalam (UBD) has set up a special collections and publications area named 'MIB Corner' in the UBD library to create an academic and research centre for MIB studies apart from the UBD Library and the Secretariat Office of the MIB Supreme Council. The MIB Corner is a user-friendly facility for those who wish to develop their understanding of the MIB philosophy and it is one of the strategic action plans of the Secretariat Office of the MIB Supreme Council which aims to further disseminate information on MIB to the general public. Thus, it is hoped that the MIB Corner at UBD will become a pioneering venture that encourages the establishment of similar MIB Corners at other educational institutions throughout the country (Universiti Brunei Darussalam, 2020d).

There is also an emphasis on the preservation of *Jawi* writing through education. *Jawi* is an Arabic writing system used in the Malay language. It is said that *Jawi* handwriting was widely used as an official written language by the government of Brunei, especially before British colonisation. *Jawi* writing was taught as a component of Malay language subject since 1989 and it still remains in the Malay subject curriculum for the primary level (Year 1 to 6) and lower secondary level (Year 7 and 8). Besides *Jawi* writing, other components in the Malay Language subject are listening, speaking, reading and writing skill (Ministry of Education, 2004a). The purpose of this inclusion is to 'retain the Malay heritage as a way to uphold Malay language as the nation's official language and at the same time to develop sense of loyalty towards religion, king and nation' (Ministry of Education, 2004a, p. 37). Moreover, MoE aims to produce primary students who are well-versed in pronouncing Arabic words in the Quran through the learning of *Jawi* writing (Ministry of Education, 2004a).

According to Rahman (2017), the teaching workforce for *Jawi* writing comprises of Malay language teachers with qualifications from diploma to postgraduate levels. She further states that *Jawi* writing is still being practised today but its uses are limited compared to the use of Roman alphabets in administration, education, business and daily communication. In his *titah* in 1988, His Majesty the Sultan of Brunei Darussalam highlighted the importance of *Jawi* and how Bruneians have the responsibility to enhance the use of *Jawi* writing. Thus, various efforts have been implemented to ensure the continuation of *Jawi* writing continues in the country (Rahman, 2017). In Brunei, we can find *Jawi* writing on signages in government buildings and business premises, including name labels, letterheads, notice boards, posters, advertisements, banners, names, road labels and so forth, and these are required to be larger than the Roman characters (Prime Minister Office Memorandum (1988) No:21/1988; see Rahman, 2017).

In the Curriculum Development Department (1996) Memorandum No: JPKT/17 J2 (36) (29 May 1996), it is stated that the MoE is responsible for the integration of *Jawi* writing as a component in the Malay language curriculum (see Rahman, 2017). According to Rahman (2017), the ministry's efforts also include the inclusion of *Jawi* questions in the Malay language examination papers at the primary and lower secondary levels and the *Jawi* spelling system used in primary and secondary schools since 1992 is the same system used by the Bruneian Institute of Language and Literature (Dewan Bahasa dan Pustaka Brunei, DBPB). DBPB has thus became the source of reference for guidance on the proper use of *Jawi* writing. Every measure effected by DBPB to improve *Jawi* spelling system must be approved by the MoE, which differs with the MoRA which has its own *Jawi* spelling system policy. Currently, textbooks that are used at religious school education in Brunei are written in *Jawi* whilst the textbooks in the general schools are written in *Jawi* script and Roman alphabets. In the latest educational system, that is, the National Education System for the 21st Century (SPN21), *Jawi* subject is still being taught to fully equipped students with spelling, reading and comprehension abilities of various articles written in *Jawi* and encourage them to present ideas and creativity through *Jawi* writing and calligraphy. The time allocated for the teaching and learning of *Jawi* education within the subject of Malay language in primary schools is an hour every fortnight (Rahman, 2017). The current development is that the *Jawi* writing is included in the religious school curriculum and IRK subject (Ministry of Religious Affairs, 2015a, 2015b, 2017, & 2020a).

In addition, institutions of higher learning such as Universiti Islam Sultan Sharif Ali (UNISSA) and Kolej Universiti Perguruan Ugama Seri Begawan (KUPU SB) are quite unique in preserving and upholding *Jawi* handwriting. Only the students attending these institutions are taught *Jawi* handwriting as an individual subject or in workshops, but it is not offered in UBD and UTB because of the limited number of courses offered in the MIB module.

Another initiative that has been done to preserve the heritage of *Jawi* writing is the establishment of the Yayasan Sultan Haji Hassanal Bolkiah Islamic Arts and Calligraphy Studies Centre and its gallery by His Majesty the Sultan of Brunei on 5 March 2020. It is an institution that offers programmes and services in developing various knowledge and skills in Islamic arts. The aim is to raise the status of *Jawi* writing, especially Islamic calligraphy. His Royal Highness Prince 'Abdul Malik officially opened the institution and the gallery. This centre is among the initiatives implemented during the third decade of Yayasan's establishment with the intention of elevating *Jawi* writing and a response to the royal decree of His Majesty the Sultan and Yang Di-Pertuan of Brunei Darussalam (Yayasan Sultan Haji Hassanal Bolkiah, 2020).

5.3 The Development of Islamic Education in Brunei Darussalam

Islam was embraced in Brunei in the fourteenth century after the first Sultan named Awang Alak Betatar converted to Islam and changed his name to Sultan Muhammad Shah (see Chap. 2). The intellectual activities then focused on preaching and teaching Islamic knowledge informally to the Bruneian people. Al-Sufri (2000) stated that the teaching of Islam became active and practised openly in the late fourteenth century, but the arrival and the spread of Islam in the Bruneian community was believed to have started before 977 CE.

According to Pehin Orang Kaya Setia Pahlawan Dato Seri *Setia* Dr. Awang Haji Ahmad bin Haji Jumat, before the establishment of formal schools, Islamic education were conducted in mosques, private houses and *balai* (community halls) (Jumat, 1989, p. 189) (see Chap. 2). During this period, another method of teaching was when the instructor commuted from house to house (Chuchu, 1990, p. 37), so Islamic teachings before the administration of the residential system are known to have been held in mosques, *balai*, *surau* (prayer halls), and residential and instructors' houses. It is not known when exactly these institutions arose due to the limited number of resources on the early teachings of Islam (Mansurnoor, 1992). The Ministry of Religious Affairs (MoRA) (1996) states that the palace was also an important place for the teaching of Islamic education in the sixteenth century (Ministry of Religious Affairs, 1996).

The Ministry of Religious Affairs Brunei Darussalam states in the book entitled *Pendidikan Ugama di Negara Brunei Darussalam* that the aim of the informal teachings in *balai* during this period was to transfer Islamic general knowledge to the Bruneian people, while also training and recruiting new *kātib* (elite scholars). The educational system was designed to fulfil the social needs of the people then (Ministry of Religious Affairs, 1996). The *balai* provided two levels of education:

1) Low Level of Islamic Education

> The curriculum was on the teaching of general knowledge. At this level, the teachings were on the basic rituals of prayer and other subjects such as: *Zikir Brunei* (a traditional Islamic *dhikr*), *Rātib Saman*, reading of the Quran and *Hadrah* (traditional music instruments or folk-music) and *salawāt* (praise) towards the Prophet Muhammad, p.b.u.h.

2) High Level of Islamic Education

> The curriculum focusing on specialised knowledge such as *Fiqh* (Jurisprudence), *Fara'iḍ* (Inheritance), *Bābu Al-Nikāḥ* (Marriage), *Taṣawwuf* (Sufism), and '*Akhlāq* (Moral).

The low level of education was taught by regular instructors, while higher levels were offered by *kātib*. These scholars must be approved by the government and those who did not get approval might set up their own houses as institutions and only taught the reading of the Holy Quran. Some scholars also taught in their students' houses. *Balai* education was restricted to male students, whilst female students could only attend intellectual activities in private residences. However, there is a lack of information regarding what kind and level of subjects were provided for them (Ministry of Religious Affairs, 1996).

Islamic traditional textbooks were used in *balai*, such as '*Sabīlu Al-Muhtadīn*' by Daud Fatani and '*Al-Mukhtaṣar Rabbi Ṣirāṭal Al-Mustaqīm*' by Ar-Raniri for teaching Fiqh. '*Ghāyat Al-Taqrīb Fī Al-'Irthi Wa Al-Ta'seeB*' for teaching *Fara'iḍ*. '*Idhahul-Al-Bāb Li Al-Murīdi Bābu Al-Nikāḥ Bi Al-Ṣawab*' for *Bābu Al-Nikāḥ*' and '*Misyāhu Al-'Afrād*' and '*Hidāyat Al-Walid Lilwalad*' for *Taṣawwuf*. The books were originally written in the Arabic language, then translated by scholars from the Indonesian archipelago into the Malay language and written in *Jawi* (Arabic script). The instructors used the Malay versions because most Bruneians in the early period were not fluent in Arabic. Students who successfully passed this *balai* level were qualified to work as teachers and could also qualify to be junior Islamic scholars (Ministry of Religious Affairs, 1996).

Mansurnoor (1992) states that Sweeney believed that the mosque mostly offered senior students advanced education, and this is to include *fiqh*, astronomy, sufism and *tafsīr* (Quranic Exegesis). On the other hand, *balai* education could be associated with broadening the knowledge of growing youth about *fiqh* and theology, whilst *surau* provided only the introduction to the Holy Quran and basic rituals to the children (see Mansurnoor, 1992). A high level of education was conducted in *balai* at Burung Pingai village and a low level one was conducted in scattered water villages situated in Brunei town centres (Jibah, 1983). Compared to other countries in the Malay Archipelago, Brunei had no *pondok* (cottage) system of schooling. The *pondok* was founded by Patani scholars in the early nineteenth century and it was an institution for learning Islamic knowledge. When the *surau* was no longer able to accommodate the increasing numbers of students, a small *pondok* was built near the *surau* for teaching. The subjects taught in the *surau* were reading the Holy Quran, *'Uṣūluddīn* (Principles of Religion) and *Fiqh* (Din & Salamon, 1988). The word *pondok* is derived from the Arabic word *funduq*, meaning 'a place of temporary residence or hotel' (Mydin & Ahmad, 2014, p.112). In the north of Peninsular Malaysia, the *pondok* has two meanings: 'a small hut temporary home' and 'institution of Islamic learning in the form of traditional and orthodox'. In Malaysia and southern Thailand, the hut is a significant Muslim educational institution and boarding. In Indonesia, *pondok* is called *'pesantren'* while it is referred to as *'madrasah'* in Javanese and *'dayah'* for those in Aceh, Sumatra.

5.4 The Development of Islamic Education During the British Protectorate (1888–1983)

As aforementioned, the state had its own informal curriculum of Islamic education in place, conducted by instructors in private houses, *surau, balai* and mosques before the arrival of the British. Brunei was under the British Protectorate in 1888 and it became part of the British Residential System in 1904. Eight years later, the first formal Malay vernacular school was established, but Islamic education was not included in the curriculum. The Islamic Education lessons were conducted privately and informally during the evenings (Jumat, 1989). It was later in 1936 that Islamic education was included in the school curriculum as a subject called *Shar'iyyat* (Legitimacy).

The content was limited to the `ibādat` (Worship) and *tawḥīd* (The Oneness of God) subjects (Mohd Daud, 2004). During the first year, these lessons were conducted twice a week in the Brunei Town school, which was attended by 150 boys and only one religious teacher was provided (Jibah, 1983, p. 6). According to Pg. Haji Abd. Rahman (1998), the evening religious class held in 1937 was not conducted consistently; the content of the subject was unorganised and there was insufficient class length. The teaching of Islamic Education was ineffective due to the lack of trained teachers who specialised in Islamic studies. The disorganisation might also have been caused by the unstable administration of the Department of Justice at the time, and these factors contributed to poor basic Islamic knowledge among the Bruneian children then (Rahman, 1998).

His Late Majesty Al-Marhum Sultan Haji Omar Ali Saifuddien recognised this problem and took an initiative by inviting two religious officers from the state of Johore, Malaysia, to conduct a study into the effectiveness of the teaching of Islamic education in Brunei's government school. Haji Othman bin Haji Mat Saad, an inspector of the Johore religious school, and Haji Ismail bin Omar Abdul Aziz, a judge from Sagamat arrived in Brunei on 31 December 1954. They reported that the weaknesses of Islamic education in Malay and English government schools were:

a) The duration for the learning of Islamic education was insufficient, because each session took only an hour and a half.
b) The religious education did not achieve most of its goals; for instance, most students did not know how to utter the *shahādāt* and did not know the basic Islamic pillars.
c) Most teachers did not have a sufficient academic and professional background.
(Mohd Daud, 2004, pp. 1–5)

The officers also suggested hiring 100 teachers from the Johore religious school so that the duration of the Islamic Education lessons can be extended. Daily evening lessons for those attending primary school should be one hour, and an hour and a half for secondary school students. Furthermore, Islamic education should be taught separately from other subjects and the religious subject which were held twice a week (Mohd Daud, 2004).

In the book entitled *Chadangan Mengenai Pelajaran Ugama dalam sistem Persekolahan Negara Brunei Darussalam* (Proposal of Religious Studies School system in Brunei Darussalam), The Religious Affairs

Department reported on the insufficiency of the time allotted for learning religious knowledge as follows:

> The fact is that religious education should comprise more than one subject as it is taught in the Malay and English schools. It cannot be treated the same as Geography, History, Science and so on, all of which represent a branch of a major discipline. Religious education comprises several disciplines. Each discipline has its own characteristics, for instance Fiqh, tawhīd, the Quran, Recitation, etc. Therefore, it is not justifiable to teach either all or a large section of these various disciplines as a subject in an allocated time of say three periods a week. Three periods per week is even insufficient to teach one or two religious disciplines effectively (3.14).
>
> The teaching of religious studies through one subject has evidently been insufficient and does not allow for the objectives to be attained. Even though it is intended to increase these periods up to five per week, this would possibly cause some negative effects on other subjects, where their allocated periods would have to be reduced as a result. Such action may not be well received by teachers of other subjects. Therefore, Religious Studies as a subject cannot be compared or even regarded on an equal footing with the Religious Schools System (3.15). (Jumat, 1989, p. 189)

His Late Majesty Al-Marhum Sultan Haji Omar Ali Saifuddien III accepted the report and agreed with these suggestions (Mohd Daud, 2004). On 16 September 1956, by His command, Brunei opened seven formal religious schools in four different towns:

1) Ahmad Tajuddin Malay School, Belait Town
2) Laila Menchanai Malay School, Brunei Town
3) Muda Hashim, Tutong Town
4) Muhammad Alam, Seria Town
5) Muhammmad Jamalul Alam Malay Schools, Brunei Town
6) Sultan Hasan, Brunei Town
7) Sultan 'Omar 'Ali Saifuddien College, Brunei Town.
   (Rahman, 1998, p. 10)

In the early stages, the Islamic education lessons were taught separately from the public Malay and English teaching, and were only conducted during the afternoon. Most of the teachers and office administrators were hired from Johore State and the educational system followed the existing curriculum in the Johore religious schools including using the same textbooks (Mohd Daud, 2004). These religious schools were administered by the Department of Customs, Religious Affairs, and Communities Welfare; then the Religious Affairs section was separated from the Customs Section on 1 May 1960 and upgraded into the Department of Religious Affairs and Community Welfare (Mohd Daud, 2004). The duration of religious studies was up to six years. Students' admission into the primary one level of religious schools was opened to those who were studying at primary three level in the Malay and English morning schools (Rahman, 1998), and this led to the Religious Primary School Certificate Examination, controlled by the Ministry of Religious Affairs.

According to Abd. Rahman Khatib Abdullah (1979), some Malay and English schools had to provide religious classes in the morning and afternoon sessions because of the increase in the number of students attending religious schools. Due to the positive responses in the Muslim community of the opening of these schools and the increasing number of students, religious classes were again held in the *balai*, *surau* and temporary buildings, provided by the local people with help from the Department of Religious Affairs (see Rahman, 1998).

In 1960, the curriculum of religious schools was changed in accordance to the state's needs and identity. The development and rapid increase in the number of students, teachers and schools in the religious sector over 28 years (1956–1983) can be seen in Table 5.1.

Islamic Religious Knowledge (IRK) was introduced in 1966 by the government as a subject in the Malay and English government schools' curriculum, whilst religious schools in the afternoon focused on Islamic education. Based on the Report on Religious Schools (1966), IRK was first taught in Sultan Muhammad Jamalul Alam's secondary school, then was gradually implemented in all schools in Brunei (see Rahman, 1998).

In response to a proposal by His Majesty Sultan Omar 'Ali Saifuddien on 15 January 1956, an Arabic secondary Hassanal Bolkiah Boys School opened with the enrolment of 50 students on 11 March 1966. In the following year, according to Abdul Aziz bin Juned (1968), the first Arabic school for girls, Raja Isteri Pengiran Anak Damit Religious Arabic Secondary School, opened with an intake of 61 female students (see Rahman, 1998).

Students are required to take a Candidates Arabic School Examination at the primary 4 level in a Malay primary school or at level 2 classes in religious schools for them to be enrolled in an Arabic school. Based on the results, the MoRA would then select students to join the Arabic schools at primary 4. The development of these Arabic schools was reported in *Penyata Sekolah-Sekolah Agama Kerajaan Brunei bagi Tahun 1968–1970* (Report on Government's Religious Schools in Brunei 1968–1970). The school system consists of two years at the primary level, three years in lower secondary school, two years in the upper secondary school, and another two years in pre-university school (see Rahman, 1998). According to Hj Serudin (1981), the Islamic knowledge subjects are taught in Arabic, while others were taught either in Malay or English (see Rahman, 1998). In general, the system of education run by the Brunei government was in three media of instruction: Malay, English and Arabic languages (BAR for the Year 1981–1984).

5.5 The Development of Islamic Education After Independence

1984 marked a historical achievement for Brunei Darussalam during which the country achieved independence from the British Protectorate. After independence, the development of the teaching of Islamic education progressed rapidly. In 1993, His Majesty the Sultan of Brunei established the Tahfiz Al-Quran Sultan Haji Hassanal Bolkiah institute, which aims to produce students who can memorise the Quran, known as *huffāz*, while studying other academic subjects such as English and Science (Ministry of Education, 2004a).

After gaining independence, Brunei implemented the Bilingual Education System. The religious and Arabic Schools remain under the supervision of the Ministry of Religious Affairs, whilst the morning Malay and English Medium schools remain under the Ministry of Education (see Chap. 2). The Tahfiz Al-Quran Sultan Haji Hassanal Bolkiah institute was first administered by the MoE then it was handed over to the MoRA on 1 January 2006 (Ministry of Religious Affairs, 2020f).

As mentioned in Chap. 2, Pehin Orang Kaya Setia Pahlawan Dato Seri Setia Dr. Awang Haji Ahmad bin Haji Jumat (1989), is of the view that the division of the national education system into religious and non-religious school is problematic for young students. Metassan (1979) suggests that it would be more effective if the administration of schools were the responsibility of one body to minimise waste of financial resources and manpower. Furthermore, most of the people responsible for administrating religious schools were not educationists, so it is better for them to concentrate on the propagation of Islam (see Jumat, 1989).

This lack of education system integration was discussed by Allahyarham Dato Paduka Seri Setia Prof. Dr Haji Awang Mahmud Saedon at the *School Curriculum Towards the 21st Century* convention in 1998. In his paper, *School Curriculum Following Islamic Perspective,* he highlighted that this dual system of education led to the misconception that religious knowledge has no link with the world or the environment, and the development of science and technology. The religious knowledge (*Naqly*) should not contradict acquired knowledge (*`Aqly*). Acquired knowledge must be guided by revelation (Saedon, 1998). In response to this convention, Integrated Education System was implemented in replacement to the Bilingual System (Ministry of Education, 2004b). Unfortunately, this system was only implemented for two years.

The current educational system, the National Education System for the 21st Century (SPN21), continues the dual system and religious schools are conducted either in the afternoon or morning. At the present time, Tahfiz Al-Quran Sultan Haji Hassanal Bolkiah institute, Arabic schools and religious schools are under the supervision of the MoRA, whilst general schools are under the supervision of MoE. IRK and subjects taught in Islamic religious schools follow the curriculum during the bilingual system but as an addition in the new curriculum, Arabic Language as a subject has been included in the religious school curriculum.

Brunei also established its first university, Universiti Brunei Darussalam in 1985 and the first intake was a total of 176 students. Today, there are eight faculties, nine research institutes and six academic service centres ranging from Islamic Studies, Business, Arts, Science, Health Sciences, Asian Studies, Policy Studies, Education, Biodiversity and Integrated Technologies (Universiti Brunei Darussalam, 2020a). In 2009, UBD introduced the GenNEXT Programme (Universiti Brunei Darussalam (2020b) which is a:

> student-centric approach to education and lays the foundation for life-long learning. It seeks to equip students with essential skills of critical thinking, reasoning, communication, quantitative analysis and with both a national and global perspective. Three principles embedded in all the GenNEXT modules are entrepreneurship, leadership and innovation, and environmental awareness.

In 2009, UBD introduced the GenNEXT Programme (see Chap. 2), which included three compulsory breadth modules: Melayu Islam Beraja (Malay Islamic Monarchy), English Language, and Islamic Civilisation and the Modern World. The Islamic Civilisation and the Modern World module is the continuation of learning Islamic education at a higher institution. Sultan Omar Áli Saifuddien Centre for Islamic Studies (SOASCIS) is the research institute that provides service in the teaching of this module, and it was established on 30 September 2010, with the consent of His Majesty Sultan Haji Hassanal Bolkiah Mu'izzaddin Waddaulah. Its main objective is:

> To produce graduates and scholars equipped with necessary knowledge and expertise to lead the Muslim community in facing the changes and challenges of today's world. This centre will also generate Islamic thinkers and intellectuals who can share and express their views and thoughts on contemporary issues.
> (Universiti Brunei Darussalam, 2020c).

Another milestone during this period is the establishment of an Islamic higher education institution named Kolej Universiti Perguruan Ugama Seri Begawan (Seri Begawan Religious Teacher University College) on 20 January 2007. KUPU SB is a university college that produces trained religious teachers, to fulfil the national needs and open their door to international students (Ministry of Religious Affairs, 2020f; see Chap. 2).

Universiti Islam Sharif Ali (Sultan Sharif Ali Islamic University) was established on 1 January 2007 in conjunction with His Majesty *Titah's* command, delivered during the UBD 17th convocation, whereby His Majesty had stated that the second university shall be an Islamic university. It had an enrolment of 125 undergraduates and 27 postgraduate students. The main aim of the UNISSA is to become a centre for the spread of Islam in the region (Universiti Islam Sultan Sharif Ali, 2020).

Although the teaching of Islamic education has been formalised after the country gained independence, informal teaching still continues at private and instructors' houses, mosques and learning centres in Brunei Darussalam.

5.6 MIB AND ISLAMIC EDUCATION AS NATIONAL CURRICULUM IDENTITY AND WAY FORWARD

The present curriculum represents the uniqueness of Bruneian identity. MIB presents the historical background of Bruneians as Malays practising Islam as a way of life in a moderate manner without neglecting the importance of other sciences, and places importance on the acquisition of twenty-first-century skills among Bruneian students. Islamic religion has played a crucial role in the structure of the national curriculum. Although Islamic education is no longer taught in the traditional *balai*, Islamic religious studies continues to be taught in formal primary, secondary and higher educational institutions and the government has made religious school compulsory for Muslim children to attend commencing with the '*Perintah Pendidikan Ugama Wajib 2012*' (Compulsory Religious Education Order 2012). According to this order, all Muslim children were obliged to attend religious school starting from 1 January 2013. This law shows the commitment to holistic education in Brunei in line with the educational mission statement on 'quality education' by the Ministry of Education:

> to provide equitable quality education to our future generation who are guided by the values of Malay Islamic Monarchy, equipping them with knowledge and 21st century skills to be future ready citizens. Developing them to become positive, responsible learners and contribute positively to the nation.
> (Ministry of Education, 2020)

Under the MoE, SPN21 aims to:

1) be the Ministry of Education's platform for achieving Wawasan Brunei 2035;
2) realise the Ministry of Education's vision and mission;
3) add value to and raise the quality of education in line with current/contemporary needs and anticipated needs in future years;
4) fulfill the needs and challenges of the social and economic development of the 21st century;
5) develop 21st century skills amongst students; and
6) uphold and develop desired values and attitudes amongst students in line with the Malay Islamic Monarchy or Melayu Islam Beraja (MIB) concept as the national philosophy.

(Ministry of Education, 2013, p.19)

These aims show that the national education in Brunei is provided to ensure the Bruneian national identity is maintained without neglecting the importance of the teaching of Islamic religion and sciences, while also focusing on developing the twenty-first-century skills among students.

One of the many challenges in the current formal religious education is that the curriculum does not cover matters pertaining to current issues such as the view of Islam on the practice of in vitro fertilisation (IVF), which is one of several techniques available to help people to conceive. It is suggested that a textbook can be provided which focuses on the discussion of selected topics in relation to current issues and practices among the Muslims. Also, the time allocated to teach each subject is only half an hour, and this presents a challenge for teachers to deliver the curriculum while helping students develop twenty-first-century skills.

Another issue is the existence of a dual system, resulting in the need for every Muslim child to attend both primary and secondary school as well as religious school. There is some overlap in the religious school curriculum textbook content with the morning IRK subject textbook, such as the topic on *Zakat* (annual alms tax) which is included in the Year 5 and 6 syllabus at religious school and it is also listed in the general school IRK syllabus for Year 9. Also, the history of Prophet Muhammad Peace be Upon Him is taught in the Year 3 religious school syllabus and again in the Year 7 IRK curriculum at general school (Ministry of Religious Affairs, 2015a, 2015b, 2020b & 2020c). The teaching of two different *Jawi* writing systems should also be reviewed as this has created confusion among students.

In view that if Brunei prefers to continue with the implementation of two different systems (general school and religious school), it must revise and refine the Islamic education subjects content in both systems to avoid the overlapping of content and ensure the connection and 'flow' of the topics. From the curriculum analysis based on the religious school's syllabus and the teaching of IRK at general school, it was found that there is a lack of knowledge content and of emphasis on development of love of the environment (Ministry of Religious Affairs, 2015a, 2015b, 2017, 2020a, 2020b, 2020c, 2020d & 2020e). Perhaps this can be examined by the relevant authorities in the MoE and MoRA so that Islamic education is delivered in a holistic manner.

To conclude, apart from MIB and Islamic education, the nation has also placed great emphasis on learning science subjects within the general school curriculum. There is a need to revise the curriculum in both general and religious schools to bridge the gap in the current dual system of education. Although, the current national systems of education portray 'dualism' of education, all children in Brunei have the opportunity to learn both religious and science knowledge and develop their twenty-first-century skill of learning.

REFERENCES

Al-Sufri, M. J. (2000). *Tarsilah (Chronicles) Brunei: The Early History of Brunei Up to 1432 AD*. Pusat Sejarah Brunei.

Chuchu, M. N. (1990). The Development of Education in Brunei Darussalam. *Jurnal Pendidikan, 1.*, Year 1, 37–64.

Din, H., & Salamon, H. (1988). *Masalah Pendidikan Islam Di Malaysia*. Academe Art & Printing Services Sdn. Bhd.

Jibah, M. (1983). Perkembangan Persekolahan Melayu di Brunei Dalam Pentadbiran Sistem Residen (1906-1959) (The Development of Malay Schools in Brunei Darussalam During the Administration of Resedential System). *Brunei Museum Journal, 5*(3), 1–26.

Jumat, A. (1989). *A Chronological Study of the Development of Education in Brunei Darussalam from 1906 to 1984: With Special Reference to Education Policies and their Implementation*. PhD thesis, California Coast University.

Mansurnoor, I. A. (1992). Intellectual Tradition in A Malay World: Ulama and Education in Brunei. *Jurnal Pendidikan, 3.*, Year 3, 34–60.

Mydin, H. H. M. M., & Ahmad, N. S. (2014). The System of Islamic Studies At Madrasah (Sekolah Pondok). *Journal of Mechanical Manufacturing (J-Mfac), 1*, 111–116.

Ministry of Education. (2004a). *Pencapaian dan Penilaian 20 Tahun Pendidikan (1984-2003) dan Perancangan 20 tahun Akan Datang (2004-2024)* (Achievement and Evaluation in 20 Years of Education (1984-2003 and Future 20 Years Planning (2004-2024). MIEDU, Brunei Darussalam: Ministry of Education.

Ministry of Education. (2004b). 'Integrated Education'. Unpublished manuscript, Ministry of Education, Brunei Darussalam.

Ministry of Education. (2013). *The National Education System for the 21st Century (SPN21)*. Ministry of Education.

Ministry of Education. (2020). Vision & Mission. Retrieved from http://MoE.gov.bn/SitePages/Homepage.aspx#

Ministry of Religious Affairs. (1996). *Pendidikan Ugama di Negara Brunei Darussalam* (Religious Education in Brunei Darussalam). Department of Islamic Studies, Brunei Darussalam: Jabatan Percetakan Kerajaan, Kementerian Undang-Undang.

Ministry of Religious Affairs. (2015a). *Sukatan Pelajaran Persekolahan Agama Negara Brunei Darussalam (Religious School Syllabus in Brunei Darussalam)*. Bahagian Kurikulum, Jabatan Pengajian Islam.

Ministry of Religious Affairs. (2015b). *Sukatan Pelajaran dan Panduan Mata Pelajaran Asas Pengetahuan Ugama Islam Tahun 1—3 Sekolah-Sekolah Rendah Negara Brunei Darussalam* (Syllabus and Guidelines for Core Subject Islamic Revealed Knowledge Year 1 -3 at Primary Schools in Brunei Darussalam). : Jabatan Pengajian Islam.

Ministry of Religious Affairs. (2017). *Sukatan Pelajaran dan Panduan Mata Pelajaran Asas Pengetahuan Ugama Islam Tahun 4 dan 5 Sekolah-Sekolah Rendah Negara Brunei Darussalam* (Syllabus and Guidelines for Core Subject Islamic Revealed Knowledge Year 4 and 5 at Primary Schools in Brunei Darussalam). : Jabatan Pengajian Islam.

Ministry of Religious Affairs (2020a). *Sukatan Pelajaran dan Panduan Mata Pelajaran Asas Pengetahuan Ugama Islam Tahun 6 Sekolah-Sekolah Rendah Negara Brunei Darussalam* (Syllabus and Guidelines for Core Subject Islamic Revealed Knowledge Year 6 at Primary Schools in Brunei Darussalam). : Jabatan Pengajian Islam.

Ministry of Religious Affairs (2020b). *Sukatan Pelajaran dan Panduan Mata Pelajaran Asas Pengetahuan Ugama Islam Tahun 7 dan 8 Sekolah-Sekolah Rendah Negara Brunei Darussalam* (Syllabus and Guidelines for Core Subject Islamic Revealed Knowledge Year 7 and 8 at Primary Schools in Brunei Darussalam). : Jabatan Pengajian Islam.

Ministry of Religious Affairs (2020c). *Sukatan Pelajaran dan Panduan Mata Pelajaran Asas Pengetahuan Ugama Islam Tahun 9 Sekolah-Sekolah Rendah Negara Brunei Darussalam* (Syllabus and Guidelines for Core Subject Islamic Revealed Knowledge Year 9 at Primary Schools in Brunei Darussalam). : Jabatan Pengajian Islam.

Ministry of Religious Affairs (2020d). *Sukatan Pelajaran dan Panduan Mata Pelajaran Asas Pengetahuan Ugama Islam Tahun 10 Sekolah-Sekolah Rendah Negara Brunei Darussalam* (Syllabus and Guidelines for Core Subject Islamic Revealed Knowledge Year 10 at Primary Schools in Brunei Darussalam). : Jabatan Pengajian Islam.

Ministry of Religious Affairs (2020e). *Sukatan Pelajaran dan Panduan Mata Pelajaran Asas Pengetahuan Ugama Islam Tahun 11 Sekolah-Sekolah Rendah Negara Brunei Darussalam* (Syllabus and Guidelines for Core Subject Islamic Revealed Knowledge Year 11 at Primary Schools in Brunei Darussalam). : Jabatan Pengajian Islam.

Ministry of Religious Affairs. (2020f). Retrieved from http://www.kheu.gov.bn/SitePages/Institut%20Tahfiz%20AlQuran%20Sultan%20Haji%20Hassanal%20Bolkiah.aspxhttp://www.kupu-sb.edu.bn/SitePages/Latar%20Belakang.aspx

Ministry of Religious Affairs. (2020g). Retrieved from https://kurikulumjpi.wordpress.com/pengenalan-2/

Mohd Daud, A. H. (2004). *Perkembangan Persekolahan Agama di Negara Brunei Darussalam dari Tahun 1956-1984 (The Development of Religious Schools in Brunei Darussalam from 1956-1984)*. Dewan Bahasa dan Pustaka Brunei.

Muhammad, N. (2014). *The Educational System in Brunei Darussalam in the Light of Al-Attas' Philosophy of Education*. UBD Press.

Othman, A. (2013). Preface. In Z. Serudin (Ed.), *The Malay Islamic Monarchy: A Closer Understanding* (pp. xxiii–xxiv). The National Supreme Council of the Malay Islamic Monarchy.

Rahman, P. A. P. H. M.. (1998). *Perkembangan Pelajaran Agama di Negara Brunei Draussalam Dalam Zaman Pemerintahan Sultan Omar' Ali Saifuddien 1950-1967* (The Development of Religious Schools in Brunei Darussalam from 1956-1984). *Jurnal Pendidikan*, Bil.6, 7-46.

Rahman, S. K. (2017). Jawi in Malay Language Education in Brunei Darussalam: A Review of Empirical Research. *International Journal of Humanities and Social Science, 7*(5), 1.

Saedon, M. (1998). Kurikulum Sekolah Mengikut Perspektif Islam: Bentuk dan Kandungannya (School Curriculum Following Islamic Perspective: It's Structure and Content)" In *Laporan Konvensyen Pendidikan: Kurikulum Sekolah Abad Ke-21*, (Education Convention Report: School Curriculum Towards the 21st Century). Brunei Darussalam: , pp. 37-50.

Universiti Brunei Darussalam. (2020a). Retrieved from https://ubd.edu.bn/about/organisation/ubd-history.html

Universiti Brunei Darussalam. (2020b). *Undergraduate GenNEXT Degree*. Retrieved from https://ubd.edu.bn/admission/ undergraduate/gennext-degree-programme/

Universiti Brunei Darussalam. (2020c). *SOAS Centre for Islamic Studies* Retrieved from https://ubd.edu.bn/research-institutes/soas-centre-for-islamic-studies.html

Universiti Brunei Darussalam. (2020d). *Additional Resources Add Value to Research Capabilities*. Retrieved from https://ubd.edu.bn/news-and-events/news/2018/10/03/additional-resources-add-value-to-research-capabilities/

Universiti Islam Sultan Sharif Ali. (2020). *About Us*. Retrieved from https://www.unissa.edu.bn/about-us/

Yayasan Sultan Haji Hassanal Bolkiah. (2020). Retrieved from http://www.yshhb.org.bn/464-majlis-perasmian-galeri-pusat-pengajian-kesenian-dan-kaligrafi-islam-yayasan-sultan-haji-hassanal-bolkiah-ppkki-yshhb-dan-pelancaran-buku-pelan-strategik-yayasan-sultan-haji-hassanal-bolkiah-2020-2025.

PART II

Curriculum and Pedagogical Issues, Teachers' Knowledge and Beliefs, and New Developments

CHAPTER 6

From Pedagogical Beliefs to Implementation: The Development of Pre-Service Teachers' Technology, Pedagogy and Content Knowledge for Student-Centred Learning

Sallimah Mohd. Salleh, Juraidah Musa, Marlizayati Johari, and Noraisikin Sabani

6.1 Introduction

Teachers play an essential role in ensuring the success of an education system that aims for high-quality teaching and learning in order to meet the global demand for quality and innovative education. Like most countries

---

Salleh, S. M., Musa, J., Johari, M., & Sabani, N. (2021). From pedagogical beliefs to implementation: The development of pre-service teachers' technology, pedagogy and content knowledge for student-centred learning. In Phan, L. H., A. Kumpoh, K. Wood, R. Jawawi, & H. Said (Eds.), *Globalisation, education, and reform in Brunei Darussalam* (pp. 107–131). Palgrave MacMillan.

S. M. Salleh (✉) • J. Musa • M. Johari
Universiti Brunei Darussalam, Bandar Seri Begawan, Brunei
e-mail: sallimah.salleh@ubd.edu.bn; juraidah.musa@ubd.edu.bn; marlizayati.johari@ubd.edu.bn

© The Author(s), under exclusive license to Springer Nature Switzerland AG 2021
Phan, L. H. et al. (eds.), *Globalisation, Education, and Reform in Brunei Darussalam*, International and Development Education, https://doi.org/10.1007/978-3-030-77119-5_6

in the world, Brunei Darussalam has introduced systemic policy change, such as the *Sistem Pendidikan Negara Abad ke-21* (The National Education System for the 21st Century) (SPN21) (Brunei-MOE, 2013).

SPN21 was introduced in 2009 as a blueprint for the country's education system throughout primary, secondary and tertiary education focusing on, among other important changes, the end of student retention from Year 1 to Year 10/11, the provision of multiple pathways to higher education, catering for the needs of students with special needs and opportunities for acquisition of marketable skills. Central to SPN21 is the focus on the development of students' twenty-first-century skills (Brunei-MOE, 2013, p. 20).

In this chapter, we describe how one of the modules in the Master of Teaching (MTeach) programme, *Technology, Pedagogy and Content Knowledge* (TPACK), develops teacher candidates' skills for teaching and learning in the twenty-first century. We hypothesised that their experiences of learning through the module would shape the teacher candidates' pedagogical beliefs and we report on that effect. We also share a framework for developing teacher candidates' technological, pedagogical and content knowledge (TPACK) to help teacher educators better understand how teacher candidates' beliefs can be shaped through their collaboration in designing and planning technology-integrated lessons. Similarly, through the experience of producing self-made documentary videos of the implementation of the TPACK-designed plans, teacher candidates learn to enhance learners' twenty-first-century skills development and enrich their understanding of the subject matter.

6.2 Technological, Pedagogical and Content Knowledge Framework for Teacher Candidates

One major emphasis for a teacher education institution in preparing teachers for the twenty-first century is to instil positive pedagogical beliefs about the use of technology to support twenty-first-century teaching and learning. As teacher education is an arena for developing and changing beliefs, it is crucial to address the connections between teacher candidates'

N. Sabani
Curtin University Malaysia, Miri, Malaysia
e-mail: noraisikin.s@curtin.edu.my

pedagogical beliefs and classroom practices (Fives & Gill, 2014). The Technological, Pedagogical and Content Knowledge (TPACK) framework (Malik et al., 2019; Mishra & Koehler, 2006) provides a platform for designing the *Technology, Pedagogy and Content Knowledge* module that helps teacher candidates develop their pedagogical beliefs about the integration of technology into classroom teaching plans. Table 6.1 shows how each of the knowledge dimensions in the module is related to the content objectives (defined using Bloom's Taxonomy, Bloom et al., 2013), the associated pedagogy and the supporting technology to enhance teacher candidates' understanding of the content.

Teacher candidates use the multiple knowledge dimensions of the TPACK framework (consisting of declarative, procedural, schematic and strategic dimensions) as tools for planning, teaching and learning activities that integrate technology to achieve the twenty-first-century goals of collaboration, critical thinking and problem solving (Atun & Usta, 2019; Chai et al., 2013; Koh et al., 2013; Voogt et al., 2013).

The learning outcomes of the TPACK module are to develop teacher candidates' understanding and application of the TPACK framework for the design of student-centred lessons that enhance learners' understanding of subject matter. Additionally, it is to develop teacher candidates' technological knowledge (TK) and skills to promote the development of learners' twenty-first-century skills. In this way, the inclusion of the TPACK module in the MTeach programme supports the goals of SPN21.

6.3 Teachers' Pedagogical Beliefs

Ertmer (2016) defines pedagogical beliefs as 'any proposition, specifically related to teaching and learning, which begins with the phrase, I believe that …'. It has been suggested that research is needed to understand the relationship between teachers' pedagogical beliefs and their use of digital technologies, particularly those that promote twenty-first-century teaching and learning (Pischetola, 2020). A focus on the importance of promoting teachers' technological beliefs is timely, as it supports the call for an increase in teachers' use of digital technologies in the classrooms (UNESCO, 2011). In order to promote teachers' technology practices, it is important to address teachers' underlying beliefs that support and facilitate the change required for technology integration in the classroom (Jung et al., 2019; Li et al., 2019; Chai et al., 2009).

Table 6.1 TPACK framework for the pedagogy, technology and content knowledge module

KNOWLEDGE DIMENSION	OBJECTIVES OF CONTENT	TEACHING AND STUDENT LEARNING (PEDAGOGY)	TECHNOLOGY
SCHEMATIC (using revised blooms' taxonomy of educational objectives: Analysing)	Teacher candidates *analyse* the usefulness of technology-enriched pedagogy and *reflect* on their personal beliefs about integrating technology for values and students, personalised learning and development of students' twenty-first-century skills	EXPERIMENT—Teacher candidates develop and plan curriculum in their learning areas collaboratively REFLEXIVITY—Teacher candidates read and reflect on their personal beliefs about using technology for values and personalised learning REAL-WORLD PROBLEM SOLVING AND INNOVATION Project-based learning: Teacher candidates identify real-world problems (e.g. students' difficulty in conceptual understanding) and implement their TPACK-designed lesson to rectify or overcome the problem	Teacher candidates read compulsory journal articles shared in UBD canvas Submit online personal reflections through UBD canvas Teacher candidates submit online group work through UBD canvas Teacher candidates exhibit their group work in a poster on the SHBIE EXHIBITION Wall for public view through HP reveal applications
STRATEGIC (using revised blooms' taxonomy of educational objectives: Evaluating Creating)	Teacher candidates *design* and *create* a curriculum in their areas of specialisation collaboratively Teacher candidates *create* a lesson plan individually on the selected topic from their curriculum that integrates content, pedagogy and technology Teacher candidates *implement* their TPACK-designed lesson plan and *evaluate* the effect of the lesson on students' learning and attainment of the twenty-first-century skills Teacher candidates *evaluate* the impact of technology on values and personalised learning		

Becker (2000) highlights several aspects that need to be in focus to cultivate technology use in the classrooms. These can be divided into internal and external aspects. Internal aspects include whether the teachers are comfortable with using technology, their level of expertise in using computers, which should be at least moderate, and teachers' personal beliefs regarding technological use for learning purposes. Recent studies have indicated that internal factors have more substantial bearing on the use of educational technology among educators (Long et al., 2019). Similarly, previous research has emphasised the necessity for teachers' beliefs, skills, attitudes and knowledge to be aligned with current technological needs and practices, to ensure the success of the application of technology in education (Bordalba & Bochaca, 2019; Ertmer, 1999).

The external factors that may determine the success or failure of technology integration include the schools' opportunities to do so in terms of the availability of technological resources and time, the availability of sufficient computer resources, the school culture and the availability of complementary assessment, in order to support the teaching and learning process seamlessly.

Chai et al. (2013) propose that research on TPACK should make five contextual factors explicit; the interdependence of which would influence the TPACK-integrated lessons designed by an educator. The five contextual factors in the current study can be described as (a) the intrapersonal dimension of context (epistemological and pedagogical beliefs that teacher candidates' hold); (b) the interpersonal dimension, where the teacher candidates design the curriculum collaboratively, and individually planned lessons for personalised learning and development of students' twenty-first-century skills; (c) the institutional factors in which the education system exerts influence on teachers' use of technology through a new national education system, such as SPN21; (d) the technological and physical provisions in schools, which influence teachers' beliefs and, lastly, (e) the school context.

6.4 Conceptual Framework

The current study focused on the inculcation of teacher candidates' pedagogical beliefs in creating innovative curriculum materials designed using the Technological Pedagogical and Content Knowledge (TPACK), shown in Fig. 6.1. It aimed to achieve this through a design-based approach,

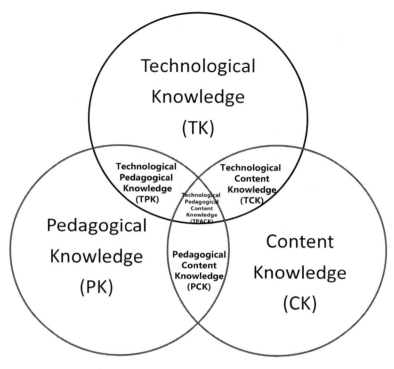

Fig. 6.1 Technological, pedagogical and content knowledge

underpinned by the combination of external and internal factors related to the TPACK framework and considering other contextual factors.

Koehler and Mishra (2009) conceptualised the TPACK framework as comprised of seven knowledge domains:

(a) Content Knowledge (CK) which is about the actual subject matter that is intended to be learnt or taught,
(b) Pedagogical Knowledge (PK) which is about the processes and practices or strategies about teaching and learning,
(c) Technological Knowledge (TK) which constitutes knowledge about operating digital technologies,
(d) Pedagogical Content Knowledge (PCK) which comprises the interaction of PK and CK,

(e) Technological Content Knowledge (TCK), which focuses on the interaction of TK and CK,
(f) Technological Pedagogical Knowledge (TPK), which highlights the interaction of TK and PK,
(g) Technological and Pedagogical Content Knowledge (TPACK), which comprises the interaction of PCK, TCK and TPK.

PCK involves the knowledge of representing content knowledge and adopting pedagogical reasoning to make the specific content more accessible to the learners (Angeli et al., 2016, p. 15). TCK refers to the technological representation of content knowledge without taking any account of teaching (Njiku et al., 2020; Cox & Graham, 2009). TPK refers to pedagogically sound ways of using technology, with no reference to any specific subject matter (Angeli et al., 2016, p. 15). TPACK is regarded as the synthesis of teacher knowledge about teaching specific content, through the use of educational technology that best supports teaching and learning, and optimally engages students of diverse needs and preferences in learning (Chai et al., 2013; Harris & Hofer, 2011).

The TPACK domains have been tested extensively and the outcomes indicate validity, although there are researchers who suggest the possibility of the inculcation of other factors (Drummond & Sweeney, 2017), which led to the design of this research project.

6.5 Methodology and Findings

6.5.1 *What Teacher Candidates Learnt from the TPACK Module that Shapes their Pedagogical Beliefs?*

Teacher candidates' responses to the completion question, 'I believe that …' were analysed using thematic framework analysis. It was applied to the students' written statements for (i) data management and (ii) abstraction and interpretation of data. Data management consists of (i) familiarisation, (ii) constructing an initial thematic framework, (iii) indexing and sorting, (iv) reviewing of data extracts and (v) data summary and display (Spencer et al., 2014).

As an illustration of the outcome of the analysis, three teacher candidates' reflections reveal the emergence of four common themes: (i) personal beliefs on technology usage, (ii) previous practices before taking the module TPACK, (iii) shift of practices after participation in the module

TPACK and (iv) the challenge faced when using technology in the classroom. The findings are presented here.

6.5.1.1 Teacher A

Teacher A is a primary science teacher. She believes that different learning strategies can be accommodated using technology as long as it is not against the teaching of Islam. This is echoed in her belief on the integration of technology in students' activities, where she mentioned that young children need a guardian present when using technology to avoid explicit content made available on the Internet.

> Teacher can provide tasks that required the pupils' to do more research on the internet. However, young children need to be supervised by the parents or guardian while they surf the net. This is to avoid visiting explicit websites on the net.

In addition, she also believes that there are limitations to using technology in science teaching, as highlighted by these two statements.

> Yet, as a teacher, we also have to advise our pupils to do more reading from educational books too. This is because not all resources or information found in the net are valid and can be trusted.

> However, not all technology can be used into teaching and learning of in Science classrooms, as most of the subject content required hands-on experiments.

In her previous practice, she used technology in her teaching, but to a limited extent. For example, she used PowerPoint to show videos and pictures for explanatory purposes only.

> This illustrates a non-interactive communication approach as pupils were sitting down and listening to what I have explained.

She revealed that this was because of her lack of knowledge and exposure to using ICT with twenty-first-century learning design (SRI International, 2013). After taking the TPACK module, her practice shifted. She decided on the technology tool selection first, and thought about how to use the selected technology to accommodate her teaching method. Only after that, would she decide on the content of the teaching and learning process.

Table 6.2 Changes in Teacher A's practice after TPACK

Dimensions	Before	After
Teaching method	Teacher-centred	Pupil-centred
Technology used	Whiteboard and marker pens, PowerPoint slides	PowerPoint slides, YouTube videos, Instagram (IG), Google search
Pupils' activities	Pen and paper activities	Pairing project—Creating e-notes
Pupils' participation	Passive learner	Active learner

> When using the TPACK model, I as the teacher have to think carefully on what kind of technologies that I will be using during the class and how will I use the technologies, accommodated with my teaching method. As soon as I have selected the appropriate tools and teaching method, then I need to think of the appropriate content needed to be put into the teaching and learning process.

Teacher A highlighted the four dimensions of her teaching and learning activities that changed after taking the TPACK module (see Table 6.2).

Teacher A elaborated with an example of her teaching method, whereby she asked students to use the Internet at home to search for information on a certain topic. Then, the students used that information during the class discussion in school. She found out that this led to the pupils taking a more active role in class. As for the technology used, she highlighted the use of Instagram, which allowed communication after school hours.

However, there are challenges faced by Teacher A in implementing technology in the classroom:

> Some problems that teachers encounter are: difficulty when handling digital technology, such as lack of ICT skills, teachers' perception on pupils using ICT and time consumed to prepare and conduct the lesson.

> I also received a response from my pupils that they were not good at using a laptop and has no access to the internet connection at home.

6.5.1.2 Teacher B

Teacher B is a secondary school mathematics teacher. She believed that the students' motivation and interest in mathematics could be increased by introducing technology in the classroom. She had positive attitude towards using technology as she believes that technology can enhance and improve students' knowledge and understanding of the topic taught, as well as develop students' twenty-first-century skills. In 2014, her institution introduced a standardised lesson plan known as Whole School ICT Development (WSID) to the staff. However, there was no coaching or professional mentorship provided on how to integrate the technology into the lesson planning.

> Teachers were given booklets on the WSID framework, but no further coaching or professional mentorship was provided.

Due to this limitation, most staff, including herself, retained their traditional teaching approach, that is, chalk and talk and direct instruction. This may have led to boredom and lack of understanding among the students.

> From my personal experience, I noticed that teaching through direct instructional approach creates boredom for the students, whereas, for some, they did not understand the concept of the lesson that needs to be learnt.

After taking the TPACK module, she perceived that technology use supports personalised learning. In addition, she learnt about game-based learning, which improved her technological knowledge (TK). This finding resonates other researchers' acknowledgement of similar circumstances as well (Hsu et al., 2020). According to her, one advantage of game-based knowledge is the visualisation aspect, and she elaborated this with an example of graphical software usage. Furthermore, she used applications such as Kahoot, Socrative and Google Forms to assess students' understanding via quizzes.

> One example of developing an interesting professional development is to introduce teachers to game-based knowledge (a form of TK).

> I realised that the use of technology encourages students to be engaged in the lesson, as well as support personalised learning.

> With the help of graphical software, teachers find it easier to plot, and they can ask a lot of questions to develop students' higher-order thinking skills.

> Using this ICT tool, it gives me an idea to design and plan my Mathematics quiz using Kahoot, Socrative and Google forms.

With these technologies, she came to believe that students can be motivated to learn mathematics by engaging them more effectively.

> I believe that, with the use of technology, it will encourage my students to be more motivated and find learning Mathematics as an interesting subject. I think as a teacher, we should limit ourselves from using too many direct instructional approaches like the "talk and chalk" method and let students have the freedom to learn independently with the aid of using technology.

Nonetheless, she identified a problem she faced regarding the use of technology in the classroom caused by the lack of support from the administration, for the provision of ICT professional development through an appropriate coaching programme.

6.5.1.3 Teacher C

Teacher C is an instructor at a vocational and technical college teaching hospitality. She believes that technology can enhance the teaching and learning processes in hospitality courses. However, the success of this technology integration depends on the teachers' initiatives and commitment towards it. This commitment is manifested through the teachers' planning, as well as their instructional and classroom practices. As in her previous teaching practice, she conducted demonstrations in class, such as the proper method to peel onions. After taking the TPACK module, she opted for resources available on YouTube for students to watch at home. Thus, the classroom sessions were dedicated to students' actual demonstration, such as peeling the onions. This practice also supports personalised learning that can be afforded by the introduction of technology in teaching. In addition, she advocates group discussions in class. She used Edmodo as a learning management platform to develop students' collaboration during group discussion.

> Based on my teaching experience, engaging students in group discussion, as a pedagogical practice is essential in developing such skill.

> I believe, by integrating digital technology, it enhances collaborative work in the classroom.

She elaborated on her use of Edmodo for student collaboration as an example of how she used technology to enrich her instruction.

For instance, in order to prepare for a cooking demonstration, students are required to search for a recipe on the internet. Each member (2-3 students) in the group shares and discuss their findings in the Edmodo. Edmodo has incredible features of chatting groups, digital storage, sharing photos, links, documents, as well as videos, which enables students to access everyone's idea instantly and paperless. Such practices help passive learners to communicate with their peers and promote literacy skills.

She concured with Teacher B's perspectives regarding the challenges faced by teachers in integrating technology in the classroom due to lack of support from administration for professional development for teachers in ICT.

The availability of technology may not transform teachers' practices in and of itself. However, technological tools have the potential to transform teacher's practices, which can influence students' achievement. It is up to subject teachers, instructional designers, and program developers, essentially every individual involved in education; to ensure that these technologies facilitated opportunities benefit learning and every child's future.

She also emphasised the importance of recognising that ICT should not be seen as a separate subject but as a tool for learning other subjects.

From my personal point of view, ICT is not considered a separate academic subject. ICT is often used as a tool for learning in other subjects.

6.5.2 What Did Teacher Educators Learn from the Teaching and Learning of the TPACK Module?

For the group assignment, the teacher candidates were required to design and plan their lessons using the TPACK framework matrix, videotape the implemented lesson and produce a 30-minute video documentary on the implementation of TPACK-designed lesson plans to illustrate the various stages of their implementation. Examples from the video documentary submitted by a group of teachers comprising of Teachers A, B and C illustrates the assessment of the designed lesson plans and implemented lessons.

From the submitted assignments, it was clear that the teacher candidates used the TPACK framework effectively as a template for discussion and decision-making about appropriate pedagogies, to deliver the respective lesson goals for each of the four knowledge dimensions and the selection of the most suitable technologies to support those learning activities.

6 FROM PEDAGOGICAL BELIEFS TO IMPLEMENTATION... 119

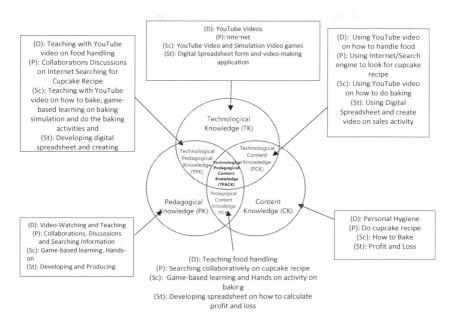

Fig. 6.2 Example of the teachers' use of the TPACK framework and knowledge dimension: (D) declarative, (P) procedural, (Sc) schematic and (St) strategic

The following examples demonstrate how the three teachers collaborated optimally using the TPACK framework matrix (see Fig. 6.2) to design and plan for all the four knowledge dimensions: declarative (knowing WHAT), procedural (knowing HOW), schematic (knowing WHY) and the strategic knowledge (knowing WHEN and WHERE). The declarative and procedural knowledge dimensions guide teacher candidates to plan for foundational content knowledge and operational knowledge. The schematic and strategic dimensions guide the teacher candidates to develop learners' higher-order thinking, and twenty-first-century skills of real-world problem solving, collaboration, knowledge construction, use of technology, skilled communication and self-regulation (Stehle & Peters-Burton, 2019).

Using the excerpts from teacher candidates' submitted lesson design and plans, as well as snapshots from the submitted video documentary, it is possible to demonstrate the assessment evaluation of an exemplary group assignment.

Figure 6.3 illustrates how Teacher C successfully planned for technology-integrated learning activities in the declarative knowledge dimension. The goals of the lessons were: first, to discover the principles of cooking methods; second, to discuss tasks given to share responsibility; and last, to present their findings using flashcards. Teacher C planned the teaching and learning strategies for student collaboration (one of the twenty-first-century skills) while searching the Internet (an integration of Technological Knowledge), for information on the subject matter (Content Knowledge) and for discussion and presentation (Pedagogical Knowledge) of their findings to the class. Then Teacher C instructed students to watch a YouTube video (Technological Knowledge) about the subject matter (Content Knowledge) to corroborate their findings. Lastly, Teacher C assessed students' understanding of the subject matter through playing an interactive game (Pedagogical Knowledge) online quiz using Kahoot (Technological Knowledge).

Teaching and learning activities		ICT and Other Resources
Students Learning Activities	**Teacher Activity Consideration**	
Declarative:	**Declarative:**	**HARDWARE/DEVICES:**
Lesson 1: State the principal methods of cooking	**Lesson 1: State the principal methods of cooking**	**Laptop (with internet connection):** (1) to explore for information on the principles method of cooking, (2) to show videos on principal methods of cooking, (3) to access and play Kahoot online.
Part 1	**Part 1**	
1. Students work collaboratively to discover the principal methods of cooking by doing internet research	1. Teacher introduces the lesson using PowerPoint slides.	
2. Students discuss among themselves on deciding which information fits and answer the task	2. Teacher instructs students to find out principal methods of cooking by using laptop and internet	
3. Students present their findings using flash card.	3. Instruct students to work in group. 3-4 persons per group.	**Mobile phones:** for student and teacher to assess and play Kahoot online.
	4. Encourage discussion among students while searching for information on the internet	**Projector:** to project (1) YouTube video, (2) online game Kahoot!
	5. Distribute flash card.	
	6. Instruct students to write down the principal on the flash cards using marker pens. Assist them during internet research activity.	**Speakers:** to allow (1) audio video projection, (2) game audio projection.
	7. Limit their time. 20minutes maximum.	
	8. Listen to their presentation	
Part 2:	**Part 2:**	**INTERNET/APPLICATION:**
1. Students watch YouTube video	9. Teacher plays YouTube video which is on principal methods of cooking.	**Web-based game Kahoot:** to play the interactive game.
2. Check their answers on the flash cards	10. Instruct students to check their answers on the flash cards.	
Part 3:	**Part 3:**	
1. Each student use laptop with internet connection they are allowed to use their mobile phones.	11. Teacher instruct students to play online Quiz Kahoot to assess their understanding and knowledge on the principal methods of cooking	
2. Students log in to Kahoot.it and enter the pin game	12. Allow students to use laptop and mobile phones to play the game.	
3. Students play the online quiz.		

Fig. 6.3 Example of teacher C's lesson plan for the declarative knowledge dimension

Figure 6.4 illustrates an example of how Teacher C successfully implemented a student-centred learning situation, where the students worked collaboratively to search for information on the Internet using Google on mobile phones or laptops (using technology to gather information) and to achieve the goals of the lesson.

For the procedural knowledge dimension, this group planned and implemented the lesson using the TPACK framework (shown in Figs. 6.5 and 6.6). In this lesson, the learning objective is to develop a cupcake recipe with *halal* ingredients. Teacher C planned the lesson with the use of an Internet search for cupcake recipes, similar to the previous task. The difference is in the procedural knowledge dimension activity, in which the students were asked to find and modify the selected cupcake recipe. Figure 6.7 shows students working together to search for the cupcake recipe using the search engine. The modified cupcake recipe is then shared via Edmodo. In this task, the twenty-first-century skills are collaboration, knowledge construction and the use of ICT.

With regard to the schematic knowledge dimension, this group planned the lesson, as shown in Fig. 6.8. This lesson focuses on the application of their previous knowledge (from declarative and procedural dimensions) to the practical activity, which is baking cupcakes, based on the recipes that

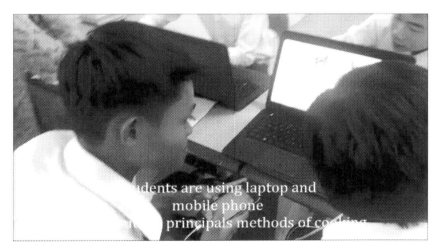

Fig. 6.4 Students using laptops and mobile phones to search for information on the Internet

Knowledge Dimension	Content Knowledge	Teaching and learning	Technology	21st CLD Dimension
Procedural	Task 4 Preparing for Bake Sales Project a) Create a recipe page	**Lesson 4:** • Working in group, students work collaboratively to discuss and decide cupcake flavour they intend to bake and sell. Each student (or pair up) in the group do internet research on the cupcake flavour that they are interested in, for example; Oreo Cupcake, Vanilla Cupcake, etc. Students then will have substantial decision among themselves on which cupcake flavour they want to bake. • Extract the chosen cupcake recipe from the website to create students' own recipe page using MS Word. Students make sure that the ingredients are halal. Modify the recipe page whenever appropriate. Below is a sample of recipe page of chocolate cupcake.	**Lesson 4:** **HARDWARE/DEVICES:** **Laptop** (with internet connection): to extract recipe on cupcakes **Mobile phones:** for students to search for cupcake recipes. **Printer:** to print out the recipe page. **SOFTWARE:** **Microsoft Word:** to create cupcake recipe page. **INTERNET/APPLICATION:** **Edmodo:** to submit softcopy of the recipe page.	- Collaboration code: 4 - Knowledge construction code: 4 - Use of ICT for learning code: 4

Fig. 6.5 Lesson plan for the procedural knowledge dimension

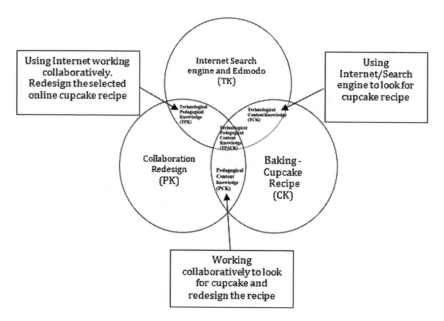

Fig. 6.6 TPACK framework of procedural knowledge dimension lesson activities

Fig. 6.7 Students searching for cupcake recipes

the students selected. Before starting the baking activity, students were asked to watch an online video (Fig. 6.9) and played an online simulation game relating to cupcake baking process. This is the technology that Teacher C used for teaching the baking process of a cupcake. In this lesson, the twenty-first-century skills highlighted are collaboration, knowledge construction and the use of ICT. For pedagogical knowledge, Teacher C has used game-based learning and a video watching activity.

As teacher educators, we learnt that, for successful implementation of the strategic knowledge dimension, teacher candidates of various subjects' backgrounds could design and plan interdisciplinary lessons effectively using the TPACK framework. For the strategic knowledge dimensions, teacher candidates designed and planned lessons for learners to apply their knowledge of different subjects to create new knowledge and to experience the real-world implementation of that knowledge (see Fig. 6.10).

Figure 6.11 illustrates how Teacher C (the Technical and Vocational Teacher), Teacher B (the Secondary School Mathematics Teacher) and Teacher C (the Primary School Science Teacher) designed and planned for the lessons on entrepreneurship through the bake sale project. The lessons' goal was focused on entrepreneurship, which was to nurture learners' entrepreneurial skills (comprising preparing for a bake sale, running

Knowledge Dimension	Content Knowledge	Teaching and learning	Technology	21st Dimension	CLD
	a) Watch videos on how to bake cupcake	• Before students do actual baking, teacher shows YouTube videos on how to make cupcake. • Students list down equipment and appliances required in baking process. Recommended videos: Kit Kat Cupcake https://www.youtube.com/watch?v=Ka64k2g6u94 Strawberry Cheese Cupcake https://www.youtube.com/watch?v=SYjH1EiJ2zI Malteser Cupcake https://www.youtube.com/watch?v=fSMcmPRlxw4	**Laptop** (with internet connection): to show YouTube videos **Projector:** to project YouTube videos **Speakers:** to allow video audio projection **Mobile phones:** for students to play cupcake games **INTERNET/APPLICATION:** Cupcake Makers 2: play simulation game on how to bake cupcakes.	- Collaboration: code: 4 - Knowledge construction code: 4 - Use of ICT for learning code: 4	
	b) Play simulation cupcake game for better foreseen baking practical	• Working in pairs, students play the simulation game on baking cupcakes to visualize the actual baking process. Recommended application on cupcake games: Wedding Cupcakes Cupcake Makers Cupcake Makers 2 Bake Cupcakes Available in Play Store for androids users and Apple Store for iPhone users.			
	c) Baking cupcake	**Lesson 8:** • Working in groups or in pair, students demonstrate the actual baking of cupcakes by using the recipe page from the previous instruction. Implement the previous topic on safe working practices during the baking practical i.e. proper hand washing, short finger nails, short hair, etc. Students must video the practical activity. • Teacher assists students in every group.	**Lesson 8:** **HARDWARE/DEVICES:** **Laptop:** to view recipe page **Mobile phone:** Mobile phone: (1) to view recipe page (2) to take videos and photos **INTERNET/APPLICATION:** Edmodo: to extract recipe page	- Collaboration: code: 4 - Knowledge construction code: 2 - Use of ICT for learning code: 2	

Fig. 6.8 Lesson plan for the schematic knowledge dimension

the sale, and calculating profit and loss). The pedagogy selected to achieve the goal was a project-based activity. The technologies appropriately and optimally chosen were students' use of computer applications to create advertising posters for social media, including Instagram. The students used Microsoft Excel applications to record expenditure for the bake sale and to calculate profit/loss. For this strategic knowledge dimension, the focus was on students applying their content knowledge, along with declarative, procedural and schematic knowledge dimensions gained from earlier lessons on baking (taught by Teacher C), keeping records and calculation of expenditure (taught by Teacher B), and health and safety precautions for food production (taught by Teacher A).

Fig. 6.9 Students watching a YouTube video on baking cupcakes

The Bake Sale project (Fig. 6.12) provides evidence of successful attainment of the lesson goals in nurturing students' entrepreneurial skills, as well as developing the twenty-first-century skills of real-world problem solving, collaboration, skilled communication and using ICT.

In summary, the teacher educators learnt that the TPACK module was effective in instilling positive pedagogical beliefs among the teacher candidates, as they developed their skills in designing and planning student-centred learning activities using the TPACK framework. The teacher educators also learnt that the teacher candidates referred to the TPACK framework as a template that guided their discussions and planning, so they could work in collaboration. Lastly, the teacher candidates of various subject backgrounds could design and plan for teaching an interdisciplinary topic. They used the TPACK framework to design and plan for the strategic knowledge dimensions that promote higher-order thinking skills and develop students' twenty-first-century skills.

6.6 Conclusion

The current emphasis within the education system on the development of twenty-first-century skills seemed to play an important role in shaping teacher candidates' readiness to utilise technology in the classroom. As

Knowledge Dimension	Content Knowledge	Teaching and learning	Technology	21st Dimension	CLD

Strategic	Task 5: Running Bake Sales Project that nurtures entrepreneurship project	**Lesson 9:**
		• Students share and distribute responsibilities and roles before running the bake sales i.e. cashier, manager, and Instagram
		  ➢ Group 2: Students working collaboratively to produce noticeboard advertisement using PosterMyWall.com
		  ➢ Students pair up to create speech for announcing the bake sales project.
		  ➢ Group 3: Work in pair, produce a log sheet to record sales activity using MS Excel. Print out the log sheet.
		  ➢ Group 4: Students collaboratively work together to record down items and equipment they require for bake sales project i.e. tables, display plates.
			HARDWARE:
			Laptop (internet connection): (1) to create relevant documents and paperwork for sales project. (2) To create advertising
			Printer: to print advertisement for school noticeboards.
			INTERNET/APPLICATION:
			PosterMyWall: to create online poster for advertising the sales activity. Available at www.postermywall.com
			Microsoft Excel: to create log sheet for sales records
			Instagram and WhatsApp: to advertise the sales activity to Official School Instagram Page and Students' WhatsApp chatting group.
				- Collaboration: code: 2
				code: 3	

	b) Run the business	**Lesson 10:** • The cupcake sales project will be carried out in the school. Teacher highlights students' implementation on safety and hygiene practices leant from the previous lesson. Record number of cupcakes sold and unsold on log sheet.	**Lesson 10:** **HARDWARE:** **Mobile phone/video cam:** to record students' activity	- Collaboration: code: 4 - Knowledge construction code: 4 - Use of ICT for learning code: 2	
	c) Create short video on Bake Sale Projects d) Calculate profit and loss from the bake sales	**Lesson 11 and 12:** • Working in group, students collaborate to produce videos based on both baking practical and sales activity. • Calculate the profit and loss from the sales project by using the purchasing spreadsheet that they have created. Using the receipts, students will key in the prices of the items bought. Total up the amount of money spent to the ingredient. Calculate the difference between selling price and the money spent (cost price) to buy the ingredients. If the selling is higher than cost price, there is profit gained. If the cost price is higher, there is loss in the business.	**Lesson 11 and 12:** **HARDWARE:** **Laptop:** to create video **Mobile phone:** to extract video data and transfer to laptop. **SOFTWARE:** **Microsoft Excel:** to calculate the profit and loss from the sales activity. **INTERNET/APPLICATION:** **Kizoa:** to create short video on baking and sales activity. Available at www.kizoa.com	- Collaboration: code: 4 - Knowledge construction code: 4 - Use of ICT for learning code: 4	

Fig. 6.10 Lesson plan for strategic knowledge dimensions

mentioned by Ertmer (1999), the alignment between current technological needs and teachers' own belief in its purpose can lead to its successful application to students' learning. With effective implementation of technology in the classroom, students' engagement and motivation to learn subject content may increase. Sampson et al. (2002) argued that more sophisticated software used in a technological learning environment, such as intelligent learning environments (ILEs) coupled with technology-enhanced learning and animated pedagogical agents may increase motivation among students.

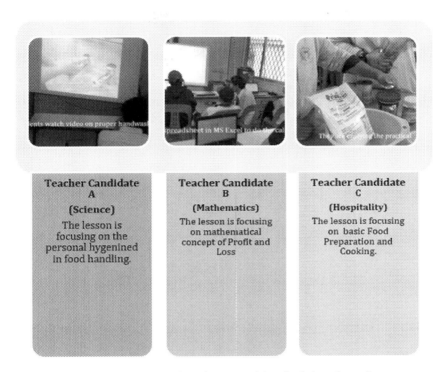

Fig. 6.11 Collaborative interdisciplinary teaching for bake sale project

The teacher candidates' pedagogical beliefs about the impact of technology use in the classroom seemed to be aligned with Becker's (2000) internal and external factors. These internal aspects include whether the teachers are comfortable with technology use and their level of expertise in using computers. However, the findings of this study seemed to highlight other important factors, particularly teacher's intention and willingness to use technology (cf. Conde Hernandez, 2019). Meanwhile, the external factors mentioned by the teacher candidates in determining the success or failure of technology integration in the classroom were limitations on technological resources, time allowances and the availability of sufficient computer resources (Becker, 2000; Ertmer, 1999; Ottenbreit-Leftwich et al., 2010). It is also pertinent for School administrators to play

Fig. 6.12 Students' bake sale

an active role in supporting and promoting the use of technology for teaching and learning (Lucas, 2020).

Finally, for teacher educators, it is argued that the TPACK framework is a logical first step on the path of development of teacher candidates' technological and pedagogical beliefs during the Initial Teacher Education Programme. These step has aided teacher candidates to design and plan lessons within their content areas that are rooted in TPACK, and allow them to build an understanding of, as well as the skills necessary to develop meaningful learning experiences for their students that integrate technology for twenty-first-century teaching and learning (Wilson et al., 2020).

References

Angeli, C., Valanides, N., & Christodoulou, A. (2016). Theoretical consideration of technological pedagogical content knowledge. In M. C. Herring, M. J. Koehler, & P. Mishra (Eds.), *Handbook of technological pedagogical content knowledge (TPACK) for educators* (pp. 11–32). Routledge.

Atun, H., & Usta, E. (2019). The effects of programming education planned with TPACK framework on learning outcomes. *Participatory Educational Research, 6*(2), 26–36.

Becker, H. J. (2000). Findings from the teaching, learning, and computing survey: Is Larry Cuban right? *Education Policy Analysis Archives, 8*(51), 1. Retrieved from: http://epaa.asu.edu/ojs/article/viewFile/442/565

Bloom, B. S., Munzenmaier, C., & Rubin, N. (2013). Bloom's Taxonomy: What's Old is New Again *Educational Objectives: The Classification of Educational Goals*: The eLearning Guild Research.

Bordalba, M. M., & Bochaca, J. G. (2019). Digital media for family-school communication? Parents' and teachers' beliefs. *Computers & Education, 132*, 44–62.

Brunei-MOE. (2013). 21st Century National Education System (SPN-21). 2013, from http://www.moe.edu.bn/web/spn21.

Chai, C. S., Hong, H. Y., & Teo, T. (2009). Singaporean and Taiwanese preservice teachers' beliefs and their attitude towards ICT use: A comparative study Singaporean and Taiwanese preservice teachers' beliefs and their attitude towards IG use: A comparative study. *The Asia-Pacific Education Researcher, 18*(18), 117–128. https://doi.org/10.3860/taper.v18i1.10-40

Chai, C. S., Koh, J. H. L., & Tsai, C. C. (2013). A review of technological pedagogical content knowledge. *Educational Technology and Society, 16*(2), 31–51. https://doi.org/10.1111/j.1365-2729.2010.00372.x

Cox, S., & Graham, C. (2009). An elaborated model of the TPACK framework. *Proceedings of Society for Information Technology & Teacher Education International Conference 2009*, 4042–4049. Retrieved from http://www.editlib.org/p/31291.

Drummond, A., & Sweeney, T. (2017). Can an objective measure of technological pedagogical content knowledge (TPACK) supplement existing TPACK measures? *British Journal of Educational Technology, 48*(4), 928–939.

Ertmer, P. A. (1999). Addressing first-and second-order barriers to change: Strategies for technology integration. *Educational Technology Research and Development, 47*(4), 47–61.

Ertmer, P. A. (2016). Understanding the relationship between teachers' pedagogical beliefs and technology use in education: A systematic review of qualitative evidence. *ETR&D*, 1–41.

Fives, H., & Gill, M. G. (2014). *International handbook of research on teachers' beliefs*. Routledge. https://doi.org/10.4324/9780203108437

Harris, J. B. H., & Hofer, M. J. (2011). *Technological Pedagogical Content Knowledge (TPACK) in Action: Journal of Research on Technology in Education, 1523*(April 2015), 211–229. https://doi.org/10.1080/15391523.2011.10782570

Hsu, C. Y., Liang, J. C., & Tsai, M. J. (2020). Probing the structural relationships between teachers' beliefs about game-based teaching and their perceptions of technological pedagogical and content knowledge of games. *Technology, Pedagogy and Education*, 1–13.

Jung, Y. J., Cho, K., & Shin, W. S. (2019). Revisiting critical factors on teachers' technology integration: The differences between elementary and secondary teachers. *Asia Pacific Journal of Education, 39*(4), 548–561.

Koehler, M. J., & Mishra, P. (2009). What is technological pedagogical content knowledge (TPACK)? *Contemporary Issues in Technology and Teacher Education, 9*, 60–70. https://doi.org/10.1016/j.compedu.2010.07.009

Koh, J. H. L., Chai, C. S., & Tsai, C. C. (2013). Examining practicing teachers' perceptions of technological pedagogical content knowledge (TPACK) pathways: A structural equation modeling approach. *Instructional Science, 41*(4), 793–809. https://doi.org/10.1007/s11251-012-9249-y

Li, Y., Garza, V., Keicher, A., & Popov, V. (2019). Predicting high school teacher use of technology: Pedagogical beliefs, technological beliefs and attitudes, and teacher training. *Technology, Knowledge and Learning, 24*(3), 501–518.

Long, T., Cummins, J., & Waugh, M. (2019). Investigating the factors that influence higher education instructors' decisions to adopt a flipped classroom instructional model. *British Journal of Educational Technology, 50*(4), 2028–2039.

Lucas, M. (2020). External barriers affecting the successful implementation of mobile educational interventions. *Computers in Human Behavior, 107*, 105–509.

Malik, S., Rohendi, D., & Widiaty, I. (2019, February). Technological pedagogical content knowledge (TPACK) with information and communication technology (ICT) integration: A literature review. In *5th UPI International Conference on Technical and Vocational Education and Training (ICTVET 2018)*. Atlantis Press.

Mishra, P., & Koehler, M. J. (2006). Technological pedagogical content knowledge: A framework for teacher knowledge. *Teachers College Record, 108*, 1017–1054. https://doi.org/10.1111/j.1467-9620.2006.00684.x

Njiku, J., Mutarutinya, V., & Maniraho, J. F. (2020). Developing technological pedagogical content knowledge survey items: A review of literature. *Journal of Digital Learning in Teacher Education*, 1–16.

Ottenbreit-Leftwich, A. T., Glazewski, K. D., Newby, T. J., & Ertmer, P. A. (2010). Teacher value beliefs associated with using technology: Addressing professional and student needs. *Computers & Education, 55*(3), 1321–1335.

Pischetola, M. (2020). Exploring the relationship between in-service teachers' beliefs and technology adoption in Brazilian primary schools. *International Journal of Technology and Design Education*, 1–24.

Sampson, D., Karagiannidis, C., & Kinshuk. (2002). Personalised learning: Educational, technological and standardisation perspective. *Interactive Educational Multimedia, 4*, 24–39.

Spencer, L., Ritchie, J., Ormston, R., O'Connor, W., & Barnard, M. (2014). Analysis: Principles and processes. In J. Ritchie, J. Lewis, C. M. N. Nicholls, & R. Ormston (Eds.), *Qualitative research practice* (pp. 269–293). SAGE.

SRI International. (2013). *21 CLD Learning activity rubrics.* Microsoft Partners in Learning.

Stehle, S. M., & Peters-Burton, E. E. (2019). Developing student 21st century skills in selected exemplary inclusive STEM high schools. *International Journal of STEM Education, 6,* 39.

UNESCO. (2011). *Education for Change: Past, Present and Future.* Paper presented at the 1st Sub-regional Country Report Meeting 2010 on Education for Sustainable Development in South East Asia, Jakarta, Indonesia.

Voogt, J., Fisser, P., Pareja Roblin, N., Tondeur, J., & van Braak, J. (2013). Technological pedagogical content knowledge - a review of the literature. *Journal of Computer Assisted Learning, 29*(2), 109–121. https://doi.org/10.1111/j.1365-2729.2012.00487.x

Wilson, M. L., Ritzhaupt, A. D., & Cheng, L. (2020). The impact of teacher education courses for technology integration on preservice teacher knowledge: A meta-analysis study. *Computers & Education, 10*(3), 9–41.

CHAPTER 7

Beginning Teachers' Use of a Constructivist Teaching Approach to Improve their Students' Understanding of Science Through Classroom Discussion

Hardimah Said

7.1 Introduction

This chapter reports on the use of a teaching approach known as the Conceptual Understanding Procedure (CUP) to help students engage in classroom discussion and assist them to develop better understanding of science concepts (Mills et al., 1999; Sukaesih, 2017). CUP uses a constructivist framework claimed to be effective in teaching science subjects. This framework explains how people construct their knowledge and understanding of the world through every day experiences and how these experiences can lead to a new level of understanding. By extending or modifying their prior knowledge, meaningful learning can take place. Cakir (2008) pointed out that constructivism is a way of seeing the world which combines the nature of reality, knowledge, human interaction and science. Research has shown that this helps students to achieve a better understanding of science concepts. In science education, constructivism supports and enhances science teaching and learning mainly because the approach takes into account students' prior knowledge and understanding.

Instruction that is designed to be personally meaningful and seen to be useful by the students can be more engaging and motivate students to learn more (Hulleman & Harachiewicz, 2009). The CUP provides students with an opportunity to be more active through the employment of classroom activities that require them to use their prior knowledge and experiences to construct and connect with new knowledge which would then lead learners to initiate conceptual change through enquiry. However, research has shown that this is not as straightforward as it may seem. Often, students' current knowledge, prior to learning in the science classroom, is not aligned with the acceptable science view. Misconceptions, or alternative conceptions, which are not attended to can impede future learning. In order for students to make sense of and link science concepts learnt in the classroom with their current everyday experiences and understanding of those concepts, it is necessary to have students reveal their current understanding and challenge it in such a way that they can abandon incorrect ideas, reorganise and incorporate new science explanations into their understanding. The CUP is seen to be able to achieve this in three stages.

Research has shown that this approach is particularly useful for abstract and complex science topics. Furthermore, the procedural and conceptual approaches provide positive learning environment for students as well as improve the process of teaching and learning compared to the use of the conventional procedural approach (Andrew, 2017). Furthermore, conceptual understanding helps students to better connect and organise their current knowledge with new ideas in a coherent way (Laswadi et al., 2016).

The author has introduced this teaching approach to her own Master of Teaching (MTeach) students following the success claimed by research on the use of the CUP in teaching science concepts effectively. This allowed the teacher candidates (TCs) to reflect on their teaching practice. The CUP was used as the means for the TCs to learn to be reflective, particularly in terms of pedagogical reflection (Carson, 1991), and to teach science conceptually rather than teaching for the sake of teaching. It is important for teachers and hence teacher educators to realise and understand that even when using effective teaching approaches, it is crucial to reflect upon their practice and ideally to reflect with other teachers either in small groups or as a department or as a school community (Shulman & Shulman, 2004). Reflection provides the space for teachers to enhance their capacity to learn and to develop their approach to teaching leading to purposeful change.

This chapter discusses the findings of a study with a group of 17 TCs on the use of the CUP in their teaching while undergoing their teacher training through the Master of Teaching degree (MTeach) in Science Education. These teacher candidates were required as part of their MTeach programme to do two ten-week semesters of professional teaching practice placement in secondary schools. During their teaching practice placement, they were observed by the author and asked to reflect upon their experiences through interviews and written reflection on the use of the CUP. Prior to applying the CUP in their teaching, the TCs underwent lectures on how to carry out this teaching approach.

7.2 The Conceptual Understanding Procedure (CUP)

The CUP was developed in 1996 by a team at Monash University, Australia. Gunstone and his colleagues introduced the CUP in Physics (McKittrick et al., 1999). It has three stages: individual, group and whole class. In the individual stage, students are required to think about a given exercise on their own and to write their answers on an A4 sheet of paper. Figure 7.1 is an example of a CUP worksheet out of 13 worksheets which is made freely accessible online (https://monahs.edu/science-education/2015/resources/conceptual-understanding-procedure) by Gunstone and his colleagues.

An example of a worksheet that was adapted from what is available online and used by one of the MTeach candidates is shown in Fig. 7.2. Stage One allows students' own prior knowledge on the topic to be identified. This is beneficial to teachers because it allows them to identify their students' misconceptions. The second stage of the CUP requires three or four students, depending on the number of students in a class, to work as a group and for the students to discuss their individual answers from the first stage. In Stage Two, students are expected to reach an agreement as

136 H. SAID

A4 sheet

Ex 12   Momentum in traffic accidents

In the Victorian Alps a minibus (**B**) travelling north crashes into the back of a parked car (**C**), as shown in Fig. 1.

(You can assume that the frictional forces between the tyres and the icy road are negligible and that the road is horizontal.)

Fig. 2 shows vectors representing the momentum p_b of the bus and p_c of the car just prior to the collision.

Fig. 3 shows the momentum p_b of the bus at an early instant **during** the collision.

Fig. 1

1 On Fig. 3 draw in a vector to represent the momentum p_c of the car at this instant during the collision.

As a result of the collision the bus and car move forward **joined together**.
The mass of the bus is three times the mass of the car.

2 On Fig. 4 draw in vectors to represent the momenta p_b of the bus and p_c of the car as they move forward joined together.

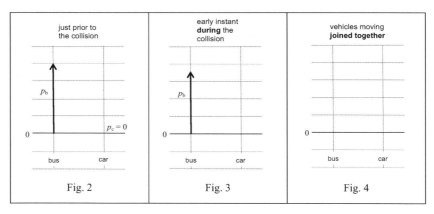

Fig. 7.1   A example of a CUP worksheet

a group with answers being written on an A3 sheet and each group is responsible to explain and defend their answers to the whole class in Stage Three. This stage brings collaboration and team work among the group members and provides a positive way of debating and discussing in order

What is the reading on the Ammeter?

The series in Fig. 1 is set up and an ammeter can be connected between various points in the circuit.

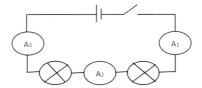

When the ammeter, A, is measured, it appears as shown below:

(i)   Before the switch is closed   (ii) after the switch is closed

 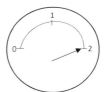

So the current supplied in the circuit is _____ A.

Mark in the approximate position of the **arrow** for the reading on ammeter.

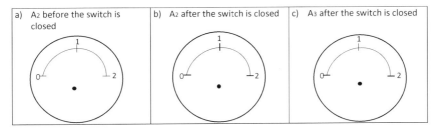

a) A₂ before the switch is closed   b) A₂ after the switch is closed   c) A₃ after the switch is closed

Fig. 7.2 A CUP worksheet designed by a teacher candidate

to get a group consensus on answers to the questions on the worksheet. At the third stage, the groups' final answers are displayed at the front of the whole class for discussion. The second and third stages allow students to learn cooperatively and achieve a class consensus while the teacher acts as facilitator. McKittrick et al. (1999) have shown that these classroom discussions make students more engaged and provide a positive collaborative learning experience.

The three stages of the CUP create opportunities for students to actively participate in discussions, which can motivate them to learn cooperatively. Thus, the CUP integrates cooperative learning and students' ideas to solve conceptual problems that allow students to be active in the process of learning (McKittrick et al., 1999). This is an aspect of student-centred learning. The group and whole class discussion allow students to give each other feedback in a structured way by actively engaging in discussion. The formation of knowledge is most likely to occur when students are engaged in social interaction (Cakir, 2008). Furthermore, active discussions can challenge students' prior understanding of a scientific explanation and reasoning. Thus, the CUP enables students to reassess their prior knowledge and change their conception of scientific phenomena (Mills et al., 1999). This has proven to be one of the crucial methods practised by science teachers for many decades. Teachers need to challenge students' alternative conceptions which are usually rooted in their epistemological beliefs (Posner et al., 1982).

In contrast, a passive learning environment where students are taught using a teacher-centred approach often leads to a lack of students' participation in discussion and to students being less creative and critical (Sukaesih, 2017). The CUP is not only about collaboration; it helps improve students' understanding of difficult topics through a communicative learning activity (Purnami et al., 2018). The CUP also increases students' participation in discussion and critical thinking.

See Figs. 7.3 and 7.4 for examples of Stage One (individual) and Stage Two (group) answers.

7.3 Findings and Discussion

Despite some challenges, all the TCs gave positive feedback on the use of the CUP, and they found the teaching approach to be stimulating and refreshing. Moreover, the TCs expressed their willingness to use this teaching method in the future with appropriate changes, which are discussed further below.

7 BEGINNING TEACHERS' USE OF A CONSTRUCTIVIST TEACHING... 139

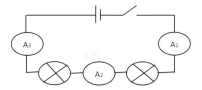

The current supplied in the circuit is ___**2**___ A.

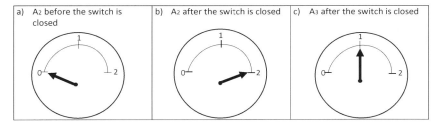

Fig. 7.3 Stage One individual answers

The current supplied in the circuit is ___**2**___ A.

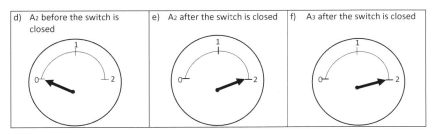

Fig. 7.4 Stage Two group answer

7.3.1 Classroom Observation

Classroom observations provided the author with more detailed evidence and verification of the events described in the teachers' written reflection. It allowed the author to have better interaction with the TCs during and after the classes to query matters which required further clarification.

7.3.2 Observation of Students' Participation

Many students were reluctant to participate in the first individual stage. Some students also hesitated to participate in group and class discussions even with encouragement from their teachers. It became clear that this resulted from their concerns about being criticised by their peers. This was especially the case for the lower ability students (Weaver & Jiang, 2005). Most were excited to proceed to the second stage, not to discuss the activity but rather to play with their friends. In contrast, more high-ability students completed the tasks more seriously and they were more involved in the discussions from the outset. This observation was discussed at length by the TCs in their reflection on the lessons.

7.3.3 Challenges for the Teacher Candidates

It was observed that the TCs faced similar issues when implementing CUP, such as group selection and timing. It was not possible to use the CUP with an ideal group size of three students as most of the classes had more than 30 students each. Thus, forming a group of three meant having at least ten groups which led to difficulty in completing the whole class discussion on time with a variety of responses. However, the exercise revealed a range of students' alternative conceptions but it challenged the teachers in completing their facilitation role. Another issue with grouping was whether or not to group on the basis of ability. Some TCs indicated that their students disagreed or showed their reluctance when the teachers made prior arrangements for the grouping. Some students even requested to form their own groups.

The TCs also faced issues with time management as students were not ready when asked to move to the next stage or task, which led to the delay in completing the observations. Other challenges include the students' level of commitment and participation in the activities, and the classroom setting. Classes in laboratories with fixed benches resulted in limiting the space for students to move around when regrouping. Students' misconceptions on abstract concepts such as electricity and atomic structure may have been problematic but they were also beneficial with the use of the CUP for many TCs.

Some TCs found it challenging to be a facilitator because they saw a need for the teacher to deliver knowledge to the students and they expressed difficulty in making their students participate in the whole conceptual understanding procedure. However, many were positive about the importance of student participation but with the caveat that some other teaching approaches which involve students' discussion can result in the discussion being dominated by the high-ability students or those who are more extroverted. In contrast, the CUP stimulates students' active involvement in defending their individual answers in the second and third stages.

The two main issues faced by TCs in using the CUP can be considered technical challenges. A challenge experienced by all of them involved the design of the CUP worksheet. Even those who adapted a CUP worksheet expressed similar challenges in adapting the worksheet:

> I chose to create the CUP activity on the topic of Energy ... by incorporating from example student worksheets available online (Monash University, 2015). My mentor's input was very crucial in the process of creating the CUP activity as I do not have the experience to be able to gauge the Year 9 students' ability to complete my CUP worksheet. The draft was changed about 4 to 5 times before it was ready to be implemented and that took me three weeks. (TC-M)

Another TC explained the difficulty she faced:

> The process of designing the first trial of the CUP exercise was really challenging for me as I struggled to come up with suitable questions. Ideally, a CUP exercise is supposed to contain question set in a 'real-world' context but I was not able to include any 'real-world' context due to the non-observable phenomena of chemistry concepts that require understanding at the sub-microscopic level and are not relatable to everyday life experiences. (TC-S)

7.3.4   *Teachers' Reflection*

The written reflection revealed the TCs' experience of implementing the CUP. They constructed meaning and gained knowledge through this learning experience, and they began to see ways on how to improve their teaching methods. Teachers' reflection is one of the main components of their professional development, and this is most important for novice teachers to see at the beginning of their professional careers. Teachers' reflection is an ongoing learning process which helps improve practice by revealing flaws and strengths as teachers learn and develop from experience (Dewey, 1933, 1938). Self-reflection also allows teachers to learn about themselves and take necessary action in order to increase their effectiveness and be successful teachers. Teachers become more aware and are able to identify their own dilemmas and perspectives on issues that they face as well as the ability to recognise the learning background and styles of their students (Sellars, 2012).

Teachers might overlook the time to reflect on the effect of their practice as they spend too much time in lesson planning and teaching (Juklová, 2015). This highlights the importance of this study: the need to encourage teachers to be reflective. Analysing the TCs' written reflection can help teacher educators to be better informed about the needs of the TCs. When teachers reflect on their work, they are not only learning from their own experience but also enhancing their capacity to learn and to develop as teachers (Shulman & Shulman, 2004). Said (2017) identified elements of reflection such as the teachers' motivation, vision, understanding and practice that should be considered when exploring and analysing their written reflection in order to better understand the teachers and their practices. Hence, in this study, the written reflections were thematically analysed according to these elements, the significance of topics being discussed and the recurring themes and patterns.

As aforementioned, the challenges for many TCs were time management and completing the intended tasks within the time allocation. Many found it a challenge to ensure completion of the three stages in one lesson and if they were able to complete all the stages, the main objective of the CUP was not achieved as the stages were done in a hurry and some students were not able to fully grasp the intended conceptual understanding. Some TCs saw this was a result of their students needing more time to reach a consensus. The TCs felt they have failed in implementing the CUP. Below are two quotes from TCs with regard to time management:

> I did not have the time to access their conceptual understanding. I asked the students to give their level of understanding using their hands. One finger being the lowest level of understanding and five fingers being the highest level of understanding. (TC-A)

> The worksheet itself contained ten questions including drawing a graph. Students provided feedback stating insufficient time to finish all the questions. I realised that I overestimated the potential of my students in com-

pleting all the questions. Hence, for future improvement, I would limit the questions to three questions in one activity. (TC-T)

Many TCs found that the CUP allowed students who showed less interest and unwillingness to engage at the start of the task to become active participants in discussion and interaction with others as the CUP proceeded to the final stage of whole class discussion. The TCs admitted that, unlike other teaching approaches that require students' discussion, CUP allowed their students to be more proactive as they needed to justify to their peers that their answers were correct. This allowed them to speak up and build their confidence. On a positive note, the TCs' reflection focused mainly on the benefits of CUP and many commented on how it was successful as a student-centred design for teaching as it allowed teachers to act as facilitators and thus provide students with the responsibility to take control of their learning. Overall, all TCs claimed that the CUP encouraged their students to participate actively and to contribute to discussion:

> I act as a facilitator … the aim is to reach a whole class consensus with the answers provided. During this stage, although it's challenging, it encourages the students to develop critical thinking and work independently. CUP promotes high level of interaction and participation which further helps the students to understand the learning experience. (TC-W)

> I believe CUP can help students to improve their communication especially during Stage 3: the whole-class mode. (TC-S)

Many TCs found that CUP allowed them to discover their students' misconceptions. This was useful and challenging to them as they have to respond to the students' misconceptions and correct them immediately. This is an issue for TCs who have a lack of subject content knowledge on certain science topics or those who were inexperienced in how to respond to students' misconceptions. Figure 7.2 shows two examples of students' individual answers to the question in Fig. 7.1. The answers reveal misconceptions about the flow of current in a series circuit. Figure 7.3 is the group's answer which was compared with other group's answers in a whole class discussion in Stage Three of the CUP.

The TC's observations about the students' responses to this CUP activity included:

> [The students'] answers mostly suggested that they assume current reduces as the ammeter are placed further away from the battery ... answers between each group mostly varied and it was time consuming to address each groups' opinions but in spite of these challenges, the activity has provided the opportunity for me to address some of the misconceptions that arose and scaffold students' lack of understanding of the topic. (TC-N)

It is clear that the CUP assisted the TCs in this study to discover their students' misconceptions and thus help them to scaffold their students' conceptual understanding.

Another teacher candidate reflected on her students' misconceptions:

> Most students are having misconception and failed to apply the concept correctly to explain the concept as observed in their answers ... However, through a heated debate-style interpretive discussion, the concept was clarified and explained clearly by those who are considered as the most-able learners. (TC-T)

Many TCs were able to be scaffold their students' conceptions in Stage Three of the classroom discussion as can be seen in the following response:

> I managed to highlight the students' misconceptions during the whole class mode discussion. (TC-S)

7.4 THE WAY FORWARD FOR A BETTER EXPERIENCE IN CONDUCTING THE CUP

Overall, the TCs felt that more time was needed to prepare a lesson using the CUP. However, perhaps time is not the issue here but the lack of confidence and techniques required to produce questions that can reveal the students' understanding of science concepts. Figure 7.5 is an example of a CUP worksheet in which the questions emphasised procedural rather than conceptual understanding. Students were expected to investigate the total resistance of the arranged circuit, but the TC failed to include written instructions on the worksheet. Perhaps this was intentional as he wanted to provide instruction verbally. Yet, this inadequacy of written instruction could lead to confusion among students about what is expected of them to do in the CUP activity. This worksheet could be improved by asking the students the significance of the variation of each circuit setting.

EX1: INVESTIGATE CIRCUIT'S TOTAL RESISTANCE

NAME:

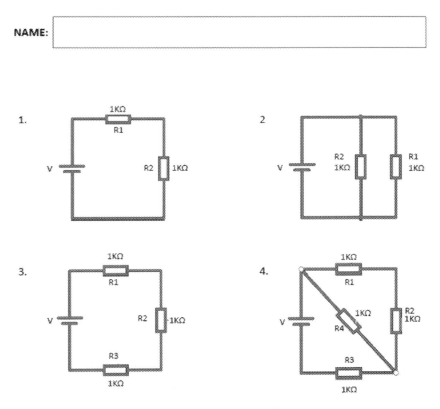

Fig. 7.5 The CUP worksheet by a teacher candidate

Some found that using the procedure meant more time is needed for the teacher to cover a lesson objective whereas more objectives can be met using other teaching approaches. This issue resulted from the worksheet created by the TCs, and either it was too lengthy or it attempted to cover too many learning objectives in the worksheet. This issue gained prominence due to their lack of teaching experience and they were still developing skills in questioning and creating students' worksheets. Some admitted that the struggle did not arise from creating questions per se but the real challenge was to produce good conceptual questions, especially for topics which are abstract in nature. Creating a worksheet that aims to help students achieve a better conceptual understanding was quite challenging for these teacher candidates. In addition, they found it was necessary to create questions that both targeted conceptual understanding and suited the school's Scheme of Work for the subject. This challenge can be met if TCs can develop the skills and design techniques that enable them to feel confident and at ease in working with their own CUP worksheets incorporated in a scheme of work that they have developed in order to achieve the intended outcomes of the curriculum.

Another technical factor is the use of an A3 paper for the whole class discussion. The TCs found it was too small and some commented on how the paper was wasted. A solution for this is to use a flip chart or educational technology in subsequent use of the CUP which was initiated by some TCs.

Grouping the students appropriately can also be seen as a technical issue. Group size, composition and social relationships are important as they could have an effect on participation. Some students were unable to work individually, so they skipped Stage One and were eager to discuss the worksheet (Stage Two) straight away. They were impatient as they wanted the answers immediately and they lacked focus. If the discussion was less lively, it might end up being taken over by the teacher. Thus, it is crucial for teachers to take the opportunity from Stage One where most of students' prior knowledge and misconceptions are identified. Grouping the students for Stage Two could be done based on class size or on their responses in Stage One.

Despite all the challenges, the most encouraging finding from the use of the CUP was the students' enthusiasm, motivation and boost in interest and confidence. As a consequence, the TCs became more motivated in their teaching. This resulted in positive and conducive learning and teaching experiences for students and teachers. This was particularly apparent during the second and third stages where students needed to interact and share their understanding to come to an agreement. Students then became responsible for their own learning to solve the issue. They were more aware of their own prior conceptions versus the accurate scientific knowledge of the concepts.

All the technical issues such as time management, resources and preparation of the CUP can be categorised according to their immediate practice (Shulman & Shulman, 2004). After the implementation of the CUP, their reflection focused on their future vision and motivation in implementing the procedure in their teaching approach. Many TCs expressed willingness to use it in their future teaching with refinements that they expected to include after their initial experience of the CUP.

Some TCs explained the difficulty they had in predicting the kind of answers their students might give. Similarly, some experienced the difficulty in how to respond to students' misconceptions in order to facilitate the development of correct scientific conceptions, which is not an issue specific to the use of the CUP. Most student-centred teaching approaches require science teachers to possess good subject content knowledge that would assist them in handling issues related to students' misconceptions. This pedagogical content knowledge comes with practice. Thus, while it is important for beginner teachers to possess strong subject knowledge, they must develop insights into their students' experience of scientific phenomena as they plan and facilitate teaching activities that reveal their students' ways of experiencing the science objects of learning (Traianou, 2006).

Despite the challenges for the TCs in responding correctly to their students' misconceptions, CUP has shown to be able to provide a pathway for teachers to elicit their students' misconceptions. The discovery of alternative conceptions held by their students should have prepared the teacher candidates to plan for their future teaching to assist their students to become aware of their ways of seeing scientific phenomena and to help them to come to more powerful ways of experiencing those phenomena or concepts. Students' misconceptions in science teaching and learning have been one of the challenges in science education for many years. Teachers, particularly teachers in training, have been identified to hold alternative conceptions just like their students (Halim & Meerah, 2002; Wandersee et al., 1994). It might be more relevant to refer to these alternative conceptions and to study the relationship between them and science ways of experiencing to improve teaching and learning (Marton & Booth, 1997). In other words, it is time for science teachers to realise the object of learning that will help them identify students' misconceptions.

7.5 Conclusion

This study aimed to explore the effect of introducing new TCs to a teaching approach based on constructing conceptual understanding in science learning. Throughout the process, the TCs were made aware of the importance of implementing evidence-based science teaching in their classroom. Specifically, this study aimed to explore the TCs' reflections on the use of the CUP, which was found to be successful in that many planned to repeat the procedures with changes to suit the context in which they teach having seen it as a way to improve their teaching and their students' learning.

Within the context of Brunei, students approach their learning as them being knowledge receivers and for teachers to be the transmitter of knowledge. Most students, if not all, listen to their teachers and remain passive students. Even when the opportunity arises, especially in the science classroom when hands-on activities are conducted, students prefer to get answers or guidance from teachers. Students show hesitation to commit to the activities because of the tradition of being exposed to teacher-centredness and are unable to understand those activities and use them effectively.

Now, the Ministry of Education is encouraging student-centred teaching approaches and the CUP has the potential to support this approach to teaching. Following this approach, it is crucial to encourage teachers to take the time to reflect upon their actions and to learn from their experience and assess their own practices. They learn about themselves, actions and thoughts which assist them to a more informed development of their own practice (Kahn & Walsh, 2006). Reflection should be an ongoing process. Only then can teachers see what needs to be done, or changed in themselves, and to achieve their own teaching goals. This study has shown how each TC reflected upon their experiences in using CUP and their concerns on how to improve their future actions.

This small-scale study could become a longitudinal study with a new intake of MTeach teacher candidates each year under the Science Education programme. It is hoped that the insight and understanding achieved in this study would lead to continuous improvements in teaching and learning in science classrooms.

References

Andrew, R. (2017). Learn implement share blog. Procedural vs conceptual knowledge in mathematics education. https://www.learnimplementshare.com/procedural-vs-conceptual-in-mathematics.html

Cakir, M. (2008). Constructivist approaches to learning in science and their implications for science pedagogy: A literature review. *International Journal of Environmental and Science Education*, 3(4), 193–206.

Carson, T. (1991). Pedagogical reflections on reflective practice in teacher education.

Dewey, J. (1933). *How we think*. Prometheus Books (Original work published 1910).
Dewey, J. (1938). *Experience and education*. Collier Books, Macmillan.
Halim, L., & Meerah, S. M. (2002). Science trainee teachers' pedagogical content knowledge and its influence on physics teaching. *Research in Science and Technological Education, 20*(2), 215–225.
Hulleman, C. S., & Harachiewicz, J. M. (2009). Promoting interest and performance in high school science classes. *Science, 326*, 1410.
Juklová, K. (2015). Reflective in prospective teacher training. *Procedia—Social and Behavioral Sciences, 171*, 891–896.
Kahn, P., & Walsh, L. (2006). *Developing your teaching: Ideas, insight and action*. Routledge.
Laswadi, K., Yaya, S., Darwis, S., & Afgani, J. D. (2016). Developing conceptual understanding procedural fluency for junior high school students through model-facilitated learning (MFL). *European Journal of Science and Mathematics Education, 4*(1), 67–74.
Marton, F., & Booth, S. (1997). *Learning and awareness*. Routledge.
McKittrick, B., Mulhall, P., & Gunstone, R. (1999). Improving understanding in physics: An effective teaching procedure. *Australian Science Teachers Journal, 45*(3), 27–33.
Mills, D., McKittrick, B., Mulhall, P., & Feteris, S. (1999). CUP: Cooperative learning that works. *Physics Education, 34*(1), 11–16.
Posner, G. J., Strike, K. A., Hewson, P. W., & Gertzog, W. A. (1982). Accommodation of a scientific conception: Toward a theory of conceptual change. *Science Education, 66*, 211–227.
Purnami, A. S., Widodo, S. A., & Pramana, R. (2018). The effect of team accelerated instruction on students' mathematics achievement and learning motivation. *Journal of Physics: Conference Series, 948*(1), 012020. IOP Publishing.
Said, H. (2017). *Explorations of the moral socio-cultural contexts of the intentional action of physics teachers, case studies to inform practice and teacher education*. Unpublished doctoral dissertation, The University of Melbourne.
Sellars, M. (2012). Teachers and change: The role of reflective practice. *Procedia—Social and Behavioral Sciences, 55*, 461–469.
Shulman, L. S., & Shulman, J. H. (2004). How and what teachers learn: A shifting perspective. *Journal of Curriculum Studies, 36*(2), 257–271. https://doi.org/10.1080/0022027032000148298
Sukaesih, S. (2017). The effects of conceptual understanding procedures (CUPs): Towards critical thinking skills of senior high school students. In *Journal of Physics: Conference Series* (Vol. 824, No. 1, p. 012070). IOP Publishing.
Traianou, A. (2006). Teachers' adequacy of subject knowledge in primary science: Assessing constructivist approaches from a sociocultural perspective. *International Journal of Science Education, 28*(8), 827–842.

Wandersee, J. H., Mintzes, J. J., & Novak, J. D. (1994). Research on alternative conceptions in science. In D. L. Gabel (Ed.), *Handbook of research on science teaching and learning* (pp. 177–210). Macmillan.

Weaver, R. R., & Jiang, Q. (2005). Classroom organization and participation: College students' perceptions. *Journal of Higher Education, 76*(5), 570–601.

CHAPTER 8

The Development and Growth of Inclusive Education in Brunei Darussalam

Siti Norhedayah Abdul Latif, Rohani Matzin, and Aurelia Escoto-Kemp

8.1 Introduction

Brunei Darussalam has an education system that consistently strives to be responsive to the needs of all students regardless of ability or background. The National Education Policy was an early milestone that was introduced in 1992 to ensure education for all (EFA) by providing quality education to students with special needs as well as students from diverse backgrounds (Ministry of Education, 1992). This continues to be the main priority in the more recent Strategic Plan 2018–2022 which focuses on ensuring

---

Abdul Latif, S. N., Matzin, R., & Escoto-Kemp, A. (2021). The development and growth of inclusive education in Brunei Darussalam. In Phan, L. H., A. Kumpoh, K. Wood, R. Jawawi, & H. Said (Eds.), *Globalisation, education, and reform in Brunei Darussalam* (pp. 151–175). Palgrave MacMillan.

S. N. Abdul Latif (✉) • R. Matzin • A. Escoto-Kemp
Universiti Brunei Darussalam, Bandar Seri Begawan, Brunei
e-mail: norhedayah.latif@ubd.edu.bn; rohani.matzin@ubd.edu.bn; 17H0384@ubd.edu.bn

© The Author(s), under exclusive license to Springer Nature Switzerland AG 2021
Phan, L. H. et al. (eds.), *Globalisation, Education, and Reform in Brunei Darussalam*, International and Development Education, https://doi.org/10.1007/978-3-030-77119-5_8

access to quality education for all students. In this globalised world, an international declaration towards inclusive education is an ideal commitment which sets a goal and provides hope and an impetus for transformation. Throughout the period of these educational reforms, change has come slowly, but the foundation has provided the framework to develop an education system that would include all children including those with special needs. This chapter describes the key milestones in the development and growth of inclusive education in Brunei Darussalam: national policies which highlighted inclusive education as a prioritised educational agenda in line with international declarations towards inclusion; the establishment of Special Education Unit (SEU) in 1994 to oversee the implementation of inclusive education in mainstream school settings and the training of Learning Assistant Teachers (LATs) to support students with special needs in schools; and, important reforms in teacher education to ensure the provision of qualified teachers to support students with special needs. The chapter concludes with some thoughts on inclusive education in Brunei Darussalam in relation to the nationwide initiatives and collaborative efforts to uphold inclusive education practices at regional and international levels.

8.2 The Direction of Educational Reform After Independence

While Brunei was under the British protection (1888–1984), the locals were actively involved in matters pertaining to the education of their people. As mentioned in previous chapters of this book, the first Malay language school began in 1912, followed by a Chinese school in 1916 and an English school in 1931. In August 1969, a major priority and concern was highlighted at the Brunei Youth Council seminar on education, where the locals expressed the need for a national education policy. This led to the Report of the Brunei Education Commission 1972 that provided the basis for further changes and development of the educational structure. The government adopted and implemented parts of the Report in 1974 which formed the basis for the present organisation and hierarchy of the Ministry of Education (MoE).

Several key educational structure and reform agendas in school curricula from the 1970s onwards helped to advance the development of inclusive education in Brunei Darussalam. The adoption of the Report of the Brunei Education Commission in 1979 imposed compulsory education for all children at the age of five beginning with enrolment in Primary 1. The Bilingual Education Policy was introduced in 1984 to ensure a high level of proficiency in both Malay and English. Under this policy, existing Malay and English medium schools were replaced with a single bilingual school system. The single bilingual system included a common national curriculum from preschool to secondary levels in 1985, thereby removing any language barrier as an impediment to accessibility for all students (Ministry of Education, 2013).

Despite the bilingual language support provided across schools, there was a tendency for students with special needs to experience school failure as the education system was strongly orientated towards academic performance (Wong & Mak, 2005). Students who fail in exams were often retained at the same grade level instead of being promoted to the next grade level. This led to repeated experiences of academic failure with students being over-aged because of grade retention or students dropping out (Omar, 2001). It was the high number of student failures which provided the impetus for special education to be introduced in schools to curb school dropouts and provide support for students with special needs (Csapo & Omar, 1996). Yet the introduction of special education in school at that time was hampered by the lack of trained teachers to meet the learning needs of students with special needs (Tait & Mundia, 2012).

Consequently, various initiatives were introduced to encourage students to stay on in school. These included the Reading and Language Acquisition (RELA) project introduced in 1989, the Cognitive Research Trust (CoRT) thinking skills programme in 1993–2008, Learning Programme Styles (LEAPS) in 1994, Specialist Mathematics and Science Teacher projects for primary schools in 1994 and the Active Mathematics in the Classroom project (AMIC) in 2004. Teachers from overseas were recruited to address the lack of qualified local teachers, new subjects were introduced in the school curriculum and a Teacher Training Centres was set up (Ministry of Education, 2013). Also, national policies and legislation were implemented to ensure that students with special needs received the required learning support to remain in schools longer. These initiatives provided professional development opportunities for teachers and generated interest in the training of new personnel whose primary role was to assist subject teachers to work with children with special needs. The new personnel were initially known as Learning Assistant Teachers (LATs) and are currently known as Special Education Needs Assistant (SENA) Teachers.

8.3 The Impact of National Policies and International Declarations on Inclusive Education

Brunei Darussalam was one of the 155 countries which attended the World Conference of Education for All organised by the United Nations Educational, Scientific and Cultural Organization (UNESCO) in Jomtien, Thailand, in 1990 (Norjum, 2002). The conference was considered a landmark in the field of special education which drew international attention to the right of every child to education but also asserted that meeting the basic learning needs of every child is a universal responsibility (UNESCO, 1990). In response to the global pressures, regions soon adopted international conventions that focus on equity and education.

The conference had a significant impact in shaping the provision of special education in Brunei Darussalam (see Table 8.1). In 1992, the National Education Policy of Brunei Darussalam described its education system as one that aimed

> to give all Bruneian children every opportunity to achieve at least an upper secondary or vocational education and to provide opportunities for all children in Brunei Darussalam to develop to their full potential so that they play a useful role in the development of the country. (Ministry of Education, 1992, p. 7)

In 1992, the National Education Policy was introduced to ensure the provision of seven years of education at preschool and primary levels, three years at lower secondary and two years either in upper secondary level or at vocational/technical level. This superseded the 9-Year Education Policy which provided six years of education at primary level followed by three years at lower secondary level (Ministry of Education, 2014).

Brunei Darussalam continued to assert its commitment to the provision of quality education for all children by attending the World Conference on Special Needs Education in Salamanca, Spain, in 1994. The outcome of the conference was the Salamanca Statement and Framework for Action in Special Needs Education which urged all countries to embrace the principles of inclusive education as either law or policy. It called for the establishment of inclusive schools as a means of developing special needs education. This was based on the affirmation that all children can learn together in the same school and that barriers impeding participation or achievement should be addressed and removed (UNESCO, 1994).

Table 8.1 The impact of national policies and international declarations on Brunei's inclusive education system (1979–2018)

Year	Milestones in Brunei's Inclusive Education System
1979	• Preschool was made compulsory for all children at the age of five years before they can be enrolled in Primary 1.
1984	• The Bilingual Education Policy was introduced.
1990	• Brunei attended the World Conference of Education for All organised by United Nations Educational, Scientific and Cultural Organization (UNESCO) in Jomtien, Thailand.
1992	• The National Education Policy ensured the provision of quality education for students with special needs as well as students from diverse backgrounds.
1993	• The 12-Year Education Policy was introduced.
1994	• Brunei attended the World Conference on Special Needs Education in Salamanca, Spain. • Special Education Unit (SEU) was established.
1996	• The First National Conference on Special Education took place.
1997	• The Inclusive Education Policy ensured the provision for students with special needs to attend mainstream school. • The First International Conference on Special Education, with the theme *Inclusive Education: Inclusive Society* was held in Brunei Darussalam.
1999	• The Second National Conference on Special Education, with the theme *Inclusive Education: Teaching to Diversity in the New Millennium*, took place.
2005	• Brunei Darussalam joined UNESCO as its 195th member state. • The Five-Year Strategic Plan (2007–2011) was launched to provide high-quality education to maximise the potential of all students. • The Second International Conference on Special Education, with the theme *Our Children Our Future: Global Approaches*, was held in Brunei Darussalam.
2007	• The introduction of the Compulsory Education Order meant every child between the ages of 6 and 15 years is mandated to complete at least nine years of compulsory education.
2009	• The *National Education System for the 21st Century* or *Sistem Pendidikan Negara Abad ke-21* (SPN21) set out to provide students with greater access to tertiary education via multiple pathways.
2012	• The introduction of the Compulsory Religious Education Order meant that every Muslim child aged between 7 and 15 years is required to attend religious school.
2018	• The Strategic Plan 2018–2022 focused on equality and equity for all students by ensuring access to quality education.

In the same year, Brunei Darussalam achieved a key milestone by establishing the Special Education Unit (SEU) to ensure the successful implementation of inclusive education in schools and support students with special needs in schools. This commitment was highlighted by the Minister of Education during the opening address of the First National Conference on Special Education in 1996:

> We must look at how the system can better serve all children, including children with special needs who require special education and related services if they are to realize their full potential.
>
> The special education, or special needs agenda in Brunei Darussalam, is an essential element of the drive for education for all. The emphasis is on inclusive education where the aim is to respond to the needs of all children. (Abdul Aziz, 1996, p. 2)

In line with global trends towards inclusion, Brunei Darussalam began to embrace the concept of inclusive education and its philosophy through the introduction of the Special Education Policy Guidelines in 1997. This meant that students with special needs were enrolled in the mainstream schools and were supported by Learning Assistant Teachers (LATs), now known as Special Education Needs Assistant (SENA) Teachers, in partnership with their class teachers. In the same year, the First International Conference on Special Education (*Inclusive Education: Inclusive Society*) took place in Brunei Darussalam which was then followed by the Second National Conference (*Inclusive Education: Teaching to Diversity in the New Millennium*) in 1999.

Brunei Darussalam solidified its commitment to the provision of an inclusive education system when it joined the UNESCO as its 191st member state in 2005. The primary objective of the organisation is to promote international collaboration in education, sciences and culture as a means of contributing to world peace and security. To achieve this, UNESCO identified Education for All (EFA) goals such as improving early childhood education (ECE), ensuring access to free and compulsory quality primary education, enhancing the learning skills for youths and adults, increasing adult literacy, achieving gender equality in education and improving quality of education (UNESCO, 1990).

In an effort to achieve the EFA goal of ensuring access to free and compulsory quality primary education, Brunei Darussalam introduced the

Compulsory Education Order in 2007 whereby every Bruneian child and those residing in Brunei Darussalam, aged between 6 and 15 years old, are mandated to attend school for at least 9 years. Within the same year, Brunei Darussalam launched the Five-Year Strategic Plan (2007–2011) which set out to ensure the provision of high-quality education to maximise the potential of all students (Ministry of Education, revised edition, 2007). This brought about the latest educational reform known as the *Sistem Pendidikan Negara Abad ke-21* (SPN21) or the National Education System for the 21st Century in 2009 which aims to provide students with greater access to tertiary education via multiple pathways (see Chap. 2). Focused changes are targeted in three main areas: Education Structure, Curriculum and Assessment, and Technical Education.

With SPN21, students with special needs are offered two programmes that aim to support their learning and development. The first programme, the Specialized Education Programme, is targeted at gifted students in specific academic fields such as science, mathematics, music, performing arts, fine arts and sports. The second programme known as the Special Educational Needs Programme caters for students whose needs fall in one or more of the following categories: Cognition and Learning Needs; Communication and Interaction Needs; Sensory Needs (Visual Impairment and Hearing Impairment); Physical Needs; Behaviour, Emotional and Social Development Needs; and Other Needs, for example, Medical Needs (Ministry of Education, 2013; Special Education Unit, 2015).

There is a unanimous call to other ministries to support the Special Educational Needs Programme in Brunei. The Compulsory Religious Education Order in 2012 stipulated that every Muslim child between 7 and 15 years old is required to attend religious school. The Order ensures the religious and moral wellbeing of Muslim students by instilling them with religious knowledge to understand and practise the teachings of Islam (Ministry of Education, 2013). This Order resulted in the establishment of the Special Religious Education Unit at the Islamic Studies Department which aims to improve the skills and competence of teaching staff to implement various programmes to assist special needs students. One key emphasis is placed on performing *Solat* (or five daily prayers) which is an obligatory act for all Muslims, including those with special needs assistance. In 2018, the Solat (Pray) programme was attended by 21 children with special needs in Temburong district. In addition, another skill offered to these is the reading of the Quran using braille (Borneo

Bulletin, 2018). This provision of an Islamic religious foundation offers the opportunity for these children to participate in daily religious practice with family, peers and their wider community.

8.4 Current Movement Towards Inclusive Education in Brunei

The issue of equity has been a major force underlying the movement towards a more inclusive educational system. Since the provision of quality education, the Ministry's top-down vision of inclusion remains to be embraced by those most involved in the process of implementation. The latest initiative in Brunei Darussalam is the MoE Strategic Plan 2018–2022 which consists of three Strategic Objectives to ensure access to quality education. Strategic Objectives 1 (SO1) focuses on capacity building of skilled personnel driven by culture, while the Strategic Objectives 2 (SO2) strives to provide equal and equitable access to higher quality education, and finally Strategic Objectives 3 (SO3) assumes a collaborate approach across stakeholders for shared accountability in the learning experience of the learners. Collectively, the three objectives set out to achieve the main aim of *Wawasan* Brunei 2035 (Brunei Vision 2035) whereby Brunei Darussalam is recognised as a nation of well-educated, highly skilled and highly accomplished people (Ministry of Education, 2019). These are all aligned to the following international declarations (see Fig. 8.1).

Currently, it is not feasible to practise total inclusion in all schools in Brunei without massive restructuring of administration and financial support. This may not be so much different from neighbouring countries such as Malaysia. While adhering to international declaration is a global commitment, it is important to frame provision of inclusive education within the local context. In Brunei, the moral values recognised under the country's national philosophy known as *Melayu Islam Beraja* (MIB) are a blend of language, culture and customs; the teaching of Islamic laws and values; and the monarchy system which must be upheld by all regardless of ability. It is central to education and taught throughout schooling, and society is encouraged to practise MIB as a way of life.

- **Southeast Asian Ministers of Education Organisation (SEAMEO) 7 Priority Areas**

Addressing barriers to inclusion is a Priority Area which Brunei Darussalam actively tackles to ensure the provision of quality inclusive

```
                    MoE STRATEGIC PLAN 2018-2022
```

Strategic Objective 1 (SO1):	Strategic Objective 2 (SO2):	Strategic Objective 3 (SO3):
Transform our organization human resource towards a performance driven culture for growth and success	Provide equal and equitable access to higher learning for opportunities to quality education	Engage and involve stakeholders for shared accountability in the learning development of our learners

BRUNEI VISION OR *WAWASAN* 2035
The attainment of Brunei as a nation of well-educated, highly skilled and highly accomplished people

INTERNATIONAL DECLARATIONS

SEAMEO 7 Priority Areas (Addressing barriers to inclusion)	United Nations International Convention on the Rights of Persons with Disabilities	United Nation Sustainable Development Goals (Goal 4: Provision of Quality Education)

Fig. 8.1 The alignment of the Strategic Plan 2018–2022 to Wawasan 2035 and international declarations (Escoto-Kemp & Matzin, 2019)

education (SEAMEO Secretariat, 2018). This is evidenced by the establishment of nine Model Inclusive School (MIS) Centres. The MIS Centre is a building annex located within a school and equipped with appropriate infrastructure, specialised equipment and learning resources where students with special needs receive remedial learning support and intervention by SENA teachers. SEU was primarily responsible in overseeing a major MoE initiative which was the establishment of nine Model Inclusive Schools (MIS). Five primary schools and four secondary schools were purpose-built in 2008 and were all fully operational by 2010. An MIS is a building annex located within a school and equipped with specialised equipment and specialised learning resources to provide quality inclusive education for students with special needs.

- **United Nations International Convention on the Rights of Persons with Disabilities**

Article 24 on Education places a strong emphasis on the provision of inclusive education at all levels and lifelong learning for all persons with disabilities. It asserts that persons with disabilities should not be excluded from the general education system on the basis of disability. Several initiatives were implemented to ensure the concept of acceptance, belonging and providing school settings in which all children with disabilities can be valued equally. There exist active local collaborations between the SEU, MoE and the Voluntary Unit of the Community Development Department, JAPEM creating awareness on hearing issues, sign language and braille skills. This was more of a voluntary invitation from public held from time to time. More of a similar initiative would benefit teachers from schools who taught those students with diverse needs which offer continuation training. Within the school administration, a training collaboration focusing on these skills for regular teachers are essential for the success of inclusion.

- **United Nations 'Sustainable Development Goals'**

In 2015, the leaders from 193 countries created a plan known as the Sustainable Development Goals to create a safe world for a better future. One of the 17 goals include quality education (Goal 4) which focuses on the provision of quality education that is both inclusive and equitable as well as opportunities for lifelong learning to occur for all (United Nations, 2015). We continue to see efforts being undertaken by the MoE to strengthen the present practice of inclusion in Brunei. Inclusion needs to be given consideration as a whole school approach (Ainscow, 1997). Teachers in schools should be persuaded not demanded by their head teachers to accept children with disabilities and then we can be united in driving a sustainable development goal towards inclusion.

8.5 The Establishment of Special Education Unit (SEU)

The SEU was set up in 1994 with the vision of education for all in Brunei, and it strives to realise the potential of children with diverse needs through provision of quality inclusive education. SEU upholds this vision with the mandate of ensuring the ten target areas of development to be addressed, which include identification of children with special needs, the provision, programmes, assessment, research, resources and public awareness (more about these targets can be accessed from Wong & Mak, 2005). A summary of the achievements of the SEU is described in Table 8.2.

There was a greater call to train teachers as SENA teachers to assist the growing number of students with special needs in Brunei 25 years ago. Being awarded the Certificate or Diploma in Special Education at that time was seen as a compensation for a teaching career for those who could not meet the additional requirements for enrolment in the Bachelor's Degree in Special Education at Sultan Hassanal Bolkiah Institute of Education (SHBIE), Universiti Brunei Darussalam (UBD). While teacher trainees are prepared to teach millennial children, they are also reminded to uphold local values which are synonymous with the Brunei identity: Melayu Islam Beraja (MIB), using religious principles as a guide for cultivating values. This MIB module in the degree programme was a compulsory module for all teacher trainees regardless of racial and religious background (see Chaps. 2 and 5). This is even more important for teachers who will work with students with special needs, as it increases the challenge compared to that for regular teachers in schools.

To date, there is a growing number of students with special needs, while there are only handful of teachers that were qualified to assist just over half of the students in schools and this is overwhelming for SEU and school partnership. Added to this challenge, the Bachelor Degree programme was phased out in 2010 and replaced by a Master's Degree. Many potential teacher candidates could not meet the current requirement for entry to the Master's Degree in Inclusive Special Education at the University of Brunei Darussalam. Hence, most of these teachers are offered continuous professional development to keep them updated. These teachers are mostly in their late 40s but because of their respected experience, they are assigned as mentors to guide pre-service Master's teacher candidates when they are in schools for teaching placement.

In January 2019, SEU embarked on a further MoE initiative which is to oversee the establishment of two Centres of Excellence (CoEs) for students with special needs in the Temburong district. These centres are located in two local mainstream primary schools built with the appropriate infrastructure and facilities, specialised equipment and specialised learning resources. The SENA teachers and teacher aides are placed in the centres to support all the students with special needs within the district (Special

Table 8.2 Summary of SEU initiatives to implement and uphold inclusive education practices in mainstream schools between 1994 and 2019

1994	• Special Education Unit (SEU) was established in Brunei Darussalam
1994–1995	• Public education was a main priority and included the publication of SEU Quarterly Reports for circulation within the Ministry of Education, Newsletters on Special Education for schools as well as the broadcast of radio and television programmes on Special Education
	• Special Education Unit and SHBIE collaborated to train Learning Assistance Teachers (LATs) by introducing the Certificate in Special Education
1996	• The newly trained Learning Assistant Teachers (later called SENA Teachers) were despatched to primary schools. They received ongoing support and continuing professional development from SEU to ensure they were effectively assisting students with special needs
	• The First National Conference on Special Education took place
1997	• The Handbook on Policy Guidelines for Special Education was published for mass distribution
	• The First International Conference on Special Education, with the theme *Inclusive Education: Inclusive Society* was held in Brunei Darussalam
1998	• A pilot project on the Pre-Vocational Programme commenced in a secondary school
	• Training for selected SENA teachers on how to address the learning needs of students with hearing impairment were conducted by invited consultants from overseas
	• A sharing session on Gifted Education was also conducted for SENA teachers
	• The Special Education Handbook was published and circulated among Headmasters, Teachers and SENA teachers
1999	• The Pre-Vocational Programme was introduced in 18 secondary schools
	• The Enrichment Programme was implemented. A total of 35 students from the Brunei-Muara district made up the first cohort of students in the programme
	• Training on the provision of learning support for students with visual impairment was held for selected SENA Teachers
	• The Bachelor of Education (Special Education) and the Master of Education (Special Education) offered by the University of Brunei Darussalam commenced with the first intake of trained SENA teachers The Second National Conference on Special Education, with the theme *Inclusive Education: Teaching to Diversity in the New Millennium* took place
2000	• The next phase of the Pre-Vocational Programme and Enrichment Programme commenced
	• A review of SEU was conducted with a recommendation to localise human resources

(*continued*)

Table 8.2 (continued)

2001–2002	• A series of teacher workshops were conducted by SEU on topics such as Remedial Teaching, Use of Various Teaching Strategies, Teaching Pre-Vocational classes, Visual impairment, Sign Language, Dyslexia and Autism • The SEU databank and the SEU Resource Center were set up • The first intake of six teachers from religious schools under the Ministry of Religious Affairs completed the Certificate of Special Education Course • The posts of Educational Psychologists, Speech Therapist and Occupational Therapist were approved by the Civil Service Department
2003	• The Special Olympics Brunei Chapter was established to develop the sports skills of students with special needs • The first Independent Living Skills Center was set up for the students in the Pre-Vocational Programme
2004	• The *Curriculum Guidelines for Students with High Support Needs* was completed and presented to the Curriculum Development Department, Ministry of Education • The proposal to hire Teacher Aides to assist SENA teachers in supporting students with special needs in schools was presented and approved • Three Senior Educational Psychologists and a Speech Therapist were appointed
2005	• The Second International Conference on Special Education, with the theme *Our Children Our Future: Global Approaches,* was held at University Brunei Darussalam
2006	• Workshop on *Braille Code* • Workshop on *Sign Language* • Publication of *Curriculum Guide Book for Students with High Support Needs*
2007	• Seminar and Workshop on *Curriculum Guide for Students with Special Needs* Training Workshop in Gifted Education
2008	• The establishment of *Model Inclusive Schools (MIS)* • Training Workshop in *Gifted Education* • Ten-day Intensive Training in *Gifted Education* • Nationwide screening for gifted students • National Seminar and Workshop in *Special Education*
2009	• Workshop on *Differentiated Curriculum, Instruction and Assessment for Gifted Learners* • Seminar and Consultation Session on B*ehavioural Intervention for Children with Autism and Other Learning Difficulties* • National Seminar and Workshop on *Special Education: Meeting the Educational Needs of Learners with Dyslexia in Inclusive Classroom*
2010	• National Workshops on *Picture Exchange Communication System (PECS)* • Training Workshops and Seminar on *Enhancing the Assessment Skills of Educational Psychologists in the Areas of Intellectual Potential, Learning Difficulties and Social-Emotional Difficulties* • Colloquium on *Diagnosis and Early Intervention for children with ASD*

(*continued*)

Table 8.2 (continued)

2011	• ASEAN Co-operative Conference on Inclusive Education (ACCIE) 2011 • Oral Health Programme for Students with Special Needs (in collaboration with National Dental Center)
2012	• ASEAN +3 Junior Science Odyssey (APT JSO) • *Creativity, Enrichment and Research Development for Advanced Students (CERDAS)* *Project* Competition
2013	• *Innovate* National Gifted Programme for Gifted Students • Workshop on *Perkins Brailler Maintenance and Repair* • *Special Education* Carnival • Launching of *Support Services Guidebook* • Series of Public Talks on *SEU Initiatives and Programmes to Support Students with Special Needs in Schools* • Sports Day for Children with Special Needs
2014	• National Literacy Seminar and Workshop in Special Education • Hearing Impairment and Visual Impairment Course for teachers • Launching of *Guidebook to Support Students with Hearing Impairment and Visual Impairment*
2015	• Launching of School-Based Team (SBT) Guide Book • Fundraising event in conjunction with International Day for Persons with Disabilities • Series of training Sessions provided annually to Brunei Darussalam Teacher Academy for new teachers • *Introductory Course in Inclusive Education* offered once yearly to primary and secondary teachers from government and private schools
2016	• National Numeracy Seminar and Workshop in Special Education • Local Information Technology Competition (LITC) for Youths with Disabilities
2017	• *Every Child is a Gift* Charity Run in conjunction with World Disability Day • Sport Competitions for students with special needs in primary and secondary schools • Culinary Competition for Pre-Vocational Students Workshop on *Parenting Skills* organised by Yayasan Sultan Haji Hassanal Bolkiah in collaboration with SEU
2018	*Open Day* for students with special needs who have completed the Pre-Vocational Programme in secondary schools • Bocce Competition for secondary school students
2019	• Three-Day consultation and workshop session to develop a curriculum package for students with high support needs • The establishment of Centres of Excellence (CoEs) in the Temburong District for students with special needs

Education Unit, 2018). Progress is currently underway to establish further CoEs in the other three districts (Belait, Tutong and Brunei-Muara).

Table 8.2 summarises the significant developments in inclusive education since the establishment of the SEU in 1994. It outlines the numerous initiatives of SEU to implement and uphold inclusive education practices in mainstream schools between 1994 and 2019. Since its establishment, SEU had been very supportive in the provision of training for their SENA teachers in the teaching and learning support of students with special needs. SEU is responsible for keeping the wheels of professional development turning, and it has been proactive in sharing knowledge of national methodology and assessment with current Master's students at UBD. To live up to the vision of SEU, it is now time to consider the next National Conference. It has been 21 years since the previous one was held. To include this in SEU, the action plan will require further collaboration with other relevant stakeholders who together could realise the next conference dedicated to bringing together leading academics, researchers, scholars and other stakeholders to discuss current trends. The past two years, MoE has collaborated with the Sultan Hassanal Bolkiah Institute of Education (SHBIE) to showcase the Teacher Conference Education. This will serve as a platform for teachers to celebrate a variety of pedagogies, and examine teaching and learning across different disciplines from early years to tertiary education.

Two previous milestones were recognised when SEU organised an inaugural conference at the ASEAN level. One was a collaboration with UBD to organise the inaugural ASEAN Co-operative Conference on Inclusive Education (ACCIE) in 2011 and the other was a collaboration with the Ministry of Development to host the inaugural ASEAN Plus Three Junior Science Odyssey (APTJSO) in 2012 which is the equivalent of the International Science Olympiad held for the first time in Asia. The eight-day international competition comprised lab skills assessments, fieldwork projects and assessments, and fieldwork presentations. A total of 63 students from 9 countries with Sweden as an observer country participated in the competition while 22 science teachers from these countries participated in a teacher workshop sharing innovative ideas, practices and research in field of gifted education. The continuation of such initiatives seems essential to ensure the active involvement of Bruneian special education needs teachers and students representing at ASEAN and international levels. Table 8.2 expands further on SEU involvement at regional level.

8.6 The Role of Teacher Education in Brunei Darussalam

Sultan Hassanal Bolkiah Institute of Education (SHBIE) is the oldest faculty in UBD. To some extent, SHBIE has always supported the inclusion of a special education module in teacher training at the certificate and undergraduate-level programmes. At that time, only one module on special education was offered to teacher trainees which aimed to equip pre-service teachers with basic knowledge of special education in general. As the only teacher training centres at that time, SHBIE institutionalised the certificate in special education (part-time) while working in tandem with the SEU. Part-time teachers were recruited to join the Certificate in Special Education, a 14-month programme which trained them to be Learning Assistance Teachers (LATs) with skills in supporting special education needs students in regular classroom (Lim et al., 2006).

It was not until 1997 during the implementation of the Special Education Policy Guidelines in Brunei Darussalam that a call was heard for more teachers to be trained and qualified to teach students with special needs. SHBIE accepted greater responsibility for providing more options with a comprehensive structure on special education for teacher preparation. SHBIE adopted a three prolonged strategy towards Inclusive Education in all its teacher education programmes in 1999 (Sim et al., 1999). During that time, the programmes appeared in three modes, namely (1) pre-service preparation, (2) in-service upgrading and (3) postgraduate specialisation.

The first strategy involved initiatives on inclusion of special education courses in both Diploma and Bachelor of Education courses. The student teachers were introduced to key concepts and policy of inclusive education, equipping them with teaching and management skills to cater for students with SEN as well as preparing them to work collaboratively with SENA teachers and parents of students with SEN (Lim et al., 2006). Other degree programmes also offered special education elective courses. In addition, methods of teaching children with learning problems were also included in several curriculum studies courses in the undergraduate programmes. The second strategy provided a new upgrading opportunity for in-service SENA teachers to earn a Bachelor of Education (Special Education). This was a four-year programme with its first intake consisting of 23 upgrading SENA teachers (Lim et al., 2006). And finally, the third strategy was realised through offering a two-year part-time professional development programme for upgrading SENA teachers to Master of Education (Special Education) in 1999. This new initiative extended professional training to include student research exercises on inclusive education and equipped with effective managerial and consultative roles in the MoE.

The McKinsey Report (2007) on the world's best-performing school systems revealed that a highly skilled and professional teaching force is crucial in providing high-quality education. The global response to this report was that the education faculties in universities upgraded their initial teaching qualification to a Masters level and UBD is no exception. By August 2009, SHBIE ceased to offer undergraduate degrees and diplomas in teacher education and has since offered programmes at the Graduate level such as Master of Education (by coursework or research), Master in Counselling (by coursework) and PhD in Education (including specialisation in special education and inclusive education). With the new Master of Education in place, teachers are more keen to upgrade their education status. On the other hand, this also brought a setback for special education teachers with certificate and diploma qualification stranded in the midst of the new curricular reform. As a result, the number of SENA teachers in schools has decreased over the last few years due to teacher retirement and teacher promotion. To counter this problem, UBD has opened a one-year diploma in education for in-service teachers who work with students in special education needs in schools. This programme is housed at the Center for Lifelong Learning at UBD.

Where once SHBIE provided an accessible programme university entry especially among sixth form school leavers, the introduction of the Master of Teaching degree was intended to raise the quality of teachers graduating from the programme. In support of SHBIE's new vision, the Initial Teacher Preparation (ITP) offers Master of Teaching (MTeach) which becomes the flagship programme for the faculty and intended to support the new national vision of the Ministry of Education (MoE) in providing quality education in Brunei Darussalam. For 11 years since MTeach was introduced, only four specialisations were offered: Early Childhood Education (ECE), Primary Education, Secondary Education, and Vocational and Technology Education (VTech). Currently, the MoE is more involved than ever in the selection process for the number of enrolments per specialisation in MTeach so as to reflect their recruitment projection. SHBIE continues to work closely with MoE on school placement for teacher trainees and providing Continuous Professional Development (CPD) for teachers.

8.7 MTeach: Inclusive Special Education (ISE)

In 2016, there were 792 students with special needs on *Individual Education Programmes* (IEPs) in government primary schools and 109 SENA teachers who provided support to students with special needs on a 1:7 teacher to student ratio. There are now 1161 students with special needs on IEPs in government primary schools and 103 SENA teachers who provide support to students with special needs on a 1:11 teacher to student ratio (September 2020). Additional SENA teachers are therefore required to reduce this ratio to ensure students' needs are supported in schools (Special Education Unit, 2020).

In response to the Strategic Objective 2 (SO2) of the 2018–2022 Ministry of Education Strategic Plan education (Ministry of Education, 2019), there was a call from the MoE to train more teachers in special education and that specialisation is now called Inclusive Special Education (ISE). The term Inclusive Special Education reflects the importance for children with special needs to receive an appropriate education which meets children's specific needs (Warnock, 2010). According to Hornby (2014), ISE

> Is a synthesis of definitions of both special education and inclusive education. It involves educating children with SEND in the most inclusive setting in which their special needs can be effectively met, with the overarching goal of facilitating the highest level of inclusion in society after school for all children with SEND. It is a process of ongoing whole-school reorganization and development in order to assist mainstream schools to effectively include as many children with SEND as possible. (Hornby, 2014, p. 36)

MTeach ISE is an 18-month programme designed to prepare teacher candidates to co-teach with subject teachers in the regular classroom and support students with moderate and profound support needs in alternative inclusive settings such as *Learning Assistance Centres*. Teacher candidates in this programme will be equipped with knowledge in special and inclusive education and a variety of supporting skills for dealing with students with special educational needs. Their school placement at primary and secondary schools for majority of the week to work with students with special needs provides the opportunity to apply what they have learnt at the university to real-life settings. This practice also enables them to reflect on current practices of special and inclusive education nationally and globally. Teacher candidates will also conduct evidence-based research on inclusive special education-related areas throughout the programmes. After graduating from this programme, they will be recognised as key persons in initiating the formation of *School-Based Team* (SBT) for the purpose of systematic planning and implementation of the *Individual Education Programme* (IEP) throughout the early years of schooling, and an individualised transition plan for students with moderate and profound needs in secondary schools to attain either post-secondary education, employment or independent living.

It is envisaged that graduates of this specialisation would be able to work as SENA teachers in schools. They may also work as Special Educational Needs consultants, administrators or researchers in government departments and agencies that may be related to education or social work, rehabilitation or community service.

8.8 Inclusive Education Practices in Brunei Darussalam

This section provides a brief discussion on the implementation of inclusive education in Brunei Darussalam and how this is aligned to international declarations such as the United Nations International Convention on the Rights of Persons with Disabilities and UNESCO's Education for All. It illustrates how inclusive education is multi-faceted in that it places importance on aspects such as raising public awareness of students with special needs, provisions to ensure their welfare as well as opportunities for them to participate in religious and sport competitions. Importance is also placed on working collaboratively with other Ministries to support students with special needs and on international co-operation. However, the current functional integration of inclusion is considered the most suitable and practical to realise acceptance and belonging, with the presence of limitations and constraints.

Inter-agency collaboration within Brunei Darussalam is evidenced by regular Inter-agency Student Progress Meetings (ISPMs) which are held to discuss students who have been referred for specialised support services. Representatives from the Ministry of Education; the Ministry of Culture, Youth and Sports; the Ministry of Health; and Ministry of Religious Affairs meet once monthly to discuss the referrals and to provide updates on students' progress and required level of specialised support services.

A caring outlook in Brunei over those people with special needs is mainly driven by the promotion of moral, social and religious values, through the nationhood education of MIB in schools. The introduction of the MIB concept in schools is intended to orientate education towards the development of MIB-driven value individuals who are lifelong learners, competent (efficient and productive), competitive and responsive to global trends. MIB as a way of life promotes social encouragement and involvement that creates awareness among society at large about those individuals who have special needs.

SEU plays a significant role in raising public awareness of students with special needs in inclusive schools. It organises events which involve the wider community. For example, a Charity Run was organised in 2018 which attracted approximately 1000 participants. The participants consisted of not only students with special needs but also their teachers and individuals from other government agencies, non-government organisations and the wider public. Nationwide road shows in schools are conducted for school staff and parents, and newspaper articles are published to raise awareness of various issues pertaining to students with special needs. On the other hand, students with special needs who have an interest in sports are provided with opportunities to participate in regional and international competitions such as the Asia Pacific Bocce Competition and Special Olympics.

In addition, various ministries have joined efforts in the provision of welfare assistance and educational allowances (Department of Community Development) including the 'Baitul-Mal' fund (Ministry of Religious Affairs). Within religious affairs, students with special needs are also encouraged to participate in the annual *Al-Quran* Memorization and Recitation Competition organised by SEU. The competition aims to maximise the potential of such students in the memorisation of verses and/or chapters from the Quran and talent development towards becoming *Qari* or *Qari'ah*. It also aspires to nurture an appreciation and instil the practice of reading verses from the Quran in their daily life.

While it is legislated for government schools (such as the model inclusive schools) to accept all children who wish to enrol, the policy for non-government schools to cater for students with special needs has different arrangements, which include fees and most likely interviews. Beside formal education, there is also growing evidence of licensed practitioners operating personal therapy sessions which offer opportunity for some parents who could not meet the requirement of the international school's policy. However, not all these facilities are always accessible to everyone and this means a large number of students with special needs continue to be dependent on government schools for education and skills development. This in return poses challenges to the government schools to recruit more qualified special needs teachers to maintain equity in education.

The latest MoE initiative has seen the establishment of two Centres of Excellence (CoEs) for all the students with special needs in the Temburong District in 2019. CoEs aim to promote equal opportunities according to students' needs and abilities in order to ensure access, engagement and active participation in all aspects of their education. The CoEs are located within local mainstream primary schools and have been fitted out with the appropriate infrastructure and facilities, specialised equipment and specialised learning resources. The number of SENA teachers and teacher aides were provided according to the needs of students which were solely based on whether they have a diagnosis. This was a straightforward process which resulted in the placement of all 21 students with diagnoses in the 2 CoEs within the Temburong district (Special Education Unit, 2018).

Establishing CoEs in larger districts does not, however, entail a straightforward process due to the substantially higher number of students in the other districts. For example, the number of students with special needs in Tutong district in 2019 was 193 (Special Education Unit, 2019). The placement of such a large number of students in CoEs would be neither ideal nor feasible as it would require a significant increase in the number of SENA teachers and buildings. This has led to the development of the Designated Priority Levels (DPLs) as an objective way of identifying students' needs that is not solely based on whether they have a diagnosis. Instead, it sets out to examine the level of support and resources required for these students in the specific domains of learning support, curriculum adaptation, physical adaptation, specialised resources and access arrangements. Each domain has its own scoring criteria which then determine a Priority Level for students with diagnoses. Once determined, the Priority Level is used to differentiate among students with special needs so as to accurately designate their placement according to whether their needs would be best met in a CoE or a non-CoE mainstream school.

There are five Priority Levels to determine each student's level of needs: Priority 1 (Diagnosis Only), Priority 2 (Mild), Priority 3 (Moderate), Priority 4 (Severe) and Priority 5 (Profound). Students on Priority Levels 1 and 2 would remain in their respective schools because they are able to follow the curriculum with minimal or regular support from their teachers. On the other hand, students on Priority Levels 3, 4 and 5 would be selected for placement in CoEs to ensure that their individual needs are adequately supported with appropriate, skilled human resources, required physical adaptations and specialised resources (Escoto-Kemp & Matzin, 2019). It is anticipated that the Designated Priority System will be used for all students with special needs during the process of establishing CoEs in the other districts. This will ensure that there is shared responsibility between SENA teachers in CoE schools and subject teachers in non-CoE schools to support all students with special needs. It will also ensure that CoEs can be established in a timely, cost-efficient manner while maximising the use of current skilled human resources, infrastructure and resources.

At an international level, Brunei Darussalam also collaborates with other countries to establish and maintain mutually supportive relationships in upholding inclusive education practices. To this end, SEU actively engages in international co-operation by participating in competitions such as Special Olympics and Global IT challenge Competitions (GITC) for Youths with Disabilities. The latter is an annual IT competition organised by the Korean Society for Rehabilitation of Persons with Disabilities for youths in the region. Brunei Darussalam is also represented during the Annual Governing Board members meetings organised by SEAMEO Regional Center for Special Education Needs (SEN) Malaysia. These meetings are held to share best inclusive practices, identify training needs and conduct training courses within the region.

8.9 Final Thoughts

While the current functional integration of inclusion in Brunei is considered the most suitable and practical way forward, it is equally important to understand the real meaning of 'Education for ALL' in terms of quality and equity. Although the concept of inclusion is not new, its impact on practices continues to be examined and debated. The focus of these final thoughts is on developing a more promising approach to better prepare everyone for inclusive education. In order to do this, we need to do the following:

- Increase resources to materialise infrastructure to ensure accessibility in all government primary schools for students with physical and sensory needs (e.g. wheelchairs, lifts, handrails and tactile signs).
- Increase capacity building with ongoing university training at postgraduate level to provide a pool of qualified SENAs to uphold inclusive education practices in schools.

- Start investing on specialist expertise to reduce the reliance on paraprofessionals personnel whose role has been to support students with special needs.
- Enhance best practice in providing curriculum differentiation to ensure that the learning of students with special needs is relevant, culturally appropriate and of good quality. In doing so, schools establish best practices in inclusive classrooms while ensuring accessibility to the mainstream curriculum.
- Create awareness and collaboration at ministerial level and public awareness as an ongoing process to ensure a shared understanding of inclusive education practices and how students with special needs can be supported in mainstream schools.

8.10 Conclusion

Brunei Darussalam is unique in the sense that it has never had a history of segregated and separate special education for children with special needs. (Ministry of Education, 2015, p. 36)

Its history of inclusive education can be traced back to a series of key milestones including the introduction of national policies to highlight inclusive education as a prioritised educational agenda which is also in line with international declarations towards inclusion. Special Education Unit (SEU) was established in 1994 as the key agency to oversee the successful implementation of inclusive education practices and provision of specialist support services for students with special needs in schools. Brunei Darussalam has since continued to demonstrate its tenacious commitment to uphold inclusive education practices and policies that are consistent with International Declarations.

As a way forward, it is believed that more collaboration with stakeholders who share the same energy and desire to see our children succeed could promote more positive development and growth of inclusive education in Brunei. In addition, this initiative will offer new research opportunities to inform practice and policy. It should be recognised that successful implementation will mean more effort and resources are needed to be directed to this project in Brunei Darussalam. This chapter showcases significant strides in the development of inclusive education which will undoubtedly continue on in the nation's journey towards realising *Wawasan* Brunei 2035.

References

Abdul Aziz bin Begawan Pehin Udana Khatib Dato Seri Paduka Haji Awang Umar, Pehin Orang Kaya Laila Wijaya Dato Seri Setia Awang. (1996). Opening Address, in Proceedings of the First National Conference on Special Education (pp. 1–5). : Special Education Unit.

Ainscow, M. (1997). Towards inclusive schooling. *British Journal of Special Education, 24*(1), 3–6.

Csapo, M., & Omar bin Haji Khalid. (1996). Development of special education in Brunei. Darussalam: The case of a developed/developing country. *International Journal of Special Education, 11*(3), 108–114.

Escoto-Kemp, A. & Rohani binti Haji Awang Matzin, Hajah. (July 2019). *The Designated. Priority Level (DPL) System: establishing priority levels for students with special needs in Brunei Darussalam*. Paper presented at the International Conference of Special Education. 2019, Surabaya, Indonesia.

Hornby, G. (2014). *Inclusive Special Education: Evidence-Based Practices for Children with Special Needs and Disabilities*. New York: Springer.

Lim, J. C., Mak, Y. F., & Koay, T. L. (2006). Special education teacher preparation in Brunei Darussalam. *Brunei Darussalam Journal of Special Education, 3*, 11–23.

McKinsey Report. (2007). Retrieved October 22, 2019, from https://www.mckinsey.com/~/media/McKinsey/Industries/Social%20Sector/Our%20Insights/How%20the%20worlds%20best%20performing%20school%20systems%20come%20out%20on%20top/How_the_world_s_best-performing_school_systems_come_out_on_top.ashx.

Ministry of Education. (1992). *National Education Policy*. Ministry of Education.

Ministry of Education. (revised edition, June 2007). The Ministry of Education Strategic Plan 2007–2011. : Ministry of Education.

Ministry of Education. (2013). *The National Education System for the 21st Century SPN21*. Ministry of Education.

Ministry of Education. (2014). *Brunei Darussalam national education for all 2015 report*. Ministry of Education.

Ministry of Education. (2019). *2018–2022 Ministry of Education Strategic Plan*. Strategic Enterprise Performance and Delivery Unit (SEPaDU).

Norjum binti Haji Yusop, Hajah. (2002). *Special education in Brunei. Darussalam*. Paper presented at the Childhood in the Millennium: Regional. Conference. September 2002, Singapore.

Omar bin Haji Khalid. (2001). *Special needs in inclusive schools in Brunei Darussalam: Perceptions, concerns and practices*. Unpublished PhD Thesis. The University of Oxford.

SEAMEO Secretariat. (2018). *Action Agenda for the 7 SEAMEO Priority Areas*. SEAMEO Secretariat.

Sim, W. K., Koay, T. L., & Liew, E. (1999). Teacher education in inclusive education. Proceedings of 2nd National Conference on Special Education (pp. 184-189). Brunei Darussalam, September 24-27, 1999 (184-189).

Special Education Unit. (2015). The School-Based Team Guidelines. Bandar Seri Begawan: Special Education Unit, Ministry of Education.

Special Education Unit. (2018). "The establishment of Centres of Excellence" project: Optimising resources, improving accessibility, strengthening engagement and achievement of students with special needs. Bandar Seri Begawan: Special Education Unit. Unpublished source.

Special Education Unit. (2019). "The establishment of Centres of Excellence" project: Tutong District. Bandar Seri Begawan: Special Education Unit. Unpublished source.

Special Education Unit. (2020, September 9-10). Brunei Darussalam Country Report for SEAMEO SEN 8th Governing Board Meeting 2020. Malacca, Malaysia.

Tait, K., & Mundia, L. (2012). Preparing teachers to meet the challenges of inclusive education in Negara Brunei Darussalam. In C. Forlin (Ed.), *Future Directions for Inclusive Teacher Education: An International Perspective* (pp. 61–70). Routledge.

UNESCO. (1990). *World declaration of education for all and the framework for action to meet basic learning needs*. UNESCO.

UNESCO. (1994). *The Salamanca statement and framework for action in special needs education*. UNESCO.

United Nations. (2015). #Envision2030: 17 goals to transform the world for persons with disabilities | United Nations Enable. Retrieved from https://www.un.org/development/desa/disabilities/envision2030.html.

Warnock, M. (2010). *Special Educational Needs: A New look* (pp. 11–46). Ed L. Terzi. London.

Wong, J., & Mak, Y. F. (2005). Special Education in Brunei Darussalam. *Brunei Darussalam Journal of Special Education, 2*, 1–15.

CHAPTER 9

Using Role-Play to Teach Minority Ethnic Languages: A Case Study at Universiti Brunei Darussalam

Norazmie Yusof and Yabit Alas

9.1 Introduction

Brunei Darussalam is a small country located on Borneo Island together with Sabah and Sarawak, Malaysia and Kalimantan, Indonesia. Despite the small size, this country is the homeland of some of the Bornean ethnic minorities. The *Brunei Constitution* (1959) has listed ethnics such as Dusun, Bisaya, Kedayan, Tutong and Murut as Malay in Brunei even though there are variations in their cultural and linguistic aspects. This study will discuss the use of role-play technique in teaching the Dusun language or known as Dusun (Level I—Basic) at The Language Centre, Universiti Brunei Darussalam (LC UBD). The two main objectives of this research are as follows:

N. Yusof (✉) • Y. Alas
Universiti Brunei Darussalam, Bandar Seri Begawan, Brunei
e-mail: norazmie.yusof@ubd.edu.bn; yabit.alas@ubd.edu.bn

© The Author(s), under exclusive license to Springer Nature Switzerland AG 2021
Phan, L. H. et al. (eds.), *Globalisation, Education, and Reform in Brunei Darussalam*, International and Development Education, https://doi.org/10.1007/978-3-030-77119-5_9

1. To investigate the effects of the role-play technique on the oral skills among the students who took Dusun elective course (LY-1433 Level I Basic) and
2. To investigate the perception of students on their learning experience in Dusun classroom.

There are limited literatures on the teaching of the Dusun language of Brunei even though this course has been introduced in UBD since 2009. Most research mainly focus on the linguistics, folklore and cultural aspects of the Dusuns. Matussin (1986) was among the first to write about the Dusun's anthropology in Brunei. Then, it was followed by the re-writing and collecting of the Dusun folklore by Bantong Antaran between 1986 and 1988. Not long after, Nothofer (1991) researched the landscape of all ethnic languages in Brunei and created the first Brunei languages Swadesh list. The linguistic aspects of Dusun such as morphology, phonology and preposition have been reported by various scholars such as Jalin (1989), Alas (1994), Buah (1996), Aini (2007), Chong (2010) and Gardiner et al. (2019). There are also studies on the vitality and status of the Dusun language (Fatimah & Najib, 2013; McLellan, 2014; Noor Azam & Ajeerah, 2016). Most recent studies were about the Dusun culture (Pudarno, 2017) and the influence of Malay language in Dusun language by Yusof and Saidatul (2019). This research project hopes to become the reference and supplement materials for any ethnic language teaching and research, especially in Brunei.

9.2 Brunei Dusun Language

Dusun is a language of the Dusun ethnic group who lives in Brunei, Sabah, Sarawak and Kalimantan (Alas, 1994). The Dusun language in Brunei is also known as '*Turan Suang Jati*' or '*Basa Sang Jati*' which means 'the language of our people'. According to Alas (1994) and Chong (2010), the Dusun language belongs to the Austronesian Language Family, categorised under the sub-category of Filipina-Formosa and Brunei Language group together with other Brunei ethnic languages such as Melayu Brunei, Tutong, Bisaya, Belait and Iban. Alas (2009) stated that there was a possibility that the Brunei Dusun language originated from North Borneo (now known as Sabah) but, today, it cannot be used to communicate with the Dusun languages spoken in Sabah. Saidatul (2012) explains that the Dusuns are the dominant ethnic group in Sabah but the speakers of those languages cannot communicate effectively among each other because there are differences in lexical, morphology and other linguistic aspects.

In Brunei, the Dusuns are much more dominant in Tutong district (Asiyah, 2011). They can be divided into three groups: (1) Valley Dusun—those who live near the valley and inland area of Tutong district; (2) Hill Dusun—those who live near hilly area in Tutong and Belait Districts; (3) Coastal Dusun—those who live near the coastal area (Pudarno, 2017). Until recently, there was no specific consensus of the Dusun population in Brunei. Aini (2013) estimated the population to be around 6000–8000 in Brunei, but Pudarno (2017) said the number might be lower, around 5000 people. However, the number of Dusuns who can speak the Dusun language was never recorded, and it was suggested that the number of Dusun speakers might be lower than the population as there have been a decline in the language use in recent decades (Noor Azam, 2012; Fatimah & Najib, 2013; McLellan, 2014; Yusof & Saidatul, 2019). To overcome this challenge, the LC UBD has introduced some of the Brunei ethnic languages, including the Dusun, Tutong and Iban as optional courses (also known as Breadth Modules) for UBD undergraduate students. This initiative is considered the first effort to teach ethnic languages formally in Brunei as it has never been offered in any education institution in this country. The LC UBD hopes this effort could raise the awareness of the ethnic languages among the students and prolong the survival of those languages.

9.3 Role-Play: Theory, Benefits and Challenges

Role-play is one of the teaching techniques used in teaching foreign and second language in education institutions (Atas, 2015; Lee, 2015; Lin, 2009; Salies, 1995; Wagner, 1998). The role-play technique theory corresponds to the Krashen (2009) Second Language Acquisition, in which his 'input hypothesis' has suggested that learners can increase their language proficiency when they are exposed to the language usage which is higher than their proficiency level. This means the proficiency level exposed to the learners has to be a level higher in order to increase the learner's proficiency. He has devised a formula of 'i + 1' to simplify this hypothesis in which 'i' is the current level of the learner and '1' is the input needed to increase their proficiency. The level of proficiency (1) could potentially be increased (+) when it obtains input (1) which is higher than the current proficiency. This theory was supported by Brown (2000) who

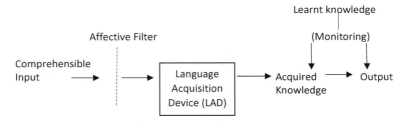

Fig. 9.1 Krashen input hypothesis (2009, p. 16)

also stated that the language exposed to learners must be higher than their prior knowledge so that they could increase their language ability. The language input in this context could originate from various aspects, such as the language input from peers or teachers through teaching techniques and activities. Figure 9.1 shows how the input hypothesis works.

According to Krashen, the comprehensible input is the main input to acquire language knowledge. In this context, the role-play technique is the communicative activity to give the input needed by the students to learn a language. Using role-play helps them by giving challenges, motivation and confidence, and acts as a mechanism to increase their desire to learn a language in a safe context of learning and to pass through the affective filter (Benabadji, 2007; Dundar, 2013; Krashen, 2009; O'Toole, 2009; Wagner, 1998). When the language knowledge passes through the affective filter, it would reach the learner's Language Acquisition Device (LAD) which Krashen believes to be the mental and instinct capability to acquire the language naturally as suggested by Chomsky (1965). Subsequently, the learner will acquire the targeted language and develop their proficiency.

Many studies have shown the benefits of using this technique in the classroom (Alabsi, 2016; Ashton-Hay, 2005; Atas, 2015; Dundar, 2013; Kholmakova, 2017; Lin, 2009; O'Toole, 2009; Wagner, 1998), such as:

1. Allowing students to learn and practise the language in a safe context of learning.
2. Enhancing their speaking proficiency.
3. Motivating students in learning a language.
4. Lowering anxiety and creating safe context of learning.
5. Allowing students to think independently.

6. Being a platform for students who have different proficiency levels to learn from each other.

Role-play also allows students to explore the language by interacting with their peers and to develop their experience by trying different possibilities of acting and talking styles (Kholmakova, 2017). According to Benabadji (2007), this situation shows that the role-play technique and natural language learning are interconnected to some extent.

Some of these benefits were proven in a research project called Drama Improves Key Competences in Education (DICE, 2010) which involved more than 4000 students. Many experts from various disciplines such as educational psychology and sociology, and drama practitioners worked together to investigate the effects of dramatic activities such as role-play for more than two years. One of the case studies conducted in Palestine showed there were positive outcomes for the students exposed to the role-play technique, such as:

1. They have confidence in public speaking.
2. They are more motivated to express their opinion.
3. They feel this technique is creative and entertaining.
4. They have positive academic achievement.

These results show that this technique could have a positive impact on language learning.

Atas (2015) also found that the students' anxiety during language learning had decreased as a result of a six-week role-play intervention. Based on the students' journals, the students were more confident in using the new language in conversations. Overall, the students enjoyed their lessons and felt that learning new vocabularies was easier than before. However, despite the positive impact, some of the students felt it was difficult to perform the role-play activity because they had to perform many things at one time, for example, intonation, translation, pronunciation and acting. These issues made some of the students refuse to participate in the activities because either they were afraid or they were not interested.

In another study, Alabsi (2016) suggested that role-play helped the students in one of the schools in Saudi Arabia who had difficulties in using correct English vocabulary. Conventional techniques such as memorisation made the students feel bored because there were too many repetitions in practising new words. She used the role-play technique as an intervention for the experimental group while the control group continued using the conventional technique. The t-test had shown that the mean of experiment group had positive significant difference ($p < 0.05$) compared to the control group. Even though the technique seems promising, she reminded that the teachers had to be given proper training in order to effectively implement the technique in their language classroom. Similarly, Lee (2015) emphasises that the role-play technique could have drawbacks if the teacher did not know how to properly conduct the role-play activity in their classroom.

To conclude, the role-play technique may be a useful tool to be implemented in any language classroom. A number of studies have shown that this technique could benefit language students such as increasing their academic achievement, motivation and language proficiency. However, this technique needs to be carefully implemented as it could give negative outcomes such as anxiety especially among the new language students. Furthermore, teachers must be properly trained before conducting their lessons using this technique.

9.4 Research Methodology

This research used an explanatory sequential mix method design to answer two research questions:

1. Does role-play have any significant impact on the students' oral proficiency of the Dusun language?
2. What is the perception of the students when they were involved in the role-play activities given by the teacher?

To answer these two research questions, this study began with a pre- and post-oral test which was conducted in week 6 and week 13, respectively. Subsequently, a survey was given to the students, followed by a focus group discussion session in week 14. The study is divided into three phases:

First phase: For the Oral test, each student was tested individually for not more than five minutes. The test was marked using the analytic rubric of The Common European Framework of Reference for Languages (CEFR) level A1—Basic User. Subsequently, in week 13, the same format of oral test was conducted but with different questions and topics. In this research, both of the groups were given oral pre- and post-test following the format below:

- Part A: the students were given a simple biodata of a person in the Malay language. Then, they had to explain the person to the examiner within two minutes using the Dusun language (10 marks).
- Part B: the students were given four questions regarding familiar topics, such as transportation, foods and drinks, fruits and their family. This session was fully conducted in Dusun language (10 marks).

A pilot test was carried out in March (pre-test) and May 2019 (post-test) for a validity check. All results were keyed into the IBM Statistical Package for the Social Sciences (SPSS v.26) for the record and data analysis.

Second phase: An online survey was distributed among the students to collect their perception on their learning experience. Ten items were given using a six-point Likert scale (1 totally disagree—6 totally agree). The survey was validated by five different experts in the field of education and linguistics. All of them checked the questionnaire and agreed on the items used in the survey. The pilot test was done between March and May 2019 to assess its reliability. The value of alpha Cronbach of the 'perception on teaching technique' sub-domain was 0.779 (item 1–5) and of 'confidence and understanding' sub-domain was 0.797 (item 6–10), suggesting that the questionnaire's internal consistency was acceptable and no item needed to be removed from the questionnaire.

Third phase: A focus group discussion was conducted in the final phase of the study. The discussion had two moderators in which one of the research assistants was the main moderator and the other one took notes as suggested by Nyumba et al. (2017). Six students (three males and three females) were given semi-structured interview questions. The length of the discussion was approximately 1 hour and 30 minutes and was recorded using a voice recorder and transcribed by the moderator.

Prior to the data collection, the researcher asked permission from the LC's Director to conduct the research in LY-1433 classes between March and November 2019. No names were recorded and any information that linked the respondents to their identity were concealed. Their registration numbers were changed to numbers from 1 to 40. During the focus group discussion, their names were also changed to protect their privacy and a consent form was given before conducting the survey and the focus group discussion.

9.5 The Process of Teaching and Learning (The Intervention)

The research focused on the students who took Dusun Level I—Basic (LY-1433) course in LC, which was offered as an elective. The LC followed the CEFR level A1 as its guide, so at the end of the course, the students

> can understand and use familiar everyday expressions and very basic phrases aimed at the satisfaction of needs of a concrete type. Can introduce him/herself and others and can ask and answer questions about personal details such as where he/she lives, people he/she knows and things he/she has. Can interact in a simple way provided the other person talks slowly and clearly and is prepared to help. (CEFR, 2011, p. 8)

Briefly, the student needed to achieve the basic proficiency, such as explaining personal information and be able to answer familiar questions such as transportation, foods and drinks, fruits and their family. This course was conducted for 14 weeks (1 semester) and restricted to students who did not have any prior knowledge on the language. The research design implemented in this research project is called 'Nonequivalent (Pre-test and Post-test) Control-Group Design' as suggested by Creswell (2014) (see Table 9.1).

The table shows that there are forty students divided into two groups, and each group has ten male and ten female students. All students who registered for this course were selected as the sample. Below is the overview of the students' timeline:

1. Weeks 1–6: Both of the groups were taught using conventional technique of memorisation and repetitions.
2. Week 7: They were given pre-oral test.

Table 9.1 Research design

Group	Research design		
A (Experimental group) ($n = 20$)	Pre-test O	Treatment X	Post-test O
B (Control group) ($n = 20$)	Pre-test O	Post-test O	

3. Week 8: Group A used role-play as intervention and Group B still used the conventional technique.
4. Week 13: All students were given post-test.
5. Week 14: Students were interviewed and surveyed.

The process of using role-play in teaching can be divided into four parts. To clarify the process, the topic of 'Buying and Selling' is used as an example.

Step 1: Explanation (30 mins): The teaching began with the explanation of vocabularies related to cooking in Dusun language, for example, buy, sell, I want to ..., please, give me ... and others.
Step 2: Activity (45 mins): The teacher divided the class into few groups (four to five students each group). Then, the teacher gave a situation to the students, for example, 'You and your mother are going to a fruit market in town. Please buy four to five items or fruits from two vendors. One of the vendors sells fruit at cheaper price. The other does not.'
Step 3: Presentation (15 mins): Each group presented their play in front of their friends for two to three minutes.
Step 4: Question and Answer (ten mins): The teacher commented each group for their presentations. Question and answer sessions would take place.

Figures 9.2 and 9.3 show the students in the class during the role-play activity. Overall, the teacher allocated 30 mins for explanation, 60 mins for the role-play activity and 10 mins for the Q&A session in every lesson for six weeks depending on the topics. There were various topics and role-play situations given to the students such as food and drinks, meeting a doctor, meeting old friends and giving excuses to a teacher. The class usually begins with an introduction to the topic by the teacher and then the students are assigned the roles to be played. The teacher was the facilitator during the activity and helped the students during their discussions. Benabadji (2007) suggested that the teacher was advised not to intervene in students' presentation as this could hinder their potential to use the language freely. The teacher then surrendered the floor to the students entirely so that their grammar and vocabulary could develop accordingly during the communicative process of their presentation, thus allowing the students to be the main role-players in the learning process (Adenan & Khairudin, 2012).

Fig. 9.2 The students during discussion

Fig. 9.3 The students during role-play

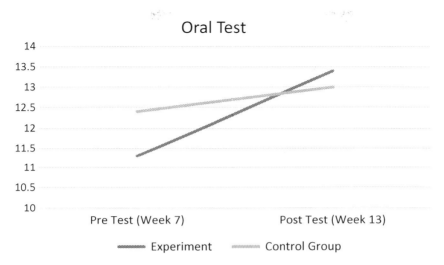

Fig. 9.4 Pre- and post-oral test

9.6 Results and Discussion

To answer the first research question, the researcher had set two null hypotheses and two alternative hypotheses. Figure 9.4 shows the result of the students in the experimental and control group after the pre- and post-oral tests.

The trend shows an increase of mean for both groups. To determine whether the difference was significant, a paired sample t-test was conducted to test the hypothesis (see Table 9.2):

Hypothesis 1
$H_0 1$: There is no significant mean difference between pre- and post-oral test of experimental group.

$H_a 1$: There is a significant mean difference between pre- and post-oral test of experimental group.

There is a significant difference in the pre-test scores ($M = 11.288$, SD $= 1.7978$) and post-test scores ($M = 13.350$, SD $= 2.2976$; $t = -6.749$, $p = 0.000$). This result rejected the null hypothesis $H_0 1$ and kept the alternative, $H_a 1$, suggesting that there was a significant difference of the

Table 9.2 Paired sample t-test of experiment group

Paired samples test

		Paired differences					t	df	Sig. (2-tailed)
		Mean	Std. deviation	Std. error mean	95% confidence interval of the difference				
					Lower	Upper			
Pair 1	Oral pre-test and oral post-test	−2.06250	1.36660	0.3056	−2.7021	−1.4229	−6.749	19	0.000

students' oral competency before and after the students in the experimental group were taught using the role-play technique.

Hypothesis 2

$H_0 2$: There is no significant mean difference between pre- and post-oral test of the control group.

$H_a 2$: There is a significant mean difference between pre- and post-oral test of the control group.

Table 9.3 shows there is no significant difference in the pre-test scores ($M = 12.4$, SD = 1.0463) and post-test score ($M = 13.0$, SD = 1.5874; $t = -1.770$, $p = 0.093$). This result failed to reject the null hypothesis $H_0 2$ and thus rejected the alternative, $H_a 2$, which suggests that there was no significant difference of the students' oral proficiency before and after the students in the control group who were taught using the conventional technique of memorisation and repetition.

In Phases 2 and 3, the researcher had collected a data survey and conducted a focus group discussion to gauge the perception of the students who were taught using the role-play technique. The responses and survey data were discussed together to determine the convergence between the survey and the discussion. Table 9.4 presents the students' perception on the teacher's teaching techniques during the classes.

Many students either agreed or strongly agreed that the teaching technique was clear, held their interest, and encouraged them to participate in

Table 9.3 Paired sample t-test of control group

Paired samples test									
	Paired differences						t	df	Sig. (2-tailed)
		Mean	Std. deviation	Std. error mean	95% confidence interval of the difference				
					Lower	Upper			
Pair 1	Oral pre-test and oral post-test	−0.6000	1.5161	0.3390	−1.3096	0.1096	−1.770	19	0.093

Table 9.4 Students' perception on teaching technique

	Item	Strongly disagree	Disagree	Slightly disagree	Slightly agree	Agree	Strongly agree
1	Teaching technique was clear	0%	0%	0%	0%	5%	95%
2	The teaching was fun and made us laugh	0%	0%	0%	0%	0%	90%
3	The teaching held my interest during class	0%	0%	0%	0%	20%	80%
4	The teaching encouraged me to participate in class discussions	0%	0%	0%	0%	30%	70%
5	The teaching encouraged us to share our ideas and knowledge	0%	0%	0%	0%	45%	55%

class discussions and to share their ideas. One of the notable responses was all students strongly agreed that the teaching technique was fun and it made them laugh. A few interview responses are as follows:

> In every classes, the teacher will give activities. All of them were fun for example role-play, drawing, communicating … The class was full of activities and was not boring. (Mary, personal communication, November 7, 2019)

Some of my family members are Dusun but I don't how to speak in Dusun. That's why I take [the course]. When I join the class, it was fun and I don't have any regret. (Jolyne, personal communication, November 7, 2019)

My friend said the class was fun … At first I was not excited because I don't have any background. I don't understand any word (in Dusun language). But over the weeks it was fun. (Shah, personal communication, November 7, 2019)

These responses also suggest that the class environment that used the role-play technique was fun and not boring, and the students were satisfied to join the class. Table 9.5 presents the students' perception on their confidence and understanding during the lessons.

From the data, 95% of the students were confident in the classroom, but those who claimed to be not confident were only in the aspects of understanding complex material and mastering the skills taught in the classroom. The rest either slightly agreed, agreed and strongly agreed that they were confident and understood what was being taught in the Dusun

Table 9.5 Students' perception on their confidence and understanding

Item	Strongly disagree	Disagree	Slightly disagree	Slightly agree	Agree	Strongly agree
6 I'm certain I can understand difficult reading material in this course	0%	0%	0%	5%	60%	35%
7 I'm confident I can learn the basic concepts taught in this course	0%	0%	0%	0%	40%	60%
8 I'm confident I can understand the complex material presented in this course	0%	0%	5%	5%	60%	30%
9 I'm confident I can do the assignments and tests in this course	0%	0%	0%	5%	55%	40%
9 I'm certain I can master the skills being taught in this class	0%	0%	5%	15%	60%	20%

Language course. Some of the students' responses showed positive signs on the role-play technique such as:

> Yes, I was more confident in front of the audience (friends). Bruneians, some of us are shy and this [technique] gave us confidence. This activity gave us confidence to speak ... to write. (Mary, personal communication, November 7, 2019)

> [The activity] helped us a lot because every week there was a different theme. For example, we did role-play in a market; there were friends who did a role-play of talking to elderly people, buying and selling ... One activity I remember the most was when my friend was cooking. From there I memorised the words that were used in the Dusun language. Thus, I understand them more and they can be used in my test. (Snickers, personal communication, November 7, 2019)

The interview responses suggest that the role-play technique could give more confidence for the students to use the Dusun language. Furthermore, the students felt that they could memorise the words when they were being used which helped them in their test.

9.7 Discussion

The use of the role-play technique has shown positive impacts on the students' oral proficiency of the Dusun language. This can be seen in the mean of pre- and post-oral test in which the mean increased significantly from $M = 11.288$ (Pre-Test) to $M = 13.350$ (Post-Test). During the pre-oral test, some of the students lacked the confidence to answer the given questions. They took more time to answer and most of them showed hesitation during the oral test. This had been taken into account in the design of the role-play as the nature of role-play was to communicate with each other, in turn helping the students to practise their oral fluency and spontaneous thinking (Booth, 1998). Overall, the intervention was a huge success in terms of their proficiency, achievements and confidence as seen from the statistics even though both groups experienced an increase in mean. Apart from that, based on the students' feedback, they felt more confident during the oral test as the role-play had taught them to be more spontaneous, suggesting that the role-play intervention was successful in teaching the ethnic language.

This study has proven that the role-play technique is not limited to teaching world languages such as English and Malay, but it can also greatly benefit the teaching of minority languages as the technique can help students achieve good results while creating an entertaining and fun learning environment (DICE, 2010; Alabsi, 2016). Apart from the students' achievements in the oral proficiency, students feel more confident as they become more proficient in using the language. A study by Atas (2015) showed almost the same result in which the role-play technique could increase the confidence of the students because the anxiety of the students decreased. In this study, 95% of the students were confident and felt they could understand the lessons and materials presented in the class. Furthermore, this technique has indirectly helped them with memorisation and utilisation of the vocabulary.

9.8 Recommendations and Conclusions

In summary, this study has shown that the role-play technique could significantly impact the students' oral proficiency, confidence and understanding. This study could be a stepping stone for a bigger research in the future as this study was limited to the Dusun language and only collected data from a small sample size. The results may differ if it was conducted with other minority languages and with a larger sample size. For future research, this study can be improved as follows:

1. Conducting the research with other ethnic languages such as Tutong, Murut, Bisaya and Belait.
2. Collecting data from larger sample.
3. Conducting research on different aspects of language learning such as listening, reading and writing skills.
4. Conducting longitudinal study of ethnic language teaching.
5. Comparing role-play with other teaching techniques that use technology such as media social and web-based learning.

Even though the conventional technique of memorisation and repetition seems less favourable, it does not mean the technique cannot be used at all. A study by Nasrollahi-Mouziraji and Nasrollahi-Mouziraji (2015, p. 871) claims that memorisation has the potential to make progress on many aspects of learning such as '1) providing the learner with linguistic data; 2) being the first step to understanding; 3) enhancing association in memory; 4) causing cognitive development as a learning strategy; 5) helping noticing; 6) providing rehearsal; 7) being especially helpful in the early stages of learning'. Moreover, the authors state that memorisation and repetition should not be seen as a rote type of learning but as a complement to other techniques. According to Khamees (2016), memorisation can be considered as low level of thinking which could be used together with high level of thinking. Ultimately, there is no single way of teaching a language and teachers have to be creative to implement other techniques in their lessons.

To conclude, this study achieved both its objectives to investigate the effects of the role-play technique on the oral proficiency of the students and to investigate the perception of students who took the Dusun language (LY-1433 level 1) module. As suggested, further research in using this technique to teach other ethnic languages is needed because role-play is not the only technique to have a positive impact on language learning (Yusof, 2012). Rhyner (1999) and Yusof (2012) suggest any teaching technique should be experimented by language teachers and facilitators. The results of the experiments might differ from this study because the languages and samples are different. In addition, trainings and workshops for ethnic language teachers should be conducted by relevant institutions before they could implement this technique in their class (Alabsi, 2016).

REFERENCES

Adenan, A., & Khairudin, M. (2012). *Kaedah Pengajaran Bahasa Melayu*. Oxford Fajar Sdn. Bhd.

Aini, K. (2007). *Preposisi Bahasa Dusun dan Bahasa Melayu: Satu Analisis Kontrastif dan Analisis Kesilapan*. Dewan Bahasa dan Pustaka.

Aini, K. (2013). Pembentukan Kata Kerja Cerminan Penakatan dan Cabaran Bahasa Minoriti: Kes Bahasa Dusun di Brunei Darussalam dalam Hajah Aminah binti. In H. Momin & M. A. Othman (Eds.), *Kepelbagaian Bahasa di Borneo* (pp. 414–469). Dewan Bahasa dan Pustaka.

Alabsi, T. A. (2016). The effectiveness of role play strategy in teaching vocabulary. *Theory and Practice in Language Studies*, 6(2), 227–234. https://doi.org/10.17507/tpls.0602.02

Alas, Y. (1994). *The reconstruction of pre-Dusun and the classification of its descendants*. University of Hawaii.

Alas, Y. (2009). Tanah Leluhur Masyarakat Dusun: Perspektif Linguisitk. In *SouthEast Asia: A Multidisciplinary Journal*, 9, 107–121. http://fass.ubd.edu.bn/staff/profiles/yabitalas.html

Ashton-Hay, S. (2005). Drama: Engaging all Learning Styles. In *Proceedings 9th International INGED (Turkish English Education Association) Conference, Economics and Technical University, Ankara Turkey*. https://eprints.qut.edu.au/12261/1/12261a.pdf

Asiyah, A. A. K. (2011). *Conversion to Islam: The case of the Dusun ethnic group in Brunei Darussalam*. Unpublished PhD Thesis. University of Leicester. https://lra.le.ac.uk/handle/2381/9804

Atas, M. (2015). The reduction of speaking anxiety in EFL learners through drama techniques. *Procedia—Social and Behavioral Sciences, 176*, 961–969. https://doi.org/10.1016/j.sbspro.2015.01.565

Benabadji, S. (2007). *Improving Students' Fluency Through Role Playing*. Unpublished Master Thesis, University of Oran. https://theses.univ-oran1.dz/document/TH2362.pdf

Booth, D. (1998). Language power through working in role. In B. J. Wagner (Ed.), *Educational Drama and language arts: What research shows* (pp. 57–76). Heinemann.

Brown, H. D. (2000). *Principles of language learning and teaching* (5th ed.). Pearson Education, Inc.

Buah, T. (1996). *Sistem Fonologi Dusun Pedalaman*. Unpublished BA Thesis, Universiti Brunei Darussalam.

CEFR. (2011). *Common European framework of reference for languages: Learning, teaching, assessment*. http://ebcl.eu.com/

Chomsky, N. (1965). *Aspects of the theory of syntax*. MIT Press.

Chong, A. F. (2010). Pronomina Persona Bahasa Dusun. *Jurnal Bahasa, 20*, 30–43.

Creswell, J. W. (2014). *Research design: Qualitative, quantitative, and mixed method approaches* (4th ed.). Sage.

DICE. (2010). *Drama improves key competences in education*. http://www.drama-network.eu/file/Policy%20Paper%20long.pdf

Dundar, S. (2013). Nine drama activities for foreign language classrooms: Benefits and challenges. *Procedia—Social and Behavioral Sciences, 70*, 1424–1431. https://doi.org/10.1016/j.sbspro.2013.01.206

Fatimah, A. C., & Najib, N. (2013). Vitaliti dan Revitalisasi Minoriti Etik Dusun dalam Situasi Semasa dalam Hajah Aminah binti. In H. Momin & M. A. Othman (Eds.), *Kepelbagaian Bahasa di Borneo* (pp. 352–389). Dewan Bahasa dan Pustaka.

Gardiner, I. A., Deterding, D., & Alas, Y. (2019). The pronunciation of Dusun. *South East Asia: A Multidisciplinary Journal, 19*, 14–21. http://fass.ubd.edu.bn/research/dusun/index.html

Jalin, L. (1989). *Fonologi Bahasa Dusun, Refleks dari bahasa Austronesia dan Tatatingkat Kekerabatan dengan Bahasa di Sekitarnya*. Unpublished BA Thesis, Universiti Brunei Darussalam.

Khamees, S. B. (2016). An evaluative study of memorization as a strategy for learning English. *International Journal of English Linguistics*, 6(4), 248–259. https://doi.org/10.5539/ijel.v6n4p248

Kholmakova, I.V. (2017). *The advantages and disadvantages of drama techniques in foreign language teaching.* http://enpuir.npu.edu.ua/bitstream/123456789/19482/1/Kholmakova.pdf

Krashen, S. (2009). *Principles and practice in second language acquisition* (Internet Edition). http://www.sdkrashen.com/content/books/principles_and_practice

Lee, S. (2015). Revisit role-playing activities in foreign language teaching and learning: Remodeling learners' cultural identity? *Electronic Journal of Foreign Language Teaching*, 12(1), 346–359.

Lin, Y. (2009). *Investigating role-play implementation: A multiple case study on Chinese EFL teachers using role-play in their secondary classrooms.* Unpublished PhD Thesis, University of Windsor.

Matussin, T. (1986). Puak Dusun dan Adatnya. In *Beriga* Bandar Seri Begawan: Dewan Bahasa dan Pustaka, pp. 15–29.

McLellan, J. (2014). Strategies for revitalizing endangered Borneo languages: A comparison between Negara Brunei Darussalam and Sarawak, Malaysia. *Southeast Asia: A Multidisciplinary Journal*, 14, 14–22.

Nasrollahi-Mouziraji, A., & Nasrollahi-Mouziraji, A. (2015). Memorization makes Progress. *Theory and Practice in Language Studies*, 5(4), 870–874. https://doi.org/10.17507/tpls.0504.25

Noor Azam, H.-O. (2012). Teaching an endangered language: Basa' Tutong in UBD. In A. Clynes (Ed.), *Selected papers from the 11th Borneo Research Council Conference, 2012.* [UBD, Online publication].

Noor Azam, H.-O., & Ajeerah, S. (2016). The state of indigenous language in Brunei Darussalam. In H.-O. Noor Azam, J. McLellan, & D. Deterding (Eds.), *The use and status of language in Brunei* (pp. 17–28). Springer.

Nothofer, B. (1991). The languages of Brunei Darussalam. In H. Steinhauer (Ed.), *Papers in Austronesian linguistics* (pp. 151–176). Australian National University.

Nyumba, T. O., Wilson, K., Derrick, C. J., & Mukherjee, N. (2017). The use of focus group discussion methodology: Insights from two decades of application in conservation. *Methods in Ecology and Evolution*, 9, 20–32. https://doi.org/10.1111/2041-210X.12860

O'Toole, J. (2009). Drama as Pedagogy. In O. John, S. Madonna, & M. Tiina (Eds.), *Drama and curriculum: A Giant at the door* (pp. 97–116). Springer.

Pudarno, B. (2017). *Budaya Masyarakat Dusun: Imbasan Kembali.* Jabatan Muzium- Muzium.

Rhyner, J. (1999). Introduction: Some basics of language revitalization. In R. Jon, C. Gina, N. S. C. Robert, & P. Y. Evangeline (Eds.), *Revitalizing Indigenous Language* (pp. v–xx). Northern Arizona University.

Saidatul, N. H. M. (2012). *Pesona Dialek Melayu Sabah*. UMS.

Salies, T. G. (1995). *Teaching language realistically: Role play is the thing*. Retrieved Januari 1, 2019, from https://files.eric.ed.gov/fulltext/ED424753.pdf

Wagner, B. J. (1998). *Educational Drama and language arts: What research shows*. Heinemann.

Yusof, N. (2012). *How can drama and performance in the classroom contribute to the moral and social development of students? A case study*. Unpublished Master Thesis, University of Warwick.

Yusof, N., & Saidatul, N. H. M. (2019). Pengaruh Bahasa Melayu dalam Bahasa Dusun Brunei. *Jurnal Bahasa, 19*(1), 96–116.

CHAPTER 10

Standardised Testing and Students' Wellbeing: A Global or Local Problem?

Siti Norhedayah Abdul Latif

10.1 Introduction

Globalisation has a significant impact across many aspects of education, and it has always been a globalised tradition to use assessments as a form of systematic evaluation to inform the quality of an educational system. The term 'globalisation' has offered a sense of the shared nature of the world, and education is seen as a key input that influences the development of the knowledge economy (Scott et al., 2016). These globalised linkages are what many countries feel they have to reform in order to be part of the international movement, and this has led to competition, sometimes competing for supremacy as international players. Educational reform is one dimension of globalisation. Participating countries aim to raise the academic standards of students, and the test is the globalised form for the assessment of students. This standardised testing is now the key measure of national competitiveness and prestige.

S. N. Abdul Latif (✉)
Universiti Brunei Darussalam, Bandar Seri Begawan, Brunei
e-mail: norhedayah.latif@ubd.edu.bn

© The Author(s), under exclusive license to Springer Nature Switzerland AG 2021
Phan, L. H. et al. (eds.), *Globalisation, Education, and Reform in Brunei Darussalam*, International and Development Education, https://doi.org/10.1007/978-3-030-77119-5_10

Standardised assessment is prevalent and useful for monitoring the quality of a country's educational system and international competitiveness. However, being compared and seen to be failing to perform, which is charted in the league table, puts pressure on policy makers from society at large and from parents who expect some form of accountability following implementation of any kind of reform that involves testing their children. It is not surprising that another educational reform will be introduced following this post-mortem and possibly the whole process will be repeated, again holding school principals, teachers and students responsible for materialising the reforms. When such reform does not work, principals are fearful of the blame that follows. Cuban (1990) suggests one of the reasons for the failure of educational policies could be the lack of rational planning that would permit the diagnosis of problems and promotion of an appropriate solution. Policy makers seldom conduct analysis and evaluation of programme effectiveness before suggesting a reform and putting it into practice (Zajda, 2010).

10.2 Academic Assessment Versus Wellbeing Assessment

It is common for adolescents to feel anxious about standardised testing due to the demand and expectation placed upon students from schools, educators and parents to perform well (Putwain & Roberts as cited in Saeki et al., 2015). The value of the test for many governments includes the capacity to evaluate their own education system (Zhang & Kong, 2012), while learning from high-performing countries on what reforms can be initiated (Sarjala, 2013). One example of a worldwide study called the Programme for International Student Assessment (PISA) developed by the Organisation for Economic Co-operation and Development (OECD) intends to measure 15-year-old school pupils' scholastic performance in Mathematics, Science and Reading for every three years. OECD produces this triennial report on the state of education around the globe which other countries can use as a tool to fine-tune their education policies.

PISA was first conducted in 2000. Brunei Darussalam participated in this comparative international large-scale standardised assessment for the first time in 2018. Of the 79 participating countries, results ranked Brunei in 60th place for Reading, 51st place for Mathematics and 50th place for Science. While overall scholastic performance of students in Brunei scored lower than the OECD average performance, the country ranked third amongst the participating ASEAN countries in all domains of PISA 2018. This achievement pleased many government educational bodies and was showcased in every local news bulletin. In contrast, public health professionals were more interested in the PISA snapshot report (Table 10.1) on Brunei students' wellbeing which surprisingly received less to no public news. PISA reported that as many as 50% of Bruneian students who participated in the study experienced bullying from others. While general bullying conduct was reportedly high, exposure to other forms of bullying was relatively low, ranging between 12% and 39%. At present, it is still not clear if those specific items were understood by Bruneian students as problematic or reflecting bullying issues. Furthermore, PISA reported that only 42% of students expressed satisfaction with life. These statistics should be worrying for many since researchers as well as practitioners have long acknowledged that both wellbeing and academic achievement are favourable outcomes for students.

Although there were no insights obtained into other related wellbeing questions and reports from PISA, we do know that some countries put more investment into students' wellbeing in general. A multicultural comparison across 25 societies from the self-administered Youth Self Report (YSR) questionnaire yielded low total problem scores of emotional and behavioural problems from Finland, Germany, Iceland and Norway (Ivanova et al., 2007). This finding is no coincidence when, for example, account is taken of Finland's commitment to free access to services and seamless support for all children and teachers throughout schooling

Table 10.1 PISA snapshot on Brunei students' exposure to bullying

Students' exposure to bullying	%
Any types of bullying act	50
Frequently bullied students	26
Other students left me out of things on purpose	19
Other students made fun of me	39
I was threatened by other student	20
Other students took away or destroyed things that belong to me	12
I got hot or pushed around by other students	15
Other students spread nasty rumours about me	17

Note: Retrieved from PISA 2018 Results (Volume III): What School Life Means for Students' Lives (https://www.oecd-ilibrary.org/sites/cd52fb72-en/index.html?itemId=/content/component/cd52fb72-en#fig6)

(Sahlberg, 2012), greater flexibility for students to move between vocational programmes and academic streams (Raisanen & Rakkolainen, 2009), and investment in the professionalism of their educators. To some extent, these commitments explain their success in the PISA rankings (Schleicher & Stewart, 2008). Recently, with the release of the latest PISA results (Schleicher, 2019), the education systems of the Flemish community of Belgium, Estonia, Finland and Germany, who scored above the average in reading, continue to report good satisfaction with life overall. The implication is that more emphasis should be placed on students' wellbeing enabling healthy academic and personal development.

10.3 Assessment of Wellbeing Across Culture

Despite the continued development of wellbeing instruments, no universally accepted measure has emerged (Layard, 2010), in part because there are no agreed conceptual criteria concerning what this instrument should contain. Depending on the theoretical principle underpinning the definition of wellbeing, different priorities are emphasised in the design of the instrument. Hence, a universally accepted measure of wellbeing may be an unrealistic goal. An exhaustive study by Linton et al. (2016) provided a detailed inventory of 99 measures of wellbeing developed over the past 50 years and made available a thematic catalogue which registered 196 dimensions. This suggested that there is little consistent agreement on how wellbeing should be measured, its design and the inclusion of dimensions. It should be understood then that the presence of different dimensions reflects wellbeing as a multidimensional construct (i.e. often with overlapping themes) and appreciating any cultural stream of thought brought into the measure. Given the breadth, and the inability to agree on a definition, it might be more advantageous to use wellbeing as an umbrella term. However, this is not always useful to inform other researchers because they will end up with a selection based on familiarity, what is most popularly used by others, or be encouraged to develop yet other new design instruments to be added to this exhaustive list.

Employing a standardised wellbeing assessment across different cultures poses its own challenges as well. The recognition of cultural differences across countries has led to several studies taking close measure into the appropriateness of using western-designed tools into study. Most of the findings revealed that some of the items used to describe predetermined problems or issues from the West did not capture the same meaning of problematic or concerning to responses when used in studies from the eastern region. In other words, it lacks validity support in informing us how items are conceptualised together based on the common dimensions. Only through some statistical validation support resulting in the replication of the predetermined dimensions will provide sound report of prevalence rate in representing responses that share the same cultural meaning in defining problems or issues from items of the tool used.

The Youth Self Report (Achenbach, 1991) is one of the most-used western measures employed within the Asian region in reporting adolescents' emotional and behavioural development (Leung & Wong, 2003). No other studies have reported evidence of factor structure within this region. This makes the existing Malay translation of the Achenbach questionnaires (in particular the YSR) more compelling for the present study to examine whether using the YSR in the Malay culture of Brunei would produce similar recognition of problems identified within western culture. This also raises questions of some studies (Salwina et al., 2013; Chu et al., 2009), where the researchers tend to report the prevalence of the problems from the existing difficulty scales of YSR without exploring the validity of the scales. Within the western samples, the use of YSR similarly could not present full validity support and suggested that a much shorter version (i.e. with the removal of some insignificant items/questions) in the way that the 7-factor form was identified as the best fit in a single study in Los Angeles (O'Keefe et al., 2006), 6-factor in Japan (Kuramoto et al., 2002), and instead a 2-factor of the broader internalising and externalising problems scale was reported in cross-cultural studies between Germany and Jamaica (Lambert et al., 2007). Since the notion of emotional and behavioural development is an idea of a deviance against a norm or social pattern (Mesquita & Walker, 2003; Nikapota, 2009), these norms are thought to vary widely from culture to culture and with time. Additionally, it was contended that most definitions of emotion reflect western emotional models and do not stand for eastern cultures. It is not impossible for this current study to present findings relative to all the above-mentioned reviews.

Taken together, these findings suggest that there is a pressing need for more statistical evidence on the use of the YSR within the Asian context, in particular with the use of the existing Malay translation. In the case of Brunei, there is no epidemiological study on this issue to date; systematic reports on emotional and behavioural-related problems among children and adolescents are scarce. At present there are no formal studies that have been conducted to provide data in relation to the mental health status of Bruneian children and adolescents that could offer valuable insights for practice. The only formal report received has shown that 429 children and adolescents have registered with the mental health clinics since 2006 (Borneo Bulletin, 2011). It was not stated how much the rate has increased since, but the emotional and behavioural problems among children and adolescents reported were mostly internalising (troubled emotions and feelings) and externalising (related problems such as disturbed and antisocial behaviours). One of the main reasons for the absence of systematic reports regarding these issues is the lack of a reliable and valid measure to identify the prevalence rates of emotional and behavioural problems among adolescents in Brunei. This study aimed to provide preliminary evidence to support the gap in presence that will guide researchers in making informed decisions involving assessment tools.

10.4 Adolescents' View of Problems Affecting Wellbeing

In cultural development, social age (i.e. expectations of the social-cultural group into which a person should fall at a certain chronological age) reveals a most interesting pattern seen universally across different cultures. Cross-cultural studies of young people's behaviours have been conducted in different societies (Chen et al., 2011). However, it is important to recognise that gender differences in the presentation of a behavioural problem are also determined by the value systems in societies: such as the extent to which such behaviours result in increased parental control and social disapproval. Consequently, higher rates of externalising problems (such as acting out) are commonly reported where externalising behaviour is not actively discouraged or disapproved of as a result of lower tolerance thresholds in some cultures. Similarly, higher rates of internalising behaviour (such as fear or anxiety) are commonly reported where interdependence is encouraged or seen as normative within the society. For instance, a study by Leung et al. (2008) showed that 77% of Chinese adolescents in the study exhibited symptoms of anxiety. However, despite this very high rate, the Chinese adolescents were not functioning in an impaired range. It was argued that shy and inhibited behaviours are observed in socially competent individuals (Chen et al., 1995). Consistent with traditional Thai values and among Asian societies, overcontrolled problems (such as shyness and fear) were viewed as less serious, less worrisome and more likely to improve with time (Ollendick et al., 1996; Weisz et al., 1988). Hence, reporting such incidence rates of externalising and internalising problems must be done with sensitivity to the culture such data represents.

In addition to cultural influence, student engagement in schools also showed a direct effect on personal growth and academic achievement. Several findings have shown that perception of school climate at a personal level can be very important since feelings about school life have a great impact on student's wellbeing (Gage et al., 2016). For instance, the lack of an appropriate toilet can affect children's education and put their physical and psychological health at risk (Vernon et al., 2003). A more adverse effect of this is that inadequate privacy combined with bullying results in many children avoiding school toilets. Another place that students report to be less safe is the school canteen where negative peer interactions, such as harassment, bullying and other forms of violence occur (Horton & Forsberg, 2020). In a study among Chinese adolescents age 11–20 from six secondary schools in China (Sun et al., 2013), peer emotional bullying was found to be significantly associated with stress in school as measured by the Educational Stress Scale of Adolescents (ESSA) (Sun et al., 2013) which can be a detrimental threat to one's wellbeing and development. Another study reported that issues like limited break time and a crowded canteen discourage students from washing their hands in their rush to get food in schools (Khaing et al., 2019).

Qualitative studies (Fletcher & Bonell, 2013) support the idea of school connectedness to peer relationships. It is suggested that young people who feel disconnected from school are commonly identified with deviant behaviours. Their circle of friends may therefore serve as a risk or undertake protective roles depending on the levels of connectedness to school, but failure to form supportive friendships with peers can be detrimental which can cause threats to one's wellbeing and development (Bukowski et al., 2010). However, it is also important to recognise that socialising processes among adolescents in particular with peers is also a reflection of what is valued according to the norm of the culture (Rothbaum et al., 2000). In this review, it was found that harmony is more valued in Japan than in the United States. In general, Japanese youth will continue to place emphasis on stability and continuity of relationships with parents and peers. In contrast, adolescents in the United States commonly need to individuate from parents and transfer their allegiance from parents to peers. Interpretations of peer relationships within the Asian region should be tackled with caution as studies continue to showcase the lack of support for reporting peer problems, when using the western design tool, such as in China (Du et al., 2008), Thailand (Woerner et al., 2011) and Malaysia (Stokes et al., 2013), signalling that peer problems might be construed differently while acknowledging the existence of peer problems.

Within the school system, students' perception of interpersonal teacher behaviour also correlated with student's wellbeing (Petegem et al., 2008). There was a negative relationship between students' perception of teachers and teachers' interpersonal behaviour of an authoritarian type (e.g. less friendly and not friendly). Instead, an authoritative type/tolerant teacher develops close relationships with students. Students felt that this type of teachers provided much attention and expectations which are more pleasant and interesting for the students. Hence, investing in high affective wellbeing offers improved students' affective and achievement outcomes.

Apart from teachers, family is regarded as a major social institution surrounding a person's social activity. This includes family affairs such as families' daily lives, parental conflicts, the parent-child relationships, maternal mental health, financial hardship and repeated changes in living arrangements, including family structure (see Buehler, 2020 for more examples). Generally, a close relationship with family is almost universally discussed as protective of substance use, subjective wellbeing and mental health.

10.5 Methodology

In agreement with many researchers in the field of quantitative assessment and to ensure reliability and validity of the adapted questionnaire assessing emotional and behavioural problems, this study explored the preliminary factor structure analysis of the YSR to establish if it can replicate the predetermined eight factors as in the original study. This study employed a cross-sectional design and factor analysis, which is a statistical method used to describe variability among observed, correlated variables to determine whether groups of variables tend to bunch together to form distinct clusters referred to as factors. In this design, quantitative data was collected at a single point in time.

A critical issue in evaluating the wellbeing of adolescents at school is the lack of valid instruments to measure many of the psychological constructs associated with the emotional and behavioural development of adolescents, particularly when used in a different culture. In this investigation, surveys were administered at the commencement of the project. The survey data from students were employed to provide measures of a range of students' emotional and behavioural functioning, and open responses on issues that concern adolescents in schools. Because this construct and the underlying items previously had not been validated, it was important to establish the reliability and validity of the measure that was adopted.

From the total of 34 secondary government schools, 10 schools were randomly selected through multi-stage sampling and contacted. The surveys were distributed to all students in the ten schools at the commencement of the project. After pairwise deletion of cases containing missing data, complete data for the analyses were available for 282 adolescents. This chapter reports on the findings from the study in relation to the adolescents' emotional and behavioural functioning via self-administered reports. It aimed to explore if the instrument could capture similar concepts of problems identified globally and/or if other problems being reported are in fact more localised.

10.6 Instrument

The Achenbach System of Empirically Based Assessment (ASEBA) for school-age children includes three instruments for assessing emotional and/or behavioural problems. One of them is the adolescents self-administered, Youth Self Report (YSR). The ASEBA offers a comprehensive approach to assessing adaptive and maladaptive functioning in children and adolescents. It is widely used in mental health services, schools, medical settings, child, family services, public agencies, child guidance, training and research. The ASEBA instruments have been translated into over 80 languages and more than 7000 publications on the use of ASEBA materials involving the work of 9000 authors from over 80 cultural groups and societies (www.aseba.org).

The behaviour profile that is the focus of this study comprises 118 items that can be scored as zero (not true), one (somewhat or sometimes true) or two (very true or often true). These items provide scores for eight narrow narrow-band scales or syndromes (*Anxious/Depressed, Withdrawn/Depressed, Somatic Complaints, Social Problems, Thought Problems, Attention Problems, Rule-Breaking Behaviour* and *Aggressive Behaviour*) and three broad-band scales (Internalising Behaviour Problems, Externalising Behaviour Problems and Total Behaviour Problems). The name given to these syndromes is empirically derived identified by factor analysis. Items from the syndromes or subscales *Anxious/Depressed,*

Withdrawn/Depressed and *Somatic Complaints* are components of the Internalising scale, while items from syndromes or subscales *Rule-Breaking Behaviour* and *Aggressive Behaviour* are components of Externalising scale. The remaining three syndromes or subscales of *thought, attention* and *social problems* are established as distinct narrow concepts. The Total Problem scale includes items from *all* syndromes. At the school's request, one item addressing sexual behaviour was removed. For each item, adolescents rated how well the item described the adolescent's wellbeing over the past six months on a three-point scale ranging from 0 ('Not true') to 2 ('Very True/Often True').

10.7 Data Analysis

Data from the questionnaire were initially subjected to Exploratory Factor Analyses with principal component extraction, and Varimax rotation was used to ascertain the reliability and validity of the survey instruments. Any missing values deliberately left by participants were completely removed from the database prior to analysis; this resulted in a 0% missing values and 282 completed adolescents' responses. This study aimed at exploring the data, not to test a hypothesis or theory, nor is it suited to full validation of instruments. The second step provided a closer observation on the items that were perceived as concerning to adolescents marked by the highest percentage as 'true' in their ratings.

10.8 Results

The preliminary factor analysis revealed as many as 29 categories which indicated that it was not the most parsimonious. A possible explanation outlined by Costello and Osborne (2005) is that failure to converge is exclusively observed in smaller samples with regard to the effects of Subject-to-Item ratio. The sample fell short of the recommendation offered by Costello and Osborne (2005) where this sample only accounted for a 3:1 subject ratio and corresponded to only 10% of the sample to produce a correct solution which was considered insufficient. Since it could not replicate the existing eight categories of the original YSR, it will be only useful to explore at item level to capture relevant cases that relate to adolescents' reports. Doing so will provide some insights into which items could inform us about the nature of wellbeing of adolescents at the time of study.

Of the total 112 items on the YSR (Fig. 10.1), as many as 25 items are being reported as true (i.e. collapse between 'sometimes true' and 'always true'). Four items had the highest percentage (>50%) marked as true. Highest fears were for items on *I am afraid I might think or do something bad, my moods or feeling change suddenly, my school work is poor* and *I have a hot temper*. The remainder of the items raised issues such as Aggressive type behaviour (e.g. *I argue a lot, I scream a lot* and *I have a hot temper*) and Withdrawn (e.g. *I would rather be alone than with others* and *I am too shy or timid*).

In addition to the predetermined items on adolescents' emotional and behavioural problem scales, an open-ended response (Table 10.2) was also invited from adolescents on any concerns they have in school. Their responses were themed as four matters: *academic, peer relationships, school facilities* and *family-related problems*.

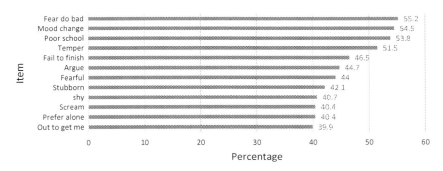

Fig. 10.1 Bar chart of highest percentage on items of Youth Self Report

Table 10.2 A summary of concerns adolescents have in schools

Theme	Description
Academic matters	Failing school exams, difficult subjects, uncertainty of what future holds for them
Peer relationship	Being bullied, some friends do not understand, some friends are not friendly
School facilities	Poor school facilities, long queue and crowded in canteen, dirty toilets, broken fans
Teacher factor	Teachers looked down at students, fierce and not approachable
Family-related problems	Family wellbeing and health, late attendance

Academic matters. A majority of adolescents reported concerns over failing school exams and mainly the related problems are linked with difficulty in learning subjects like English, Mathematics and Science. For some students, this resulted in uncertainty about what the future holds for them.

Peer relationship. Several adolescents reported fear of being bullied by 'naughty kids'. Lack of understanding by some friends emerged, some students are not friendly and some prefer to avoid friends.

School facilities. Several adolescents reported poor school facilities that let them down. The most reported concern was the long queue and crowded situation at the canteen. Several adolescents complained about the dirty toilets in schools with some broken (unable to lock) doors. A few students reported hot classrooms with some having broken fans.

Teacher factors. A few students felt the teachers looked down on them and that teachers are fierce as well (not approachable).

Family-related problems. Adolescents' responses were not limited to only school concerns. Several students included family factors. Many mentioned about family wellbeing and health of parents. A few mentioned being late to school and fear of attendance problems.

10.9 Discussion

Findings show that while employing scholastic standardised assessment on students can be used to compare students' academic achievement across countries, the use of standardised wellbeing must be treated with sensitivity to the culture of the country it represents. In other words, while academic performance can be used to measure education quality with the aim of improving education standards, we cannot normalise wellbeing because culture influences the viewpoints that adolescents have regarding their own wellbeing. The present study supported the argument that culture plays an important role in influencing adolescents' self-report (Nikapota, 2009). When a standardised measure like the YSR was adopted, it could not provide any useful interpretation of the best fit of categories to describe the emotional and behavioural difficulties of adolescents in Brunei. This is no surprise as studies continue to report on reliability, but they focus less on validity when it comes to the use of YSR as a tool.

The reliability of a tool is easily achieved because a longer instrument usually increases the reliability of the test regardless of whether the items are homogeneous or not (Tavakol & Dennick, 2011). An instrument can be reliable but not necessarily valid without steering away from the original predetermined subscales. This was evident in studies which report YSR has different 'validity versions' from the original scales when used across various countries (Kuramoto et al., 2002; Lambert et al., 2007; O'Keefe et al., 2006). Like the present study, an attempt to explore validity was not successful. It is important then to be mindful to continue reporting prevalence rates for existing categories of the YSR. Since other studies did not run the overall factor structure, it signals the possible lack of desirability of using the questionnaire to describe problems that were designed from the western perspective. Perhaps within this Asian region, it is expected that factor analysis of YSR may lack support in producing the existing eight-factor structure, which explains the absence of this validity analysis across the region (Leung & Wong, 2003). This study has implications for the recent PISA wellbeing results that revealed that Brunei students had the lowest wellbeing performance among the 72 participating countries using a standardised measure. A critical review of 99 self-report measures for assessing wellbeing (Linton et al., 2016) argued that there exists ambiguity and identified substantial heterogeneity in how wellbeing was defined and used. The review reiterated that the most appropriate measure of wellbeing will depend on the dimensions of wellbeing of most interest, in coordination with psychometric (i.e. validation) guidance.

While we know that adolescents tend to report similar concerns or problems universally thought to affect their wellbeing, a higher report of cases does not necessarily mean that it is viewed as problematic and has dampened psychological functioning among children and adolescents. For example, the current study reported the highest case (55%) for *fearing to do bad* by adolescents at the time the study was carried out. This is not an unusual response from anyone, but excessive fear is driven by anxiety and can lead to extreme shyness which may in turn lead to avoiding their usual activities or a refusal to engage in new experience. This anxiety symptom also appears to be more prevalent in societies that value inhibition, compliance with social expectations and social evaluation, such as in the Asian countries (Ollendick et al., 1996; Weisz et al., 1988). Alternatively, shyness and inhibition in young people are regarded by parents and teachers in western cultures as signs of incompetence and immaturity requiring protection, intervention and sometimes reprimand. Hence, the outcome of these behaviours in Asian society is seen less likely as clinical problems, but rather desired behaviours perceived within the culture. When this current study indicated 41% of adolescents being shy, this is perhaps a desirable behaviour that is valued by the culture in Brunei. This is somehow relatable to studies by Leung et al. (2008). Within the Confucian and Taoist philosophies, shy and inhibited behaviours are valued and encouraged in Chinese culture, and that shy-anxious children in China are regarded as socially competent and understanding (Chen et al., 1995).

Issues around bullying and unfriendly 'friends' are quite commonly reported by adolescents elsewhere (Horton & Forsberg, 2020; Sun et al., 2013), including Brunei adolescents in this study. Experiencing failure to form supportive friendships with peers can be detrimental which can cause threats to one's wellbeing and development (Bukowski et al., 2010). However, seeing this issue as a threat to adolescents in different culture requires some sensitivity. While adolescents in Asia value harmony and emphasise stability and continuity with peers (Rothbaum et al., 2000), it is not surprising that avoiding conflict or some confrontation is what most adolescents are in favour of. So, this again does not necessarily indicate true peer problems relationships if such cases are reported as high. This brings back the PISA snapshot on Brunei students' exposure to bullying. The striking surprise was that although general act of bullying was reportedly high (50%), other bullying-related items were reportedly low (see Table 10.1), implying that predetermined bullying items might not necessarily be perceived as problematic. Instead, this 50% rate would be meaningful if only PISA could actually identify what exactly did Brunei adolescents mean with 'general bullying act' if none of them could be relatable to PISA bullying items. Moreover, it was argued that reporting peer problems using predetermined items is not advisable because of the lack of validity support in other related studies (Du et al., 2008; Stokes et al., 2013; Woerner et al., 2011). Research to understand peer problems among adolescents within the Asian region appears to be lacking.

Interestingly, the YSR scale did not touch on items that are outside of student factors influencing their so-called emotional and behavioural problems in schools. The open-ended question added some insights into additional concerns that might be overlooked by many researchers to inform problems that are probably more localised than expected. We do know that feelings about school life have a great impact on students' wellbeing (Gage et al., 2016). At the time of study, students in Brunei mainly reported the lack of cleanliness of the toilets with broken doors that discouraged them from going to the toilet. This lack of privacy put their physical and psychological health at risk (Vernon et al., 2003). While other studies identified school canteens as less safe which are susceptible to negative interactions and bullying (Horton & Forsberg, 2020), adolescents in Brunei were more concerned over the crowded canteen leaving less time for quality break time with friends. Another concern of students relates to teacher factors. Adolescents in Brunei mainly felt that teachers are very authoritarian and to some extent this affects their study life in school. In the long run, many students felt uncertain about their future. This is not a surprising response as studies (Petegem et al., 2008) have also indicated that students' wellbeing is negatively affected by the presence of poor student-teacher relationships in school. Finally, there is the family, a well-known factor that plays a crucial role in ensuring adolescents' positive functioning and wellbeing whilst in school. Instead of concern over the universal problems mentioned by Buehler (2020) such as parent-child relationship, parent conflicts and financial issues, the problems were rather specific such as worrying about their parents' wellbeing and the fear of late attendance at school.

10.10 Conclusion

This chapter has provided some insights into how adolescents responded to the Malay translation of the YSR. Drawing on the above discussion, expectations based on adolescents' report of YSR provided mixed support and are still inconclusive. Many of these items were recognised as sensitive questions, and the low or underreporting of these sensitive problems may have contributed to the low loadings on both factor structure and item interrelatedness to total difficulties scores. This also signals for researchers the importance of investigating the factor structure of the YSR to confirm the appropriateness of adapting the western assessment tools to report and describe emotional and behavioural development of adolescents in Brunei. The notion of western emotional and behavioural models does not necessarily stand up in eastern cultures. Not all problems then are globalised since acceptable norms are the products of socially and culturally created behaviour within the community under study. Hence, some concerns in one culture may not necessarily be acknowledged as problems in another culture. Ignoring this could create unnecessarily issues of labelling in school which can be stigmatising.

The findings of study also showcase what it means to report a prevalence rate of wellbeing when adopting an assessment tool from a different culture. Depending alone on the predetermined items or factors from the YSR might lack consideration of other relevant factors. Despite the importance of gaining understanding from the internal or personal factor to inform us about Bruneian adolescents' wellbeing, the open-ended questions generated more important themes that were external to them (such as peers, teachers, school and family factors). An external dimension was seen to become a growing concern over time and to interfere with not just adolescents' wellbeing but also their health and academic achievement. Today, the COVID-19 situation has brought everyone together with a similar goal to improve students' health and wellbeing. Through the new norms of socialising processes, schools begin to notice and take measures to ensure cleanliness of the toilets, washing hands and reducing crowded places in school compounds. There is a greater emphasis on wellbeing and acknowledgement of its acceptability as an umbrella term. Researchers need to take care when drawing findings pertaining to another's wellbeing.

References

Achenbach, T. M. (1991). *Manual for the Youth Self-Report and 1991 profile*. University of Vermont, Department of Psychiatry.

Borneo Bulletin. (2011). Retrieved April 10, 2012, from http://www.brudirect.com/index.php/Local-News/mental-health-problems-among-children.html

Buehler, C. (2020). Family processes and children's and adolescents' wellbeing. *Journal of Marriage and Family, 82*, 145–174.

Bukowski, W. M., Laursen, B., & Hoza, B. (2010). The snowball effect: Friendship moderates over-time escalations in depressed affect among avoidant and excluded children. *Development and Psychopathology, 22*, 751–759.

Chen, X., Chung, J., Lechcier-Kimel, R., & French, D. (2011). In P. Smith & C. Hart (Eds.), *Wiley Blackwell handbook of childhood social development* (2nd ed., pp. 141–160). Wiley-Blackwell.

Chen, X., Rubin, K. H., & Li, B. (1995). Depressed mood in Chinese children: Relations with school performance and family environment. *Journal of Consulting and Clinical Psychology, 63*, 938–947.

Chu, C., Thomas, S. D. M., & Ng, V. P. Y. (2009). Childhood abuse and delinquency: A descriptive study of institutionalized female youth in Singapore. *Psychiatry Psychology and Law, 16*(Suppl 1), S64–S73.

Costello, A. B., & Osborne, J. W. (2005). Best practices in exploratory factor analysis: Four recommendations for getting the most from your analysis. *Practical Assessment, Research, & Evaluation, 10*, 1–9.

Cuban, L. (1990). Reforming again, again and again. *Educational Researcher, 19*, 3–13.

Du, Y., Kou, J., & Coghill, D. (2008). The validity, reliability and normative scores of the parent, teacher and self report versions of the Strengths and Difficulties Questionnaire in China. *Child and Adolescent Psychiatry and Mental Health, 2*(1), 8.

Fletcher, A., & Bonell, C. (2013). Social network influences on smoking, drinking and drug use in secondary school: Centrifugal and centripetal forces. *Sociology of Health & Illness, 35*(5), 699–715.

Gage, N. A., Larson, A., Sugai, G., & Chafouleas, S. M. (2016). Student perceptions of school climate as predictors of office discipline referrals. *American Educational Research Journal, 53*, 492–515.

Horton, P., & Forsberg, C. (2020). Safe spaces? A social-ecological perspective on student perceptions of safety in the environment of the school canteen. *Educational Research, 62*(1), 95–100.

Ivanova, M. Y., Achenbach, T. M., Rescorla, L. A., Dumenci, L., Almqrist, F., Bilenberg, N., Bird, H., Broberg, A. G., Dobrean, A., Dopfner, M., Erol, N., Forns, M., Hannesdottir, H., Kanbayashi, Y., Lambert, M. C., Leung, P., Minaei, A., Mulatu, M. S., Novik, T., ... Zukauskiene, R. (2007). The generalizability of the Youth Self-Report syndrome structure in 23 societies. *Journal of Consulting and Clinical Psychology, 75*(50), 729–738.

Khaing, A. M., Ameen, A., & Isaac, O. (2019). Analysis of consumption habit on safety and healthy foods at school' canteens of basic education schools: A qualitative study on factors that influence students' food choice. *International Journal of Management and Human Science, 3*(3), 12–25.

Kuramoto, H., Kanbayashi, Y., Nakata, Y., Fukui, T., Mukai, T., & Negishi, Y. (2002). Standardization of the Japanese version of the Youth Self-Report (YSR). *Japanese Journal of Child and Adolescent Psychiatry, 43*, 17–32.

Lambert, C., Essau, C. A., Schmitt, N., Samms-Vaughan, M., & E. (2007). Dimensionality and psychometric invariance of the Youth Self-Report form of the child behavior checklist in cross-national settings. *Assessment, 14*, 231.

Layard, R. (2010). Measuring subjective well-being. *Science, 327*, 534–535.

Leung, P. W., Hung, S. F., Ho, T. P., Lee, C. C., Liu, W. S., Tang, C. P., & Kwong, S. L. (2008). Prevalence of DSM-IV disorders in Chinese adolescents and the effects of an impairment criterion: A pilot community study in Hong Kong. *European Child & Adolescent Psychiatry, 17*(7), 452–461.

Leung, P. W., & Wong, M. M. (2003). Measures of child and adolescent psychopathology in Asia. *Psychological Assessment, 15*(3), 268–279.

Linton, M. J., Dieppe, P., & Medina-Lara, A. (2016). Review of 99 self-report measures for assessing well-being in adults: Exploring dimensions of well-being and developments over time. *British Medical Journal Open, 6*(7), e010641.

Mesquita, B., & Walker, R. (2003). Cultural differences in emotions: A context for interpreting emotional experiences. *Behavior Research and Therapy, 41*(7), 777–793.

Nikapota, A. (2009). Cultural issues in child assessment. *Child and Adolescent Mental Health, 14*, 200–206.

O'Keefe, M., Mennen, F., & Lane, C. J. (2006). *The factor structure for the Youth Self Report on a multiethnic population*. Research on social work practice 16,315 OECDiLibrary PISA 2018 results (Volume III): What school life means for students' lives. Retrieved June 11, 2020, from https://www.oecd-ilibrary.org/sites/cd52f-b72en/index.html?itemId=/content/component/cd52fb72-en#fig6

Ollendick, T. H., Yang, B., King, N. J., Dong, Q., & Akande, A. (1996). Fears in American, Australian, Chinese, and Nigerian children and adolescents: A cross-cultural study. *Journal of Child Psychology and Psychiatry, 37*, 213–220.

Petegem, K. V., Creemers, B., Aelterman, A., & Rosseel, Y. (2008). The importance of pre-measurements of wellbeing and achievement for students' current wellbeing. *South African Journal of Education, 28*, 451–468.

Raisanen, A., & Rakkolainen, M. (2009). Social and communicational skills in upper secondary vocational education and training. *US-China Education Review, 6*(12), 36–45.

Rothbaum, F., Pott, M., Azuma, H., Miyake, K., & Weisz, J. (2000). The development of close relationships in Japan and the United States: Paths of symbiotic harmony and generative tension. *Child Development, 71*, 1121–1142.

Saeki, E., Pendergast, L., Segool, N. K., & von der Embse, N. P. (2015). Potential psychosocial and instructional consequences of the common core state standards: Implications for research and practice. *Contemporary School Psychology, 19*(2), 89–97.

Sahlberg, P. (2012). A model lesson: Finland shows us what equal opportunity looks like. *American Educator, 36*(1), 20–27.

Salwina, W., Ruzyanei, N. J., Nurliza, A. M., Irma, A. M., Hafiz, B., Lew, K. X., Rozhan, M. R., & Iryani, T. (2013). Emotional and behavioural problems among adolescent off-springs of mothers with depression. *Malaysian Journal of Medicine and Health Sciences, 9*(2), 35–43.

Sarjala, J. (2013). Equality and cooperation: Finland's path to excellence. *American Educator, 37*(1), 32–36.

Schleicher, A. (2019). *PISA 2018. Insights and interpretations*. Paris: OECD Publishing.

Schleicher, A., & Stewart, V. (2008). Learning from world-class schools. *Educational Leadership, 66*(2), 44–51.

Scott, S., Scott, D. E., & Webber, C. F. (2016). *Assessment in education*. Springer.

Stokes, M., Mellor, D., Yeow, J., & Hapidzal, N. F. M. (2013). Do parents, teachers and children use the SDQ in a similar fashion? *Quality & Quantity, 48*(2).

Sun, J., Dunne, J., Hou, M. P., Xu, X. Y., & Qiang, A. (2013). Educational stress among Chinese adolescents: Individual, family, school and peer influences. *Educational Review, 65*(3), 284–302.

Tavakol, M., & Dennick, R. (2011). Making sense of Cronbach's alpha. *International Journal of medical Education, 2*, 53–55.

Vernon, S. J., Lundblad, B., & Hellstrom, A.-L. (2003). Children's experiences of school toilets present a risk to their physical and psychological health. *Child Care Health and Development, 29*(1), 47–53.

Weisz, J. R., Suwanlert, S., Chaiyasit, W., Weiss, B., Walter, B. R., & Anderson, W. W. (1988). Thai and American perspectives on over- and undercontrolled behavior: Exploring the threshold model among parents, teachers and psychologist. *Journal of Consulting and Clinical Psychology, 56*, 601–609.

Woerner, W., Nuanmanee, S., Becker, A., Wongpiromsam, Y., & Mongkol, A. (2011). Normative data and psychometric properties of the Thai version of the Strengths and Difficulties Questionnaire (SDQ). *Journal of Mental Health of Thailand, 19*(1).

Zajda, J. (2010). *Globalisation, ideology and education policy reforms*. Springer.

Zhang, M., & Kong, L. (2012). An exploration of reasons for Shanghai's success in the OECD Program for International Student Assessment (PISA) 2009. *Frontiers of Education in China, 7*(1), 124–116.

PART III

MIB in Teacher Training, Curriculum, Classroom Practice, and Society

CHAPTER 11

Training MIB Among Teachers in Brunei's Religious Teachers University College

Nazirul Mubin Ahad and Mohammad Hilmy Baihaqy

11.1 Introduction

Brunei Darussalam has adhered to its national philosophy of Malay Islamic Monarchy or *Melayu Islam Beraja* (MIB) for nearly four decades. As mentioned in the earlier chapters of this book, MIB was formally proclaimed by His Majesty the Sultan of Brunei on the 27 Rabi al-Awwal 1404H, corresponding to 1 January 1984, in the Decree of Independence Declaration of Brunei Darussalam:

> Brunei Darussalam and with the permission and grace of Allah *Subhanahu wa Ta'ala* will forever remain a Malay Islamic Monarchy State, an indepen-

N. M. Ahad (✉)
Seri Begawan Religious Teachers University College,
Bandar Seri Begawan, Brunei

M. H. Baihaqy
Universiti Islam Sultan Sharif Ali (UNISSA),
Bandar Seri Begawan, Brunei
e-mail: hilmy.yussof@unissa.edu.bn

© The Author(s), under exclusive license to Springer Nature Switzerland AG 2021
Phan, L. H. et al. (eds.), *Globalisation, Education, and Reform in Brunei Darussalam*, International and Development Education, https://doi.org/10.1007/978-3-030-77119-5_11

dent, sovereign and democratic, holding on to the teachings of Islam according to *Ahlus Sunnah wal Jama'ah*. (The Collection of His Majesty's *Titah* Year 1984 and 1985, 2017)

The Malay Islamic Monarchy philosophy is the driving force behind the practices and policies of the nation (see Chap. 3). The Declaration reflects the intention of His Majesty the Sultan that the nation should be a Malay, Islamic, Monarchy State and that this vision should be upheld by all Bruneians. The MIB identity includes race, language, sciences, economics, self-esteem, attitude and vision for the future. Without MIB values, the system of administration, trust and principle would be undermined.

Many have contributed to the understanding of MIB in local intellectual circles, such as senior government officials who are known as the 'establishment intellectuals' (Wahsalfelah, 2016) and those among the ordinary people such as teachers or 'public intellectuals'. Teachers play a vital role in the portrayal and spread of MIB values to the nation and to instil a sense of appreciation for MIB among their students. Teachers are seen as role models for students, so it is important for them to adopt and demonstrate a noble personality in accordance with the values of the Malay Islamic Monarchy philosophy.

This highlights the importance of teaching MIB as a subject in school, and for prospective teachers to practise these values to become the next generation of connectors with the mould of MIB identity (see Chap. 5). Although the education system in Brunei is bilingual, the use of English should not detract one's identity. English is the language of knowledge and international relations, but each teacher should have a sound knowledge of the Malay language and the culture of Brunei.

11.2 Teacher Training and Education in Brunei Darussalam

Pillai (2012) stresses the importance of a teacher education programme inculcating good manners, the avoidance of excessive control, the proper use of pedagogical aids and high morale. Such programmes can enrich the educators with teaching arts, pedagogy, techniques, tricks, tips, methods, processes and procedures of teaching. Without this training, most would have no acquaintance with basic psychology nor would they be conversant with the art of teaching. Teachers must have the patience to deal with underachievers or students constantly creating trouble. Consequently, a teacher's productivity is viewed as their contribution to student achievement, holding other inputs constant. To measure the impact of education and training on teacher productivity, it is necessary to first develop a model of student achievement (Harris & Sass, 2006). This is the most commonly used method of research to determine the effectiveness of a particular educational method.

The first school was built in Bandar Seri Begawan, Brunei, during the British Protectorate in 1914 (see Chap. 2). This was followed by two more schools built in Tutong and Kuala Belait in 1918. However, teacher education development lagged behind school development. Initially, English-medium schools were staffed entirely by expatriate teachers whilst teachers in Malay vernacular schools were all untrained (Loo, 2019). This continued until a British initiative to train local people to undergo training started in the 1930s and teachers were sent overseas for college training. In the 1930s, three teachers were sent to Sultan Idris Teachers College in Tanjong Malim, Perak, to receive their teacher training. Later in 1946, the first batch of female teachers was sent to Durian Daun Women Teachers College, Malacca.

Subsequently, students were trained to be teachers in the Malaysian States such as Kelantan, Sabah and Sarawak. Meanwhile, teachers from Malaysia were recruited to serve in Brunei Darussalam, to educate not only students but also the local teachers. By 1956, the first teacher training college, Brunei Teachers Training Center (BTTC), was established in a temporary campus at the Sultan Omar Ali Saifuddien College in Brunei Town. The BTTC then moved to a permanent building in Berakas and was renamed as the Brunei Malay Teachers College (BMTC). The teaching staff were Singaporeans and Malaysians until the first local teacher was appointed in 1960. In addition, a bilingual education system was introduced in 1985 to replace the Malay language as the sole medium of instruction (see Chap. 2).

In the field of Islamic studies, religious teachers were sent abroad to attend training courses such as al-Azhar University in Egypt. The Seri Begawan Teachers College (SBTC) was established in 1972 to cater for the growing need for teachers to teach religious subjects in schools. The college opened with its first intake of 30 students and it offered a three-year course to qualify as a trained teacher. This is where potential teachers have been educated in both secular and religious learning that includes a range of subjects including teaching sciences. In 2007, the college was upgraded to a university college and was renamed as Seri Begawan

Religious Teachers University College or *Kolej Universiti Perguruan Ugama Seri Begawan* (KUPU SB). Apart from KUPU SB, Sultan Omar Ali Saifuddien Centre for Islamic Studies (SOASCIS), which is part of Universiti Brunei Darussalam (UBD), and Universiti Islam Sultan Sharif Ali (UNISSA) also offer Islamic studies, although there is no specific module in the field of education as at KUPU SB (see Chaps. 2 and 5).

To date, there are two types of teacher training in Brunei Darussalam: Sultan Hassanal Bolkiah Institute of Education (SHBIE) and KUPU SB. SHBIE focuses on 'worldly' academics whereas KUPU SB emphasises on the 'afterworld' path for Islamic religious teachers. The existence of these institutions is very significant in producing future teachers who will serve the needs of the nation. Both institutes offer certificate, diploma, first degree and postgraduate certificate levels (MTeach, MEd and PhD) to both local and foreign students.

11.3 The MIB Curriculum in Teacher Training

MIB is one of the core subjects in teacher training in KUPU SB. The goal is for students to learn, understand and respect the culture and to raise awareness among prospective teachers.

KUPU SB is one of the higher learning institutions that emphasises the value of MIB in everyday life by allowing the students to practise these values such as respect and having a strong commitment to religious orders by doing congregational prayers. There is also a weekly gathering called the MIB *sahsiah* (identity) held every Monday morning. Also, MIB is a compulsory module for the students in the university and each week the lecture will be delivered by different presenters who are government officials (Panduan Kursus Negara Zikir Melayu Islam Beraja). These efforts aim to preserve MIB within students who are trained to become educators and to give future educators a true understanding of the definition of MIB as there has been a lack of understanding of the concepts among some student teachers. This could result in more confusion among school students if they are not taught properly. Therefore, it is important to learn MIB from the government's understanding as it is reflected in the precepts of His Majesty Paduka Seri Baginda Sultan Haji Hassanal Bolkiah, Sultan and Yang Di-Pertuan of Brunei Darussalam through several series of his *titah* (royal decree) (see Chap. 4).

As the national philosophy, this concept should be understood and appreciated by all segments of society. However, reaching all the target groups is not an easy task. Consequently, the education system has emphasised the teaching and learning of MIB at all levels, from the Primary school level to higher education since the 1990s. The syllabus of MIB is designed to suit the level and psychological development of students and to ensure students develop a strong awareness of the concept. As such, teacher training students are given several tasks and assignments in addition to attending lectures to explore MIB which they are required to fulfil to graduate.

11.4 The Importance of Preserving MIB in Seri Begawan Religious Teacher University College (KUPU SB)

In KUPU SB, the MIB course is conducted three hours a week consisting of two hours' seminar sessions and an hour *halaqah* (tutorial) session.

(1) **Seminar Session**

   a. Seminars will be presented by a lecturer in the selected subject.
   b. The students are required to make important notes for report and discussion session.
   c. The students are encouraged to deliver comments, suggestions or questions after the seminar.

(2) **Halaqah Session**

   a. The students will be divided into several groups based on their course namely PhD, SPU (Masters Students), DPULI (Postgraduate Certificate of Education Students), SMPU (Degree Students) and DTPU (Higher National Diploma Students).
   b. Each student will present their selected subject. Others are required to record important information for the discussion session after the presentation.
   c. A total of 14 essay topics based on 14 weeks of training will be presented.

In addition to seminars and *halaqahs*, the students will undergo practicals and simulations of MIB manners followed by a workshop on MIB values and ethics. Subsequently, the MIB practical training and simulation will be conducted according to the topics provided. Through the simulation, all trainees will practise the MIB manners and values in the session. During the simulation, the practical will be evaluated for inclusion in the coursework scoring. Among other tasks that need to be completed are the preparation of MIB essays and videos. It can be concluded that the approaches used in the teaching of MIB at KUPU SB are as follows:

1. Seminars
2. Lectures
3. Halaqah (Tutorial)
4. Stories
5. Dialogue
6. Practice
7. Simulation
8. Practical

All of these are integrational aspects with the purpose for the trainees to maximise their level of MIB understanding. The integrated values are as follows:

1. MIB values and manners
2. The Vision of 2035 (*Wawasan* 2035)
3. Professional Attitude and Teacher Competence
4. Trainee Teacher experience
5. Current issues related to Brunei's social, political, religious, educational and economic issues

The trainings are very focused on preparing future teachers for their life as educators, while guiding students on the value of MIB. Among the importance of this MIB in the Teacher Training Education (TTE) is its focus on the following:

1. The background of the *Negara Zikir* (Zikir Nation), MIB, the history of MIB, the concepts and values of MIB as the Philosophy of Brunei Darussalam.
2. Implementation of MIB as a way of life in leadership, administration, education, law, customs and public life.
3. MIB values and manners in the culture and life of Brunei Darussalam.
4. MIB education in educational institutions.

5. Issues, challenges and role of religious teachers in strengthening and upholding MIBs as a National Philosophy.
6. The identity of MIB and *Negara Zikir* among the trainee teachers as future educators in the community.

With a well-organised and comprehensive compulsory core module set up by the university, the future generation of teachers will be able to express the values of MIB in everyday life.

11.5 The Importance of Highlighting Islamic Values in MIB

Islam is considered the core value in the MIB philosophy. According to the papers of the National Supreme Council of the Malay Monarchy, Islam is

> the official religion of the nation which is, according to *aqidah Ahli Sunnah Waljama'ah* and the *Syafi'e* sect, a complete, perfect and ideal lifestyle. (Serudin, 2013, p. 62)

The above statement not only accepts Islam as the official religion enshrined in the Constitution of Brunei Darussalam, but it is also a way of life of the Malay Bruneians that are rich in Islamic values. Thus, it is highly critical to highlight Islamic values in the MIB curriculum at all levels including at the TTE institution.

In an effort to strengthen the MIB Curriculum at all level, it is also important to strengthen the curriculum with the pillars of Islam that have become the dominant policy in the MIB philosophy. As written in the 1959 Constitution, the official religion of Islam is in accordance to *Ahl as-Sunnah Wa al-Jama'ah* and the *Syafi'e* sects as fundamental part of the practice of *fatwa* (a ruling on a point of Islamic law given by a recognised authority) in accordance to the law. *Ahl as-Sunnah Wa al-Jama'ah* referred as the people of the Sunnah and the community, where in matters of creed, their tradition upholds the six pillars of *imān* (faith) and comprises the Ash'ari and Maturidi schools of rationalistic theology as well as the textualist school known as traditionalist theology. In the other, *Syafi'e* sect is one of the four schools of Islamic law in *Ahl as-Sunnah Wa al-Jama'ah*. In advancing this through education in general, it must require the students with high degrees of knowledge to explain the following questions (Serudin, 2013):

1. What is the faith of Islam that distinguishes belief from non-Muslims?
2. What is the meaning of *aqidah Ahl as-Sunnah Wa al-Jama'ah*?
3. What is the *Syafi'e* sect and how it differs from other sect?

The above questions are critical to be emphasised in the curriculum of MIB as a way to strengthen the Islamic values in the curriculum.

11.6 THE STUDY

A qualitative approach (Creswell, 1994) based on interviews and descriptive analysis was used throughout the study in order to reach the research objectives (Lapan et al., 2012). Interviews were held with different people, including a person-to-person conversation between the researcher and the informants in order to collect relevant information for the study. The interview questions were prepared in structured themes and were given to the informants prior to the actual interview. The languages used during the interviews were Malay and English.

The study analyses and describes the characteristics of the population or phenomenon that is being studied (Thyer, 2000). It does not answer questions about how/when/why the characteristics occurred; rather, it addresses the 'what' component. Through readings of various types of sources, consisting of primary and secondary resources, several answers to the research questions could be attained.

Purposive sampling was used with six informants involving the students who took the MIB course during the recent semester. It was a non-probability sample selected based on the characteristics of a population and the objective of the study. Random Sampling was used during the process with the informants chosen based on their different backgrounds and importance in this study as they had taken the MIB course during the last recent semester. They were labelled as Respondent 1, Respondent 2, Respondent 3, Respondent 4, Respondent 5 and Respondent 6. These interviews ended once the information reached saturation to prevent unnecessary information from the respondents.

The primary questions to the respondents were as follows:

1. What are your thoughts and perception of having MIB curriculum in the TTE institution?
2. How effective is the MIB curriculum in TTE institution?

3. What are the problems that you had experienced in taking MIB curriculum in the TTE institution?
4. What are the three (3) important issues that need to be highlighted in the MIB curriculum?
5. What are your thoughts and opinions in advancing MIB curriculum in the TTE institution?

11.7 Thoughts and Perception of Having MIB Curriculum in TTE Institution

From the interview, all respondents agreed that MIB should be conserved and sustained in the TTE curriculum. Respondent 1 claimed that MIB must be conserved in the TTE curriculum as it is an integral part of the Bruneian identity and it is beneficial in constituting Brunei history. Respondent 1 added that learning MIB is also about learning the *adab* (courtesy), which comprises ethics and values of respecting the elderly and teachers. This was also highlighted by other respondents except Respondent 3.

Respondent 2 stated that apart from learning the history of Brunei and *adab*, which matures the identity of the students, it also teaches them to be a good future leader of the country who prioritises Islamic teachings and values. Respondents 3 and 4 claimed that MIB is important to develop the self-discipline of the students and to enhance the communication skills with the community especially with the royal families and those who are endowed with titles or ranks such as '*Pengiran*' and '*Pehin*'. Respondent 4 also mentioned the importance of learning the customs and cultures as well as traditional Malay foods which were seldom obtained from the public markets.

Respondent 5 stated that it is critical for future teachers to know more about MIB. It is also a fundamental subject to instil the MIB core values among the students who will become future teachers. Respondent 6 added that the MIB subject should be offered in TTE because some students were not offered MIB subject during their two years' pre-university studies, and if it were offered, the respondent feels it would be inadequate. Furthermore, Respondent 6 claimed that the future teachers will forget about the importance of understanding and practising the values and philosophy of MIB if MIB was excluded from TTE.

11.8 The Effectiveness of the MIB Curriculum in TTE Institution

Generally, the respondents noted that the effectiveness of MIB curriculum is dependent on the interest of the students. Three respondents said that the MIB course offered was not effective for them because the subject focuses more on the history of Brunei without any relation to the current context and issues faced by the people and the youth of the country. Respondent 3 mentioned that the effectiveness of the MIB course depends on the students. If the students actively participate during the discussion in lectures and tutorials, the effectiveness of the MIB course would be noticeable. In addition, Respondent 4 stated that the course is not effective because students did not pay attention during the lecture and some were sleepy. Moreover, the respondent reported that some of the students do not have any determination to recall the topic discussed during the lecture unless they are given assignments.

In contrast, Respondent 5 found the MIB course to be effective as there were several invited speakers who were well-versed in their respective areas to deliver the MIB lecture. The invited speakers were among the country's important public figures such as historians and ministers. This could add interest for the students as they can learn from the valuable experiences shared by the speakers. According to Respondent 6, the effectiveness of the MIB course relates closely to the students' awareness and interest. The course was effective because the lecture successfully instilled important values in the students such as showing respect while communicating with the teachers. However, it is still dependent on the awareness of the individual students. Respondent 6 also noticed that the lecture would be ineffective if the lecturer was just reading the slides. Thus, it is important for the lecturer to interact regularly with the students during the lecture as to capture the attentiveness of the students.

When the researcher asked the respondents whether the mass lecture or the tutorials were more effective, all six respondents agreed that the latter was more effective in nurturing the understanding of the concepts and applications about the issues that they learned during the lecture.

11.9 Challenges in Taking MIB Curriculum in the TTE Institution

The third research question focused on the issues faced by the students in the TTE institution, which were mainly challenges in advancing the development of the MIB course in TTE institution. According to the first respondent, some lecturers showed less interaction during the lecture. Students need regular interaction in order for them to follow the flow of the lecture well and become more attentive during lecture.

The second respondent claimed that some of the topics taught during the mass lecture were mind-numbing as not all students will be interested in the same subject. In addition, students prefer that the lecture topics are relevant to current issues while developing some discussions and interactions with the students. On the other hand, according to Respondent 3, some of the problems faced during the lecture are technical in nature such as difficulty to find a conducive class as the availability of classes is limited. Respondents 4 and 6 highlighted that the two-hour lectures are more favourable if they were held in the morning rather than in the afternoon because they had observed a number of students not being attentive and falling asleep in the later classes. Also, some lecturers gave a number of presentation slides which will make the lecturer less interactive as they tend to read from the presentation slides. However, Respondent 5 did not state any major challenges during the MIB class as they were preventable and resolvable.

11.10 Important Issues that Need to Be Highlighted in the MIB Curriculum

Respondent 1 claims that the main issue in the MIB curriculum is the local wedding traditions because there are various wedding traditions that exist among the various tribes in Brunei such as the *Melayu Brunei*, *Kedayan*, *Tutong*, *Murut*, *Bisaya*, *Belait* and the *Dusun* tribe. This was also highlighted by Respondents 3, 4 and 6. The two issues according to Respondent 1 is not about the content of the curriculum; instead, the respondent highlighted the two technical issues which could be taken as enriching the MIB curriculum itself such as the educational field trips and a dialogue between the students and the representative of the seven indigenous tribes in Brunei. From this approach, the student would be able to comprehend deeply about the way of living of the tribes.

Respondent 2 stated that the curriculum must relate and compare historical events with the context of the current situations to develop the student's interest on the history of the country. The second and third issues, which were also brought forth by Respondents 4 and 5, are in relation to the traditional games and music that have existed among the various Bruneian tribes.

In addition, Respondent 3 stated that the curriculum should include the many interesting historical places in Brunei that are associated with the various tribes. The respondent also suggested for the students to learn the history of the selected schools and the higher institutions that have contributed to the development of education as well as the country under the leadership of MIB philosophy.

Respondent 4 indicated the importance of having practical activities such as demonstrating how to wear the traditional attires of various tribes. For Respondent 5, highlighting the philosophy of *Negara Zikir* would make the curriculum more interesting apart from learning about the royal customs and traditions such as the royal wedding customs and ways of communicating with the royals. These issues were also highlighted by Respondent 6, in addition to the importance of preserving and discussing the various traditional dance and food of the Bruneian cultures.

11.11 Thoughts and Opinions in Advancing MIB Curriculum in the TTE Institution

One of the critical factors in preserving the philosophy of MIB in TTE institution is to discover the ways of advancing the MIB curriculum itself. The fifth research question aimed to detect the opinions of the students in advancing the MIB curriculum so as to increase students' interest in learning MIB at TTE institution. Respondent 1 suggested to include educational visits during the MIB course.

Apart from that, TTE students in general would be interested to learn if there are practical activities and demonstrations on how to wear traditional customs among various tribes in Brunei and the ways to prepare traditional Bruneian foods. All respondents agreed that the educational visits to certain historical places would advance the MIB course at TTE. Respondent 5 added that it would be better for the students to have educational visits to '*Batu Tarsilah*' (Historic Tablet) to develop their awareness on *Jawi* handwritings. The tablet is a historical artefact which has *Jawi* engravings of the genealogy of the first king of Brunei who embraced Islam in the Year 1368 AD, Awang Alak Betatar (see Chap. 2), until Sultan Muhammad Tajuddin, the 19th Sultan of Brunei who reigned between 1795 and 1807 AD. Studies have shown that students who go on field trips become more empathetic and tolerant which could develop their socio-emotional growth (Kennedy, 2004). Therefore, by having some educational trips, students could enjoy the learning experience throughout the MIB course.

11.12 Conclusion and Recommendations

From the observations made above, one of the ways to preserve the philosophy of MIB among the teachers is to make the MIB course a compulsory course in the TTE institution. For KUPU SB, The Centre for Core Knowledge or *Pusat Ilmu Teras* plays an important role in offering MIB course to the students at KUPU SB, as the only religious teachers training education institution in Brunei. They are also responsible for reviewing the curriculum based on the social and current needs as shown on by the respondents above. Nevertheless, there are several challenges that need to be considered such as the pedagogical issues, the content of the curriculum and the technical issues related to the learning environments. For the pedagogical issues, the respondents stated that regular interactions between the lecturers and the students during the mass lecture would increase students' attention and interest. Almost all respondents agreed that having educational visits to historical places would improve students' learning experience as well as their interest as they could discover for themselves the evidence and facts that they have learned from the mass lectures. From the responses given, students prefer to have dialogue, as well as practical sessions on wearing the traditional costumes of the Bruneian tribes.

In terms of the content of the curriculum, the respondents have explained that there are several issues that need to be highlighted and readdressed. There are issues about highlighting the development of *Negara Zikir*, understanding deeply the wedding cultures, studying traditional music as well as the traditional foods of the Bruneian tribes, apart from analysing the Islamic views on each aspect. The learning environment is also found to be one of the critical aspects of advancing the MIB curriculum. On the timing of the lectures, all respondents agreed that the morning two hours' mass lecture is more efficient compared to the afternoon session. Apart from that, the facilities provided during the lecture and the tutorials have made a positive impact on students' learning interest.

From the above study, there are some recommendations for advancing the MIB curriculum in TTE. Firstly, educational visits should be included during the MIB course. Apart from that, active interactions between the lecturers and the students during the mass lecture would increase student's attentiveness. Furthermore, from the study conducted, there is a need to review the content of the curriculum to improve its relevance to current issues and contexts. Through these efforts, the researchers believe that the MIB course could be preserved, sustained and developed.

References

Creswell, J. W. (1994). *Research design: Qualitative & quantitative approaches.* Sage Publication.

Harris, D. N., & Sass, T. R. (2006). *The effects of teacher training on teacher value-added.* Florida State University.

Kennedy, M. D. (2004). *The benefit of field trips* [University Honours Program Thesis]. Georgia Southern University. https://digitalcommons.georgiasouthern.edu/honors-theses/60

Lapan, S. D., Quartaroli, M. T., & Riemer, F. J. (Eds.). (2012). *Qualitative research: An introduction to methods and designs.* Jossey-Bass.

Loo, S. P. (2019). Teacher training in Brunei Darussalam. In K. G. Karras & C. C. Wolhuter (Eds.), *International handbook of teacher education world-wide: Issues and challenges* (Vol. I & II, pp. 99–116). Athens-Atrapos Editions 2010.ab.

Panduan kursus negara Zikir Melayu Islam Beraja [Course guideline]. (2018). Fundamental Knowledge Centre, Seri Begawan Religious Teacher University College.

Pillai, D. S. (2012). *The importance of teacher training in professional colleges.* ICPOE 2012. Volume: ISBN 97881 89843 496.

Serudin, Z. (2013). *The Malay Islamic Monarchy: A closer understanding.* National Supreme Council of the Malay Islamic Monarchy Brunei Darussalam.

Thyer, B. (Ed.). (2000). *The handbook of social work research methods* (2nd ed.). Florida State University.

Titah Kebawah Duli Yang Maha Mulia Paduka Seri Baginda Sultan Haji Hassanal Bolkiah Mu'izzaddin Waddaulah, Sultan dan Yang Di-Pertuan Negara Brunei Darussalam Tahun 1984, 1985. (The Collection of His Majesty's Titah, Year 1984, 1985). (2017). Unit Penerbitan Melayu, Bahagian Penerbitan dan Seni Grafik, Jabatan Penerangan, Jabatan Perdana Menteri Negara Brunei Darussalam.

Wahsalfelah, S. N. K. (2016). Peranan golongan intelektual Brunei dalam konsep Melayu Islam Beraja. In *Brunei merdeka—Kumpulan artikel sempena memperingati sambutan 30 tahun hari kebangsaan Negara Brunei Darussalam* (pp. 183–198). Yayasan Sultan Haji Hassanal Bolkiah.

CHAPTER 12

Internalisation Strategies of the Malay Islamic Monarchy Philosophy in Year 7 Curriculum in Brunei Darussalam

Abu Bakar Madin, Rozaiman Makmun, Suraya Tarasat, Noradinah Jaidi, Sri Kartika A. Rahman, and Najib Noorashid

12.1 Introduction

Undoubtedly, globalisation contributes to interconnected info-technology, communication and mobility, internationalisation opportunities, and the greater diffusion and assimilation of different cultures and lifestyles across the world. However, it is also inevitable that excessive acceptance towards 'a global village' may expose the prevalence of social problems within a

---

A. B. Madin (✉) • R. Makmun • S. Tarasat • N. Jaidi • S. K. A. Rahman
N. Noorashid
Universiti Brunei Darussalam, Bandar Seri Begawan, Brunei
e-mail: bakar.madin@ubd.edu.bn; rozaiman.makmun@ubd.edu.bn; suraya.tarasat@ubd.edu.bn; noradinah.jaidi@ubd.edu.bn; kartika.rahman@ubd.edu.bn; najib.noorashid@ubd.edu.bn

© The Author(s), under exclusive license to Springer Nature Switzerland AG 2021
Phan, L. H. et al. (eds.), *Globalisation, Education, and Reform in Brunei Darussalam*, International and Development Education, https://doi.org/10.1007/978-3-030-77119-5_12

society, especially when local norms and traditions have become common value and practices among the people. In this respect, Tamuri and Abdul Razak (2004) describes social problems as a deviating way of life opposing the common value of people in a society. The diffusion of social problems amid globalisation has consistently raised a wide-ranging debate on how to understand and to appreciate the notion and practice of manner, morality, nobility and common values among the younger generation, such as school students. Other studies have found a decline of morality and social value which are strongly correlated with the increase of youth problems (Abd Rahim & Hashim, 2005; Engku Alwi, 2009; Haji Othman et al., 2013).

Brunei Darussalam (henceforth Brunei) have also seen such problems. In 2014, the Brunei's Centre for Strategic and Policy Studies and Universiti Brunei Darussalam conducted a national survey involving 2868 youth respondents (of age 15 to 26 years old) in the Sultanate, and identified nine major categories of social problems including truancy, violence and public disorder, drugs abuse and trafficking, vandalism, theft, sexual deviation, personal safety, bullying and exploitation, and financial hardship (Centre for Strategic and Policy Studies, 2014). Meanwhile, in 2017, Brunei also recorded a high rate of truancy and social problems involving its adolescents among other ASEAN countries (Pengpid & Peltzer, 2017). Similar social problems involving the youth in Brunei has raised awareness on strategies to overcome these national issues (Pelita Brunei, 2015). The statistics were alarming as Brunei is also known as the Abode of Peace and the state has upheld its national philosophy and practical ideology of *Melayu Islam Beraja* (also known as Malay Islamic Monarchy, henceforth MIB). Although the spread of social problems in the country may not be linked directly to education, there are still debates on the efficacy of the MIB curriculum to help inculcate moral values to the younger generation.

12.2 MIB AND NATIONAL EDUCATION IN BRUNEI

As the national philosophy of the country, Bruneians have accepted MIB as the ideal and comprehensive way of life, which includes upholding the Malay language, embracing Islam and showing obedience towards monarchical institution, customs and laws in the Sultanate (Haji Mail et al., 2019). This also includes embracing Islamic spiritual and human values, cultural communal life of a Bruneian and the traditional administration of Brunei Law Code, Islamic law and principles, royal customs and traditions and traditional code of conduct (Haji Serudin, 2013).

One of the most effective strategies to internalise morality and common values adhering to MIB is through education. This is postulated in one of the aims of the National Education System of Brunei Darussalam since 1984. As explained in previous chapters of this book, MIB was established as a subject in the national curriculum since 1992, starting from the early education of Year 1 until 6 in the primary level and continue to Year 7 until 11 in the secondary level. After the reformation of the National Education System for the 21st Century (also known as SPN21) in 2012, MIB has become a core subject for various levels of education in the country, explicating the importance of the subject in the curriculum and the national development. MIB is also offered as a core module at the university level and is compulsory for all students. In line with the introduction of SPN21, the MIB curriculum is further improved in accordance to the needs of the country and to meet the challenges of the new millennium. Hence, the content of the latest curriculum is more emphasised on the development of students' personality (Brunei Curriculum Development Department, 2010).

Looking into the Year 7 MIB curriculum, the content of the Year 7 textbook entitled *Negaraku Brunei Tercinta* (My Beloved Country, Brunei) was developed by the Curriculum Development Department (CDD) at the Brunei's Ministry of Education (MoE), and published by Star Publishing Pte Ltd, Singapore. According to the Director of the CDD, the aim of the new textbook is to align its content with the latest reformation of the MIB curriculum in SPN21. Whilst the development of the new textbook also implies that MIB is not a static subject, it still aims to inculcate morality and Bruneian values as part of everyday practices. The textbook was first introduced in 2011 and used as part of MIB curriculum nationwide since 2012. The Year 7 MIB textbook is also complemented with an activity book.

Although studies have shown the importance of the MIB curriculum for human and national development in Brunei, and for internalising morality and social values through education, not many have investigated the process of deliverance and internalisation, especially using the textbook as part of a pedagogical approach. Most studies in respect of MIB education tend to review the historical development of the curriculum (Abu Bakar, 1997; Abdul Latif, 2003; Haji Mail, 2013; Makmun et al., 2019) and the attitudes of students towards the curriculum (Haji Omar, 2016; Hj Tassim, 2019).

This chapter thus attempts to fill in this research gap by providing a content analysis of the Year 7 MIB textbook, including incorporated implicit and explicit aspects of morality and social values, and internalisation strategies implemented in the latest reformed Year 7 MIB textbook used in secondary schools in Brunei. However, this chapter will exclude the analysis of the Year 7 MIB activity book.

The focus on the Year 7 curriculum is significant as it deals with students in their adolescence (between the age of 11 to 13), which is also the critical transitioning period from childhood to adulthood. At the adolescent stage, these students are exposed to risk-taking, high exploration, novelty and sensation seeking, social interaction, and playful behaviours that will stimulate acquisition of maturity and independence, while developing knowledge, skills and character-building (Spear, 2000). Whilst more likely to be exposed to negative behaviours at this age (Sarah et al., 2013; Spear, 2000), the adolescence period is also the crucial stage where inculcation of morality and social values will be mostly adapted by this demographic, thus, raising the importance of investigating internalisation strategies in the Year 7 MIB textbook. Year 7 also marks the first stage of secondary school in Brunei.

This study also draws its significance from its timely relevance due to reports on the lack of disciplinary actions and immorality among school students and the youth in the country amid the expected success of the MIB curriculum to meet these challenges since 1991. This study is also in line with the requirement of the educational objectives of MIB, which among others is to cultivate more understanding towards moral values, particularly involving the qualities of being Bruneian (Brunei Curriculum Development Department, 2010). Thus, the findings in this chapter are expected to produce pedagogical implications and recommendations that can be utilised by various academic stakeholders, including educators, students, school managers and the public.

12.3 Content Analysis of Year 7 MIB Textbook

From the content analysis of the textbook (see Table 12.1), there are three major sections based on three themes in the Year 7 MIB curriculum: (1) responsibility towards oneself; (2) responsibility for family, neighbours and community; and (3) responsibility towards the country and the environment.

Each theme is divided into several topics. Theme 1 consists of three topics on self-care and responsibilities pertaining to healthy life practices, Theme 2 consists of two topics focusing on doing charity and goodwill, while Theme 3 consists of three topics which are submission to the monarch, preserving national treasures and artefacts, and protecting the environment. Each theme is highlighted with morality and social values, whether they are described explicitly or/and infused implicitly, which is aimed to raise students' awareness on social issues.

In the textbook, each topic consists of a number of sequential segments: (1) reading text of various genres, (2) a 'Knowledge Info' section which intends to provide additional information and increase students' awareness on contemporary issues, (3) a 'Word Meaning' section which enlists important words and their synonyms, (4) a list of 'Commendable Values' highlighted in the topic, and is ended with (5) a 'Think and Discuss' section comprising of comprehension exercises. Each topic has colourful illustrations, both drawings and real-life photos, that serve to support the content of the topic. At the end of each theme, one practical activity and a collaborative project are included to further reinforce moral values among students.

It is apparent that the development of the textbook is to support the MIB philosophy by incorporating moral education that emphasises on commendable social values to students at the secondary school level. This can be seen from the consistent infusion of contexts involving adolescents or secondary school students, which makes the content relatable to the demographic audience (secondary school students). Arguably, the book only contains traits of morality and social values which are exclusive to Bruneians and MIB, but these common noble characteristics can be shared with other cultures and traditions across the globe. Moreover, the textbook has an obvious and strong infusion of Islamic principles that influence the notion of obedience towards the Monarchy and the traditional Brunei Malay aspects. This can also be seen on how the textbook consistently contextualises different situations or issues pertaining to Brunei settings and being Bruneian. Thus, it can be concluded that the content development in the Year 7 MIB textbook is solely to support character and nation building, focusing on aspects of moral education adhering to MIB concepts, which supports the claim that MIB is constantly programmed as part of nation building through education system (Haji Serudin, 2013, p. 47). Moreover, this can be inferred by the introduction of a new Social Studies curriculum in Brunei education for primary and secondary level of

Table 12.1 Content analysis of year 7 MIB textbook

Theme 1		
Theme	Topic	Subtopic
Theme 1 Responsibility to oneself	Practice healthy lifestyles	Benefits of being courteous
		Knowledge info: Loyal and obedience Practice clean attitudes
		Knowledge info: Clean thought
		Practice of supplication
		Knowledge info: Manners and benefits of supplication
	Self-reliance	Ability to self-manage
		Knowledge info: Reward of studying
	Honest	Fostering trust
		Knowledge info: Manners and benefits of being honest

Morality and social values based on contents	Notes
Reading text explains the values of politeness and describes polite characteristics such as honesty, sincerity, good behaviour and avoid acting violent, abide by laws and regulations, and wear decent clothing as a student. This unit also shows the adaptation of outfits of every Brunei indigenous group to the decency of MIB. Reading text describes that the value of loyalty and obedience is one of the most commendable values in Islam. Reading text explains the necessity of practising clean attitudes at work. This is to avoid chaos, argument, breach of trust, corruption unfair treatment. This is further reinforced with righteous attitudes of the head class in school. Other explicit examples given are being careful and meticulous related to being responsible in completing duties impeccably and carefully. The info section explicitly mentions the importance of having clean thought and the benefits gain from the community and oneself. This includes being honest, be courteous and avoid conflicts with people. A narrative about a student who is admitted to a hospital accompanied by a good friend who advises him to be patient, and always pray to Allah Subhanahu WaTaala (the Divine Power) to ease his discomfort. This account implicitly teaches the readers to be amicable and supportive when somebody else is in difficult situation, while practising supplication wholeheartedly. Reading text explains the proper manners and steps in supplication, and its benefits from Islamic perspective. The text also shows the importance of supplication for the Muslims. The text is also accompanied with a website address to increase accessibility of knowledge on the importance of supplication. Reading text explains the importance and purpose of self-care, the traits of self-reliant people, the benefits of studying diligently and making plan to carry out tasks efficiently. A creative work of poem is incorporated to allude the benefits of studying diligently. The poem implicitly tells that a diligent student will be rewarded with bright future, will become an intelligent individual and will be respected by many. Reading text describes the value of honesty associated with fostering a sense of trust between mankind. Honesty should be practised in speech and behaviour for the betterment of oneself and the community. The text also suggests several bad implications to those who are not trustable. The value of practising sincerity, honesty, trustworthy and obedience is emphasised through a *Hadith* by Prophet Muhammad and a *titah* (royal decree) by His Majesty the Sultan of Brunei. Both accounts also explicitly mention the punishment of dishonesty and breach of trust in this life and hereafter.	• Total number of illustrations related to topics are 30 images, including painting and real-life photos. • Total number of pages for theme 1 is 36 pages.

Theme 2

Theme	Topic	Subtopic
Theme 2: Responsibilities to the family, neighbour and society.	Practise courtesy	Family (Parents, siblings, relatives)
		Knowledge info: Consequence of not respecting family and community
		Neighbours and community
		Knowledge info: Noble characters
	Participation in good and bad times, and worshipping places	Respect the mosques
		Blissful and mourning ceremonies
		Knowledge info: Life and death as Allah Subhanahu WaTaala's will

Morality and social values based on contents	*Notes*
Reading text details proper manners to respect parents, siblings and relatives, as well as maintaining a family's good name in a society. The text also explicitly lists out many positive traits that ought to be embraced by a good son/daughter, as it also describes worldly and hereafter retribution for those immoral ones. Reading text explains the consequences of disrespecting parents through Islamic perspective. This is bolstered by a Quranic verse that encourages the practice of being kind towards one another and forbid disrespectful behaviours. A narrative about three school students practising healthy socialisation and activities such as participating a football competition organised by their school. In this account, it implicitly encourages the readers to fill in their free time with meaningful activities. This is accompanied by an advisory poem on the values of comradeship, tolerance and respectful in society and in a nation. This section shows a *Hadith* by Prophet Muhammad and its interpretation detailing about coveted honourable characters that are attributes of heaven residents. These are further cemented by detailing the exemplary qualities of Prophet Muhammad that should be emulated by others. The section is also closed with advices to reflect oneself continuously and practice nobility. Reading text explains the definition of mosque, steps of respecting mosque as a worship place, maintaining the cleanliness of mosque and manners entering mosque. These are also contextualised in the setting of Brunei where the mosques are occupied not just for worshipping, but also to celebrate Islamic and national events, and tourist attraction, thus detailing the significance of taking care of them. Reading text details about thanksgiving and funeral, through Islamic perspectives and practices, representing blissful and mourning events, respectively. The text clarifies proper manners, clothing and etiquette while attending thanksgiving and funeral to ensure the harmonious functionality and comradeship as a Brunei-Muslim society. Reading text explains that every living creature, including humans, animals and plants will perish. All are upon provisions of Allah Subhanahu WaTaala. Even when the text explicitly states that remembering death is encouraged in Islam, it simultaneously implies that nothing is eternal, but the Divine Power. The excerpt also lists out four necessary steps when preparing a Muslim's funeral.	• Total number of illustrations related to topics are 20 images, including painting and real-life photos. • Total number of pages for theme 2 is 26 pages.

Theme 3

Theme	Topic	Subtopic
Theme 3: Responsibilities to the country and the environment	Loyal to the king	Loyal to the king
		Knowledge info: Obedience to the king
		Benefits of obeying law and regulations
		Knowledge info: Living as a commanded citizen
		Disadvantages of loitering culture, smoking, drug abuse and promiscuity
		Knowledge info: Anti-corruption education
	Nurturing treasures and national heritage	Bruneian traditional musical instruments
		Knowledge info: Decree 1997
		Bruneian Malay traditional songs
		Knowledge info: Playing *gambus*
	Loving the environment	Sustaining greenery
		Knowledge info: Keeping the environment clean

Morality and social values based on contents	Notes
Poetry '*Rajaku Payung Negara*' (My King, The Nation Ruler) showcases the success of the Sultanate due to the caring nature of the King to his people and their wellbeing. The poem is used to highlight the wisdom and the virtuousness of the Monarch to attract the readers embracing the Monarch in the process. Reading text explains the necessity of obedience to the King through Islamic perspectives. The text also details that the notion of obedience to the King is to embrace every order and the Monarch affairs as part of nationalism spirit. Reading text explains the significance and the benefits of complying with the national law and regulations, and further details several examples of illegal actions. The text also includes a list of warnings and punishments for those who do not abide by the law and regulations imposed by the government. Reading text, an excerpt from the website of Ministry of Religious Affairs, highlights the commanded way of life for every Bruneian citizen. The text, based on the 27th anniversary of National Day in 2011, calls upon the people of Brunei to continue instilling and practising the sense of obedience towards the Monarch, the national government, law and regulations, and its national philosophy among others. This section incorporates an oratory speech highlighting the disadvantages of committing prohibited activities in Brunei, including truancy, loitering, smoking, drug abuse and promiscuous activities, which among others due to the lack of Islamic guidance and education among the youth. The text also calls upon the youth to abide by Islamic principles, the law and regulations and wisdom thinking and advices and never succumb to worldly pleasures. Reading text class upon the necessity to avoid committing bribery and support anti-corruption, and further exemplifies the negative impacts of corruption to community and the nation. Reading text describes the use, the purpose of Bruneian traditional musical instruments and the necessity to maintain them as part of national and ethnic heritage. The text also encourages Bruneians to be proud of their national artefacts and preserve them. Extract from His Majesty the Sultan of Brunei's *titah* on the obligation for every Bruneian to uphold purity in Islam, the essence of Malay culture, customs and national unity. Reading text lists out original traditional Bruneian Malay songs for children and adults. The text briefly describes the use and the symbolism of these songs as part of introducing and upholding Bruneian culture and traditions. Reading text which features the experience of a local man who possesses skills of making traditional string musical instruments especially *gambus*. Taken from a local newspapers, the text also aims to implicitly introduce certain cultural practices of local indigenous groups in Brunei to the readers. Reading text describes the importance of taking care of the environment, including public amenities, recreational parks and beaches. The text is also aimed to nurture the sense of responsibility among the readers and galvanising a sense of reflection to unhygienic practices and its consequences to the environment, the society and the nation. Reading text explains the importance of environmental hygiene and certain measures to avoid and overcome sanitary problems. This text also calls upon collaborative efforts from parents to school community, the government and non-government bodies to maintain good environment for collective betterment.	• Total number of illustrations related to topics are 25 images, including painting and real-life photos. • Total number of pages for theme 3 is 34 pages.

education since 2011, which focuses on developing knowledge, skills and values to achieve the Brunei Vision 2035, while the MIB curriculum emphasises on internalising morality and social values to Bruneian students.

Whilst the textbook is aimed to nurture moral and social values which are strongly correlated to Bruneian values, it is also imbued with cause-and-effect teachings to be reflected by the students. Therefore, the textbook is designed not only to become a guideline of morality teaching, but also to encourage its targeted audience to think creatively and critically through series of activities, including reading, reciting, doing exercises and collaborative projects.

12.4 Internalisation Strategies in Year 7 MIB Textbook

Four major internalisation strategies can be identified in the development of moral education and social values in the textbook, which are channelled through approaches of modelling, integration, multimodal and reinforcement.

12.4.1 Modelling

Modelling is an internalisation strategy implemented through displaying exemplary form of behaviours, particularly through worshipping and instilling morality (Nata, 2001). Modelling is claimed to be the most effective method in shaping morality, social and spiritual values among young adults (Anam et al., 2019; Pratiwi, 2018). In the Year 7 MIB textbook, modelling is predominantly used in two ways: one is channelled explicitly through human-model instructional behaviours adhering to MIB and the other indirectly through the inclusion of familiar and prominent human models and relevant activities.

Direct modelling is strategised through themes, topics and subtopics, insertions of knowledge information that repetitively raise the awareness towards morality and guiding principles (can be seen from Table 12.1). Morality, spiritual and social values are fostered through the necessity of practising mutual good behaviours to the masses, for instance, being courteous, honesty, self-reliant, loyalty and taking responsibility, not only for oneself but also to the community and the nation. The essence of the textbook contents also attempts to redirect the notion that any deviant act to nobility will cause inharmonious, argument, oppression, and hatred, and further punishment. In this case, direct modelling is strategised by highlighting explicit instructional of noble characters that ought to be followed by the students.

Meanwhile, through indirect approach, modelling is strategised by incorporating a prominent figure in Islam and also in the hierarchical monarchy system in Brunei. This can be seen by consistent inclusion of Prophet Muhammad and His Majesty the Sultan of Brunei as role models in embracing and accepting moral and commendable spiritual and social behaviours. These figures are also known across generations in Brunei, making them relatable to the younger generation. Whilst Prophet Muhammad as the Messenger of Allah Subhanahu WaTaala is a paragonistic human model for the Muslims that can be found across verses in the Quran and *Hadiths*, His Majesty the Sultan of Brunei is also the idolised figure of Bruneian ruler that must be respected and followed by the people of Brunei.

Through the exemplary figure of Prophet Muhammad, the essence morality, spiritual and social values are instilled through the inclusion of Quranic verses and prophetic *Hadiths* (sayings and traditions of the Prophet Muhammad and his companions), while various *titahs* (royal decree) by His Majesty the Sultan of Brunei consistently call upon the significance of obedience and contribution to the nation, practising commendable traits in individual and in community, and the awareness of a citizen in supporting MIB for the country's betterment. These materials, which encompasses life guidance, rewards and punishments, are carefully selected to internalise moral values and a sense of obedience to Allah Subhanahu WaTaala, His Messenger, the Monarch, in this world and the hereafter. This is understood as the Quran and the Hadith are used as the foundation of Islamic guidance and education for the Muslim.

In this case, indirect modelling through exemplary figures can be seen as the best strategy expected to contribute to more extensive, influential and clearer effects to the secondary school students, rather than listing out the coveted traits of morality without the presence of a role model. This is due to the human nature, specifically among adolescents, who tend to emulate others either impersonating good behaviours or otherwise (Haji Othman et al., 2013).

Further analysis also found that the textbook development used indirect modelling approach by instilling commendable traits through illustrations. In the textbook, illustrations are used to inculcate the moral values through pictures that emphasise well-mannered behaviours, appropriate dress codes and ethics, and practising responsibilities for individual, religion and nation. In this case, various illustrations strongly adhered to morality, spiritual and social values imbued with MIB are used to portray an ideal Bruneian who students can emulate. This is amid claims that the inclusion of illustrations in teaching materials can become an effective pedagogical approach in local curriculum (Al-Johary, 2003).

The indirect approach is also strategised from the expected outcomes from proposed activities such as hot seat, role-playing, acting, identifying, understanding and analysing characters and crafting. It is clear that these pedagogical activities are used to teach noble behaviours through portraying and exemplifying them. Furthermore, these activities instil the value of cooperation and responsibility among the school students, while also imparting moral and social values and further enhancing their interpersonal skills (Long et al., 2010), which support students' character-building pertaining to MIB principles.

12.4.2 Integration

In the Year 7 MIB textbook, the integration approach is implemented in the supporting material for the MIB curriculum. Integration is a way of connecting skills and knowledge from multiple sources and experiences or applying skills and practice in various settings. It simply means bridging connection between academic knowledge and practice (Kanwar et al., 2017). Integrated learning incorporates multiple subjects, which are usually taught separately, in an interdisciplinary method of teaching. The goal is to help students remain engaged from inculcating multiple sets of skills, experiences and sources to accelerate the learning process.

Whilst the content of the textbook is instilled with the essence of the national philosophy, there are also integrations of other related subjects including Islamic education, Civic, Social Studies, History, Geography and language. The concept of integration by instilling morality and social education can be applied in various subjects in schools, either through pedagogical activities or extra-curricular activities (Haji Othman et al., 2013), as seen in the MIB subject where the curriculum content includes education of morality, integrity and nobility (Haji Omar, 2016).

As one of the core pillars of MIB, the teachings of Islamic Education is prevalent in the Year 7 MIB textbook. Malay elements, specifically moral traits and social values including being respectable, honest, friendly, courteous, having good hygiene, giving greetings (*salam*), practising supplication, dressing appropriately, and managing one's mosque and home are all noble and commendable qualities advocated by Islam. As an independent and sovereign Islamic and Malay state in Southeast Asia, the teachings of Islam certainly take precedence in the education system in Brunei, and this is not unusual as the elements of Malay and Islam are synchronised and embraced by the people in the Sultanate; hence, the MIB curriculum is integrated with Islamic teachings not only as a spiritual guidance but also as reminders for the students. In this case, integration occurs when a topic is merged with relevant lesson content, as it can be seen where the Year 7 MIB textbook offers various factual accounts, narratives, illustrations and activities related to the cultivation of MIB values through its curriculum.

The integration of Islamic Education is also evident in the inclusion of the knowledge of the Quran and Prophet Muhammad's *Hadith* as supporting materials, guidance and lessons in the textbook. For example, Quranic verses highlighted in the textbook such as *Surah Al-An'am* verse 120 is used to remind of punishments for those who commit sins, *Surah An-Nisaa* verse 59 is included to call upon piety and devotion to Allah Subhanahu WaTaala, His Messengers and *Ulil Amri* (the rightful leader), while several *Hadiths* by the Prophet of Muhammad are used to highlight about human models, including the act of honesty and moral attitudes. All teachings overlapping with morality and social values in the textbook lead to upholding kindness and prosperity, adhering to Islamic principles. These teachings also maintain a system of value or law which ensures good welfare of human's relations with God, human's relations with other human beings and human's relations with nature—a life principle strongly highlighted in Islam (Omar et al., 2014).

The integration with Social Studies can be seen from the accentuation of teachings in managing oneself from developing personality, self-esteem, and a sense of responsibility to family, community and for the nation. These are clearly highlighted from the consistent call upon instilling attitudes and morality and showing respect to oneself, to the community and the nation. The incorporation of upholding social values here are objectified to uphold dignity, maintaining harmony and joint prosperity in socialism. These can be easily detected from the composition of three themes highlighted in the textbook that summon the importance of an individual and their contribution to family, community and the whole nation (see Table 12.1).

The significance of sustaining the environment and greenery can be identified in the textbook, which overlaps with the study of Health Science and Geography (Natural Science). Whilst the textbook highlights the basic knowledge on taking care of the environment and public places, it further incorporates the knowledge of health science by summoning the significance of cleanliness to avoid potential viruses or diseases. These values are also consistent with Islamic principles which emphasise on cleanliness, preserving property, and hereditary and preserving rights and independence (Omar et al., 2014).

The textbook also integrates the anthropological study of Bruneian culture and music that are highlighted in Theme 3 which emphasises the significance of maintaining traditional musical instruments such as *gulingtangan*, *tawak-tawak* and *gendang labek* and Bruneian traditional songs including *Cabuk-Cabuk Bertali Rambai*, *Laila Mencanai*, *Nakhoda Manis* and *Kampong Ayer* which highlight the cultural history of Brunei. The integration of traditional music as part of Bruneian traditions in the textbook also allows the students to recognise and appreciate the nation's heritage and history.

In this case, the integration of various subjects aims to cultivate MIB values in a more comprehensive way in order to balance the development of students in terms of intellectual, spiritual, emotional and physical aspects. This also shows that the essence of MIB philosophy overlaps with moral education, sociology, psychology, history, civic and language studies where it can also become part of Bruneian lifestyles—traditionally and modernity (Ahmad Effendi, 2017; Haji Serudin, 2013; Tuah, 2002). This also shows the flexibility of MIB curriculum and the textbook which can provide more alternatives for educators to maximise the teaching and learning for Year 7 students.

12.4.3 Multimodal

Multimodal is one of the potential strategies to be used in teaching and learning of MIB in Brunei Darussalam and it refers to an embodied learning situation which engages multiple sensory systems and action systems of the learner (Massaro, 2012). It also refers to multiple modes of representation that combine elements of print, visual and design to create an exciting learning environment in classroom (Jewitt, 2008).

In the textbook, internalisation strategy through multimodal approach can be seen from the amalgamation of various materials including articles, poetry and stylistic materials, drama scripts, proverbs or words of wisdom that are used to convey, discuss and support moral and social values relating to MIB. For instance, the use of multimodal approach using narratives (story-telling) entitled 'Practice of Supplication' (in Theme 1) and 'Neighbours and Community' (in Theme 2) illustrates the duties and responsibilities of young people to their surrounding and community in a more relatable and understandable way.

Various teaching materials such as articles, writings and digital contents are also used as supporting resources to strengthen the students' appreciation towards morality and social values associated with obedience, national law and regulations, and prohibitions. Moreover, His Majesty the Sultan of Brunei's decrees are used to emphasise moral values relating to honesty and prevention of corruption. Materials such as factual articles are also included to inculcate moral attitudes and commendable traits in socialism, and these are further supported by special reference to the Quranic verses. Meanwhile, several *Hadith*s excerpts are used to emphasise the demands of morality and honesty.

The multimodal strategy of incorporating a series of illustrations also provides opportunities for students to internalise a sense of morality and social attitudes. Real-life photos and cartoons are used to portray self-reliant attitudes, harmonious community and nation. The diversity of images used in the textbook also enhances the students' knowledge and appreciation of Malay culture, in terms of heritage, traditions, relationships, manners and clothing. These illustrations are designed to show awareness related to upholding respect and compliance to the ruler, the government and the nation, while they also encourage healthy socialism in community by portraying collaborative activities, human interactions, sports activities and community works. The illustrations are further diversified by incorporating relevant charts and symbols to make them easier to understand by the students.

It is evident that the inclusion of diversifying illustrations in the textbook is used to assist students' understanding and appreciation towards moral values, by enlightening them with real-life knowledge and surrounding outside of the curriculum. In this sense, the variety and diversity of contents and materials in the MIB textbook allow the interaction and communication in teaching and learning through various means.

12.4.4 *Reinforcement*

The understanding of all sense of morality and social values in the MIB curriculum is also strengthened by the reinforcement strategies found in the Year 7 MIB textbook such as the use of comprehension and practical activities, which can further consolidate the knowledge of MIB and its essence.

In general, the textbook is strongly committed to implementing a consolidation strategy of the knowledge of Malay, Islamic and Monarchy, and these are organised through themes and further enhanced with supporting activities that encourage communicative approach, self-reflection and critical thinking. For instance, at the end of each subtopic, the Think and Discuss section instructs students to answer four critical-thinking questions in the form of defining, explaining, asking opinions and giving examples. The purpose of questioning activities is to test the students' understanding and provide practical exposure which indirectly assists the internalisation process of morality and social values highlighted in every theme and subtopic.

Moreover, a reading comprehension activity can potentially enhance the knowledge and internalisation process due to the active involvement of students in expressing their opinions, while offering them the opportunity to analyse, reflect and think critically. Furthermore, pedagogical activities such as discussions have been claimed to help increase students' comprehension on learning contents, while providing opportunities for peer-learning (Othman & Jaidi, 2012). Various proposed activities suggested at the end of each theme under the heading of 'Practical Activity and Project' are designed to support groupworks, role-playing and self-reflection. All activities in the textbook encourage students to interact with teachers and friends concerning moral values in accordance to the themes and subtopics provided.

Through a series of comprehension and practical activities in the textbook, the reinforcement strategy focuses on active interactions between individuals, peers and with educators, in pairs or groupwork in the classroom. In this case, the role of the educator is significant particularly in providing feedback that can motivate students to engage in desirable behaviours because students tend to accept knowledge and understanding through feedback and have a penchant to repeat commendable behaviours (Smith, 2017).

It is important to implement the reinforcement strategy in every lesson as it is a form of consolidation through stimulus-response in effective teaching and learning. It also strengthens knowledge management, behavioural change and academic achievements (Alfred, 2008; Tshomo, 2015). Through the MIB curriculum, this is fostered from active involvement in the classroom, where students can share and discuss their opinions and experiences through learning opportunities and a wide selection of activities. This is expected to further enhance their understanding of the concepts taught and to embrace the essence and practice of MIB.

12.5 Pedagogical Implications and Opportunities for Educators

It is undeniable that the content development of the Year 7 MIB textbook are incorporated with multimodal of relevant materials that are designed and used to inculcate and further consolidate the understanding, morality, spiritual and social values pertaining to the essence of Malay, Islamic and Monarchy philosophy in Brunei. The three aspects of MIB are mutually interconnected and integrated in every topic in the textbook. Thus, the content development of the textbook also reflects the culture and tradition of the Malays, who embrace the religion of Islam and uphold the Monarchy system as the state of administration in the Sultanate.

As analysed in the previous sections, the Year 7 MIB textbook can be utilised by educators as a responsive material to teach morality and social norms and to help curb seven out of nine major categories of social problems among the youth in Brunei as highlighted by Centre for Strategic and Policy Studies (2014) and issues of truancy (Pengpid & Peltzer, 2017). Although the teaching materials covering aspects of bullying and exploitation, and financial hardship are not highlighted in the book, the issues are discussed in the later academic years as the MIB curriculum continues up to Year 11. Thus, the textbook content is an ample resource for educators for Year 7 MIB curriculum.

In this case, the educators should also be able to use the textbook as a guide to correlate and discuss its contents with contemporary issues surrounding the youth and environment in Brunei, which is in line with the requirement of implementing student-centre learning approaches and experience in SPN21 (Brunei Curriculum Development Department, 2009). This also supports the growing scholarship that claims learning by doing and experimenting is more effective than the traditional method of 'chalk-and-talk'. As the Year 7 MIB curriculum is relatable to the students' surrounding and environments and can be associated with real-life learning process and contemporary issues, it is imperative for educators to be able to redirect the learning content not just through deliverance of knowledge but also as life practices.

Overall, the four strategies (modelling, integration, multi-model and reinforcement) can be implemented simultaneously in the teaching and learning of MIB at school. For instance, in a topic such as 'good hygiene', the internalisation of noble values using these strategies can be implemented by exemplifying the teacher as the role model, moral educator, instructor, facilitator and exemplar (Anam et al., 2019; Balakrishnan, 2010). Here, the teacher can inculcate content knowledge by practising good etiquette, dress neatly and maintain proper hygiene, which is encouraged by Islam. In addition, the teacher can use multi-capital strategies through various media such as creative works and visual materials for a stimulating learning environment in a classroom. Meanwhile, the reinforcement strategy can be carried out at the end of the lesson by questioning, discussing, doing activities and reflecting the lesson content to ensure the topic is well received by the students.

Although the textbook provides multiple exercises and proposed activities, MIB educators should also prioritise the feedback approach to lesson learning as a form of consolidation to morality and social values. Thus, the consolidation process through reinforcing internalisation strategies in the textbook can be utilised by educators to foster positive feelings to the students, which can improve behaviour and develop a healthy self-image and positive attitude not only among the students themselves, but also towards educators and the school community (Downing et al., 2005).

The textbook contains moral education and social values that are considered universal and relevant for the Malays or non-Malays, and the Muslims or non-Muslims. In this case, the flexibility of contents in the textbook also provides vast opportunities to educators to explore their pedagogical initiatives to cater to different themes and topics, and fully optimise content learning and appreciation. Thus, the MIB curriculum can be utilised through the diversification of pedagogical approaches and deliverance to the students. This is also complemented by incorporating and integrating various teaching materials strategised to inculcate morality and social values in the textbook. For instance, incorporating multimodal approaches in teaching and learning process which can be applied in various ways, creativities and by exploiting various sources that have been claimed to be more effective in internalising moral behaviours (Haji Abu Bakar, 2018; Makmun, 2018; Marchetti & Cullen, 2016). Moreover, the willingness and the aptitude of educators utilising various teaching materials and methods can also help consolidate content learning and deliverance to the students, and further create a conducive learning environment (Hamdi, 2013; Oman & Hashmeni, 2015). Endless possibilities in pedagogy may occur in a MIB classroom if both teachers and students reciprocally decide to use various skills to maximise teaching and learning efficacy.

One of the essential skills of an educator is the ability to transform the content delivery method to become more comprehensible to the students (Shulman, 1986a, 1986b, 1987). This skill should also become one of the prerequisite characters of MIB educators. This is due to the limitations of the textbook in terms of activities, practices, and it requires further understanding of the content and the essence of MIB to optimise its efficacy. By comprehending the essence of the textbook, its moral education and internalisation strategies, MIB educators will be able to select the best approach and teaching model complementary to the expected outcomes. In this case, it is important for the educators to understand their roles and responsibilities as an MIB facilitator and to perceive the textbook as a supporting material, where they can further incorporate other teaching materials and aids—including using relevant initiatives of info-communication technology and electronic media—to maximise their pedagogical deliverance.

12.6 Conclusion

This chapter has provided an overview of the content in the Year 7 MIB textbook pertaining to the essence of moral education, and spiritual and humanistic values imbued in it. The new MIB textbook for Year 7 was aligned and introduced accordingly to the latest reformation of SPN21, and its aim is still to nurture and inculcate morality and character values infused with the essence of MIB. Whilst understanding the content of textbook and its internalisation strategies is significant to align effective pedagogical deliverance for the educators, it also provides wide-ranging opportunities for the educators to fully utilise its content and curriculum providing that they can offer serious commitment to the curriculum and their students.

Based on the discussion in this chapter, the textbook can become a moral and social guide for educators and students and a reminder for Bruneians in general. The contents in the textbook uphold and support the philosophy of MIB as part of character and nation building, and they can be diversified using creativity and relevancy, and utilised to overcome real-life contemporary issues involving the youth. This responsibility lies on the shoulder of the public and various academic stakeholders, particularly MIB teachers.

Therefore, as part of the ongoing MIB curriculum throughout the different academic levels in the national education system, the textbook can be perceived as providing direct and indirect approaches of internalising moral education and social values to be utilised by educators to enhance commendable behaviours among the students. Thus, the educator's ability to incorporate pedagogical strategies to enhance the learning content is one of the critical elements in transforming students' behaviour inside and outside the classroom positively.

Whilst previous studies have focused more on the historical aspects of moral education and student attitudes in relation to the MIB education in Brunei, this chapter provided an in-depth content analysis of the new MIB textbook and further explore strategies that can potentially help teachers in designing their teaching and learning strategies. Moreover, the four internationalisation strategies can also be used in more details in various forms of delivery measures, guidance, facilitation, learning techniques for MIB teaching and learning process. This chapter has bridged a significant research gap in identifying internalisation strategies of MIB curriculum for Year 7 in secondary schools in Brunei that can become a teaching guidance to MIB teachers and researchers. It also opens more possibilities in scrutinising teaching materials at various levels in primary and secondary schools, or even at the university level in the Sultanate.

Furthermore, this chapter raises the chances of juxtaposing the MIB curriculum with similar moral education and curriculum in Malaysia and Indonesia. For instance, Malaysia introduced their *Rukun Negara* curriculum in 1970 with an intention of providing guidance for nation-building effort such as pledging their people to be united, believe in god, loyalty to king and country, upholding the constitution, sovereignty of the law, and good behaviour and morality. This is aligned to the national curriculum of Moral Education that aims to integrate and create a harmonious environment between ethnic groups in the multicultural country. Meanwhile as Pancasila is philosophical basis for the foundation of independent

Indonesia, as prescribed in the Indonesian Constitution, it has also become the key philosophical concept in its curriculum of moral education. The moral education is also imbued with inseparable and mutually qualifying principles of among others believing in One God and unifying Indonesia with democracy, humanity and social justice. As the teaching materials used in the respective curriculum in Malaysia and Indonesia are expected to adhere to the suitability of the nation's national philosophy (Anam et al., 2019; Balakrishnan, 2010; Nishimura, 1995; Tan et al., 2018), this opens another research scope in comparing the situation in Brunei to these two Malay countries for the future direction of this study.

References

Abd Rahim, R., & Hashim, N. H. (2005). Penerapan nilai-nilai murni dalam pendidikan sekolah rendah. *Proceeding of Seminar Pendidikan JPPG 2005*. Universiti Sains Malaysia.

Abdul Latif, H. I. (2003). Pengajaran dan pembelajaran MIB dan sejarahnya: Permasalahan dan kesinambungan. *Janang: Warta Akademi Pengajian Brunei, 8*.

Abu Bakar, P. H. S. (1997). Melayu Islam Beraja dalam sistem pendidikan Negara Brunei Darussalam. *Janang: Warta Akademi Pengajian Brunei, 7*.

Ahmad Effendi, A. H. (2017). *Falsafah Melayu Islam Beraja hubungannya dengan modeniti*. Dewan Bahasa dan Pustaka Brunei.

Alfred, G. C. (2008). *Seven strategies for building positive classrooms*. http://www.ascd.org/publications/educational leadership/sept08/vol66/num01/Seven-Strategiesfor-Building-Positive-Classrooms.aspx

Al-Johary, Z. S. (2003). *Kaedah pengajaran dan pembelajaran Sejarah*. Universiti Brunei Darussalam.

Anam, S., Degeng, I. N. S., Murtadho, N., & Kuswandi, D. (2019). The moral education and internalisation of humanitarian values in pesantren: A case study from Indonesia. *Journal for the Education of Gifted Young Scientists, 7*(4), 815–834. https://doi.org/10.17478/jegys.629726

Balakrishnan, V. (2010). The development of moral education in Malaysia. *Asia Pacific Journal of Educators and Education, 25*, 89–101.

Brunei Curriculum Development Department. (2009). *Sistem Pendidikan Negara Abad Ke-21 (SPN21)*. Curriculum Development Department, Ministry of Education.

Brunei Curriculum Development Department. (2010). *Pendidikan kenegaraan Melayu Islam Beraja: Peringkat rendah dan menengah*. Curriculum Development Department, Ministry of Education.

Centre for Strategic and Policy Studies. (2014). *National study on social problems among youth people in Brunei Darussalam.* http://www.csps.org.bn/research/social-policy/social-problems/

Downing, J., Keating, T., & Bennett, C. (2005). Effective reinforcement techniques in elementary physical education: The key to behavior management. *Physical Educator,* 62(3), 114–122.

Engku Alwi, E. A. Z. (2009). Didik generasi muda bertanggungjawab setiap muslim. *Berita Harian.* http://www.bharian.com.my/CurrentNews/BH/Monday/Agama/20090524214952/Article/index.html

Haji Abu Bakar, S. N. (2018). *Kesan penggunaan alat bantu mengajar pendekatan multimodaliti dalam pemelajaran soalan konteks Kesusasteraan Melayu.* Unpublished thesis. Universiti Brunei Darussalam, Tungku Link, Brunei.

Haji Mail, H. A. A. (2013). Dasar-dasar pendidikan Negara Brunei Darussalam (1950–2010): Kemunculannya dan hubungannya dengan falsafah Melayu Islam Beraja. *Susur Galur,* 1(2), 151–166.

Haji Mail, H. A. A., Ampuan Haji Tengah, A. H. B., Haji Abu Bakar, N. S., Haji Ahmad Kumpoh, H. A., & Haji Abu Bakar, H. T. (2019). *The Malay Islamic Monarchy in Negara Brunei Darussalam prior to 1906: A historical study.* Brunei Historical Society (PESEBAR).

Haji Omar, H. M. H. (2016). *Amalan nilai murni guru mata pelajaran Melayu Islam Beraja bagi tahun 10 di sekolah menengah: Kajian eksplorasi.* Unpublished thesis. Universiti Brunei Darussalam, Bandar Seri Begawan, Brunei.

Haji Othman, M. K., Suhid, A., Rashid, A. M., & Roslan, S. (2013). The relationships between social factors and the internalisation of noble values among students at secondary school. *Journal of Applied Research in Education,* 17, 56–76.

Haji Serudin, H. M. D. (2013). *The Malay Islamic Monarchy: A closer understanding* (trans. Haji Muhammad Tahir, D. H. Z., & Haji Abdul Majid, D. H. N.). The National Supreme Council of the Malay Islamic Monarchy.

Hamdi, S. (2013). Menguatkan keyakinan diri siswa dalam pemelajaran matematik melalui pendekatan multi-modal strategy (MMS). *Proceeding of Seminar Nasional Matematika dan Pendidikan Matematika.* https://eprints.uny.ac.id/10801/

Hj Tassim, M. N. (2019). *Penerapan Nilai-Nilai Melayu Islam Beraja di Kalangan Pelajar Institut Pengajian Tinggi Melalui Perlaksanaan Projek Khidmat Masyarakat.* Unpublished thesis. Universiti Brunei Darussalam, Tungku Link, Brunei.

Jewitt, C. (2008). Multimodality and literacy in school classrooms. *Review of Research in Education,* 32, 240–267.

Kanwar, G., Shekhawat, M., Saxena, N., & Mehra, M. C. (2017). Introduction and impact of integrated teaching learning method for first professional medical students. *IOSR Journal of Research & Method in Education,* 7(1), 10–13.

Long, J., Minhad, I. S., Tarasat, S., & Abu Bakar, N. (2010). Pembelajaran koperatif dalam pengajaran dan pembelajaran Bahasa Melayu. In J. Long (Ed.), *Kaedah Pengajaran dan Pembelajaran Bahasa Melayu* (pp. 133–153). UKM.

Makmun, R. (2018). *Refleksi dan inovasi proses pengajaran dan pembelajaran Kesusasteraan Melayu*. Dewan Bahasa dan Pustaka Brunei.

Makmun, R., Madin, A. B., Tarasat, S., Abd Rahman, S. K., Jaidi, N., & Abu Bakar, R. (2019). Strategi penghayatan lima tema falsafah MIB dalam pengajaran dan pembelajaran di peringkat sekolah di Negara Brunei Darussalam: Cadangan awal. *The International Conference on Teachers Education 2019 (ICOTE 2019)*, Kolej Universiti Perguruan Ugama Seri Begawan, Brunei.

Marchetti, L., & Cullen, P. (2016). A multimodal approach in the classroom for creative learning and teaching. *CASALC Review, 41*.

Massaro, D. W. (2012). Multimodal learning. In N. M. Seel (Ed.), *Encyclopedia of the sciences of learning* (pp. 2375–2378). Springer.

Nata, A. (2001). *Filsafat pendidikan Islam*. Logos Wacana Ilmu.

Nishimura, S. (1995). The development of Pancasila Moral Education in Indonesia. *Southeast Asian Studies, 33*(3), 303–316.

Oman, A., & Hashmeni, S. S. (2015). Design and redesign of multimodal classroom task – Implication for teaching and learning. *Journal of Information Technology Education: Research, 14*, 139–159.

Omar, A. Z., Shuid, M., Aris, M., Sam, M. F., & Syratnu, R. (2014). *Penghantar pendidikan moral: IPTA, IPTS, IPG & Kolej*. Multimedia Sdn. Bhd.

Othman, Y., & Jaidi, N. (2012). The employment of metacognitive strategies to comprehend texts among pre-university students in Brunei Darussalam. *American International Journal of Contemporary Research, 2*(8), 134–141.

Pelita Brunei. (2015). *Semua pihak perlu tangani masalah sosial*. Jabatan Penerangan. www.pelitabrunei.gov.bn/Lists/Dari%20Sidang%20Pengarang/NewDisplayForm.aspx?ID=315&ContentTypeId=0x010013DFE879A136E44D9DB252C8690975A2

Pengpid, S., & Peltzer, K. (2017). Prevalence, demographic and psychosocial correlates for school truancy among students aged 13–15 in the Association of Southeast Asian Nations (ASEAN) member states. *Journal of Child & Adolescent Mental Health, 29*(3), 197–203.

Pratiwi, J. I. (2018). *Penggunaan metode kisah dan penanaman nilai keteladanan dalam meningkatkan minat belajar siswa kelas x pada mata pelajaran Pai di SMKN 1 Jenangan Ponorogo*. Unpublished BA thesis. IAIN Ponorogo.

Sarah, A. S., Lauren, W., Marc, A. Z., Rebecca, M. C., Stephen, T. C., & Maureen, A. W. (2013). The relationship between cumulative risk & promotive factors & violent behaviour among urban adolescents. *AMJ Community Psychology, 51*, 57–65.

Shulman, L. S. (1986a). Those who understand: Knowledge growth in teaching. *Educational Researcher, 15*(2), 4–14.

Shulman, L. S. (1986b). Paradigms and research programs in the study of teaching: A contemporary perspective. In M. C. Wittrock (Ed.), *Handbook of research on teaching* (3rd ed., pp. 3–36). Macmillan Publishing Company.

Shulman, L. S. (1987). Knowledge and teaching: Foundation of new reform. *Harvard Educational Review, 57*(1), 1–22.

Smith, K. (2017). *Positive reinforcement a proactive intervention for the classroom.* https://ceed.umn.edu/wp-content/uploads/2017/05/Positive-Reinforcement.pdf

Spear, L. P. (2000). The adolescent brain and age-related behavioral manifestations. *Neuroscience and Biobehavioral Reviews, 24,* 417–463.

Tamuri, A. H., & Abdul Razak, K. (2004). Dakwah dalam menangani isu-isu sosial di kalangan remaja. In A. S. Long, J. Awang, & K. Salleh (Eds.), *Islam: Past, present and future* (pp. 828–838). UKM.

Tan, B. P., Naidu, N. B. M., & Osman, Z. J. (2018). Moral values and good citizen in a multi-ethnic society: A content analysis of moral education textbook in Malaysia. *The Journal of Social Studies Research, 42,* 119–134.

Tshomo, U. (2015). Cultivating and improving classroom reinforcement strategies to optimise pre-service student teachers' learning. *Journal of Educational Action Research Centre for Educational Research & Development, 1*(1), 24–44.

Tuah, H. D. (2002). *Brunei Darussalam nation building.* Prime Minister's Office.

CHAPTER 13

Malay Language and MIB Teacher Educators' Perceptions of the Year 7 MIB Curriculum

Abu Bakar Madin, Rozaiman Makmun, Suraya Tarasat, Noradinah Jaidi, Sri Kartika A. Rahman, and Najib Noorashid

13.1 Chapter Background

In the previous chapter, our findings reveal the four major internalisation strategies (modelling, integration, multimodal and reinforcement) are designed to inculcate morality and character values in the Year 7 *Melayu Islam Beraja* (Malay Islamic Monarchy, henceforth MIB) textbook and curriculum in secondary school in Brunei Darussalam (henceforth Brunei). We further discussed the pedagogical implications drawn from the analysis

---

Madin, A. B., Rozaiman, M., Tarasat, S., Jaidi, N., A. Rahman, S. K., & Noorashid, N. (2021). Internalisation strategies of the Malay Islamic Monarchy philosophy in Year 7 MIB curriculum in Brunei Darussalam. In Phan, L. H., A. Kumpoh, K. Wood, R. Jawawi, & H. Said (Eds.), *Globalisation, education, and reform in Brunei Darussalam* (pp. 235–260). Palgrave Macmillan.

© The Author(s), under exclusive license to Springer Nature Switzerland AG 2021
Phan, L. H. et al. (eds.), *Globalisation, Education, and Reform in Brunei Darussalam*, International and Development Education, https://doi.org/10.1007/978-3-030-77119-5_13

of textbook content and its internalisation strategies of morality, spiritual and social values for the educators as well as the students.

As also explained in Chap. 12, the empirical-based research involving the newly reformed MIB textbook and curriculum are still limited. Whilst several studies have looked into the curriculum development over the years and as part of the nation building (Ahmad Effendi, 2017; Haji Mail, 2013; Tuah, 2002), some have attempted to study several pedagogical approaches and prospect of the MIB education and curriculum (Abdul Latif, 2003; Abu Bakar, 1997), but less studies have been conducted involving teacher educators and their beliefs and perceptions towards the curriculum. Similar research, particularly involving curriculum and textbooks in moral education have been conducted elsewhere (Almonte, 2003; Asif et al., 2020; Han et al., 2018) where the outcomes are expected to provide additional yet comprehensive guidelines for the teachers. While bridging the gap in previous literature, this chapter further examines the educators' perceptions towards the recently introduced Year 7 MIB textbook as a pedagogical material and the newly reformed MIB curriculum after the introduction of *Sistem Pendidikan Negara ke-21* (National Education System in the 21st century, henceforth SPN21), through the spectacle of MIB and Malay language teacher educators. The perception of teacher educators in evaluating curriculum and textbook is significant as 'teachers are a key factor in the successful implementation of curriculum changes and particularly in textbook' (Bhanegaonkar & Mahfoodh, 2013, p. 2).

In Brunei, prospective teachers who have a bachelor's degree in MIB, Malay Language and Malay Literature are certified as having the ability and qualification to teach all three subjects in schools because the three subjects are relevant in at least two aspects. First, these subjects emphasise the element of noble values in their contents of knowledge and the process of teaching and learning. For instance, in Malay language, noble values are associated with language skills such as speaking politely and being able to

---

A. B. Madin (✉) • R. Makmun • S. Tarasat • N. Jaidi • S. K. A. Rahman • N. Noorashid
Universiti Brunei Darussalam, Bandar Seri Begawan, Brunei
e-mail: bakar.madin@ubd.edu.bn; rozaiman.makmun@ubd.edu.bn; suraya.tarasat@ubd.edu.bn; noradinah.jaidi@ubd.edu.bn; kartika.rahman@ubd.edu.bn; najib.noorashid@ubd.edu.bn

read and understand morality and nobility through selective reading material, and to write proficiently using appropriate skills and incorporate suitable registers. This overlaps with the teaching and learning of MIB which also upholds morality and nobility in according to the local norms and traditions.

Second, the three subjects also use the same medium of instruction: Malay. Every prospective teacher who wishes to teach either MIB, Malay or Malay Literature should attain good to excellent results in Malay language at the Cambridge GCE 'O' and 'A' level, which are significant examinations used as a benchmark for prospective students to enrol in the Bachelor's degree programmes in MIB, Malay Language and Malay Literature at the tertiary level. Furthermore, achieving good results in a Bachelor's degree programme in the area of Malay Language is required for a prospective teacher who wants to pursue teaching degree courses in MIB. Prospective teachers who then successfully completed their Master of Teaching in Malay Language and Malay Literature are qualified to teach MIB subject. They may be instructed to teach one or two of these subjects, and in some cases these teachers are required to teach all three.

Furthermore, a recent study conducted to elicit appreciation of morality and values among local teachers facilitating Malay Language, Malay Literature and MIB at secondary schools in Brunei showcases that 270 out of a total of 329 teachers (82.1%) taught Malay language and 281 out of 329 teachers (85.4%) taught MIB (Makmun et al., 2020). The statistical figures show that the teachers who teach Malay Language have also taught MIB. This also shows the correlation of teaching and learning of subjects in Malay Language and MIB in Brunei, further validating the purpose of incorporating perceptions of teachers in respective subjects in this study.

In this study, four highly experienced teacher educators—two males and two females—at the Sultan Hassanal Bolkiah Institute of Education (SHBIE), Universiti Brunei Darussalam (UBD), comprised of two experts in the subject of MIB and two experts in Malay language, were interviewed to get their comprehensive perceptions on the Year 7 MIB textbook as a supporting material in pedagogy in secondary schools in Brunei. All four teacher educators have at least 13–22 years of teaching experiences in either MIB or Malay language subject, thus their familiarity and expertise on the content knowledge, the development of curriculum and pedagogical approaches in their respective fields in the context of Brunei is unquestionable.

Ten interview questions eliciting their beliefs and perceptions on the role and responsibility of educators, relevant pedagogical initiatives, and the uniqueness, the limitation and the prospect relating to the MIB Year 7 textbook and curriculum were used as trajectory of discussion in this chapter (see Appendix for the interview questions).

13.2 The Role of Educators

To ensure the success of pedagogy of MIB curriculum in Brunei, including the use of the Year 7 MIB textbook, all the teacher educators believe that every MIB teacher should be equipped with the knowledge of the essence of each pillar of the national philosophy: Malay, the religion of Islam and the system of Monarchy in Sultanate. This also means that every teacher should be able to understand not only the content and the knowledge of MIB curriculum, but also MIB as the life guidance in Brunei. This is highlighted because the MIB curriculum is not only taught by MIB teachers but can also be taught by teachers of different expertise. This however should not compromise the need to have a comprehensive understanding of MIB, as mentioned by one of the educators:

> *Guru MIB harus mempunyai pemahaman yang mendalam mengenai asas MIB dan tujuan utama MIB dalam pendidikan. Guru MIB yang berkualiti dan berkelayakan bukan sahaja mempunyai pengetahuan mendalam tentang MIB, tetapi juga peka dengan kaedah atau aktiviti pengajaran terkini dan keperluan pelajar, dan adalah menjadi bonus jika guru MIB dapat mengabungkan pengajaran dengan ilmu dan kemahiran teknologi. Oleh kerana MIB berkaitan dengan nilai dan moral, aktiviti-aktiviti berunsur penghayatan dan afektif amat diperlukan dalam pengajaran dan pembelajaran.*

(MIB teachers should have in depth understanding on the basics of MIB and the main purpose of MIB in education. A good and qualified MIB teacher does not only possess in-depth knowledge of MIB, but is also updated to the latest teaching methods, activities, and the needs of their students. It is a bonus if a MIB teacher is able to incorporate their teaching with technological knowledge and aptitude. This is because MIB itself is related to enhancing values and morals, appreciation and affective activities that are essential in teaching and learning.)

The teacher educators claim that one of the reasons on the synchronous content and sentiment in both subjects is due to the progressive nature of MIB curriculum that are stretched from early childhood in the primary school level up until at the tertiary university level, amid comprising of social norms and traditions among the people of Brunei. In this case, MIB teachers should be familiar with the MIB philosophy, education and curriculum to ensure the efficacy of teaching and learning in accordance with the level of acceptance and cognitive of the students. Therefore, MIB teachers ought to be proactive in researching the needs in teaching and learning for this curriculum, while utilising the resources provided by the MIB Curriculum Development Department at the Ministry of Education. For instance, many studies have concluded that teachers should be able to understand various aspects including teaching beliefs and principles, respective curriculum, pedagogical approaches and goals as well as their role and responsibilities towards their students (Alexander, 2004; Florian & Linklater, 2010; Husbands & Pearce, 2012). Therefore, MIB teachers must play their role in providing appropriate knowledge and skills according to the targets and recommendations set out by the national curriculum and in the MIB textbook.

Furthermore, the role and responsibility of MIB teachers are more intricate in comparison to other subject teachers. Amidst the use of relevant textbooks and teaching resources, MIB teachers are also accountable to nurture and inculcate moral education and social values for students to practice. This is because the establishment of the MIB curriculum was not intended for students to obtain excellent results on paper, but it aimed to internalise morality and common values adhering to MIB through systematic approach of formal education, which is also postulated as one of the aims of the National Education System in Brunei since the Sultanate gained independence (Brunei Curriculum Development Department, 2010). Thus, the role and responsibility of MIB teachers in this respect are not restricted to teaching and learning of the content knowledge, but also cultivating the development of students' behaviours, spiritual and mentality through holistic approach because the nature of the MIB curriculum and education focuses more on the immersion of knowledge and guidance of morality, spiritual and social values, and the appreciation of these standards as life practices of every student.

Therefore, MIB teachers should be 'role models' for the students and the academic community in an institution. Interestingly, one teacher educator also remarked that every MIB teacher should possess an ideal personality aligned with the 21 core values of MIB as shown in Fig. 13.1. In this case, every MIB teacher is expected to instil, apply and portray these core values not only for themselves as an educator, but also as a reflection

1	Obedience to religion	8	Compromise	15	Comradeship
2	Obedience to monarchy	9	Discipline	16	Mutually responsible
3	Awareness	10	Polite	17	Loving and devotion
4	Unity	11	Caring	18	Committed
5	Mutual understanding	12	Honest and since	19	Harmonious
6	Respectful	13	Dedicated	20	Sociocultural purity
7	Tolerate	14	Working together	21	Socioeconomic improvement

Fig. 13.1 The core values of MIB (Brunei Curriculum Development Department, 2010, p. 10)

for the students as the recipient of knowledge. This is concurrent with previous studies that have suggested the profound impact of teacher's character, portrayal and identity to their students in facilitating moral and character education (Asmani, 2013; Chowdhury, 2016; Lapsley & Narvaez, 2006; Lapsley & Yeager, 2013).

In another aspect, both Malay language teacher educators also highlight the significance of possessing a good command of the language to increase the efficacy of the MIB curriculum in the teaching and learning process. Therefore, MIB teachers are expected to have a good proficiency in the Malay language as the curriculum is also designed to be taught in the medium of the national language of the Sultanate. In this case, the role of teachers with excellent Malay language is believed to strengthen the comprehension of the MIB curriculum among themselves and further increase the efficacy of the teaching and learning of moral education to their students. This is perhaps overlapped with the well-accepted notion of '*Bahasa Jiwa Bangsa*' (Language is the Soul of the Nation) which is upheld by the Malays in Brunei, if not the whole Malay World, thus the sociocultural contents embedded in the MIB curriculum should be delivered in Malay. In Brunei, this practice strongly correlates to the maintaining of the status of Malay language as the official language in the Sultanate through its Constitution of Brunei 1959. Thus, although this has never been explicitly mentioned in previous literature pertaining to MIB education, the significance of using the mother tongue or/and national language in teaching moral education can be seen as part of nation building in Brunei, as a way to preserving the language and identity of the Malays. Moreover, the teachers are also expected to develop various language skills in oral, reading and writing in Malay through the curriculum.

In this case, the teacher educators are also aware of how the teaching of MIB and Malay language can support and enrich one another even though both subjects have slightly different emphasis: Malay Language focuses more on the correct use of language, while MIB focuses more on the application of nobility and politeness in speech and writing. They believe both subjects stress complementary efforts to teach, internalise and refine morality and socialisation through language skills among students. These concepts of moral and social values are deemed significant for students to master. Thus, in this sense, all the teacher educators also believe that high competence in using Malay language can further help the students to put their MIB values in practice, especially through speech and written at various levels of socialisation, including the practice of language politeness. For instance, the significance of using a suitable naming system and appellation—involving the use of proper pronouns within family, community, the nobles and the royal family—which are strongly imbued with the essence of MIB in the Bruneian society may also be refined through good competence in using the Malay language. This suggests that the teacher educators realise that there are overlapping sentiments and synchronous content knowledge in both subjects as planned by the Ministry of Education and they can be fully optimised by teachers of both subjects.

Moreover, Makmun et al. (2020) found two values that are nurtured through the teaching and learning of Malay Language and MIB: general values and speech and written values. The former includes morals, cooperative attitude and discipline, while the latter emphasises on the use of appropriate language skills in socialisation. In light of this, all the interviewed teacher educators acknowledge the symbiotic relationship between the knowledge, competence and usage of both knowledge and practices in MIB and Malay language and inevitably support the use of curriculum in both subjects for the teachers and the students.

13.3 Flexibility of the MIB Curriculum

According to the teacher educators, the flexibility of the MIB curriculum is seen on how the curriculum and the textbook can be optimised and fully utilised in teaching other subjects. For instance, both teacher educators of the Malay language are aware that the MIB curriculum emphasises on social values in living as a community on the basis of Islamic principles while adhering to the Monarchy. In this case, the focus of the MIB curriculum also exists in Malay language education where the essence of MIB can also be found throughout reading materials and textbooks used for teaching Malay subject. This change is observed due to the reformation of education and curriculum content after the introduction of SPN21 which adheres more towards infusing the surrounding as part of 'learning from real experience' and practical approach (Brunei Ministry of Education, 2009; Mundia, 2010). One teacher educator admits to using the MIB textbook as a supporting material in Malay language subject and claims that the overlapping sentiments and materials in both subjects can be merged and be potentially used to maximise either subject, as the essence of morality, spiritual and social values in MIB curriculum can also help enhance the contents in Malay subject.

Secara tidak langsung, guru Bahasa Melayu juga menyentuh, menekankan, mengajar kandungan dan unsur-unsur MIB dalam pengajaran dan pembelajaran Bahasa Melayu. Oleh itu, peranan guru Bahasa Melayu adalah untuk memantapkan lagi kandungan nilai-nilai yang ada di dalam pengajaran Bahasa Melayu agar kefahaman mengenai unsur-unsur MIB dapat pelajar serap dengan baik. Peranan guru Bahasa Melayu juga adalah untuk menggabungjalinkan unsur-unsur MIB dalam pengajaran kemahiran-kemahiran lisan, membaca dan menulis. Selain itu, bahan bacaan yang berunsurkan hidup masyarakat Brunei, maklumat mengenai Negara Brunei dapat dijadikan bahan untuk pengajaran aspek bacaan dan kefahaman dan bahan rujukan pelajar bagi membantu mereka dalam penulisan karangan.
(Indirectly, Malay language teachers also touch upon, emphasise, and teach contents and elements of MIB during teaching and learning Malay language. Therefore, the role of Malay language teachers is to enhance the content values in their curriculum by incorporating MIB elements that can be instilled upon them. The role of Malay language teachers is to integrate elements of MIB in teaching language skills, including oral, reading, and writing. In addition, reading materials in MIB curriculum which emphasise the life of the people of Brunei, information about the country can be used as teaching materials in terms of reading and understanding, as it can also become a reference for students in writing essays.)

Aside from its use in the teaching and learning of the Malay language in school, all four teacher educators also believe that the MIB curriculum and the new textbook can also be used to teach Islamic studies or specifically Islamic Religious Knowledge subject as there are strong elements and teachings of Islam found throughout the textbook pages. These elements are further reinforced with the inclusion of Quranic verses, Prophetic

Hadiths and the *titah* (royal decrees) of His Majesty the Sultan of Brunei which also adhere to the Islamic teaching. This may not be an unusual integration in moral education for a Sultanate such as Brunei as religious sentiments and moral values always go together among Islamic countries and the Muslims (Halstead, 2007). Therefore, the MIB curriculum is not only restricted to teaching morality and social values, but it can also be further utilised to enhance spiritual values and behaviours among the students. In this case, the teacher educators' perception on the flexibility of MIB curriculum which can be fully optimised by integrating other subjects, including humanities and science subjects, is also in line with the findings that we raised in Chap. 12 where the internalisation strategies of inculcating morality and social values can be used as a method of teaching through and using the Year 7 MIB curriculum and textbook.

The teacher educators also believe that the flexibility of the MIB curriculum and MIB textbook can be used as supporting materials in pedagogy of early education. This is due to the acceptance of the morality, spirituality and social values imbued in the formal curriculum that are in line with the idealism of lifestyles in Brunei. This supports the claim made by three teacher educators who believed the MIB curriculum can be implemented beyond the Sultanate, due to its flexible essence of humanity and spirituality that can be inculcated to all people of different races, religions and systems. Several Bruneian intellectuals (Ahmad Effendi, 2017; Haji Abdul Ghani, 2015; Haji Serudin, 2013; Tuah, 2002) have made similar claims on the flexibility of MIB principles and how it can be practised across generation, eras and people, given that the people have an in-depth understanding of the principles. In response to this, one teacher educator believes the MIB curriculum should be exposed further not only through formal education, but also to the global communities for it can create a better understanding of the national philosophy and the curriculum itself.

> *Salah satu jalan yang mungkin dapat diusahakan supaya kurikulum MIB dapat dilihat, dibaca malah dipraktis oleh masyarakat global ialah melalui penulisan. Penulisan yang telus, berkualiti dan berhemah boleh membuatkan masyarakat luar ingin tahu mengenai Brunei, masyarakatnya, budayanya, agamanya, ekonomi dan politiknya malah segala aspek kehidupan bangsanya sendiri yang unik yang mungkin berbeza dengan masyarakat lainnya. Penyebaran melalui media sosial, eletronik dan teknologi yang lain juga berperanan penting bagi mengembangluas penyebaran falsafah dan kurikulum*

MIB agar masyarakat luar dapat pengetahuan dan menilai dan membanding perbezaan yang ada dengan kurikulum mereka sendiri khususnya yang melibatkan falsafah negara dan pembangunan bangsa.

(One of the possible ways so that MIB curriculum can be seen, read, and even practised by the global community is through writing. Transparent, quality, and prudent writing about MIB curriculum can resolve the curiosity from the outside community. This includes understanding about the society, culture, the religion, the economy, and politics in Brunei and even all aspects that are unique and may be different from other global societies. The dissemination through social media, electronics and other technologies also plays an important role in the dissemination of MIB philosophy and curriculum so that the outside world can gain knowledge and further evaluate and compare the differences with their own curriculum [moral education], especially those involving national philosophy and nation development.)

As briefly suggested in Chap. 12, the newly reformed Year 7 MIB textbook can be strategised as a responsive teaching material to reduce the social problems in Brunei. Following their understanding on the youth and social problems in the Sultanate, all the teacher educators also believe that the MIB education is not only effective in cultivating social norms and traditions among younger generation, but it is also flexible enough to be utilised in curbing these social problems. However, they still raised the concern of not implementing these pedagogical approaches properly in the classroom.

For instance, Haji Omar's (2017) analysed the designated syllabus and content of MIB curriculum for Lower Secondary from 1991 until mid-2000 which focused on the application of values pertaining to national security and it was found that MIB was not taught satisfactorily in school. This is further bolstered by the increasing statistics of disciplinary problems reported by researchers and local media (Haji Gharif, 2010; Haji Talipuddin, 2013). Moreover, the statistics released by the *Jabatan Pembangunan Masyarakat* (Department of Community Development) in 2013 show that there was an increase in the number of admissions to welfare home rehabilitation involving students with moral problems and juvenile cases from 2009 to 2013 (Haji Talipuddin, 2013).

Despite this worrying trend, the teacher educators believe that the local Ministry of Education has worked hard by providing appropriate platforms and channels to address these problems, such as offering various seminars, conferences and workshops for MIB teachers and incorporation efforts made by and with *Majlis Tertinggi Melayu Islam Beraja* (The

Supreme Council of Malay Islamic Monarchy). The Supreme Council is also the government body that is responsible for guiding and monitoring the lifestyle of the people of Brunei at all levels based on MIB, which has made a strategic plan to ensure the objectives of its establishment are met. In this case, the teacher educators also believe in the prospect of these efforts and continue to support their initiatives to build a peaceful Bruneian nation.

Although these teacher educators believe that the provision of MIB textbooks is a suitable medium to channel the formal education of MIB in an organised manner, they still believe that the impact on the use of the latest textbook should be studied comprehensively, particularly through the students' perspectives. Nevertheless, based on one teacher educator's experience, the average teachers in schools often manage to convey the contents of MIB textbook quite well, even though measuring the practice of social norms and values as part of daily practice consistent to MIB education is still complex. In this case, it also leaves more room for further research in this respect which can divulge more aspects of flexibility of the MIB curriculum and its impact on the people and the surrounding.

13.4 New Textbook Provides Endless Opportunities

As suggested in Chap. 12, the newly reformed MIB textbook can provide endless prospects and opportunities for teaching and learning and success of MIB curriculum and practice. In the interviews, the teacher educators stated that the new textbook has its own uniqueness as part of a supporting teaching material in MIB education.

The most apparent feature in the new textbook raised by the teacher educators is the design and the new layout of the textbook which is in line with the contemporary teaching and learning of MIB. In comparison to the old textbook which has black and white still images, the new textbook provides more colourful and eye-catching illustrations that can be utilised by MIB teachers. The new textbook also includes relevant cartoons, sketches, real-life images and diagrams to accompany the content of the book. Thus, the reformed design can assist the students to better understand the MIB knowledge highlighted in the book. Studies such as Schallert (1980), O'Donnell (1983) and Hannus and Hyona (1999) have postulated that the inclusion of relevant images and illustration may benefit teaching and learning in various subjects. In this case, images and illustrations can be seen as a tool to stimulate student's mind and creativity. In a closer context, Al-Johary (2004, 2010) also claims that the use of colourful and attractive illustrations and images has increased more understanding amongst student in the History curriculum in Brunei, thus such finding can also be implied in the use of appealing illustrations in the new MIB textbook. Moreover, the inclusion of Internet sources and media in the textbook, through the use of Internet links and social media such as Facebook, shows an attempt of the curriculum to integrate contemporary use and familiarity of info-technology in MIB education.

Another unique feature of the new MIB textbook is the inclusion of Bruneian sociocultural and anthropological elements. In addition to highlighting moral education and social values that are universally shared with other cultures or societies around the world, the textbook also incorporates the knowledge of Brunei and its heritage as part of morality, spiritual and social acknowledgement to be known and appreciated by teachers and students. The three core pillars of MIB are designed and imbued in every theme, section, discussion, activity and content in the book. Thus, the textbook is considered distinctive for its attempt to depict the true essence and the pure identity of the people of Brunei that adhere to the Islamic principles and abide by the Monarchy system and traditions. In this case, although the MIB curriculum highlights the significance of being a moral individual and member of a society, it further applies these notions to real the setting and context in Brunei. This can be seen from the content analysis of the new textbook and the internalisation strategies used to inculcate these elements to the students (see Chap. 12).

Furthermore, all the teacher educators stated that the new reformed textbook presents a more systematic and organised knowledge of MIB than the previous textbook. The contents in the new textbook are designed into three specific themes: (1) the responsibility to oneself; (2) the responsibility to family, neighbours and society and (3) the responsibility to the country and the environment, which cover the relationship of three levels of individualism, societal and nation. Each theme includes several units that contain highlighted morality, spiritual and social values pertaining to MIB, and complementary knowledge info, word meaning, discussion, proposed activities and projects. The diverse materials that are designed using a systematic approach in the textbook will be convenient for the educators to fully utilise and convey their creativity in teaching and learning. In contrast, the content of the previous textbook was less interactive and too simplistic.

Furthermore, according to the teacher educators, another distinguished feature of the textbook is the inclusion of Quranic verses, and Prophetic *Hadiths* as well as royal decrees as part of the modelling and reinforcement strategies use to strengthen MIB principles in the textbook and in the MIB curriculum in general. Thus, the eccentricity within the diversification of Bruneian elements of the MIB textbook and its curriculum in cultivating morality, spiritual and social values to the students are also seen as a positive approach to develop human model as part of nation building in Brunei.

Therefore, the inclusion of various stimulating design and contents in the textbook can be fully utilised by MIB teachers. The new textbook is also deemed to be more comprehensible and systematic in terms of its content and approach, and thus easier to be used by teachers. As the new textbook creates more opportunities in pedagogy, teachers can explore and enhance their creativity using the book in content deliverance and to apply these in their teaching and learning in the classroom. In this case, every MIB teacher can optimise their own knowledge of pedagogy or art, relevant teaching strategies and techniques in order to achieve the learning objectives in MIB.

Although the teacher educators believe that the newly reformed textbook aligns with the standards and objectives of SPN21, they claim that the development of the textbook can also be improved in some areas. For instance, the title and unit should have been provided with teaching and learning objectives that will assist the teachers and the students to understand and to achieve specific pedagogical objectives more explicitly. This suggestion is a response to the nature of the MIB curriculum that focuses more on intangible processes of learning and skills of cultivating human model by teaching and learning abstract concepts, which is a covert process of learning. Furthermore, one teacher educator also commented on the lack of emphasis on the social impacts of MIB in the textbook. This might also become a limitation as students do not understand social context and impacts through written statements where more challenging and high cognitive argumentative materials should be incorporated to stimulate their socio-cognitive levels.

Besides these limitations, MIB teachers are encouraged to provide appropriate teaching materials or aids and incorporate relatable materials and discussion to the topics and themes in the textbooks. MIB teachers are also advised to incorporate self-reflection methods in their teaching in order to understand the affectivity process received by the students. Therefore, the initiative and commitment made by MIB teachers also play an important role to ensure the success of teaching and learning of MIB, and further making the learning process more fun and interesting for the students.

13.5 Diversifying of Pedagogical Approaches

After the reformation of the national education system through SPN21, the objectives of teaching and learning in school shifted to produce globally competitive and competent younger generation through a series of comprehensive and holistic approaches (Brunei Ministry of Education, 2009). This also means that the pedagogical approaches of every subject taught in school can be diversified and experimented to maximise the potential of the students and to maintain the efficacy of all curriculums, including the MIB curriculum.

As part of providing teacher training courses at SHBIE in UBD, all four teacher educators are familiar with diversifying pedagogical approaches and the incorporation of info-communication technology (ICT) as part of teaching and learning of MIB. According to one of the teacher educators, local student teachers in MIB and Malay language normally undergo teaching training for two semesters in different schools for the first and second semesters to enrich their teaching experience in a real education environment. These student teachers are encouraged to apply various teaching methods, aids and teaching and learning materials in accordance with the requirements of SPN21 that they have learned in theory at UBD. These student teachers are assessed based on their abilities to incorporate various teaching methods, including cooperative learning method to instil a cooperative attitude among students, while boosting good nature among students by encouraging students to respect each other, listen to other opinions, give good suggestions, debate issues thoughtfully and prudently, and practising language politeness.

Whilst practising various ICT materials and resources for their own lectures and tutorials, the teacher educators also acknowledge the selection of good and suitable materials for their student teachers to use in schools. Amidst the proliferation of teaching materials, these teacher educators believe in being selective about teaching materials, particularly those involving the use of ICT that are beneficial and suitable in adherence to the requirement of SPN21. For instance, one teacher educator provided an example where the school teachers can use video or recordings related to the content of the lesson which contain good teaching and morality from various media platforms such as Facebook and YouTube or make use of Pinterest to pin educational resources. In another example, the school teachers can encourage cooperative groupwork by setting up quizzes using the Kahoot application, and using YouTube as part of flipped classroom or blogs such as blogger and WordPress to set up homework and interactive quizzes and activities. This shows the significance of incorporating innovative and interactive pedagogy and ICT in the teaching and learning of moral education to create a more conducive and effective learning environment that will not only achieve pedagogical objectives but also inculcate the needed values among the students (Ghavifekr et al., 2016; Narinasamy & Wan Mamat, 2013; Schuitema et al., 2007).

All the teacher educators acknowledge that the MIB curriculum gives freedom and more opportunities for teachers to undertake collaborative teaching and learning as well as individual learning. Among the teaching approaches suggested to optimise the MIB curriculum is to implement projects or roadshows that are fully managed by students. According to the teacher educators, such activities can help instil the interest towards MIB among the students as they can experience the whole process themselves. These projects should not be implemented for short term, but they should be carried out throughout the year based on the topics in the textbook and the MIB curriculum. This is to ensure the students continuously learn and instil the morality and commendable behaviours pertaining to MIB through social interactions between peers, their teachers and the public. One teacher educator further suggested that the MIB curriculum can be fully utilised as part of collaborative learning and it can also be strengthened through independent learning using various activities inside and outside a classroom.

Selain itu, pementasan lakonan situasi nilai-nilai murni juga dilaksanakan sepanjang projek jerayawara bagi memberi kefahaman mendalam maksud atau konsep nilai yang terkandung atau nilai yang perlu diterapkan dalam diri pelajar berdasarkan konteks lakonan yang dipentaskan. Selain itu, mengadakan lawatan ke tempat-tempat bersejarah yang berkait dengan sistem Beraja agar pelajar lebih memahami dan melihat sendiri sistem Beraja yang dimaksudkan. Kesimpulannya, pedagogi yang berbentuk pengalaman kendiri lebih dapat menerapkan unsur MIB dengan lebih mendalam lagi ke dalam jiwa para pelajar.

(Besides, the students can set up stage performances relating to good values, and this can be undertaken throughout the roadshow project to provide in-depth understanding on the concept of social values. In addition, they can do a visit to historical places related to the Monarchy system, so they can understand better and be able to experience the system holistically. In short, pedagogy in the form of self-experience can be applied to inculcate the essence of MIB among the students.)

Furthermore, the teacher educators also acknowledge the importance of incorporating additional or supporting materials in diversifying pedagogical approaches in maximising the efficacy of teaching MIB curriculum. This includes the use of appropriate and relevant teaching aids. Overviewing the pedagogical analysis of curriculum involving Malay-medium subjects in Brunei, Makmun and Mahamod (2015) found that the use of teaching aids should be varied and fully optimised depending on the needs and appropriateness. Thus, in this case, every MIB teacher should be able to understand and use suitable teaching aids to determine the success of teaching and learning of MIB. Furthermore, as explained earlier, the nature of the MIB curriculum involves teaching abstract concepts of morality, life practices and skills which may impose certain consideration for the teachers in choosing suitable teaching aids. Hence, a complementary physical object may assist the efficacy of teaching and learning of MIB. For instance, Makmun (2018) formulated that teachers put more initiative to diversify ways and teaching resources if they were dealing with students who with learning difficulties, hence the creativity of a teacher is significant in this respect. Aside from that, the teacher educators also believe that the students' needs in learning MIB should be prioritised in the decision-making and design of the MIB curriculum. Similarly, studies including Husbands and Pearce (2012) and James and Pollard (2011) strongly advise on the involvement of students in designing effective curriculum and teaching practices. This is also in line with Haji Abu Bakar's (2018) and Makmun's (2018) findings that show an increase of students' achievements following an intervention of teaching and learning in classroom involving the use of multimodal pedagogical strategy. Thus, the ability of every teacher to modify their methods requires relevant creativity and skills.

Since the introduction of the new reformed MIB curriculum, various efforts have been made by MIB teachers to deliver the curriculum using the Year 7 MIB textbook. Various teaching methods and techniques as well as the use of teaching aids have been experimented to increase the efficacy of MIB curriculum, including acting or role play, story-telling and drama techniques (Haji Awang Matassan, 2013; Haji Yaakub, 2014; Saidin, 2018), by implementing Jigsaw II learning and Buzz techniques (Bahrin, 2020; Janudin, 2020), the use of games, poster and crossword puzzles (Haji Md Yassin, 2014; Haji Rashid, 2018; Haji Tarsat, 2013) and boardgames (Haji Awang Damit, 2020). At the same time, several secondary school teachers also maximise the use of MIB textbooks by incorporating other contemporary media such as ICT, interactive power-point (Haji Jaili, 2015; Haji Tahamit, 2016), social media such as Facebook (Besar, 2016) and animation technology (Hj. Md Jalaluddin, 2015).

Every effort made by MIB teachers and the teacher educators must ensure that the teaching process can be fully optimised and engaging for student learning, and most importantly, to guarantee the teaching objectives are achieved. The studies mentioned above further show that the newly reformed MIB textbook and curriculum can be diversified in many ways if the teachers and the students accept the teaching and learning process of MIB creatively and cooperatively. In this case, innovative teaching and learning process among others can be implemented to encourage cooperative learning and further prompting stimulus reactions among students which are not only designed to achieve teaching and learning objectives but also to put the content knowledge into practice.

13.6 Conclusion

Indeed, there are concerns that the continued exposure to globalisation and secularisation in the world today will impose a challenge on the development of human models in Brunei today, and it may even continue in the future, but the confidence towards MIB as a life guidance should continue to be maintained and strengthened as a thriving legacy in this modern age. This should also continue to be channelled through formal education and school curriculum because the MIB concept comprises of positive values that can be used to shape and nurture the Bruneian identity among the younger generation, following the Malay proverb '*melentur buluh biarlah dari rebungnya*' (bend the bamboo from the shoot).

From the perspective of experienced teacher educators, this chapter has shown that the MIB curriculum and the use of the newly reformed textbook have met the needs, preferences and suitability with the current education system in Brunei. To date, the MIB curriculum has provided a guideline for the teachers—who are the important stakeholder in education that can guide and inculcate young generation to embrace the true identity of being Bruneian.

Therefore, every teacher needs to be prepared to respond to the challenges in today's education as well as their surrounding such as participating in re-skilling or up-skilling programmes or other various efforts made by relevant agencies. Such skills assist in improving the MIB teaching and learning in schools, in accordance with the curriculum provided by the Ministry of Education. Through their successful teaching and learning, it will transcend to improving life skills and morality among the students, and further help into curbing social problems in the country.

Bridging the scholarly gap on the perception of teacher educators specifically on the MIB curriculum for secondary education in Brunei, the feedback from these teacher educators are able to provide explanations of the relationship between the MIB curriculum and the teacher roles, responsibilities and expertise from different perspectives. Most previous studies have focused more on reviewing the efficacy of pedagogical approaches of MIB, but the study on the teacher educators' views as attempted in this chapter is more relevant in understanding the basis of curriculum requirements and how these are connected to the education philosophy, while providing new perspective of reviewing the MIB curriculum across subjects and national curriculum through the spectacle of experienced stakeholder in training local teachers. Thus, this chapter also provides a needed guideline for teachers and teachers-in-training on the potential of the MIB curriculum. A similar intention can be maximised by understanding the curriculum itself, for instance, as how the authors of this chapter also attempted in deciphering the content analysis and internalisation strategies of the MIB textbook and curriculum. Hence, both complementary chapters can be fully utilised in practice of teaching and learning of MIB as well as for research purposes.

This chapter also opens more opportunities to conduct further research involving the beliefs and perceptions towards the MIB curriculum after the introduction of SPN21. Perhaps, more studies should be accomplished in understanding the viewpoint of the students who are the recipient of the MIB knowledge, in order to provide all rounded comprehension on the efficacy of the MIB curriculum, particularly due to the elusiveness on teaching and learning and the inculcation of morality and social values towards this important agent in education. Also, more studies should be conducted using comparative analysis in juxtaposing the curriculum MIB with other moral education subject taught across the globe. This could perhaps offer more prospect in understanding the curriculum that may provide more potentials of the curriculum not just for the educators, the students and the public, but also to policymakers in Brunei.

Appendix: Interview Questions

1. As a teacher educator yourself, could you explain what is the role of a MIB/Malay teacher in utilising the MIB curriculum (at the secondary-level education) as a whole?
2. What (how) about the role of a MIB/Malay teacher at secondary school in using the latest Year 7 MIB textbook specifically?
3. How do you think a MIB/Malay teacher at secondary school can fully utilise the use of the latest Year 7 MIB textbook?
4. What do you think the uniqueness and the limitation of the latest Year 7 MIB textbook?
5. Aside from the usual pedagogical approaches of teaching and learning in classroom, how do you think a MIB/Malay teacher can make use of the latest Year 7 MIB textbook? Do you have any evidence or any efforts that have been done or accomplished by school teachers?
6. How do you think the use of the latest Year 7 MIB textbook can help into curbing social problems among the youth in Brunei today?
7. How do you think a MIB/Malay teacher can make use the latest Year 7 MIB textbook to instil and internalise morality and character building to their students? Is there any specific trait or quality of the teacher/facilitator/educator and the pedagogical strategy/approach to successfully utilise this textbook?
8. Why do you think the Ministry of Education decided to reform its MIB curriculum (including the use of the latest MIB textbook for Year 7)? What was lacking in the previous curriculum/textbook? How does the newly reformed MIB curriculum/textbook in line with SPN-21?
9. How do you think the reformation of MIB curriculum, including the use of the latest MIB textbook for Year 7, can help into supporting the national philosophy and ideology of MIB? You can provide some hard evidence to strengthen your argument.

10. Is there any potential that the use of the new reformed MIB curriculum (including the use of the new MIB textbook for Year 7) to be globalised or internationalised, not just for the people of young generation in Brunei, but also beyond. If there's any, could you explain how?

References

Abdul Latif, H. I. (2003). *Pengajaran dan pembelajaran MIB dan sejarahnya: Permasalahan dan kesinambungan* (p. 8). Warta Akademi Pengajian Brunei.

Abu Bakar, P. H. S. (1997). *Melayu Islam Beraja dalam sistem pendidikan Negara Brunei Darussalam* (p. 7). Warta Akademi Pengajian Brunei.

Ahmad Effendi, A. H. (2017). *Falsafah Melayu Islam Beraja hubungannya dengan modeniti*. Dewan Bahasa dan Pustaka Brunei.

Alexander, R. (2004). Still no pedagogy? Principle, pragmatism and compliance in primary education. *Cambridge Journal of Education, 34*(1), 7–33. https://doi.org/10.1080/0305764042000183106

Al-Johary, Z. S. (2004). *Kaedah pengajaran dan pembelajaran sejarah*. Institut Pendidikan Sultan Hassanal Bolkiah, Universiti Brunei Darussalam.

Al-Johary, Z. S. (2010). *Kaedah pengajaran dan pembelajaran mata pelajaran Melayu Islam Beraja, Pelajaran Am, Sejarah dan Sivik*. Institut Pendidikan Sultan Hassanal Bolkiah, Universiti Brunei Darussalam.

Almonte, S. A. (2003). National identity in moral education textbooks for high school students in the Philippines: A content analysis. *Asia Pacific Education Review., 4*, 19–26. https://doi.org/10.1007/BF03025549

Asif, T., Guangming, O., Haider, M. A., Colomer, J., Kayani, S., & Amin, N. (2020). Moral education for sustainable development: Comparison of university teachers' perceptions in China and Pakistan. *Sustainability, 12*(7), 1–20. https://doi.org/10.3390/su12073014

Asmani, J. M. (2013). *Tips menjadi guru inspiratif, kreatif, dan inovatif.* Diva Press.

Bahrin, N. A. (2020). *Kaedah Pembelajaran Teknik Jigsaw Dalam Mata Pelajaran MIB Di Kalangan Pelajar Tahun 10 Di Sekolah Menengah Kerajaan.* Unpublished BA thesis, Universiti Brunei Darussalam, Tungku Link, Brunei.

Besar, S. N. (2016). Students' perceptions of social media within the MIB module. *ASEAN Journal of Open Distance Learning, 8*(2), 1–11.

Bhanegaonkar, M., & Mahfoodh, M. (2013). New approach for evaluating EFLM: An eclectic developed checklist. *International Journal of Scientific and Research Publications, 3*(10), 1–8. https://doi.org/10.17507/tpls.0602.06

Brunei Curriculum Development Department. (2010). *Pendidikan Kenegaraan Melayu Islam Beraja: Peringkat Rendah dan Menengah.* Curriculum Development Department, Ministry of Education.

Brunei Ministry of Education. (2009). *Sistem Pendidikan Negara Abad Ke-21 (SPN21).* Curriculum Development Department, Ministry of Education.

Chowdhury, M. (2016). Emphasizing morals, values, ethics, and character education in science education and science teaching. *The Malaysian Online Journal of Educational Science,* 4(2), 1–16. https://files.eric.ed.gov/fulltext/EJ1095995.pdf

Florian, L., & Linklater, H. (2010). Preparing teachers for inclusive education: using inclusive pedagogy to enhance teaching and learning for all. *Cambridge Journal of Education,* 40(4), 369–386. https://doi.org/10.1080/0305764X.2010.526588

Ghavifekr, S., Kunjappan, T., Ramasamy, L., & Anthony, A. (2016). Teaching and learning with ICT tools: Issues and challenges from teachers' perceptions. *Malaysian Online Journal of Educational Technology,* 4(2), 38–57.

Haji Abdul Ghani, S. (2015). Hayati MIB hadapi cabaran globalisasi. *Pelita Brunei.* Brunei: Jabatan Penerangan. http://pelitabrunei.gov.bn/Lists/Berita/NewDisplayForm.aspx?ID=9056&ContentTypeId=0x0100BC31BF6D2ED1E4459ACCF88DA3E23BA8

Haji Abu Bakar, S. N. (2018). *Kesan penggunaan alat bantu mengajar pendekatan multimodaliti dalam pemelajaran soalan konteks Kesusasteraan Melayu.* Unpublished BA thesis, Universiti Brunei Darussalam, Tungku Link, Brunei.

Haji Awang Damit, S. (2020). *Kesan permainan papan ular dan tangga dalam pembelajaran Melayu Islam Brunei bagi Tahun 7 di sekolah menengah kerajaan Negara Brunei Darussalam.* Unpublished BA thesis, Universiti Brunei Darussalam, Tungku Link, Brunei.

Haji Awang Matassan, M. E. A. (2013). *Lakonan Dalam Pembelajaran Melayu Islam Beraja: Satu Kajian Tindakan Untuk Tahun 7.* Unpublished BA thesis, Universiti Brunei Darussalam, Tungku Link, Brunei.

Haji Gharif, H. R. (2010). *Penerapan nilai-nilai moral Islam dalam pengajaran dan pembelajaran di sekolah-sekolah menengah.* Unpublished MA thesis, Universiti Brunei Darussalam, Tungku Link, Brunei.

Haji Jaili, F. (2015). *Kesan Penggunaan Perisian Interaktif Powerpoint Dalam Pembelajaran Mib Dalam Topik "Titih Dan Lutanan" Terhadap Pelajar Tahun 7 Di Sekolah Menengah Brunei Darussalam.* Unpublished BA thesis, Universiti Brunei Darussalam, Tungku Link, Brunei.

Haji Mail, H. A. A. (2013). Dasar-dasar pendidikan Negara Brunei Darussalam (1950–2010): Kemunculannya dan hubungannya dengan falsafah Melayu Islam Beraja. *Susur Galur,* 1(2), 151–166.

Haji Md Yassin, H. S. S. (2014). *Pembelajaran Berasaskan Projek Poster Dalam Subjek Melayu Islam Beraja Tahun 8.* Unpublished BA thesis, Universiti Brunei Darussalam, Tungku Link, Brunei.

Haji Omar, H. M. H. (2017). *Amalan nilai-nilai murni guru mata pelajaran Melayu Islam Beraja bagi Tahun 10 di sekolah menengah: Kajian eksplorasi.* Unpublished MA thesis, Universiti Brunei Darussalam, Tungku Link, Brunei.

Haji Rashid, W. (2018). *Keberkesanan penggunaan teka silang kata dalam pembelajaran MIB.* Unpublished BA thesis, Universiti Brunei Darussalam, Tungku Link, Brunei.

Haji Serudin, H. M. Z. (2013). *The Malay Islamic Monarchy: A Closer Understanding* (D. H. Z. Haji Muhammad Tahir & D. H. N. Haji Abdul Majid, Trans.). Bandar Seri Begawan, Brunei: The National Supreme Council of the Malay Islamic Monarchy.

Haji Tahamit, Z. (2016). *Kesan penggunaan ICT terhadap pelajar Tahun 7 dalam pembelajaran Melayu Islam Beraja.* Unpublished BA thesis, Universiti Brunei Darussalam, Tungku Link, Brunei.

Haji Talipuddin, H. K. A. (2013). *Manifestasi Pendidikan akhlak: Kajian komparatif antara guru subjek Pengetahuan Ugama Islam dan guru Subjek Melayu Islam Beraja.* Unpublished MA thesis, Universiti Brunei Darussalam, Tungku Link, Brunei.

Haji Tarsat, A. H. (2013). *Penggunaan Kaedah Permainan dalam Pembelajaran mata Pelajaran Melayu Islam Beraja.* Unpublished BA thesis, Universiti Brunei Darussalam, Tungku Link, Brunei.

Haji Yaakub, H. M. (2014). *Kesan Penggunaan Kaedah Bercerita Dalam Pembelajaran MIB.* Unpublished thesis, Universiti Brunei Darussalam, Tungku Link, Brunei.

Halstead, J. M. (2007). Islamic values: A distinctive framework for moral education. *Journal of Moral Education, 36*(3), 283–296. https://doi.org/10.1080/03057240701643056

Han, H., Park, S. C., Kim, J., Jeong, C., & Kim, S. (2018). A quantitative analysis of moral exemplars presented education textbooks in Korea and Japan. *Asia Pacific Journal of Education, 38,* 62–77. https://doi.org/10.1080/02188791.2018.1423950

Hannus, M., & Hyona, J. (1999). Utilization of illustrations during learning of science textbook passages among low- and high-ability children. *Contemporary Educational Psychology, 24*(2), 95–123. https://doi.org/10.1006/ceps.1998.0987

Hj. Md Jalaluddin, N. M. (2015). *Kesan penggunaan teknologi animasi dalam pengajaran dan pembelajaran MIB bagi pelajar tahun 7 di sekolah menengah Negara Brunei Darussalam.* Unpublished BA thesis, Universiti Brunei Darussalam, Tungku Link, Brunei.

Husbands, C., & Pearce, J. (2012). What makes great pedagogy? Nine claims from research. *Research and Development Network National Themes: Theme One,* 1–16. https://assets.publishing.service.gov.uk/government/uploads/system/uploads/attachment_data/file/329746/what-makes-great-pedagogy-nine-claims-from-research.pdf

James, M., & Pollard, A. (2011). TLRP's ten principles for effective pedagogy: rationale, development, evidence, argument and impact. *Research Papers in Education*, 26(3), 275–328. https://doi.org/10.1080/02671522.2011.590007

Janudin, A. A. (2020). *Aplikasi Kaedah Buzz dalam Mata Pelajaran MIB bagi Pelajar Tahun 9 di Sekolah Menengah Kerajaan Negara Brunei Darussalam.* Unpublished BA thesis, Universiti Brunei Darussalam, Tungku Link, Brunei.

Lapsley, D., & Yeager, D. S. (2013). Moral-character education. In I. Weiner (Ed.) & W. Reynolds & G. Miller (Vol. Eds.), *Handbook of psychology. Vol. 7. Educational psychology* (pp. 147–177). New York, NY: Wiley. https://doi.org/10.1002/9781118133880.hop207007

Lapsley, D. K., & Narvaez, D. (2006). Character education. In W. Damon, R. Lerner, A. Renninger, & I. Siegel (Eds.), *Handbook of Child Psychology. Vol. 4. Child Psychology in Practice* (6th ed., pp. 248–296). Wiley. https://doi.org/10.1002/9780470147658.chpsy0407

Makmun, R. (2018). *Refleksi dan inovasi proses pengajaran dan pembelajaran Kesusasteraan Melayu.* Dewan Bahasa dan Pustaka Brunei.

Makmun, R., Madin, A. B., Tarasat, S., Abd Rahman, S. K., Jaidi, N., & Abu Bakar, R. (2020). *Amalan Terbaik Guru dalam Menyerapkan Nilai Murni – Kemahiran Berbahasa. Research Report for Universiti Brunei Darussalam.* Universiti Brunei Darussalam.

Makmun, R., & Mahamod, Z. (2015). *Teknologi, pedagogi dan pengetahuan kandungan.* Universiti Brunei Darussalam.

Mundia, L. (2010). Implementation of SPN21 curriculum in Brunei Darussalam: A review of selected implications on school assessment reforms. *International Education Studies*, 3(2), 119–129. https://doi.org/10.5539/ies.v3n2p119

Narinasamy, I., & Wan Mamat, W. H. (2013). Utilization of ICT by moral education teachers. *The Malaysian Online Journal of Educational Technology*, 1(4), 44–53.

O'Donnell, H. (1983). The use of illustrations in textbooks. *The Reading Teacher*, 36(4), 462–464. https://www.jstor.org/stable/20198251

Saidin, S. (2018). *Keberkesanan aktiviti lakonan dalam mata pelajaran melayu islam beraja bagi meningkatkan penglibatan pelajar dalam kelas.* Unpublished BA thesis, Universiti Brunei Darussalam, Tungku Link, Brunei.

Schallert, D. L. (1980). The role of illustrations in reading comprehension. In R. J. Spiro, B. C. Bruce, & W. F. Brewer (Eds.), *Theoretical issues in reading comprehension* (pp. 503–524). Routledge.

Schuitema, J., Dam, G., & Veugelers, W. (2007). Teaching strategies for moral education: A review. *Curriculum Studies*, 40. https://doi.org/10.1080/00220270701294210

Tuah, H. D. (2002). *Brunei Darussalam nation building.* Prime Minister's Office.

CHAPTER 14

The Integration of Quranic Spiritual Knowledge in Brunei Darussalam's Science Education Curriculum

Mohammad Hilmy Baihaqy

14.1 Introduction

In the era of modern sciences, scholars have expressed concerns about the moral and political aspects of science and technology. Ravetz (1984), the author of *Scientific Knowledge and Its Social Problems*, argued that there are two critical problems that must be examined in the discussion of science and values: the approach from the standpoint of the Muslim world and the total system of science and technology that so largely defines the civilisation of the Occident. In many respects, science and technology have become a part of liberation for mankind, yet from the Islamic perspective it can also be seen as a threat, cultural as well as material. Nevertheless, it also can be seen as a subject that can enhance human spirituality.

M. H. Baihaqy (✉)
Universiti Islam Sultan Sharif Ali (UNISSA),
Bandar Seri Begawan, Brunei

© The Author(s), under exclusive license to Springer Nature Switzerland AG 2021
Phan, L. H. et al. (eds.), *Globalisation, Education, and Reform in Brunei Darussalam*, International and Development Education, https://doi.org/10.1007/978-3-030-77119-5_14

As noted by Ali (2013), revivalists argued that if we ponder upon the history of civilisation and the critical assessment of realities around the world, it reveals that the lack of spirituality is the root cause of the chaos and crisis in the contemporary world, including the education system itself, because Muslims view spirituality as the essence and basis of life (Benard, 2003).

Before the modern era, people were dependent on religion for guidance in the face of adversity and hardship, thus people put their faith in God. However, as the concept of modernity and rationalism flourished, and as science refuted certain basic tenets of the Church especially in Western history, people are focusing their mind on science as a solution for their difficulties. Therefore, the world becomes materialistic and impoverished in spirituality. Regrettably, science brought mixed blessings to humanity. As stated by Ali (2013), this would create new difficulties for each problem that is being solved, which also tend to disorient and confuse people. Due to this, the industrialisation of economies has caused social upheaval and political change (Iqbāl, 1994). Thus, it is important to include the role of science in developing human spirituality.

14.2 The Meaning and Significance of Quranic Spirituality

To understand the significance of spirituality in science education, one must understand that man has a dual nature, consisting both body and soul, and man at once a physical being and a spirit. In other words, a person consists of physical and spiritual aspects (Syed Muhammad Naquib al-Attas, 2001). According to Ewert (1992), spirituality can be defined as an ultimate or an alleged immaterial reality. It is an inner path enabling a person to discover the essence of his/her being, and it is described as the deepest values and meanings by which people live (Sheldrake, 2007).

Becker (2011) argued spirituality is often viewed as more subjective and personal. Pargament (1997) stated that spirituality refers to a 'search for significance' in ways one regards to be sacred, which is the opposite of secularism. Becker added that once spiritual life develops through relationship with self an inspirational power will begin to develop. According to Wright (1999), spirituality can be described as the summation of our values, which determines the process of how we interact with the world, whereas religion is seen as a pathway to follow the practices, and thoughts that are appropriate to the God or Gods of a particular faith. Spirituality is crucial because it reflects one's deepest sense of worth, meaning and connections with the ultimate reality (Puchalski et al., 2009). From the religions point of view, spirituality is an integral aspect of religious experience of human life experiences.

In Islam, the conception of spirituality is related to all aspects of life since the main purpose of man's creation is to worship God (Rulindo et al., 2011). In Islamic tradition, as stated before, human being consists of two parts: the body or the physical dimension, and the spiritual dimension that consists of spirit or '*nafs*' and soul or '*ruh*'. According to Nasr (1987), spirituality in Islam deals primarily with the inner dimension of a person's life. Nasr (2008) added that the main principle of Islamic spirituality is the realisation of God as expressed in the Quran. One of this can be obtained from observing the creation of God. Spiritual knowledge is not only limited to the world of the pure spirit. It is also concerned with the manifestations of the spirit in the different orders of reality that make up the whole universe. A basic component of a Muslim's knowledge of God is the knowledge of the universe as an effect of the divine creative act. It is the knowledge of the relationship between God and the world, between Creator and creation, or between the Divine Principle and cosmic manifestations that includes the most fundamental basis of the unity of science and spiritual knowledge. In Islam, the most important sources of this type of knowledge are the Quran and the prophetic *hadiths*.

Osman Bakar (2008) stated that there are two strong reasons why Islam insists on a spiritually motivated appreciation of nature. The first argument is that Islam teaches Muslims to view nature as a sacred book that serves as a counterpart of the revealed Quran. As discussed before, the book of nature contains precious spiritual messages for man's constant reflection. Through these reflections, men will be able to know its Creator better and thereby, get closer to Him. With the guidance given from the Quran, men would be able to arrive at a more complete understanding of the spiritual significance of nature compared to the one that relies solely on reason and external physical senses. Secondly, Islam teaches human beings to use nature in accordance with the laws that God has laid down in His revealed book, the Quran. Thus, with the development of spirituality that arises from reflections on nature, men will be motivated to protect and be responsible towards nature as dictated by the Revealed book.

In addition, Sayyed Hossein Nasr (1993) emphasised that the Islamic natural sciences cultivated in Islamic civilisation by Muslim scientists were based on a careful and analytic study of nature within the matrix of Islamic revelation which stimulates spirituality. The essence of this revelation is *al-tawhid* which is the principle of unity professed by every member of the Islamic community. Kalin (2001) adds that this principle underlies the unity and interrelatedness of the world of nature.

Even though *al-tawhid* in its ordinary sense refers to the theological dictum that there is no divinity but God, its ontological and metaphysical meanings enter the picture as a corollary of it by construing the world of nature as issuing forth from a single source, the Divine. The main goal of Islamic sciences from medicine to geometry is to disclose this underlying unity and to show 'the unity and interrelatedness of all that exists' (Nasr, 1993, p. 58). There are verses that relate the study of natural phenomena with the acquisition of true faith and the realisation of *al-tawhid*. One of these verses is:

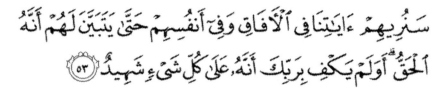

> We will show them Our signs in the horizons and within themselves until it becomes clear to them that it is the truth. But is it not sufficient concerning your Lord that He is, over all things, a Witness? [*Surah Al-Fussliat*, 41:53]

This verse shows how God invites His servants to see and reflect upon the natural phenomena. Through the reflection and observation of the order and the coordination in the system that He created, men will be able to get close to Him and these could develop their level of spirituality.

14.3 The National Philosophy of Education

One of the arguments on the integration of spiritual knowledge and science is for the national philosophy of the education. The philosophy of education in Brunei Darussalam states that:

> National education of Brunei Darussalam is a continuous endeavour based not only on revealed knowledge from the holy Qur'an and the Hadith (the

sayings and actions of Prophet Muhammad), but also on logical reasoning. (Ministry of Education, 2004, p. 4)

This statement affirms that, apart from the application of logical reasoning, which is widely applied in secular education, the philosophy of education in Brunei is also based on the teachings of the Quran as well as prophetic *hadiths* (see Chap. 5). Thus, science education according to the national philosophy of education is meant to not only improve the people's logical reasoning and thinking capacity, but also to appreciate the Quran as well as *hadiths* as fundamental sources of knowledge which could develop the spirituality of the learners and the teachers.

As stated by the Ministry of Education (2004), the main aim of national education in Brunei Darussalam is to develop individuals to their fullest, so as to produce people who are 'knowledgeable, devout, faithful, pious, trustworthy, responsible and of noble character' (p. 4). To be knowledgeable means not only to know knowledge related to the sciences, but also knowing how to integrate these sciences with spiritual knowledge that are based upon the Quran.

14.4 The Need for the Islamisation of Science

Due to the secularisation of science, which first took place in the West after the Age of Renaissance, there is a need for the Islamisation of science (Bakar, 2008). According to Osman Bakar (2008) and Mulyahdi Kartanegara (2009), Western scholarship was very much influenced by Islamic scholarship around the twelfth and thirteenth centuries, especially after the translation of Islamic scientific and philosophical works into Latin and Hebrew. Thus, the science developed was still religious (i.e. Islamic) in nature, or at least motivated by Islam itself. Unfortunately, after the Renaissance era from the fourteenth century onward, there was the so-called revolution in scientific field which shifted towards the secular view. As a result, this new scientific view did not get along with religion (Ibid.).

Brohi (1979), a Pakistani philosopher, also argued that during the last 200 years or so, the foundation of religious belief has been questioned and, to a considerable extent, undermined. He added that in the modern era, people are living in God-less times, and man does not acknowledge the Higher Presence any more especially in the world of science education.

Islamisation of modern empirical knowledge such as science is indeed an effort to assimilate this knowledge in an Islamic framework with a view to utilise this knowledge for the good of the Muslim education and society. It is also an attempt to comprehend and perhaps embrace all that is beneficial in this knowledge by integrating it with traditional Islamic knowledge that is rooted in the Quran as well as the prophetic *hadīth*. Thus, the next critical questions to ask are: How can this be done for the case of science education? How should science be taught and learned as a part of Islamic curriculum in the Muslim educational institutions form the lower secondary schools to the universities, and what are the methodologies and procedures implemented in planning a course of instruction in science? How can we establish the relevance of Islamic knowledge to contemporary scientific progress, and what parameters need to be identified and studied to bring this change? (Kazi, 1982). Indeed, the inclusion of relevant Quranic verses in the science textbook is an important move towards Islamisation of science. In the context of Brunei Darussalam, it is crucial to assess the Quranic verses that have been inserted to see whether they conform with the subjects that will be taught.

Sulaiman (2000) argued that there are four major reasons for the need for Islamisation of knowledge including science. First, the mixing of real knowledge with false beliefs (e.g. myths), ideas and theories in the curriculum content. Second, the widespread view that knowledge is neutral with respect to values. Third, science is influenced by the paradigms of study that are chosen. Scientific knowledge is discovered, classified, taught and utilised in accordance with certain paradigms. There are many such paradigms. For instance, Western paradigm of science necessarily reflects Western values, which is secular in nature. Knowledge is compartmentalised into various disciplines. Their focuses, methodologies and epistemologies are all different with respect to paradigms. In respect to this, Muslims need to rearrange and channel their educational system in accordance with Islamic paradigms. This is one of the reasons why Islamisation of science should go beyond recasting or remoulding disciplines that have been developed within the secular paradigms.

The fourth reason is the new developments in various fields of knowledge and technological products that earlier Muslim scholars and jurists did not witness in their lifetimes show the need for modern scholars to embark upon the Islamisation projects. The issue of cloning in biological sciences is one such example. New concepts and theories in science that are rapidly gaining acceptance in Muslim nations need to be tamed through the Islamisation of knowledge undertaking to prevent Muslims from accepting ideas that are opposed to the Islamic faith. If Muslim scholars fail to explain the new issues in line with the teachings of Islam, the uniqueness of Islam in terms of its philosophy and epistemology will not be seen. Inferiority complex will also be embedded in the Muslim minds when they are trained to believe that Islam has no provisions or explanations for the new issues.

14.5 THE QURANIC INCLUSION IN THE YEAR 7 SCIENCE CURRICULUM TEXTBOOK

As observed in the Secondary Science Year 7 Science textbook for Brunei, every chapter begins with a translation of a Quranic verse (see Fig. 14.1). This chapter presents the text analysis of these Quranic verses based on scientific exegesis or '*tafsīr ʿilmī*' of the Quran.

Since there is a need for a contemporary understanding of the Quran through scientific knowledge, scientific exegesis is needed. The scientific exegesis or '*tafsīr ʿilmī*' is based on revelations concerning scientific issues in areas such as astronomy, biology, geology and others, or on passages that are viewed as anticipations of modern scientific discoveries. One clear objective of contemporary Muslim scientific exegesis is to find further proof of the inimitability of the Quran and the miraculous nature of its content. Al-Ghazālī, for instance, stated that the Quran does not contain 'all the sciences', but it undoubtedly includes the key giving access to all of the sciences (Campanini, 2011). Moreover, in his view, representations of the inimitability of the Quran refer to everything that it comprises from which the sciences emerge, including astronomy, astrology and medicine. According to Ushama (2013), many Muslims scholars followed al-Ghazālī in justifying the use of scientific method (*al-manhaj al-ʿilmī*) in interpreting the Quran, which of course depends on employing knowledge in pure and applied sciences such as when interpreting the signs of the cosmos mentioned in many verses of the Quran (Al-Najjār, 2009).

14.5.1 Chapter 1: Introducing Science

This introductory chapter discusses the definition and importance of science. It also explores various scientific techniques and equipment that are often used by scientists. It also discusses the methodology of a scientific investigation to solve the given problem. In this introductory chapter, the following Quranic verse is used:

Fig. 14.1 Chapter 1 from the Year 7 secondary science textbook

$$\text{فَالِقُ ٱلْإِصْبَاحِ وَجَعَلَ ٱلَّيْلَ سَكَنًا وَٱلشَّمْسَ وَٱلْقَمَرَ حُسْبَانًا ذَٰلِكَ تَقْدِيرُ ٱلْعَزِيزِ ٱلْعَلِيمِ ﴿٩٦﴾}$$

'(He is the) Cleaver of the daybreak. He has appointed the night for resting and the Sun and the Moon for reckoning. Such is the measuring of the All-Mighty, the All-Knowing' [Al-An'am,6:96]. The Secondary Science for Brunei Darussalam Textbook for Year 7 did not state the Arabic verse from the Quran. It only states the translation of the Quran. For the purpose of explanation, the researcher intends to insert both Arabic as well as its translation in this work.

In the view of the researcher, the above verse is not closely related to the chapter entitled 'Introducing Science'. The above verse is about the power and knowledge of Allah in His creation on the phenomena of a day and a night. The verse also stated that the function of a night is for human beings to rest and the purpose of the sun and the moon is to help them in time calculation and time keeping activities. Although these issues are related to science, it does not concern with the content of the chapter. A better alternative to serve as a Quranic guide or source of inspiration to this chapter entitled 'Introducing Science' would be the following verse:

$$\text{سَنُرِيهِمْ ءَايَٰتِنَا فِى ٱلْءَافَاقِ وَفِى أَنفُسِهِمْ حَتَّىٰ يَتَبَيَّنَ لَهُمْ أَنَّهُ ٱلْحَقُّ أَوَلَمْ يَكْفِ بِرَبِّكَ أَنَّهُ عَلَىٰ كُلِّ شَىْءٍ شَهِيدٌ ﴿٥٣﴾}$$

We will show them Our Signs in the universe, and in their own selves, until it becomes manifest to them that this (the Qur'ān) is the truth. Is it not sufficient in regard to your Lord that He is a Witness over all things? [*Fuṣṣilat, 41:53*]

According to Ibn Kathīr in his *Tafsīr*, the above verse means that the study of external signs (in the universe) as well as signs within the human beings themselves will provide evidence that the Quran is indeed a true revelation. In the Islamic perspective the study of science is a study of God's signs. Therefore, by studying science, it also appreciates and reflects the greatness of God that could enhance human spirituality.

14.5.2 Chapter 2: Classification

This chapter of the textbook discusses the classification of creation into living and non-living things. As an introduction to this chapter, the following Quranic verse is presented:

$$\text{وَٱللَّهُ خَلَقَ كُلَّ دَآبَّةٍ مِّن مَّآءٍ فَمِنْهُم مَّن يَمْشِى عَلَىٰ بَطْنِهِۦ وَمِنْهُم مَّن يَمْشِى عَلَىٰ رِجْلَيْنِ وَمِنْهُم مَّن يَمْشِى عَلَىٰٓ أَرْبَعٍ يَخْلُقُ ٱللَّهُ مَا يَشَآءُ إِنَّ ٱللَّهَ عَلَىٰ كُلِّ شَىْءٍ قَدِيرٌ ۝٤٥}$$

> Allah has created every moving (living) creature from water. Of them there are some that creep on their bellies, some that walk on two legs, and some that walk on four. Allah creates what He wills. Verily! Allah is Able to do all things. [*an-Nur*, 24:45]

This time, the selection of the quoted verse seems justified, at least as far as living things are concerned. According to Ibn Kathīr, the above verse illustrates Allah's power in His creation of the animals. He has power to create all kinds of forms, colours and ways of movement. Some of His living creatures creep on their bellies such as snakes and caterpillars. The part of the verse, 'some that walk on two legs' refers to humans and birds, and the part, 'some that walk on four' refers to such animals as cattle and many other kinds. The verse ends with a stress on God's power to create diversity in His creation of animals. This means that through a scientific study of animal's human beings can have a better appreciation of God's infinite power and knowledge.

14.5.3 Chapter 3: Matter

While the second chapter illustrates the classification of objects into living and non-living things, the third chapter discusses about 'matter' which is defined as anything that has mass and takes up space. In the beginning of this chapter, the textbook displays the following verse:

14 THE INTEGRATION OF QURANIC SPIRITUAL KNOWLEDGE IN BRUNEI...

ثُمَّ ٱسْتَوَىٰٓ إِلَى ٱلسَّمَآءِ وَهِىَ دُخَانٌ فَقَالَ لَهَا وَلِلْأَرْضِ ٱئْتِيَا طَوْعًا أَوْ كَرْهًا قَالَتَآ أَتَيْنَا طَآئِعِينَ ۝

Then He rose over (Istawā) towards the heaven when it was smoke, and said to it and to the earth: "Come both of you willingly or unwillingly." They both said: "We come willingly". [*Fuṣṣilat*, 41:11]

In the view of the researcher, the choice of the above verse to be placed at the beginning of Chap. 3 is inconsistent with its overall content. Moreover, the researcher believes that the verse above was inserted in this chapter due to the English translation of the word '*dukhan*' that denotes 'smoke' as one of the states of matter (i.e. gas). Even though smoke is considered to be under the properties of gas, the smoke mentioned in the verse refers to the gaseous stuff from which the heavenly objects were made. The verse stated that the heaven and the earth and all cosmic objects were originally created from smoke. This smoke gave rise to the stars and galaxies followed by the formation of the solar system and the earth.

In this context, matter is mostly defined as any substance which has mass and occupies spaces. Today, matter is used lightly as a general term for the substance that makes up all observable physical objects (Penrose, 1991). Thus, everything that we observe which has mass and takes up space is referred as matter. In the Quranic perspective, everything that we observe as consisting of matter forms part of God's creation. Thus, a suitable verse to serve as an introduction to the third chapter that discusses about 'matter' would be:

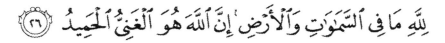

To Allah belongs whatsoever is in the heavens and the earth. Verily, Allah, He is Al-Ghani (Rich, Free of all wants), Worthy of all praise. [*Luqmān*, 31:26]

According to *tafsīr Jalālaīn*, the above verse is emphasising the power and majesty of God. Whatever is in the heavens and the earth, whether as our possessions, as creatures or as servants, all belong to God. Matter in any form—solid, liquid or gas—whether known or unknown to human beings is an aspect of the physical universe, which is His creation.

14.5.4 Chapter 4: Water

This fourth chapter illustrates several concepts concerning water. In the first few sub-topics, it urges the readers especially students to state the three states of water, namely solid (ice), liquid (water) and gas (steam). Then it explains the changes of states of water with reference to boiling, melting, condensation, freezing as well as evaporation. The Quranic verse selected to be placed at the beginning of this chapter is as follows:

مَرَجَ ٱلۡبَحۡرَيۡنِ يَلۡتَقِيَانِ ١٩ بَيۡنَهُمَا بَرۡزَخٌ لَّا يَبۡغِيَانِ ٢٠ فَبِأَيِّ ءَالَآءِ رَبِّكُمَا تُكَذِّبَانِ ٢١ يَخۡرُجُ مِنۡهُمَا ٱللُّؤۡلُؤُ وَٱلۡمَرۡجَانُ ٢٢

> He has let loose the two seas (the salt and fresh water) meeting together (19). Between them is a barrier which none of them can transgress (20). Then which of the Blessings of your Lord will you both (jinn and men) deny? (21). Out of them both come out pearl and coral (22). [*al-Rahmān*, 55:19–22]

The main scientific issue that is stated in the above verse is the separation between salt and fresh water. The separation between salt and sea water is due to the differences in their densities (UCSB; National Science Foundation, 2014). Since the concept of 'density' is not included in this chapter, the usage of verses 19 to 22 of *Surah al-Rahmān* seems inappropriate to be used to introduce this chapter.

Since the chapter is concerned with the topic of water, it would be more appropriate if the following verse is chosen:

أَفَرَءَيۡتُمُ ٱلۡمَآءَ ٱلَّذِي تَشۡرَبُونَ ٦٨ ءَأَنتُمۡ أَنزَلۡتُمُوهُ مِنَ ٱلۡمُزۡنِ أَمۡ نَحۡنُ ٱلۡمُنزِلُونَ ٦٩ لَوۡ نَشَآءُ جَعَلۡنَٰهُ أُجَاجًا فَلَوۡلَا تَشۡكُرُونَ ٧٠

> Have you observed the water that you drink? (68). Is it you who cause it from the rainclouds to come down, or are We Who cause it to come down? (69). If We willed, We verily could make it salt (and undrinkable), why then do you not give thanks (to Allah)? (70). [*al-Waqiāh*, 56:68–70]

The above verses invite human beings to think and reflect about the water that they used to drink. It can be either pure, distilled or water as a solvent. Science tells us that unpolluted rainwater is the purest form of water. Verse

69 invites man to think about the Creator who causes the water to fall from the rainclouds. This is how the Quran invites men to think about science. Through a scientific study of the production of rainwater and its nature and numerous benefits to their life human beings will better appreciate pure drinkable water as one of God's greatest gifts to mankind. If all of the water that comes down from the rainclouds were to be salty, then human life on earth would be beset with hardships. There is first of all the need to distil the salty water in order to use it for everyday life such as planting, drinking as well as bathing.

14.5.5   Chapter 5: Cell Structure and Organisation

In this chapter, students will explore the differences between animal and plant cells, as well as how cells are organised in the human body. To begin the chapter, the textbook furnishes the following Quranic verses:

يَٰٓأَيُّهَا ٱلْإِنسَٰنُ مَا غَرَّكَ بِرَبِّكَ ٱلْكَرِيمِ ٦ ٱلَّذِي خَلَقَكَ فَسَوَّىٰكَ فَعَدَلَكَ ٧ فِىٓ أَيِّ صُورَةٍ مَّا شَآءَ رَكَّبَكَ ٨ [سورة الانفطار, ٦-٨]

> O man! What has made you careless about your Lord, the Most Generous? (6). Who created you, fashioned you perfectly, and gave you due proportion (7). In whatever form He willed, He put you together (8). [*al-Infitār*, 82:6–8]

According to *Tafsir al*-Jalalaīn, the above verse reminds the disbelievers about the bounties and blessings that Allah has given to human beings, who were created in perfect proportions. The perfect creation can be observed from the construction of cells in human beings as well as plants. Furthermore, there are specific functions in every part of the human, animal as well as plant cells. By observing these functions, man will be reminded about the perfect and beauty creation of God. Thus, human spirituality would be presence as they appreciate the God's creation.

14.5.6   Chapter 6: Force and Pressure

In this chapter, students will learn the concept of forces and its effects, work done and pressure. The textbook provides the following Quranic verse in its introduction:

$$\text{وَهُوَ ٱلَّذِي خَلَقَ ٱلَّيْلَ وَٱلنَّهَارَ وَٱلشَّمْسَ وَٱلْقَمَرَ كُلٌّ فِي فَلَكٍ يَسْبَحُونَ ٣٣ [سورة الأنبياء,٣٣]}$$

And He it is Who created the Night and the Day, and the Sun and the Moon, each in an orbit floating (33). [*al-Anbiyā'a*, 21:33]

The relation between the above verse and science is through the concept of 'gravitational force'. The constant orbital motion of the moon around the earth and of the planets around the sun is due to the constant gravitational force between the two planets. The above verse is therefore closely related to the subject matter discussed in this chapter. This verse will also help to instil in human mind that God is causing the gravitational force to withhold the planets striking with the earth. Therefore, it will instil the spiritual appreciation of human towards the creation of God.

14.5.7 Chapter 7: Energy

As an introduction to the above chapter, the following verse is presented:

$$\text{ٱلَّذِي جَعَلَ لَكُم مِّنَ ٱلشَّجَرِ ٱلْأَخْضَرِ نَارًا فَإِذَآ أَنتُم مِّنْهُ تُوقِدُونَ ٨٠ [سورة يس,٨٠]}$$

He Who produces for you fire out of the green tree, when behold you kindle therewith. [*Yasin*, 36:80]

In the researcher's view, the above verse is related to the concept of fossil fuels as well as biodiesel. In addition, Ibn Kathīr quoted Ibn 'Abbas (may Allah be pleased with him) as saying that the trees stated in the verse refer to the *Markh* and '*Afar* trees, which are grown in the *Hijaz*. He stated that if one wants to light a fire but has no kindling with him, then he could take two green branches from these trees and rub them against each other so as to produce fire. Therefore, they are similar to kindling. When fire is produced, it can be used as a source of energy.

Undoubtedly, energy is also stored in trees. Trees that remained under the ground for long periods of time can be a great source of energy. For instance, fossil fuels are formed when heat and pressure act on the remains of dead plants over millions of years. In addition, when the word 'tree' is mentioned, the adjective 'green' is applied. This indicates that the layer of plants that covers the earth continuously emits oxygen, a caustic substance for burning. With the medium of oxygen, combustion for creating energy can be made possible. Furthermore, the findings in the field of biodiesel are also closer to the understanding of the stated verse. Through experiments that were carried out, it has been shown that green plants are able to produce biodiesel used as fuel to produce energy for human use (Ramli et al., 2014).

14.5.8 Chapter 8: Magnetism

The final chapter of the textbook is on magnetism. In this chapter, students will explore the characteristics and the uses of magnets. It also illustrates the formation of magnetic field. The Quranic verse that was inserted in the beginning of this chapter is:

وَأَنزَلْنَا ٱلْحَدِيدَ فِيهِ بَأْسٌ شَدِيدٌ وَمَنَٰفِعُ لِلنَّاسِ وَلِيَعْلَمَ ٱللَّهُ مَن يَنصُرُهُۥ وَرُسُلَهُۥ بِٱلْغَيْبِ إِنَّ ٱللَّهَ قَوِيٌّ عَزِيزٌ ٢٥ [سورة الحديد,٢٥]

> .... And We brought forth iron wherein is mighty power (in matters of war), as well as many benefits for mankind, that Allah may test who it is that will help Him (His religion) and His Messengers in the unseen. Verily, Allah is All-Strong, All-Mighty. [*al-Hadīd*: 57,25]

The important magnetic material that is stated in the above verse is iron. This verse explicitly mentions iron as a source of power such as for making weapons and its many other benefits for mankind. For instance, in modern times, apart from making weapons, iron which is a magnetised material is a useful element in the field of transportation, electronics as well as communications. However, with the reference from the above verse, it invites men to realise the power of God, which cultivated human spirituality.

From analysing the verses of the Quran shown on every chapter of the Year 7 Secondary Science Textbook, it is shown that three out of eight Quranic verses that were not aligned with the content of the topics. These verses are in Chap. 1 (Introducing Science), Chap. 3 (Matter) and Chap. 4 (Water). These shortcomings are mainly due to the lack of specialisation in the field of scientific exegesis among the textbook committee members. Table 14.1 provides a list of the chapters and the verses provided in the textbook as well as the suggested verses for the three chapters that are deemed unrelated with the content from the given chapter:

Table 14.1 Summary of chapters and verses in the Year 7 secondary science textbook

Name of the chapter	Provided verses	Is the verse related to the given chapter? If no, what is/are the alternative verse(s)
Chapter 1: Introducing Science	(He is the) Cleaver of the daybreak. He has appointed the night for resting, and the Sun and the Moon for reckoning. Such is the measuring of the All-Mighty, the All-Knowing	No. The alternative verse is: 'We will show them Our Signs in the universe, and in their own selves, until it becomes manifest to them that this (the Quran) is the truth. Is it not sufficient in regard to your Lord that He is a Witness over all things?' [*Fuṣṣilat*, 41:53]
Chapter 2: Classification	'Allah has created every moving (living) creature from water. Of them there are some that creep on their bellies, some that walk on two legs, and some that walk on four. Allah creates what He wills. Verily! Allah is Able to do all things.' [*an-Nur*, 24:45]	Yes. The alternative verse is: And We have made from water every living thing. Will they not then believe? [*al-ʿAnbiyā*, 23:30]
Chapter 3: Matter	'Then He rose over (Istawā) towards the heaven when it was smoke, and said to it and to the earth: "Come both of you willingly or unwillingly." They both said: "We come willingly".' [*Fuṣṣilat*, 41:11]	No. The suitable verse is: 'To Allah belongs whatsoever is in the heavens and the earth. Verily, Allah, He is Al-Ghani (Rich, Free of all wants), Worthy of all praise.' [*Luqmān*, 31:26]

(*continued*)

Table 14.1 (continued)

Name of the chapter	Provided verses	Is the verse related to the given chapter? If no, what is/are the alternative verse (s)
Chapter 4: Water	'He has let loose the two seas (the salt and fresh water) meeting together (19). Between them is a barrier which none of them can transgress (20). Then which of the Blessings of your Lord will you both (jinn and men) deny? (21). Out of them both come out pearl and coral (22).' [*al-Raḥmān*, 55:19–22]	No. The alternative verse is: 'Have you observed the water that you drink? (68). Is it you who cause it from the rainclouds to come down, or are We the Causer come down? (69). If We willed, We verily could make it salt (and undrinkable), why then do you not give thanks (to Allah)? (70).' [*al-Waqiāh*, 56:68–70]
Chapter 5: Cell structure and OrganizationOrganisation	'O man! What has made you careless about your Lord, the Most Generous? (6).Who created you, fashioned you perfectly, and gave you due proportion (7). In whatever form He willed, He put you together (8).' [*al-Infiṭār*, 82:6–8]	Yes.
Chapter 6: Force and Pressure	'And He it is Who created the Night and the Day, and the Sun and the Moon, each in an orbit floating (33).' [*al-Anbiyā'a*, 21:33]	Yes. Comment: The picture inserted in the introduction is not related with the illustrated verse. Thus, it will be better to illustrate a picture of the orbiting planets
Chapter 7: Energy	'He Who produces for you fire out of the green tree, when behold you kindle therewith' [*Yasin*, 36:80]	Yes

(*continued*)

Table 14.1 (continued)

Name of the chapter	Provided verses	Is the verse related to the given chapter? If no, what is/are the alternative verse(s)
Chapter 8: Magnetism	'…. And We brought forth iron wherein is mighty power (in matters of war), as well as many benefits for mankind, that Allah may test who it is that will help Him (His religion) and His Messengers in the unseen. Verily, Allah is All-Strong, All-Mighty' [*al-Hadīd* : 57,25]	Yes

14.6 Conclusion

The central epistemology for the integration of spiritual knowledge and science is a *tawhidic* worldview that considers Allah, as the Creator and Sustainer of the universe. According to this theory, it is possible for science to serve as an epistemological instrument to recognise the greatness and attributes of God. Therefore, it is critical to understand the universal Quranic theory of science education that is God-centric rooted from the Islamic revelation, the Quran. The *tawhidic* approach to science education emphasises both knowing God's creations through the scientific method and knowing the attributes and names of God mentioned by the Quran. In the *tawhidic* theory of science education, scientific knowledge and spirituality are viewed as being closely related to each other.

From the observations made, it is shown that the science education in Brunei Darussalam was influenced to a certain extent by this new modern global movement called Islamisation of knowledge, which aimed to integrate spirituality with sciences. This influence may be seen to have positively impacted the country's national philosophy of education. As demonstrated in this book chapter, there have been attempts aimed at integrating spiritual knowledges rooted from the Quran with their embodied concepts and values into the science education curriculum. However, there are several Quranic verses from a few chapters of the Year 7 Science textbook that are not certainly connected with the scientific content of the given chapter. Therefore, there is a need for corrections and improvements to develop the connections between the Quranic verses and the scientific content from the respective chapter.

In the context of Brunei Darussalam, the integration of Quranic spiritual knowledge and science could be made possible if there are adequate trainings given to the science teachers especially the Muslims teachers as to appreciate the source of spiritual and scientific knowledge, the Quran. Through adequate teacher training programme, teachers would be aware about the fundamental aspects of spiritual knowledges in science education.

References

Al-Attas, S. M. N. (2001). *Risalah untuk kaum muslimin*. ISTAC.

Al-Ghazālī. (2010). *Risālah al-Laduniyyah (Message from on high)* (M. Smith, Trans.). Islamic Book Turst.

Ali, M. M. (2013). *The history and philosophy of islamization of knowledge* (3rd ed.). International Islamic University Malaysia Press.

Al-Najjār, Z. R. (2009). *I'jāz al-I'lmī fī al-Qur'ān al-Kārīm*. Al-Maktabā Shoroūk.

Al-Quran.

Brohi, A. (1979). Education in an ideological state. In S. A. Ashraf, & S. M. al-Attas (Eds.), *Aims and objectives of Islamic education* (pp. 63–74). Jeddah: Hodder and Stoughton; King Abdul Aziz University.

Bakar, Osman. (2008). *Tawhid and science: Islamic perspective on religion and science* (2nd[nd] ed.). Arah Publication.

Becker, H. (2011). Research in spirituality, religion, and aging: An emerging era. Retrieved December 7, 2020, from http://www.britishgerontology.org/DB/gr-editions-2/generations-review/research-in-spirituality-religion-and-aging-an-eme.html

Benard, C. (2003). *Civil, democratic Islam: Partners, resources, and strategies*. RAND Corporation.

Campanini, M. (2011). *The Qur'ān: Modern muslim interpretations*. Routledge; Taylor & Francis Group.

Curriculum Development Department. (2013). *Secondary science for Brunei Darussalam textbook: Year 7*. Marshall Cavendish & Curriculum Development Department.

Ewert, C. (1992). *Preface to Antoine Faivre and Jacob Needleman, modern esoteric spirituality*. Crossroad Publishing.

Iqbāl, M. (1994). *The Reconstruction of Religious Thought in Islam*. New Delhi: Kitab Bahavan.

Kalin, I. (2001). *The sacred versus the secular: Nasr on science*. Open Court Press.

Kartanegara, M. (2009). *Secularization of science and its Islamic answer.* i-epistemology.net: http://i-epistemology.net/news-a-events/news/610-seminar-on-integration-of-knowledge-a-science.html

Kazi, M. (1982). Islamization of modern science and technology. In *Islam: Source and purpose of knowledge* (pp. 175–186). The International Institute of Islamic Thought.

Ministry of Education. (2004). *Education in Brunei Darussalam.* Public Relations Unit, Ministry of Education.

Nasr, S. H. (1987). *Islamic art and spirituality.* State University of New York Press.

Nasr, S. H. (1989). *Knowledge and the sacred.* State University of New York Press.

Nasr, S. H. (1993). *The need for a sacred science.* State University of New York Press.

Nasr, S. H. (2008). *Islamic spirituality* (Vol. 48). Routledge.

Pargament, K. (1997). *The psychology of religion and coping: Theory, research, practice.* Guilford.

Penrose, R. (1991). The mass of the classical vacuum. In S. Saunders & H. Brown (Eds.), *The philosophy of vacuum* (p. 21). Oxford University Press.

Puchalski, C., Ferrel, B., Virani, R., Otis-Green, S., Bird, P., Bull, J., Chochinov, H., Handzo, G., Nelson-Becker, H., Prince-Paul, M., Pugliese, K., & Sulmasy, D. (2009). Improving the quality of spiritual cae as a dmension of palliative care: The report of the consensus conference. *Journal of Palliative Medicine*, 885–904. https://doi.org/10.1089/jpm.2009.0142

Ramli, S., Murad, S. Z., & Husin, A. F. (2014). Biodiesel in holy Quran: Among the review of the Arabic lexicography and modern science. *Mediterranean Journal of Social Sciences, 5*(19), 336–342.

Ravetz, J. (1984). Science and values. In Z. Sardar (Ed.), *The touch of Midas: Science, values and environment in Islam and the west* (pp. 43–53). Butler & Tanner Ltd.

Rulindo, R., Hidayat, A., & Mardhatillah, S. E. (2011). The importance of spirituality for successful entrepreneurs. In R. I. K. Ahmed (Ed.), *Issues in Islamic management* (pp. 366–372). IIUP Press.

Sheldrake, P. (2007). *A brief history of spirituality.* Wiley-Blackwell.

Sulaiman, S. (2000). *Islamization of knowledge: Background, models and the way forward.* The International Institute of Islamic Thought.

UCSB; National Science Foundation. (2014, April 14). UCSB ScienceLine. http://scienceline.ucsb.edu/getkey.php?key=183

Ushama, T. (2013). *History and sciences of the Qur'ān.* International Islamic University Malaysia Press.

Wright, S. (1999). How to be happy at work. *Nursing Times, 95*, 26–28.

CHAPTER 15

MIB Beyond the Classroom: Local Influencers and Their Impact on the Public Understanding of the State Philosophy

Nazirul Mubin Ahad

15.1 Introduction

The significance of MIB for Bruneians is made clear in this extract from His Majesty's *titah* (decree) at a public event in 2015 with Bruneians residing in the United Kingdom and Northern Ireland:

> We are now thankful to Allah, that we are blessed by Allah with the system of the Government of Malay-Islamic-Monarchy (MIB). MIB is our value system. No matter where we are, MIB stays with us. Do not neglect it. Delegating MIB means giving up our value system. The pillar of MIB is pure Islamic teaching. Let's not turn away from this teaching. Hold it tight without having to look anywhere else. This is a hereditary legacy; we must be proud of it.

N. M. Ahad (✉)
Seri Begawan Religious Teachers University College,
Bandar Seri Begawan, Brunei

There are three essential elements in the concept of MIB (Haji Othman, 1995):

1. Malay: The rights of the Malay; which consists of seven tribal identities of the Malays which secures dynamic and dominant monarchical life, family, community, nation and state.
2. Islamic: The country's official religion in accordance with *Ahl as-Sunnah Wa al-Jama'ah* of the *as-Shafi'i* school of thought in which to be followed, perfected and the superior way of life. *Ahl as-Sunnah Wa al-Jama'ah* is a Sunni Islamic sect of Islam, while *the as-Shafi'i* school of thought is one of the four schools of Islamic law in Sunni Islam founded by Muhammad ibn Idris as-Shafi'i.
3. Monarchy: The reigning monarch, the Sultan as the leader and patron of the people holds the trust of God to exercise the highest authority over the nation.

These are the three pillars of MIB which any social influencer must not violate. Islam is seen as the core or catalyst of MIB and is regarded as the most important component of the 'soul' or 'heart' of MIB; without Islam, MIB will be paralysed and unable to function (Haji Yahaya, 2014), while the Malay and the Monarchy will assure harmony, peace and security, welfare and happiness of the people (Haji Serudin, 1998). With the status of a social influencer, one has to play their role and show responsibility as best they can by maintaining their spirituality in their delivery, behaviour and ethics. They are bound to the MIB philosophy as it is the legacy of the country's identity. Malaysia has its '*Rukun Negara*', Indonesia has its '*Pancasila*', and Brunei has its *Melayu Islam Beraja* to reflect its national identity. Thus, a local influencer must be seen to uphold the Malay-Islamic-Monarchy philosophy.

15.2 Social Media and Influencers

The use of social media has grown rapidly as seen in the latest statistics in January 2020 where there are approximately 3.8 billion users around the globe, which is a 9.2% increase in global social media usage since January 2019. This means that more than 49% of the world population (7.8 billion as of April 2020 according to the most recent United Nations estimates elaborated by Worldometer) are social media users. Based on the statistics released in 2020, the report stated that Brunei Darussalam was the second highest in terms of social media use by eligible audiences (13 years and above) with a use rate of 117% or 410,000 users. In terms of penetration rates, users in the Sultanate ranked fourth globally with 94% which is approximately 410,000 users (Othman, 2020). Among the platforms that are frequently used in Brunei Darussalam are Facebook (53.26%) making the users in the Sultanate the tenth highest globally, with 89% or 310,000 users (13 years and above) in terms of population ratio, followed by Twitter (19.98%), Instagram (11.2%) and YouTube (5.45%) as reported on Statcounter—Globalstat in 2020 (Othman, 2020).

With the world's Internet users spending an average of 6 hours and 43 minutes online each day, the typical user now spends more than 40% of their waking life using the Internet, and humanity will spend a combined total of 1.25 billion years using the Internet during 2020 (Othman, 2020). Inevitably, the platform will produce influencers who will have their followers. The rise of social media has opened up trends in a celebrity culture where the celebrities from 'mainstream' or 'traditional' spheres 'have embraced social media to create direct, unmediated relationships with fans, or at least the illusion of such' (Marwick 2013).

These influencers will regularly publish posts related to current issues, their social life, or any information or influence on any topic on their preferred social media channels and eventually generate large followings of enthusiastic and engaged people who pay close attention to their views. While the followers of social media will naturally look up to influencers in social media to guide them with their decision making, the way they think and dress. Influencers on social media are generally those who have built their reputation because of their knowledge, expertise and popularity. With the rise of the social media, and their possibilities for immediacy, interactivity and self-authorship, celebrities have taken up new forms to control the way that they communicate with their audiences, without the intermediation of celebrity media. Thus, according to Jerslev and Mortensen (2018), 'Celebrities themselves perform their private lives and selves in abundance on social media.' Some will take initiatives by creating trends and encouraging their followers to buy products they promote. This trend seeming to bypass the traditional brokers of celebrity attention like agents and managers according to Marwick (2013).

The same is happening in Brunei Darussalam. Through social media, influencers share new corners of their private lives (Jorge, 2019). Although the social media influencer (SMI) phenomenon is not as massive as that of any other country, it is undeniable that its existence plays a role in contributing to the thoughts, ideas and influences of its followers. As proof of their influence in the country, they have the ability to help local sellers to streamline sales in a timely manner with product reviews that they do. This is due to the fact that the majority of their followers are among the youths. The media scholar who first coined the term micro-celebrity defined the phenomena as 'a new style of online performance that involves people "amping up" their popularity over the Web using technologies like video, blogs and social networking sites' (Senft, 2008). The term *celebrification* came from the process of people's transformation into celebrities. This trend of celebrification or 'the changes at the individual level, or more precisely the process by which ordinary people or public figures are transformed into celebrities' (Driessens, 2013) has been afforded by technology.

In terms of the type of influencers in the country, these social media influencers have not only reached the status of mega influencers, but rather around Macro-Influencers (people with followers in the range between 40,000 and 1 million followers on a social network), Micro-Influencers (Micro-influencers considered as having between 1000 and 40,000 followers on a single social platform) and Nano-Influencers who only have a small number of followers, but they tend to be experts in an obscure or highly specialised field. In many cases, they have fewer than 1000 followers—but they will have keen and interested followers, willing to engage with the Nano-influencer and listen to his/her opinions. Among the influencers in the country are those from different groups, some of them starting from blogging, some are celebrities, entrepreneurs and preachers such as Rano Iskandar, Alin of Kurapak, Thanis Lim, Aming Gunawan, Gzul Yusof, Amirul Adli to name a few. All of them bring a similar approach, namely, sharing their knowledge about some specialist niche. Some of these influencers also use their social media to promote and advertise products, whether theirs or owned by another company where they will expect some form of payment.

According to Freberga et al. (2010), these social media influencers represent a new type of independent third-party endorser who shape audience attitudes through blogs, tweets and the use of other social media. Due to the persuasive power of social media influencers, technologies have been developed to identify and track the influencers relevant to a brand or organisation (Basille, 2009; Straley, 2010).

15.3 The Study

To help achieve the objectives of the study, a qualitative approach was adopted (Lapan et al., 2012). The data was collected via face-to-face interviews between the researcher and the study's informants (Creswell, 1994).

The interview questions were prepared in three 'structured' themes and were given to the participants prior to the actual interview. The interviews were conducted in both Malay and English.

Purposive sampling was used whereby the author interviewed seven different informants, four are among the currently known public influencers in Brunei, while the remaining three are drawn from the public. It was a non-probability sample that was selected based on the characteristics of a population prepared for each of the social media influencers. The informants were chosen based on their different backgrounds and importance in society.

Influencer One is a DJ and television presenter. He was a part-time radio broadcaster from June 2000 until 2017 and a part-time television host of Rampai Pagi. From 2006 to 2010, he went on to become a part-time news reader of 'News at 10' and one English radio station. In addition, during his tenure at Radio Televisyen Brunei (the national broadcasting company of Brunei) from 2000 to 2020, he was a commentator on English TV and radio for national events such as the royal wedding ceremony, royal birthday celebration and religious events. He hosted several shows, wrote scripts and became an emcee and organiser for events at various levels; royal (official and unofficial), national, embassy, ministry, department and personal.

Influencer Two is a religious Preacher who is a counsellor at the Counseling and Religious Understanding Unit (KAFA), Office of the Permanent Secretary, Ministry of Religious Affairs, a Muraqib Unit member as well as a religious speaker. Influencer Three has an entrepreneurship background. She is a social media influencer in the *hijab* (headscarf) culture in the country. She engaged in business since 2015, started as a drop shipper before having her own office in 2017. Throughout her business, she has been interviewed several times by a radio station as one of the successful female entrepreneurs in the country.

Influencer Four is a stand-up comedian in the country. He is one of the comedians from Bruhaha Comedy where they organise shows and perform stand-up comedy. Influencer Four also ventured into acting roles for a few series for RTB and other local production houses. He has also appeared in advertisements for many products of private companies. As an influencer, he has created short comedy sketch videos where he has his own team and posted their videos on a weekly basis on his Instagram. The content of his videos is mainly on what Bruneians go through in their daily lives. The other three interviews were conducted with three public informants.

A descriptive analysis was used in this study to describe the characteristics of a population or phenomenon that was being studied by looking through its attribute (Thyer, 2000), but it does not answer questions about how/when/why the characteristics occurred; rather, it addresses the 'what' question. It is through the reading of multiple sources that the researcher could reach a certain level of understanding towards the 'what' question. This chapter focuses on the 'what' question in particular.

15.4 The Philosophy of Malay Islamic Monarchy in the Eyes of Bruneians

The majority of Bruneian society, whether among the influencers and followers, understands the Malay-Islamic-Monarchy philosophy and the principles of life enshrined in the constitutional of Brunei Darussalam. These have become the foundation, core and the 'Standard Operating Procedure' (SOP) for the people of Brunei especially if they identify themselves as a Malay, Muslim (according to *Ahl as-Sunnah Wa al-Jama'ah*), and living under a sovereign government and monarchy. In the constitution of Brunei Darussalam in 1959, Part 2/3 (1 & 2), Islam has been explicitly stated as the official religion of the country thus: 'The official state religion-state is Islam according to the *Ahl as-Sunnah Wa al-Jama'ah*, but other religions can be practiced by those who practice it.'

Brunei's religious leader is the Sultan. Thus, the position of Sultan, Chief Minister, the Deputy Prime Minister and the Secretary of State can only be held by Muslims. The constitution also emphasises that non-Muslims are given the freedom to practise any religion. Hence, Brunei Darussalam guarantees the freedom of religion for all its inhabitants. In addition, in His Majesty's *titah* during the celebration of *Isra' Miraj* in 2019, regarding the importance of MIB, he stated, 'This is the reality of Brunei, the MIB country, where besides, it is not Brunei.'

According to an interview with an influencer (Religious Preacher, 2020),

> *Malay in the MIB is not to be understood as coercion to become Malay rather the great traditions in culture, language and ethics of the Malay should be applied in life. Similarly, Islam in the MIB does not oblige the people of Brunei Darussalam to embrace Islam but Islam must be recognised as the official religion in Brunei Darussalam. While the monarchy kingdom is a system of government that rules through the leadership of His Majesty the Sultan, as the highest ruler in the country.*

Another influencer, the stand-up comedian, stated,

> *MIB is a way of life, applied to our daily lives, (such as) being ethical, respectful, competent, always obeying the law of God through the teachings of Islam and all of His commands and prohibitions. On top of that, there is love towards the Sultan.*

Most Bruneian influencers did not deny the importance of MIB and its relevance as it reflects their identity. The same goes for all residents of Brunei. This is why it can be seen that even the non-Malays and non-Muslims were also embracing the concept in the Sultanate since it is their identity as Bruneians whether in the nation, abroad or on the Internet. It is this identity that sets out the direction of a person's life and characteristics. They see the importance of upholding MIB so that the people will live in a harmonious society under the leadership of a ruler; without any political turmoil that could disrupt the unity of society and to ensure its citizens are properly served.

In an interview, the influencer (Religious Preacher, 2020) stated that there is a need for this concept to remain relevant in today's modern setting. The more sophisticated the age becomes with the overload of information, the less everyone has the ability to choose between right and wrong. Therefore, influencers have their reserved responsibility so that the concept of MIB will become the policy, guidelines and guidance. Besides, in modern times, many were exposed to foreign cultures that have somewhat changed the way Bruneians live. Most of the influencers that were interviewed emphasised the importance of this concept, especially entering the era of globalisation. They regarded this philosophy as a gift from God bestowed for the citizens and residents of Brunei Darussalam therefore it must be honoured and maintained. However, not all influencers in this country are practising MIB at all times, and there are some who lack this identity in their lives. This is evident at some point where the controversy that has occurred contradicts the concept of MIB which will be explained later. The average Brunei community understands MIB but there is no denying that there is a number among the community who are ignorant, due to education, environment and external influences. This is why His Majesty the Sultan often emphasises the importance of raising Bruneian's understanding of this concept as mentioned in several *titahs*.

15.5 The Role and Impact of Influencer on the Public Understanding of MIB

Social media influencers are but a sign of a wider trend for self-branding (Genz, 2015). It is important to look at the leading role of the influencer in Brunei Darussalam and the purpose of becoming an influencer. It is known that the culture of entrepreneurship was the rhetoric on which social media grew and prospered by proclaiming that they would offer greater possibilities for cultural creators to succeed as there are other several reasons such as the desire to generate income, gain popularity, hobbies, or related to their career. If an influencer upholds the MIB concept, no matter how young, modern and sophisticated, he/she will be able to express the MIB well through his/her posts. This is because the influencers are responsible for providing the correct understanding towards the community, maintaining order and harmonious community life, as well as to strengthen the community's commitment towards the nation.

In assessing the extent to which they influence the MIB's portrayal of the people of Brunei, influencers are among the important front liners who are followed by the younger generation. Therefore, their actions will have an effect on their followers. Therefore, they must obey the constitution and laws of the country, and uphold the highest values of Malay Islam Brunei in themselves, educating and preaching to the people of Brunei according to their capacity and ability. For instance, Influencer One uses whatever knowledge and ability in broadcasting to set the best example. Meanwhile, another influencer who is a business owner and an image consultant claims that her career has garnered popularity among social media users. Hence, by understanding MIB, she will take care of her career through her manners as a Malay and Muslim.

Most influencers are not trying to promote MIB directly, but rather indirectly because some claim that they just portray their true selves on social media (DJ/television presenter, 2020). They also acknowledge that in the early days of using social media, they were still naive and were learning about life and how to behave properly. Among other influencers, some believed they are more pressured to dress modestly and cover themselves, using a language of full modesty, the use of Malay language as well as referring to the Quran, *Hadith* and Muslim scholars. Moreover, the emergence of laypersons that assume the roles of 'social media influencer' or 'micro-celebrity' (Senft, 2008) that promote modesty and *hijab* lifestyles on their social networking platforms is preferred by discerning social-media-savvy Muslim women over religious content and teachings on traditional media, thus imprinting the significance of Muslim societies globally today.

The rise of self-made *hijabi* (women who wear the *hijab*) micro-celebrities or social media influencers in Southeast Asia comes at the right time as we witness the exponential growth of ordinary individuals gaining fame from their everyday social media posts and the recent interest of celebrity studies to move away from media to a more social and political focus (Mohamad & Hassim, 2019). Among the positive impact of this phenomena are the resurgence of Islam experienced in the region through global media flows that encouraged Muslims to embrace emergent Islamic identities as a form of solidarity against Islamophobia and discrimination; while the *hijab* was meant to differentiate and authenticate Islamic practice among Muslim women, its representation in media has become more recursive and prominent (Grine & Saeed, 2017; Hassim, 2014; Hochel, 2013). This can be seen with the emergence of Vivy Yusof, Neelofa and others in the neighbouring country of Malaysia.

While influencers among the comedians are also trying to make sense of speech and conversation, sentences used, socialisation and filtering humour to avoid causing negative effects. Based on interviews conducted with social influencers in the country, the majority believed that the best way for an influencer to provide an understanding of MIB to the public is through morals and manners as one's manner is a reflection for anyone to demonstrate their understanding of the concept of MIB. Undoubtedly, this can be seen in some of the influencers interviewed. Looking at their social media, there is evidence of the value of the MIB in their posts. For example, generally, one does not have to be a religious preacher or an MIB teacher to showcase their association with MIB, but according to Mohamad (2017), performing some forms of religiosity even the minuscule ones such as sharing (typing) '*Alhamdulillah*' (praises to Allah), '*InsyaAllah*' (If God Wills) and including them in their comments have positive impacts on their self-image as this is closely tied to the performance of religiosity, Muslim self, or a Bruneian Muslim.

Each influencer has different abilities and talents to contribute to society. Diversity in these abilities and talents was utilised in order to achieve optimal impact. This was expressed either through the influencer's writing, actions or his involvement in educational activities. According to the Stand-up Comedian Influencer, based on his experience, activities through video recordings would have more impact than just posting sentences of advice on social sites, which led to his involvement in several video recordings.

This is the reality in Brunei, where influencers are emerging in the midst of the globalisation era. When it comes to the impact of local influencers, most of them use social media such as Instagram, blogs and YouTube as a sharing platform. Famous for the MIB, home-based influencers are always portrayed in terms of morals, dress, ways of thinking and acting, however, this is not always the case. This is the case where some of the influencers overlook the application of MIB values that should serve as a guide in presenting themselves and their content. This is in contrast to what is portrayed by the government, such as through the radio and television, where the absorption of MIB elements can be seen through their production. This is clearly evident in the differences between the two types of content and presentations, between private or personal and public parties. The simplest example is the Islamic values that can be seen and heard on the radio and television. In addition to Islamic greetings, Islamist elements are also rarely seen through an influencer's content or any use of words that clearly reflect Islam.

Undoubtedly, as role models, they are the role-model in giving a positive impact on society. As the citizens or permanent residents of Brunei, influencers should have a value, or at least, an understanding of the concept of MIB as a social responsibility to ensure and maintain harmony and peace of nationhood, religion, monarchy and state. Their followers will be inclined to the shape that the influencer describes. If this is the case, whether the influencer is a resident of Brunei, then it is very important to uphold the MIB as its influence is high on the public. It would be dangerous if the influencer accepts the falsehood doctrine contrary to the MIB concept.

Here it can be seen that religious or motivational activities are no longer confined to the forms of mass preaching at the mosques but also in an online space and at an individual level. Private performance of religiosity in the forms of subtle or direct preaching to others, constant self-reminders and written prayers shared in online sites in the forms of photo uploads, status updates, sharing links to religious sites, and liking religious pages also can be performed by social media influencers. Thus, as stated by Mohamad (2017), 'performance of religiosity is contextually transformed and performed in non-conventional ways'.

15.6 Issues of Using New Media in Relation to Malay-Islamic-Monarchy Concept

The fast-growing on the emergence of influencers have made them a spotlight among the younger generation in the country. In reality, not many local influencers use the media and applications as an approach to infuse MIB in life. In addition, it should be acknowledged that any social media platform is limited to a particular group. For example, television and radio may be less attractive to the younger generation who are more likely to use the newest media, while older people may be more comfortable watching television and listening to the radio. Due to this, SMIs who are good at engaging with these media might have a better chance of attracting followers. Hence, influencers with interesting content should attract followers while promoting MIB values, and vice versa.

Nonetheless, as mentioned before, several issues concerning manners and morals have arisen. When the MIB philosophy is only found as a subject in the school curriculum, through improper methods and learning styles, then it will only be used as memorised information that is not well understood, appreciated and practised. This is why some influencers fail to apply the values of MIB in their lives to the public. The problem arose mainly when 'Malay' was eroded, and religion began to be set aside, which leads to the Bruneian norms to no longer be embodied in their performances. For example, a few influencers acted indecently in a fast-food restaurant in Brunei in October 2018, which provoked anger and criticism from netizens (users of the Internet, especially a habitual or keen one).

Another example of a social media post that sparked outrage among the public was in June 2019, when one of the influencers uploaded his video which showed him touching the hand of a woman who was not his *mahram* (a member of one's family with whom marriage would be considered *haram* or proscribed by Islamic law) as a joke. Later, several issues followed with influencers doing 'marketing' that was inappropriate and sensitive in Brunei Darussalam. Furthermore, several local influencers involved in the business world started to see that even 'bad publicity is publicity' as a way to gain traction and marketing. This creates unhealthy conditions and is forbidden in Islam. In fact, Islam forbids traders to do extreme marketing due to fraud, which is giving an excessive and false impression of the goods offered.

Another issue raised was when society began entering into the influencer's private life as stated by Genz (2015), 'Contemporary audiences are invited to share in celebrities' personal experiences and feelings and access those parts of their lives that are normally labelled 'private' where as a normal human being, of course, there are times when influencers fail to portray the pure values of MIB into their daily lives. This is where, the bad value will also be seen and can influence the audience and followers.

Another major problem on social media is the possibilities for non-normative identities to be expressed as subcultural micro-celebrities (Jorge, 2019). Although, this is not an issue in Brunei. The normalisation of beliefs that are against Islamic values such as those from liberal and LGBT supporters could start a trend-based culture in Brunei as it is accepted in some foreign countries. This is proven with Mohamad, a gay Malay Muslim, who does not share any Islamic materials on his Facebook to keep his image as a homosexual, which he openly expressed on his profile through photos and status updates (Mohamad, 2017).

In addition, the existence of Tik Tok and YouTube contents that are contrary to the norms of an Islamic country is not something that can be avoided. For example, prank culture as showed by Yousef Erakat, a 29-year-old Arab-American who is known for his pranks, acting and parodies on his YouTube channel called FouseyTube are among the examples of celebrification (Marshall & Redmond, 2016) which can influence others to follow in his footsteps. It is believed that some of his pranks have tarnished the value of being a Muslim.

There is no denying the fact that there are influencers who take good care of themselves, morally, in the manner of how they dress themselves, their behaviour and by being sensitive to religion and race. However, some are committing wrongly in highlighting themselves. This can be seen with the emergence of influencers in social media who focus on attracting followers by performing acts or jokes that do not fit the values of MIB. In fact, there are among the influencers willing to imitate the act of the opposite sex (men imitate women or vice versa) which is forbidden in Islam as narrated by Ibn 'Abbas 'The Messenger of Allah (ﷺ) cursed the women who imitate men and the men who imitate women' to attract the audience, while some are willing to do thoughtless actions to attract the audience. These influencers felt that society will still follow them because such behaviour easily attracts human interest. This exemplifies the process of normalisation that has been applied intentionally or not by some social users. Also, the attitude of wanting to be the first to be recognised, and going viral the hottest issue in town among a handful of influencers has caused the spread of false information to society.

The spread of confusing and inaccurate information will destabilise the MIB stronghold, especially in the soul of the younger generation. This is why the true value of understanding MIB needs to be sharpened as it is voiced repetitively by His Majesty himself. In terms of culturing the MIB, it appears that local influencers have a lesser role to play in everyday life in social media. For example, it is seldom heard of Bruneian languages, which can be inadvertently educational to followers. If not accustomed or cultivated, it will be awkward and this makes it difficult for the current generation to feel good about the values of MIB.

In fact, Brunei does not have comprehensive legislation on online engagement yet. Mohamad (2019) stated, 'In recent years, the explosion in the use of WhatsApp in Brunei to disseminate false information has resulted in growing concern over the use of such media platforms.' She added, this is where the Laws of Brunei, Section 34, Public Order Act, Cap 148, 1984, 'Dissemination of false report' has been contextually applied to prevent the dissemination of false information.

15.7 The Public Perceptions of Local Influencers

For the public, the main role of the influencer is to set a good example to his followers, to spread awareness of the MIB philosophy based on the teachings of *Ahl as-Sunnah Wa al-Jama'ah* and *Negara Zikir* (a nation where many people carry out devotional acts). According to an interview with the public (2020), they stated that the rise of influencers in the country has inspired others to immerse themselves in the social media world. However, there is still much work to do as the role of influencers in absorbing the MIB to society is still lacking. Despite the fact, the practice of MIB still can be seen today, and the government's efforts undeniably play an important role in educating the people of Brunei as declared in the meeting of the Supreme Council Committee of Malay Islamic Monarchy, stating that the understanding and perception of the values of Malay Islamic Monarchy of the citizens of Brunei has improved (Haji Salleh, 2020). The Minister of Education added,

The Supreme Council Committee of Malay Islamic Monarchy always tries to improve further the practice, appreciation of the people and the country's population towards the Malay Islamic Monarchy concept. (Haji Salleh, 2020)

Meanwhile, in the form of electronic media, the government has prepared several television programmes, talks on MIB twice every month in collaboration with RTB. This is an effort by the government to ensure the MIB values always remains intact. However, speaking in reality, there are numbers among the younger generation that are also undeniably attracted to foreign cultures. The same goes for some local influencers in the country, where foreign cultures have to some extent affected them. This is due to the trends around the world where fame is prioritised and sought after. As stated during an interview with one local Bruneian, she expressed that most of the local influencers are thought to be in the quest for attention and in the race to become famous people.

However, the majority of these local influencers are still in the religious framework and the right frame of mind. Some often share knowledge through social media as this is how they reach out to their followers. According to public interviews, they expect an influencer to make more videos about Brunei in their exploration of Bruneian customs and traditions to showcase the beauty of Brunei. Therefore, the pride of Bruneian identity must exist in every influencer so that they will not only bring positivity to their followers but indirectly influence the values of MIB in their followers' identity.

15.8 Requisites and Guidelines for the Influencers

In the interviews conducted, one influencer emphasised the important elements that can enhance the understanding of the MIB to the public. He stated that there is a need for cooperation among the influencers in their approach to normalising the public with MIB indirectly and naturally in the current environment through the mass media and social media. In response to the government's call to inculcate good values and MIB, there are several guidelines to be followed by local influencers, such as:

1. Practising MIB in themselves and educating the Bruneian people on this concept.
2. Combating the teachings, elements, doctrine and everything that goes against the principle of Malay Islamic Monarchy in everyday life.
3. Filtering information before sharing any unauthorised facts, religious and government officials and others.
4. Refraining from having the desire to be the first to share sensational information.

5. Self-awareness before posting something that is of public benefit or worthless.
6. Censoring to safeguard public disgrace, misgivings and sensitivities and to appear politer and civil in delivering the right things.
7. Controlling emotions and anger as well as gathering more facts and data before posting something to be fair and civilised.
8. Making sure that what is presented is reader-friendly so that the expressed desire is met, accepted and felt by the reader.
9. Refraining from engagement in any kind of futile debate in the comments and chat section.

For this group of micro-celebrities or influencers, it is crucial to emphasise the above matters (Jorge, 2019). As their availability and connectedness to the audience are vital (Abidin, 2015), creating strong, close and friend-like relationships (Andò, 2016), such that they can adjust to the community norms and tastes while attempting to maintain the perception of their authenticity. In sharing their ordinary lives, celebrities and social media influencers should also explore promoting MIB directly and indirectly.

15.9 Conclusion

There is no denying that the MIB philosophy is a complete way of life that colours the life of the people of Brunei. Therefore, looking at the existence of local influencers, it is the responsibility of these people to portray themselves with the value of MIB in their lives because they are seen as role models for some followers. Looking at their impact on the MIB among the people of Brunei, most influencers are still bound by the concept of MIB in presenting themselves in public. They still bind themselves as Malay, as a Muslim and one who obeys the ruler. They express the value of MIB in their speech, behaviour and dress.

However, there are also a small number of influencers who have acted contrary to the MIB concept and contributed to several controversial issues that caused public outrage. This may be due to several factors, such as educational factors, environment and external influences. The existence of these factors at the same time has further strengthened their effect. Therefore, local influencers need to be aware of their role and their social responsibility as Bruneian citizens who adhere to MIB as the core of life as this matter is clearly emphasised repeatedly by His Majesty the Sultan in several of his decrees.

References

Abidin, C. (2015). Communicative intimacies: Influencers and perceived interconnectedness. *ADA: A Journal of Gender, New Media, and Technology, 8.* https://doi.org/10.7264/N3MW2FFG

Andò, R. (2016). The ordinary celebrity: Italian young vloggers and the definition of girlhood. *Film, Fashion & Consumption, 5*(1), 123–139.

Basille, D. (2009). Social media influencers are not traditional influencers. http://www.briansolis.com/2009/11/social-mediainfluencers-are-not-traditional-influencers/

Creswell, J. W. (1994). *Research design: Qualitative & quantitative approaches.* Sage.

Driessens, O. (2013). The celebritization of society and culture: Understanding the structural dynamics of celebrity culture. *International Journal of Cultural Studies, 16*(6), 641–657.

Freberga, K., Grahamb, K., McGaugheyc, K., & Frebergc, L. A. (2010). Who are the social media influencers? A study of public perceptions of personality. *Public Relations Review.* https://doi.org/10.1016/j.pubrev.2010.11.001

Genz, S. (2015). My job is me. *Feminist Media Studies, 15*(4), 545–561.

Grine, F., & Saeed, M. (2017). Is hijab a fashion statement? A study of Malaysian Muslim women. *Journal of Islamic Marketing, 8*(3), 430–443.

Haji Othman, H. A. B. (1995). *Melayu Islam Beraja: Masa kini dan masa depan.* Melayu Islam Beraja Course for School Administrators, September 2–3.

Haji Salleh, S. M. (2020, June 21). Penghayatan MIB kekal subur di kalangan masyarakat. *Pelita Brunei.* http://www.pelitabrunei.gov.bn/Lists/Berita/NewDisplayForm.aspx?ID=888

Haji Serudin, M. Z. (1998). *Melayu Islam Beraja: Suatu pendekatan.* Dewan Bahasa dan Pustaka.

Haji Yahaya, M. (2014). *"MIB" Misi global ke arah negara zikir berdasarkan Teori 'Umran.* Universiti Islam Sultan Sharif Ali.

Hassim, N. (2014). A comparative analysis on hijab wearing in Malaysia Muslimah magazines. *SEARCH: The Journal of the South East Asia Research Center for Communications and Humanities, 6*(1), 79–96.

Hochel, S. (2013). To veil or not to veil: Voices of Malaysian Muslim women. *Intercultural Communication Studies, 22*(2), 40–57.

Jerslev, A., & Mortensen, M. (2018). Celebrity in the social media age: Renegotiating the public and the private. In A. Elliott (Ed.), *Routledge handbook of celebrity studies* (pp. 157–174). Routledge.

Jorge, A. (2019). Celebrity bloggers and vloggers. In *The international encyclopaedia of gender, media and communication.* https://doi.org/10.1002/9781119429128.iegmc004

Lapan, S. D., Quartaroli, M. T., & Riemer, F. J. (2012). *Qualitative research: An introduction to methods and designs.* Jossey-Bass/Wiley.

Marshall, P. D., & Redmond, S. (2016). *A companion to celebrity*. Wiley Blackwell.
Marwick, A. (2013). *Status update: Celebrity, publicity, and branding in the social media age*. Yale University Press.
Mohamad, S. M. (2017). Performance of religiosity on a 'techno-religious' space. *Advanced Science Letters*, *23*(5), 4918–4921.
Mohamad, S. M. (2019). Self-disclosure on social media in Brunei Darussalam. In M. Caballero-Anthony & M. Sembiring (Eds.), *The face of disruptions* (pp. 46–56). Nanyang Technological University.
Mohamad, S. M., & Hassim, N. (2019). Hijabi celebrification and hijab consumption in Brunei and Malaysia. *Celebrity Studies*. https://doi.org/10.1080/19392397.2019.1677164
Othman, A. (2020, June 17). Bruneians rank high social media usage. *Borneo Bulletin*. https://borneobulletin.com.bn/bruneians-rank-high-social-media-usage/
Prime Minister's Office – Brunei Darussalam. Titah View – Collection of His Majesty's Sermon.
Senft, T. M. (2008). *Camgirl: Celebrity and community in the age of social networks*. Peter Lang.
Statcounter – Globalstat. (2020, June 19). Social media stats Brunei Darussalam. Retrieved June 19, 2020, from https://gs.statcounter.com/social-media-stats/all/brunei-darussalam
Straley, B. (2010). How to: Target social media influencers to boost traffic and sales. Retrieved September 24, 2020, from http://mashable.com/2010/04/15/socialmedia-influencers/
Thyer, B. (2000). *The handbook of social work research methods* (2nd ed.). Florida State University.

PART IV

COVID-19, Society and Education

CHAPTER 16

COVID-19: Educational Practices and Responses in Brunei Darussalam

Masitah Shahrill, Najib Noorashid, and Chester Keasberry

16.1 Introduction

Since the first recorded case of coronavirus disease 2019 (COVID-19) in Wuhan, Hubei Province, China, in December 2019, the pandemic has significantly affected many aspects of human lives, including the future and the quality of life globally, and Brunei Darussalam (henceforth referred to as Brunei) is no exception. The first recorded case of COVID-19 was reported on 9th March 2020 (Ministry of Health, Brunei Darussalam, March 9 & 10, 2020a, 2020b; Wong, Koh et al., 2020b). As a result, the

---

Shahrill, M., Noorashid, N., & Keasberry, C. (2021). COVID-19: Educational practices and responses in Brunei Darussalam. In Phan, L. H., A. Kumpoh, K. Wood, R. Jawawi, & H. Said (Eds.), *Globalisation, education, and reform in Brunei Darussalam* (pp. 325–354). Palgrave Macmillan.

M. Shahrill (✉) • N. Noorashid • C. Keasberry
Universiti Brunei Darussalam, Bandar Seri Begawan, Brunei
e-mail: masitah.shahrill@ubd.edu.bn; najib.noorashid@ubd.edu.bn; chester.keasberry@ubd.edu.bn

© The Author(s), under exclusive license to Springer Nature Switzerland AG 2021
Phan, L. H. et al. (eds.), *Globalisation, Education, and Reform in Brunei Darussalam*, International and Development Education, https://doi.org/10.1007/978-3-030-77119-5_16

pandemic has affected the working environment and the education sector among others. All levels of education in Brunei have had to implement various distance communication and learning strategies to quickly adapt to the 'new normal'. These are enforced as part of the delivery of formal education, amid inevitable measures of lockdown and quarantine.

The impact of COVID-19 on the education in Brunei can be illustrated with some key government decisions imposed within a few days of the first reported case of COVID-19: the announcement of temporary closures of educational institutions on 11th March (Ministry of Education, Brunei Darussalam, March 10, 2020b), the implementation of social distance learning for higher education institutions (HEIs) including Universiti Brunei Darussalam (UBD) on 12th March, the pronouncement of a national lockdown on 16th March and the recall of Bruneian students from abroad in early to mid-March. Whilst Brunei has been successful in flattening the curve, with schools due to partially re-open on 2nd June, there are still concerns among the people and the academic community on the effects of the pandemic. To date, the Brunei government, through the Ministry of Education and multi-sectoral departments, has imposed stricter rules and regulations to maintain health and safety while ensuring the efficacy of educational affairs and simultaneously establishing the new normal in educational settings.

Focusing on Brunei, this chapter reviews the state of educational affairs in all levels of education prior to and during the pandemic and at the time of this writing. Therefore, this chapter is divided into two sections: the first section examines the abrupt changes in educational policy and practices imposed by the government, schools and higher educations in the country, as well as challenges and issues raised from the sudden adjustment; and the second section looks into responses from educators at the primary, secondary and tertiary levels, reflecting on their roles in dealing with pedagogical issues and global health concerns.

16.2 Education Policy and Practices in Brunei Darussalam

16.2.1 *Education System in Brunei*

The education system in Brunei and the policies governing it has evolved substantially over the last century or so. Below is an excerpt that provides a brief history of formal educational policy in Brunei:

Formal education in Brunei Darussalam began in 1912. ... The earliest draft on education policy was introduced in the First National Development Plan (1954–1959). It laid down the basic foundation for the infrastructure of Brunei's education system. An important provision was six years of free education in Malay schools for Brunei Malay children aged 6–14 years. ... Brunei achieved full independence in January 1984. The historic event provided the impetus for the acceleration of reforms and development in all aspects of education. In an effort to streamline the Malay medium and English medium schooling systems, and to ensure that learners attain a high level of proficiency in both Malay and English, the Bilingual Education Policy was formulated in 1984 and implemented in 1985. With its implementation, all government schools followed a single system with a common national curriculum from preschool until pre-university. The policy was later extended to private schools (except International Schools) in 1992. In 1993, the 9-Year Education Policy was replaced with the 12-Year Education Policy. Every student was provided with 12 years of education: even years in preschool and primary, three years in lower secondary, and two years in upper secondary or vocational/technical education. (Ministry of Education, 2013, pp. 5–6)

The Ministry of Education in Brunei officially launched the National Education System for the 21st Century or *Sistem Pendidikan Negara Abad Ke-21* (SPN21) in January 2009. SPN21 brought about three major changes in the education system, which consisted of the education structure, curriculum and assessment, and technical education (Ministry of Education, 2013). There were several major changes conducted through various stages of implementation in the years that followed. Among the differences between the previous education system and SPN21 are the following:

- The differences in class labelling, with Primary 1 to Primary 6 now called Year 1 to Year 6, and Secondary 1 to Secondary 5 called Year 7 to Year 11;
- The introduction of Student Progress Assessment in Year 8;
- The differences in the duration of schooling from five years of secondary education (three years in lower secondary and two years in upper secondary) in the previous system, to students being channelled to either the four-year General Secondary Education Programme (Year 7 to Year 10) or the five-year General Secondary or the five-year Applied Secondary Programme (Year 7 to Year 11).

- Other programmes offered in SPN21 are the Specialised Education Programme for the gifted and talented students, and the Special Educational Needs Programme that caters to students with special educational needs.

The Ministry of Education in Brunei regulates all government and private education institutions. Meanwhile, the Ministry of Religious Affairs oversees the educational institutions that mainly provide aspects of Islamic religious education. According to the comprehensive data provided in the Brunei Darussalam Education Statistics 2018 (Ministry of Education, 2019a, 2019b), under the government sector, there are a total of 117 primary schools, 32 secondary schools, 4 sixth-form centres (pre-university), 7 vocational and technical institutions (from April 2016, referred to as the Institute of Brunei Technical Education [IBTE] Campuses), and 4 classified as higher education institutions including 1 Polytechnic, all of which are under the purview of the Ministry of Education.

The public or government primary and secondary schools in Brunei are allocated into six clusters (Table 16.1), each led by its respective cluster leader ("Government Education Institutions", n.d.).

The clustering of schools is divided according to the four districts, namely Brunei-Muara, Tutong, Belait and Temburong. The largest concentration of primary and secondary schools in the nation can be found in the Brunei-Muara district where the capital city Bandar Seri Begawan is located. Meanwhile, there are a total of 76 private institutions in the country, of which 3 are categorised as vocational and technical institutions and 2 as higher education. As of 2018, there are 108,553 students and 10,934 teachers in the country (Ministry of Education, 2019b).

16.2.2 Vignettes of Typical Lesson Practices

Government primary and secondary schools in Brunei typically start at 7:00 in the morning with morning prayers, singing the national anthem and class teachers taking students' attendance. Normal class hours resume

Table 16.1 The number of schools in each cluster

School levels	Cluster 1	Cluster 2	Cluster 3	Cluster 4	Cluster 5	Cluster 6	Total
Primary	19	20	18	20	24	16	117
Secondary	5	5	7	6	4	5	32
Pre-university	1	1	0	1	1	0	4

at 7:30 a.m. Class timetables of subjects are scheduled differently for every school. Depending on the school, students have their break time after 2 to 2.5 hours of lessons in the first part of the morning, and the end of the school day is at 12:30 in the afternoon.

Subject classes are taught either in single-period or in double-period lessons, with one period being 25 or 30 minutes. The standard class sizes in Brunei government schools range from 21 to 30 students for both primary and secondary levels, though there are times the number can be greater. Students' seating arrangements in the classroom vary from students sitting with tables arranged in rows and columns individually, in pairs or in groups of three or four. It is expected that male and female students will be seated separately in the classrooms. The whiteboards situated at the front of the class are usually the main focal point of the lesson.

In contextualising the lessons in Brunei, the classroom practices and the teaching and learning process may appear the same to the general public. However, careful observations may reveal different and distinctive depictions contributing to the uniqueness within the classroom, the students and importantly, the teacher. As the teacher walks into the classroom, the students will stand to greet the teacher with the usual Arabic and English greetings '*Assalamualaikum Warahmatullahi Wabarakatuh*' (in Arabic السلام عليكم ورحمة الله وبركاته which in English is 'Peace be upon you with God's mercy and blessings'), and 'Good Morning Sir/Teacher'. This is usually followed by the Muslims reciting '*Doa*' or a short prayer, a short verse from the Quran to bless the lesson. This action is believed to make the lesson flow and knowledge imparted be retained by the students easily. Non-Muslim teachers and students remain silent out of respect. Not only is this gesture carried out at the beginning of each lesson, it is also done at the end of each lesson. These practices are normally observed at all school levels including at the post-secondary levels (pre-university and IBTE) but interestingly, not so at the higher education levels.

In relation to the teaching and learning process, teachers generally prepare a lesson plan document before the start of the lesson as reference and as per required by the school administration. The lesson plan is typically filled for a single topic that spans either a one-period lesson or at most a one-week continuous lesson. The lesson plan template document varies for each school, but the main content commonly observed is as follows:

- Statements of Learning Objectives—Identifying what the students should be able to do by the end of the lesson;
- Steps to Success (S2S)—Listing the pedagogical steps on achieving the topic of the particular lesson;
- Planning the specific learning activities—Starter and main activities;
- Plenary or Closure—Recapping or summarising the lesson and assessing students' understanding by checking back with the lesson objective and S2S; and finally
- The Evaluation—Reflections by the teachers about their students, what went well during the lesson and suggested improvements for the next lesson.

It should be noted that some schools have gone to further lengths in specifying the different types of resources used for the lesson, the formative and summative assessments, integration with other subjects and the SPN21 skills such as critical thinking or problem solving; collaboration and cooperation; communication; creative thinking; ICT or Financial literacy; cultural and civic literacy; research; data interpretation; reading, writing, speaking and listening skills; and drawing skills.

16.2.3 Time Spent in Teaching and Other School-Related Activities

Teachers in schools have many responsibilities, both related and unrelated to the subject they are teaching (Hiebert et al., 2003). According to Lampert (2001), '[Teachers] have a limited amount of time to teach what needs to be taught, and they are interrupted often. The litany is so familiar' (p. 1). Shahrill (2009) reported that the secondary Brunei Mathematics teachers in her study spent on average 21 hours per week on teaching and other school-related activities, such as additional administrative tasks and organising events.

Meanwhile, a nation-wide study in collaboration with the Brunei Ministry of Education that investigated the teaching of *Bahasa Melayu* (Malay Language), English Language and Mathematics in Years 4, 5 and 6 in government primary schools (Shahrill et al., 2014; Sithamparam et al., 2014; Tarasat et al., 2014; Abdullah et al., 2018) found that 20–28% of teachers spent between 41% and 50% of their time specifically teaching lessons in a typical week. The remaining time was spent working with their students during the lessons (individually or in small groups of students), conducting administrative duties (e.g. subject coordinator, class teacher), maintaining discipline in schools, on involvement in co-curricular activities, and managing other work responsibilities such as attending professional development workshops or courses, relief teaching, work-related meetings and extra teaching duties such as enrichment and remedial classes.

16.3 COVID-19 AND CHANGES IN EDUCATIONAL PRACTICES IN BRUNEI DARUSSALAM

16.3.1 Core Education: Primary and Secondary Education

Upon detection of the first COVID-19 case in the country, the government of Brunei through its multi-sectoral ministries was quick to mull over and impose necessary precautions for each institution. As the most important agency in educational affairs in the country, the Ministry of Education also joined hands with other ministries and departments to come up with relevant initiatives to ensure the safety and wellbeing of the academic communities, while maintaining the functionality of academic institutions in the country.

Whilst the Ministry of Education took the first necessary step to shut down all academic institutions temporarily two days after the first confirmed case, the ministry progressively introduced a one-for-all Business Continuity Plan (BCP) through its 'Schools Operation Protocol Matrix during COVID-19' (Ministry of Education, 2020), which aligns with the Brunei Government Measures (Government of Brunei, 2020) undertaken in addressing the impact of COVID-19 as part of the 'Whole of Nation Approach' implemented by the government and supported by the people of Brunei. Based on the two main guidelines released by the Ministry of Education and the Government of Brunei respectively, this section reviews abrupt changes in educational practices and policies, which have affected several educational practices both during the height of COVID-19 and today. This review will be based on two main areas: (1) school and learning activities; and (2) the health, safety and wellbeing of academic communities.

16.3.1.1 School and Learning Activities
At the core level of education, throughout the first closure of schools in March and the progressive re-opening of schools over the following months, the Ministry of Education implemented de-escalation stages for primary and secondary schools. These stages brought about changes in

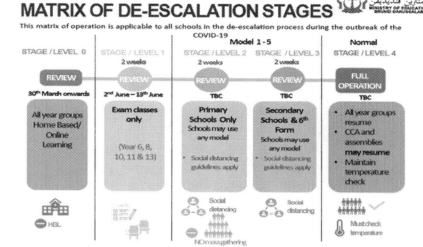

Fig. 16.1 De-escalation stages of school operation amid COVID-19 (Ministry of Education, 2020, p. 2)

pedagogical approaches, operating hours, school activities and movement that schools must follow and implement (Fig. 16.1).

As schools slowly returned to standard operation, social distancing was still mandatory at both primary and secondary schools, and schools that had small-sized classrooms were encouraged to use large spaces such as conference rooms, libraries, school halls and suraus. As part of BCP in the classroom, the ministry also urged a minimal number of students in teaching spaces, and thus schools were advised to implement a mixture of pedagogical approaches of Studying At School (SAS) and Home-Based Learning (HBL). In the case of the latter, teachers were encouraged to teach via video-conferencing, especially for students who have access to the Internet at home, while those who had limited to no Internet access were advised to undertake SAS at school with safety precautionary measures. This also meant that the number of students in each classroom was limited when compared with normal classes before COVID-19. As part of the pedagogical approach, teachers also provided Home-Learning Packs (HLP) containing subject knowledge, class and homework exercises. During the shift from face-to-face to the virtual realm, teachers opted for virtual media, particularly Zoom and Microsoft Teams, for both teaching and learning for students and communication platforms between colleagues (Kon & Roslan, 2020).

For certain secondary schools, such as boarding schools, students were advised to stay at home while doing HBL for certain days in a week. For instance, Sports School temporarily closed their hostel and students were instructed to do HBL for five days a week. Meanwhile, Pre-Vocational and Individualised Education students were instructed to do SAS for a day and HBL for four days a week, and Remedial Education students had to do SAS for three days and HBL for two days in a week. SAS was only encouraged for subjects involving projects and practical classes, and only when it was needed. Meanwhile, as part of precautionary measures, HBL for five days for a week was also required for vulnerable students and any students who showed flu-like symptoms.

In the classroom, teachers were not allowed to stand or teach near students, conduct student group activities or even share physical study materials that were not cleaned using the proper procedures. As part of the social distancing mandate, students were not allowed to sit less than 1 metre apart. Therefore, learning activities were restricted as the movement of teachers and students and their social spaces were limited. As part of the whole school modification, the changes of educational policy and practices during the COVID-19 period also included no activities such as assemblies or mass gatherings, curricular activities, physical education, drama classes and the modification of timetables; many of these policy changes are still being practised by schools today.

As part of the government initiatives to support online learning activities and platforms in schools and the Ministry of Education's efforts, various schools received provisions of bandwidth and data to facilitate continuous learning, while the government also encouraged the public to donate new or used electronic devices for the use of academic communities. During the COVID-19 period, *Program Rancangan Pembelajaran Di Rumah* (Home-Based Learning Television Programmes) for primary school students were shown on government media, namely RTB Aneka and RTB Go. These were established to facilitate students' learning during their stay-at-home period.

16.3.1.2 Health, Safety and Wellbeing
In terms of taking care of the health, safety and wellbeing of academic communities and schools, the Ministry of Education imposed certain

restrictions and Standard Operating Procedures (SOP), which followed the Ministry of Health's guidelines, to be abided by teachers, students and parents.

For teachers:

- Teachers should be equipped with SOP and BCP as required by the government and respective schools.
- Teachers who are unwell should not come to school.
- Vulnerable teachers should only attend school for their lessons.
- Teachers should ensure social distancing with students and colleagues in classrooms and the staffroom.
- Teachers should wear facemasks at all times, especially while teaching.
- Teachers should practise personal hygiene, wash their hands regularly, and practise sneeze and cough etiquette as advised by the Ministry of Health.
- Physical Education teachers should help supervise students during recess and at the canteen.
- Teachers are to help check body temperatures for students before they enter school premises.

For students:

- Students should be equipped with necessary personal hygiene items, for example, tissue, face towel and hand sanitisers (if any) and personal drinking bottles.
- Students should practise personal hygiene, wash their hands regularly, and practise sneeze and cough etiquette as advised by the Ministry of Health.
- Students are recommended to wear facemasks at all times.
- Students who are unwell should not come to school.
- Students should minimise their movement in school, including having their food in respective classrooms (during break time).
- Students should not share personal items or food.
- Students should ensure social distancing with teachers and schoolmates in classrooms and in school and should not shake/hold/touch their friend(s) hands, among others.

For parents:

- Parents should provide their child(ren) with necessary personal hygiene items, for example, tissue, face towel and hand sanitisers (if any), personal drinking bottle and pocket money with exact change.
- Parents should remind their child(ren) to not share personal items/food and to practise social distancing and personal hygiene and etiquette in school.
- Parents should not send their child(ren) to school if they are sick.
- Parents should not enter the school premises if they are sick, and are only allowed when they are not sick and have an appointment at the school.
- Parents should drop off and pick up their child(ren) at the designated area provided by the school, where one adult per family is allowed to accompany their child(ren) to avoid overcrowding.

All teachers, students and parents were encouraged to follow all the guidelines provided by the schools and the government through its multi-sectoral ministries. Throughout the process and the de-escalation stages, all government sectors were implementing the 'Whole of Nation Approach' where the ministries were kept informed through open channels and communication in order to succeed in combating the impact of COVID-19, while maintaining academic functionality throughout the nation. Furthermore, even though the initiative was never explicitly mentioned for or involving the academic community in Brunei, specifically for teachers, the government of Brunei also implemented continuous support of providing job security for government servants as well as individuals; thus, there were no reports of loss of jobs from COVID-19 recorded in the country.

The initiative of maintaining the wellbeing of the whole nation also came from different ministries. For instance, in line with the country upholding its national philosophy of *Melayu Islam Beraja* (Malay Islamic Monarchy), the Ministry of Religious Affairs also distributed a total of 15,000 copies of a collection of *Dhikr* (reminder) and prayer books in dealing with COVID-19 to government and private sectors throughout the nation, and a downloadable virtual book was also made available at the ministry's official website. The Islamic effort was further bolstered by the production of a series of books entitled *COVID-19: Apa Kata Mufti* (COVID-19: What The Mufti Says) by *Jabatan Mufti Kerajaan* (The Department of Government Mufti), made available to the public, which aimed to raise awareness on the importance of Islamic faith and religion to wellbeing in the efforts to combat the COVID-19 pandemic (Haji Yahya, 2020).

Therefore, in comparison to the pre-COVID-19 situation, the changes in educational practices is observed from the number of hours spent in teaching and learning, conducting activities to maintain the efficacy of teaching and learning, and the role of every member in the academic community. Restrictions are still present in many schools throughout the country, as schools are encouraged to minimise teachers' and students' movement while social distancing is still enforced at large today. As such, the educational practices of learning through grouping activities and hands-on experience, which follows SPN21, have been disrupted and cannot be undertaken at large. Furthermore, the roles of teachers in both primary and secondary schools have expanded beyond simply managing teaching affairs and now include taking care of the wellbeing of their students. Teachers are also often expected to come up with their own initiatives to provide the best pedagogical experience for their students, their schools and themselves. In this case, teachers have to work together with students and parents in order to follow the guidelines and the BCP implemented by the Ministry of Education. In addition, alongside the Ministry of Education's BCP, each school is encouraged to come up with their own BCP following the guidelines made by the Ministry of Education and the government of Brunei in general. This is because each school in Brunei—whether at the primary or secondary level—has their own unique academic community and environment.

16.3.2 Higher Education

Among the roles of the Higher Education Division at the Ministry of Education is to regulate and facilitate the governance of the six higher education institutions in the country ("Higher Education Division", n.d.), while the Ministry of Religious Affairs oversees the Islamic Religious Teachers' Training College that was established in 1975 and upgraded to a university college in 2007. Table 16.2 lists the seven higher education institutions in Brunei and their year of establishment. Note that for Universiti Teknologi Brunei (UTB) and Kolej Universiti Perguruan Ugama Seri Begawan (KUPU SB), the year indicates the upgrading of the institutions to a university status.

The Brunei Darussalam National Accreditation Council, established in 1990 by decree of His Majesty the Sultan of Brunei Darussalam, is the

Table 16.2 The government and private higher education institutions in Brunei

Higher education institution	Year of establishment
Universiti Brunei Darussalam (UBD)	1985
Universiti Islam Sultan Sharif Ali (UNISSA)	2007
Universiti Teknologi Brunei (UTB)	2008
Politeknik Brunei (PB)	2012
Kolej Universiti Perguruan Ugama Seri Begawan (KUPU SB)	2007
Kolej International Graduate Studies (KIGS)	2002
Laksamana College of Business (LCB)	2003

only accrediting agency and quality assurance agency in the country. 'All higher education providers conducting an accredited programme or awarding an accredited qualification or providing consultancy services on education shall comply with the Brunei Darussalam Qualification Framework' (Ministry of Education, 2014, p. 8). The following subsections will, first, review the changes in educational practices within the higher education sector and, second, consider the approaches to teaching, learning and assessment. Both subsections focus on transpired events *during* the COVID-19 pandemic.

16.3.2.1 Changes in Educational Practices Within the Higher Education Institutions

While most higher education institutions in the country remained open and the daily operations of relevant facilities continued, all the necessary and important precautions in ensuring the health, safety and the wellbeing of students and staff were carefully monitored following the guidelines provided by the Ministry of Health in order to minimise the risks of any possible transmissions (Wong, Chaw et al., 2020a). These included temperature screening checkpoints at strategic and selected main entrances of campus buildings, mandatory social distancing practices, enforcing a strict 30-minute limit for visitors to the library and 'Work from Home' schedule arrangements for staff as was stipulated by the Prime Minister's Office of Brunei (Prime Minister's Office, 2020).

Concurrently, all institutions were informed to complete their respective BCPs, which entailed cascading the task to respective leaders of faculties, centres, departments and offices, as well as the controlled entities under its operation. The main goal in preparing such a document was to minimise any disruptions to core services due to the high probability of the continued COVID-19 pandemic threat. What needed to be understood was the probable threat and the impact it might cause to daily operations, as well as the potential loss of man-hours, data and property. Critical staff roles and contact details were updated and compiled, and internal and external communication plans in the event of an emergency were provided. These communication plans described how officers, staff, students, parents and so on were to communicate with one another in the event of a crisis, such as the use of fax and/or email for official matters, telephone calls or instant messaging (Short Message Service or SMS) for urgent matters, and utilising WhatsApp, Skype, Zoom or other teleconferencing applications for group discussions.

For higher education institutions, there were many essential functions that needed to be identified for the BCP in relation to its risk, impact, recovery time, details of activities and the mitigation or prevention strategies. The main core business of any education provider is the teaching and learning delivery and other student-related services. It was important to identify how the closure of classes, libraries and teaching facilities could jeopardise students' academic and practical activities such as classroom and laboratory learning, clinical or industrial practices, assessment or examinations, and the impending students' graduation. The mitigation strategies given included alternative modes of teaching using online platforms; accessing library services remotely; postponing any scheduled seminars, forums and conferences; changing the assessment mode to 100% coursework; and allocating examined courses with a high number of students into smaller groups across several examination venues.

16.3.2.2 Teaching, Learning and Assessment Approaches

In following through with the BCP and in anticipation of any possibilities of pending risks, all higher education institutions revised their teaching, learning and assessment approaches to delivery using online media. From the available information gathered via the institutions' respective websites, social media pages and press releases in the national newspapers, we learned that after the first case was reported on 9 March 2020, adjusting to such approaches took between three days to about three weeks. A summary of the changes for each institution is given in Table 16.3.

For UBD in particular, online learning had begun several years prior and thus transitioning lectures and tutorials to online platforms was relatively smooth. Additionally, academics whose modules had examination components were given the option to convert their modules to 100% coursework.

Table 16.3 Summary of teaching, learning and assessment approaches during the pandemic (Taken and adapted from Shahrill & Hardaker, in press)

HEI	Teaching, learning and assessment modes	Start date in 2020
UBD	• Online via Canvas • Options given for modules to be converted to 100% coursework • Online examinations	12th March
UNISSA	• Online via Learning Management System (LMS) and other Teaching and Learning technology • Studies on campus deferred from 14th March to 28th March	13th March
UTB	• Online Teaching using Online Education Platforms (OEP) and other non-face-to-face delivery methods of teaching and learning • No on-campus examination • All assessments converted to 100% coursework	16th March
PB	• Online using LMS	11th March
KUPU	• School facilities closed	22nd March
SB	• Online programme	
KIGS	• Online classes using the Microsoft Team apps	28th March
LCB	• Online classes	Date in March not specified

This in turn often necessitated modifying existing coursework assignments and immediately restructuring and replanning due dates (Shahrill et al., 2020; "UBD in the COVID-19 Pandemic", 2020; Tong & Daud, 2020). Although conducting online examinations came with its own set of logistical challenges and concerns—such as preventing cheating (Boitshwarelo et al., 2017), plagiarism, academic misconduct and absenteeism (Day et al., 2020; Khan & Khan, 2019)—the relevant offices were well prepared with the option of open or closed book examinations and clear available guidelines for all such circumstances conveyed in advance to all academic staff and students of the university (Shahrill et al., in press; Tuah & Naing, 2020).

16.4 Student Teacher Responses Towards Changes in Educational Practices

The Sultan Hassanal Bolkiah Institute of Education (SHBIE), a graduate faculty of education in UBD, offers an initial teacher preparation programme called the Master of Teaching or MTeach for short. A three-semester programme provides professional training on a full-time basis to graduates who have chosen to become qualified teachers, while a four-semester programme is offered to part-time students who are categorised as Work-Based. There were 93 students in the first semester of the January 2020 Intake. The MTeach timetabling is not like other programmes or modules in UBD such that students attend classes intensively every workday for two weeks in Weeks 2 and 3, and the whole of each Saturday is blocked for core and option modules including the learning area modules starting in Week 1, and subsequently from Week 4 to Week 14. On 12th March 2020, UBD announced that all lectures and tutorials were to be delivered online (Shahrill et al., in press; Tong & Daud, 2020; "UBD in the COVID-19 Pandemic", 2020), and the university was already in Week 9 of a 14-week semester. By this time, most of the MTeach lectures, typically delivered via face-to-face sessions, were mostly completed. The remaining classes moved online and were used for assignment presentations by students using platforms such as Canvas, Zoom and Microsoft Teams.

However, challenges arose for the MTeach school practicum sessions. As part of the core requirements of the MTeach programme, all students are placed in schools and institutions around the country for their school placements starting in Week 4 until Week 14 from Monday to Thursday. Experienced teachers within the school, in collaboration with MTeach Clinical Specialists, will mentor each student during the placement. On 25 March 2020, five days before the second school term were due to resume, the Ministry of Education announced that all teaching and learning sessions in all schools under its purview, as well as under the purview of the Ministry of Religious Affairs, were to be conducted online (Ministry of Education, Brunei Darussalam, March 25, 2020b). A press release made by the Programme Leader of School Partnership in SHBIE quickly followed the next day stating that MTeach school placements at the students' respective schools would end early on 30 March 2020, with the exception of one MTeach student enrolment mode, specifically the students under the *Program Perantis* or Apprentice Programme. This was the start of Week 12 with three weeks remaining for school placements. In order to compensate for the three-week shortage in placements, assessment methods were revised: (1) Students would create one online material for submission to a Clinical Specialist and present it (via online modes) during the final seminar session as additional to the last topic and (2) the five seminar sessions by the Clinical Specialist would take place as usual but be conducted synchronously online.

The Apprentice Programme mentioned earlier is a new teacher induction initiative by the Ministry of Education that started in 2019, where applicants go through numerous stringent selection procedures before enrolling in the MTeach programme. There were 44 MTeach apprentice student teachers in total—31 specialising in Secondary Education, 9 in Primary Education and 2 in Early Childhood Education and Care. Based on the press release by the Programme Leader, all MTeach apprentice student teachers were required to continue their school placements at their earlier assigned schools with the following provisions: firstly, the arrangement followed the BCP of the respective schools (e.g. flexi-hours, following shifts) as per instructed by the school leader and mentor, and, secondly, the expectations from schools would carry on following school arrangements with regard to supporting students' online learning and also assigned tasks from the mentor and school leader.

Fourteen MTeach students were asked to share about their school practicum experiences during the COVID-19 pandemic by reflecting on their teaching, students' learning and respective school situations. All respondents stated that the initial news about the changes they needed to make in their teaching came from their corresponding leaders through the mobile application WhatsApp. The given instructions on preparing teaching materials for their students were mainly similar across all schools. For example, Halim, an MTeach apprentice student teacher based in a government secondary school located more than 100 km from the country's capital city Bandar Seri Begawan, shared the following:

> After receiving the news on COVID-19, the school leader at our school informed us through WhatsApp group to prepare a 1-month worth of home learning pack in 2 weeks. Teaching was to be done through an online platform, preferably Microsoft Teams. Students were given their respective email accounts to be used to login using Teams for their lessons. That said we were also given options to do the class through Zoom or through WhatsApp considering the availability of technologies that the students have.

Meanwhile, Maya, who is based in a government secondary school less than 20 km from the city centre, shared similar preparations in her school. She further stated:

Changes on tactics that the school decided to adopt were made and informed via WhatsApp with no heads up and required immediate action i.e. the time allowed to conduct our teaching lessons, the amount of (Home-Based Learning) HBL allowed as well as students' schedule to attend online lessons.

Maya persevered during the preparation and implemented several revisions to her teaching activities that included asynchronous teaching lessons in which she uploaded short video lessons on YouTube for her students to watch anytime. In ensuring that her students watched the videos, she assigned lesson quizzes through the *Kahoot!* online quiz platform. Maya also conducted live online discussions using Zoom during her students' scheduled timetable for Mathematics lessons in order to interact with them if they have any questions pertaining to the uploaded video lessons. Similar teaching activities were also observed for student teachers teaching at the primary school levels, with one of them emphasising that the duration of the video created lasted a maximum of six minutes only. Perhaps she may have duly researched about the six-minute online video rule, which has since been refuted as a myth (Geri et al., 2017; Lagerstrom et al., 2015).

The challenges presented to these student teachers during COVID-19 affected them intellectually, physically, spiritually and emotionally. Not only had the expectations been set high—especially since they were part of the graduate-level teacher training programme—they were also faced with the different levels of challenging demands from the schools, school leaders, mentors, students and parents. Noreen, who is an MTeach apprentice student teacher specialising in Early Childhood Education and Care, had her school placement in a government primary school. She shared that among the challenges she encountered were the difficulties in keeping track of her students' learning progress, as well as the dependence of some parents with no experience in teaching who relied heavily on her to teach their children. This made her anxious, particularly as there were also parents who did not give their full cooperation in their child's learning. Rahimah, who specialises in Early Childhood Education and Care, shared the same sentiments as Noreen:

> [I was] worried about children's learning if they could comprehend the lesson and answer themselves on the worksheet given. Less stress as not to deal with students physically, but more to dealing with parents, videos, Google form link and worksheet, and going through them before giving them to the students. Some of the parents were not cooperating well to collect HBL and help with their children's learning.

In contrast to the MTeach apprentice student teachers, those who enrolled as full-time students were required to end their practicums earlier than anticipated following the press release by the Programme Leader. Nadia and Rizal were fortunate to resume the current semester practicum without facing the challenges as experienced by their peers in the previous semester. Nadia stated that she spent more time in front of her laptop exploring the numerous free online applications and resources. However, there was limited Internet access because everyone in her house was connected online using the same Wi-Fi server. There were mixed reactions from the respondents on the use of online learning at the school level. While some welcomed it as a new and worthy experience, others still preferred the face-to-face physical classes citing the ease of getting students to respond to questions, being able to reciprocate in terms of expressions and the need to rebuild essential teacher-student rapport in the classroom.

16.5 Educator Responses Towards Changes in Educational Practices

In the face of the COVID-19 pandemic, government-mandated measures included social distancing, restrictions on mass gatherings, the enforcement of mask-wearing and the use of digital contact tracing through *BruHealth*, a mobile phone app which was swiftly created and promoted to ensure that the Ministry of Health had better access to data to help combat any potential contagion. These measures had cascading effects across all areas of life in the country, and the educational sector was no exception. Remote meetings became a way of life almost overnight, resulting in an exponential upsurge in the usage of online tools, programmes and learning environments such as Zoom, Canvas and Microsoft Teams. Along with these changes came new challenges—students (and their parents) suddenly found themselves having to deal with studying and working from home, with each person vying for Internet bandwidth and relevant devices needed for their particular tasks. Younger students also needed extra parental attention and supervision, which for many people would often prove to be a scarce resource.

Between the school closures in March, the beginning of the de-escalation plans in mid-May and the eventual resuming of the normal academic term at the end of July, educators at multiple levels had to consider how to best do their jobs while navigating all the new rules. Those with institutional support, who were already comfortable with technology or could afford to invest in it themselves, had a few less hurdles to clear. Even so, the new requirement for online teaching would be a test for everyone, given Brunei's nascent foray into digital education. Cursory conversations with different educators revealed some interesting anecdotes with regard to new institutional policies, tools provided or used, and their overall experiences with teaching during the pandemic (Keasberry, 2020).

Many of the policies implemented placed immense pressure on teachers (Phan et al., 2020). One such example could be seen in a number of primary schools, where teachers were often expected to prepare Home-Based Learning (HBL) packs that would be collected by parents on designated days. Thus, much more preparation time was needed, which meant higher strains on teachers' time and effort. Moreover, teachers did not have full discretion over what material to include in the HBL packs; they needed to justify whatever topics they would put in the packs.

One common result of the new policies was that even with schools re-opening, many students would be spending part of their week studying from home. This meant that the HBL material had to be digitised and uploaded online, usually on a cloud service or the school website. Regardless, there were still students without proper Internet or access to a PC or laptop, and so physical HBL packs still had to be prepared and distributed every week. In some cases, teachers often had to contact parents personally to ascertain their circumstances with regard to Internet connectivity, device availability and even preference for hardcopy or softcopy assignments.

Teachers also found that continual adjustments had to be made to the curriculum and content as they navigated this new online asynchronous teaching. It was difficult to tell what young students were able to digest over the Internet and delivery methods had to adjust for differences in Internet connections and speeds. As a result, some teachers opted to skip the more difficult topics until such a time when students were allowed to return to proper face-to-face classes. This was compounded by Internet issues that teachers faced themselves, as there were times that the school Internet connection was unreliable.

While the new policies were designed in preparation for the re-opening of the new academic term, exactly how these policies were to be implemented on the ground level often seemed to be unclear. Teachers were frequently left to their own devices—both literally and figuratively—and had to cobble together their own pedagogies using tools that were either foisted on them or already familiar to them before the pandemic. Suddenly, setting and marking assignments no longer took place in a physical classroom, but an online one. Face-to-face teaching gave way to screen recordings, uploaded class sessions or live video conferences. Existing content had to be reworked for online classes, which ended up being massively time-consuming. Ultimately, teachers had to decide for themselves what worked best and work accordingly, which itself frequently led to discrepancies between school levels, with primary sections tackling the challenge one way and secondary sections doing it another way.

With all these new digital tools, it seems almost inevitable that teachers would quickly encounter their next big hurdle: technical ability (or lack thereof). The rapid rise in online teaching caused some teething problems as many educators were not used to providing online education. However, beyond their own proficiency, they were also faced with the varying capacities of students and their parents. How would a teacher get their students into a Google Classroom if neither the students nor their parents knew how to navigate it? How would students access their online exercises and videos on Microsoft Teams if they did not know where to look?

All of these issues together often compounded teachers' already busy work life. Each new obstacle presented new challenges and necessitated a lot more communication between teachers and their heads of department, between teachers and their administrative staff, as well as between teachers and parents, all of which lead to even more pressure in terms of time and commitment. To say that teacher stress levels increased during the pandemic might be something of an understatement. While teachers' mental health and safety is something to be concerned about in and of itself, students' stress levels also need to be considered as there has been research to suggest that teachers' occupational stress is linked to students' physiological stress levels (Oberle & Schonert-Reichl, 2016). Teacher burnout means less effective teaching and classroom management, and students are consequently affected.

Similar issues also existed at the tertiary level. Based on early observation and responses from educators at UBD as reported by Noorashid (2020), the abrupt transitioning from classroom learning to online-distance learning had undoubtedly imposed various challenges to the educators.

Educators, particularly those who were more mature, yearned for more support in terms of the knowledge and skills to manoeuvre online-distance learning platforms and applications during the height of the pandemic.

The limitations of technical skills in using devices and platforms in e-learning have been consistently suggested to cause limitations to the teaching and learning process (Aljawarneh, 2020; Dunlap et al., 2016; Peachey, 2017), thus raising concerns over the post-COVID effects on students, as well as on the educators themselves. Along similar lines, the abrupt transition caused challenges in terms of preparing teaching materials, where in some cases, educators had to restructure and reorganise their courses to much simpler ones in order to accommodate the demand of effective online pedagogy and successful deliverance of knowledge to their students. The situation also affected assessment practices among these educators. Some had to adopt a more lenient approach in assessing their students' works and reconsider relevant tasks to support their students' final grades. A few educators also reported that they had to opt for 100% coursework as a way to find common ground with their students, as well as to adjust to the restriction of movement during the height of COVID-19 in the country. Nevertheless, a handful of teacher educators still divulged that the pandemic had severely impacted the way they work with students, the students' teaching practice opportunities and conducting school research.

A few studies in international contexts have described current pedagogical challenges in higher education and academic communities' efforts in coping with the effects of COVID-19 (Karalis, 2020; UNESCO, 2020; Ya, 2020). In Brunei, whilst considering pedagogical effectiveness using distance learning, some educators took the initiative to share knowledge with their peers in and outside of the country in an attempt to find the best approach and platforms for online learning that would be preferable by the university and academic communities. This included mulling over various aspects, such as cost effectiveness and convenience for both themselves and their students. While such approaches helped the educators to consider their pedagogical initiatives to ensure equal opportunities of learning for the students during those challenging times, some educators also reported taking into account their students' wellbeing at the same time. In these cases, it can be seen that the role of educator has also expanded, from being just a teacher to including research and counselling. Moreover, there have been less restrictions and involvement of other sectors and departments in managing BCPs for higher education, in comparison to their core-level education division. This has possibly given more opportunities for these educators to explore their potential and initiatives in dealing with pedagogical issues and challenges during COVID-19. For instance, Suhaili (2020) reported that upon the announcement that higher education institutions were required to come up with their own BCP, UTB and its academics launched various initiatives to cater to the needs of their students, such as utilising online educational platforms and preferable non face-to-face teaching and learning methods.

Nevertheless, judging from distance interviews undertaken with educators in UBD, it became clear that amid their resilience in ensuring the efficacy of their pedagogy, almost all the educators hinted at their exhaustion and unstable emotions in dealing with various challenges faced while keeping up with the unprecedented phenomenon. For example, a number of them referred to the whole situation as 'a lonely time', 'a stressful event', an 'exhausting period' and feeling 'frustrated', stating that the abrupt changes as not being 'conducive to [one's] emotional and mental wellbeing'. Whilst more in-depth studies are needed to probe further into the educators' discourse of wellbeing, it cannot be denied that the pandemic has also affected the psychological and sociological equilibrium of their lives both personally and professionally. Moreover, a few expatriate educators also reported their frustration at not being able to travel and meet their families abroad, the uncertainties about transnational benefits they normally receive and their general wellbeing. This is perhaps inevitable as claims of psychological and sociological effects from COVID-19 have also been reported in previous accounts in international contexts (Hughes, 2020; Karalis, 2020; Karalis & Raikou, 2020), where it is also consistently claimed that the psychological aspects can strongly impact the whole efficacy of pedagogy in higher education institutions. Furthermore, Moorhouse (2020) claims that the pandemic may have caused certain detrimental effects in our post-crisis society, including distancing effects between educators and their students. These effects have been raised and also reflected on by a number of the local and expatriate educators at the university.

A Global Survey Report was recently launched and conducted by the International Association of Universities (IAU) and was undertaken during the height of COVID-19. The report aimed to identify and to understand disruption caused to and responses made by HEIs all over the world (IAU, 2020). According to the report, there were three major pedagogical challenges found in the following areas: (1) technical infrastructure and accessibility; (2) distance learning competences and pedagogies; and (3) the field of study.

Based on Noorashid's (2020) and Shahrill et al.'s (2020, 2021) early observations on the impact of COVID-19 on the educators in the university, the factors of 'technical infrastructure and accessibility' and 'distance learning competences and pedagogies' are apparent in the educators' reports. Moreover, the aspect of 'the field of study' or subject is also observed, particularly from a few teacher educators' claims that the research students at the teacher education institution was strongly impacted by the restricted movement during the height of the pandemic. The closure of schools, as well as limitations of entry and time for these students, disrupted their academic endeavours. Whilst such claims demonstrate impacts on students, a larger assessment reported by Noorashid et al. (2020) has shown more comprehensive pedagogical and sociological experiences during COVID-19 based on the educators' responses involving four major public higher institutions in Brunei, including UBD, UTB, KUPU SB and Universiti Islam Sultan Sharif Ali (UNISSA). Whilst the article highlights several pedagogical issues experienced by the educators in these higher education institutions, it also entails the quick adjustments, approaches and initiatives that have been implemented by these educators through continuous support from their universities, the ministries and the government. These attempts are to support the 'Whole of Nation Approach' promoted by the government while continuing to play their roles to ensure higher education functionality.

Even when faced with challenges, educators at all levels of education took them in stride, doing their best to engage their students using the new tools and bridge any gaps so that no student is left behind. Many educators supported one another, shared stories and anecdotes about different policies, and aided others in the use of new technologies. Upon the announcement of Phase 4 of the de-escalation plan at the end of July, there seemed to be a collective sigh of relief from the majority of teachers. Things could now go back to normal or as normal as things could be while the outside world still roiled in the midst of a global pandemic.

16.6　Conclusion

Undoubtedly, the COVID-19 pandemic has affected educational affairs in various ways, particularly the academic communities, educators and students, both in Brunei and across the world. The pandemic has forced the academic community in the country to mull over various implementations and come up with necessary measures to ensure the pandemic does not affect educational affairs in the country for too long. The roles and responsibilities of everyone in the academic community have also expanded as a result.

Nevertheless, amidst these challenges, educators at all levels in Brunei have been able to cope and strategise necessary pedagogical affairs in support of the government and show resilience in dealing with the inevitable limitations and restrictions of COVID-19. In line with this, the government through the Ministry of Education and other relevant agencies continues to find ways to support the academic communities across Brunei, including educators and their students. Although there are still concerns over the future state of education and its management, to date the approach of open communication and continuous support between agencies for the education sector in the country was triumphant in dealing with the challenges during the pandemic.

Within the completion of this chapter, Brunei successfully flattened the curve and managed to curb the impacts of COVID-19 on the nation. Simultaneously, the multi-sectoral initiatives implemented by various ministries under the 'Whole of Nation Approach' promoted by the government of Brunei have received adulation from the public in Brunei and from international agencies and organisations. This has also provided opportunities to gain a deeper look into how Brunei has managed its educational affairs and pedagogical approaches involving important stakeholders at all levels of education. Whilst this chapter only focuses on reviewing changes of policy and practices and analysing responses from educators amid COVID-19, further research will need to be undertaken to fully understand and resolve other related issues, by considering the perspectives of students and the managerial stakeholders in Brunei education.

As the pandemic is an ongoing phenomenon experienced by various communities globally, more investigations should be carried out on educational affairs in Brunei, which will contribute to new knowledge and further benefit the international academic communities in many ways. Furthermore, as few studies have looked into such issues, particularly in contextualising Brunei as a case study, additional insight and research would produce more comprehensive perspectives on the current situation of education in Brunei amid COVID-19.

References

Abdullah, N. A., Shahrill, M., Yusof, J., & Prahmana, R. C. I. (2018). Identifying the factors affecting students' performances in primary school mathematics. *Journal of Physics: Conference Series, 1097*(1), 012137.

Aljawarneh, S. A. (2020). Reviewing and exploring innovative ubiquitous learning tools in higher education. *Journal of Computing in Higher Education, 32*(1), 57–73. https://doi.org/10.1007/s12528-019-09207-0

Boitshwarelo, B., Reedy, A. K., & Billany, T. (2017). Envisioning the use of online tests in assessing twenty-first century learning: A literature review. *Research and Practice in Technology Enhanced Learning, 12*(1), 1–16.

Day, T., Chang, I. C. C., Chung, C. K. L., Doolittle, W. E., Housel, J., & McDaniel, P. N. (2020). The immediate impact of COVID-19 on postsecondary teaching and learning. *The Professional Geographer,* 1–13. https://doi.org/10.1080/00330124.2020.1823864

Dunlap, J., Verma, G., & Johnson, H. (2016). Presence + Experience: A framework for the purposeful design of presence in online courses. *TechTrends, 60*(2), 145–151. https://doi.org/10.1007/s11528-016-0029-4

Geri, N., Winer, A., & Zaks, B. (2017). Challenging the six-minute myth of online video lectures: Can interactivity expand the attention span of learners? *Online Journal of Applied Knowledge Management, 5*(1), 101–111.

Government Education Institutions. (n.d.). http://www.moe.gov.bn/SitePages/Government%20Education%20Institutions.aspx

Government of Brunei. (2020, May 8). Measures Undertaken by the Government in Addressing the Impact of COVID-19 in Brunei Darussalam. http://www.moe.gov.bn/Articles/Measures%20Undertaken%20by%20the%20Government%20in%20Handling%20the%20Impact%20of%20COVID-19%20%20issued%2027.04.2020%20v7.pdf

Haji Yahya, S. (2020, April 20). *Jabatan mufti terbitkan buku mengenai COVID-19. Media Permata.* https://mediapermata.com.bn/jabatan-mufti-terbitkan-buku-mengenai-covid-19/

Hiebert, J., Gallimore, R., Garnier, H., Givvin, K. B., Hollingsworth, H., Jacobs, J., Chui, A., Wearne, D., Smith, M., Kersting, N., Manaster, A., Tseng, E., Etterbeek, W., Manaster, C., Gonzales, P., & Stigler, J. (2003). *Teaching mathematics in seven countries: Results from the TIMSS 1999 Video Study.* U.S. Department of Education, National Center for Education Statistics.

Higher Education Division. (n.d.). http://www.moe.gov.bn/SitePages/Higher%20Education%20Division.aspx

Hughes, C. (2020). Some implications of COVID-19 for remote learning and the future of schooling. https://unesdoc.unesco.org/ark:/48223/pf0000373229

IAU. (2020). Covid-19: Higher Education challenges and responses. https://www.iau-aiu.net/Covid-19-Higher-Education-challenges-and-responses

Karalis, T. (2020). Planning and evaluation during educational disruption: Lessons learned from COVID-19 pandemic for treatment of emergencies in education. *European Journal of Education Studies, 7*(4), 125–142. https://doi.org/10.5281/zenodo.3789022

Karalis, T., & Raikou, N. (2020). Teaching at the times of COVID-19: Inferences and implications for higher education pedagogy. *International Journal of Academic Research in Business and Social Sciences, 10*(5), 479–493. https://doi.org/10.6007/IJARBSS/v10-i5/7219

Keasberry, C. (2020). *Zoom in: Perceptions and perspectives of pandemic pedagogy.* Seminar presented at International and Comparative Education (ICE) Seminar Series, Universiti Brunei Darussalam, Tungku Link, September 1.

Khan, S., & Khan, R. A. (2019). Online assessments: Exploring perspectives of university students. *Education and Information Technologies, 24*(1), 661–677.

Kon, J., & Roslan, W. (2020, September 23). Rising to the COVID-19 challenge. *Borneo Bulletin.* https://borneobulletin.com.bn/2020/09/rising-to-the-covid-19-challenge/

Lagerstrom, L., Johanes, P., & Ponsukcharoen, M. U. (2015). The myth of the six-minute rule: Student engagement with online videos. Proceedings of the American Society for Engineering Education, June 14–17, 2015, Seattle, WA. https://www.asee.org/public/conferences/56/papers/13527/download

Lampert, M. (2001). *Teaching problems and the problems of teaching.* Yale University Press.

Ministry of Education. (2013). *The national education system for the 21st century: SPN21* (2nd ed.). Ministry of Education.

Ministry of Education. (2014). *Brunei Darussalam qualification framework.* Ministry of Education.

Ministry of Education. (2019a). *Brunei Darussalam Education Statistics 2018.* Educational Data Management Section, Department of Planning, Development and Research, Ministry of Education. http://www.moe.gov.bn/DocumentDownloads/Education%20Statistics%20and%20Indicators%20Handbook/Brunei%20Darussalam%20Education%20Statistics%202018.pdf

Ministry of Education. (2019b). *Brunei Darussalam Education Statistics and Indicators Handbook 2014–2018.* Educational Data Management Section, Department of Planning, Development and Research, Ministry of Education. http://www.moe.gov.bn/DocumentDownloads/Education%20Statistics%20and%20Indicators%20Handbook/Brunei%20Darussalam%20Education%20Statistics%20and%20Indicators%20Handbook%202018.pdf

Ministry of Education. (2020). *Schools Operation Protocol Matrix during COVID-19.* Ministry of Education. http://www.moe.gov.bn/Articles/School%20Reopening%20Plan%20Protocol.pdf

Ministry of Education, Brunei Darussalam. (2020a, March 10). *Surat Pemberitahuan Kementerian Pendidikan Bilangan*: 2/2020 – Ministry of

Education Notice No. 2/2020 (*Perubahan Tarikh Cuti Penggal Pertama Persekolahan* – Changes to the First Term School Holidays). http://www.moe.gov.bn/SitePages/NewsArticle.aspx?AID=637

Ministry of Education, Brunei Darussalam. (2020b, March 25). *Pembelajaran Dan Pengajaran Secara Dalam Talian (Online) Penggal Persekolahan Ke-Dua* – Second School Term Online Teaching and Learning. http://www.moe.gov.bn/SitePages/NewsArticle.aspx?AID=645

Ministry of Health, Brunei Darussalam. (2020a, March 9). Detection of the First Case of COVID-19 Infection in Brunei Darussalam. http://www.moh.gov.bn/Shared%20Documents/2019%20ncov/press%20releases/FINAL%20Press%20Release%20(eng)%20-%20First%20Case%20COVID-19%20in%20Brunei%20Darussalam%20(2).pdf

Ministry of Health, Brunei Darussalam. (2020b, March 10). Media Statement on the Current COVID-19 Infection in Brunei Darussalam. http://www.moh.gov.bn/Shared%20Documents/2019%20ncov/press%20releases/FINAL%20PRESS%20STATEMENT%20COVID-19%20INFECTION%2010%20MARCH%202020%20(ENG).pdf

Moorhouse, B. L. (2020). Adaptations to a face-to-face initial teacher education course 'forced' online due to the COVID-19 pandemic. *Journal of Education for Teaching*, 1–3. https://doi.org/10.1080/02607476.2020.1755205

Noorashid, N. (2020). *COVID-19 and responses from university teachers and students in Brunei: An initial overview and implications for research and pedagogy*. Seminar presented at International and Comparative Education (ICE) Seminar Series, Universiti Brunei Darussalam, Tungku Link, August 11.

Noorashid, N., Phan, L. H., Alas, Y., & Yabit, V. M. (2020, October 10). Beyond the pandemic, integrating online learning. *University World News*. https://www.universityworldnews.com/post.php?story=20201009150047136

Oberle, E., & Schonert-Reichl, K. A. (2016). Stress contagion in the classroom? The link between classroom teacher burnout and morning cortisol in elementary school students. *Social Science, 159*, 30–37. https://doi.org/10.1016/j.socscimed.2016.04.031

Peachey, N. (2017). Synchronous online teaching. In M. Carrier, R. M. Damerow, & K. M. Bailey (Eds.), *Digital language learning and teaching* (pp. 143–155). Routledge.

Phan, L. H., Yabit, V. M., & Alas, Y. (2020). *Effects of COVID-19 on educational policy and stakeholders in Brunei, Malaysia and Indonesia*. Seminar presented at International and Comparative Education (ICE) Seminar Series, Universiti Brunei Darussalam, Tungku Link, August 25.

Prime Minister's Office. (2020). *Guideline for Business Continuity Plan on COVID-19 for Civil Service*. Prime Minister's Office. http://www.pmo.gov.bn/SiteCollectionDocuments/covid19/bcp-eng.pdf

Shahrill, M. (2009). *From the general to the particular: Connecting international classroom research to four classrooms in Brunei Darussalam* (Unpublished doctoral dissertation), University of Melbourne, Melbourne.

Shahrill, M., Abdul Aziz, A. B. Z., Naing, L., Petra, M. I., Yacob, J., & Santos, J. H. (2020). *The developments and findings of online learning in UBD during the COVID-19 pandemic.* Seminar presented at International and Comparative Education (ICE) Seminar Series, Universiti Brunei Darussalam, Tungku Link, September 15.

Shahrill, M., Abdullah, N. A., & Yusof, J. (2014). Research Report: Teachers and Teaching of Mathematics in Primary Schools in Brunei Darussalam. Department of Planning, Development and Research, Ministry of Education, Brunei Darussalam.

Shahrill, M., & Hardaker, G. (in press). Country case study for Brunei Darussalam. In M. R. Panigrahi & B. Phalachadra (Eds.), *Handbook on online education in commonwealth Asia: Case studies.* Commonwealth Educational Media Centre for Asia (CEMCA).

Shahrill, M., Hardaker, G., Yacob, J., & Petra, M. I. (in press). Institutional case study for Universiti Brunei Darussalam. In M. R. Panigrahi & B. Phalachadra (Eds.), *Handbook on online education in commonwealth Asia: Case studies.* Commonwealth Educational Media Centre for Asia (CEMCA).

Shahrill, M., Petra, M. I., Naing, L., Yacob, J., Santos, J. H., & Abdul Aziz, A. B. Z. (2021). New norms and opportunities from the COVID-19 pandemic crisis in a higher education setting: Perspectives from Universiti Brunei Darussalam. *International Journal of Educational Management, 35*(3), 700–712. https://doi.org/10.1108/IJEM-07-2020-0347.

Sithamparam, S., Tan, J. P. S., & Raju, C. J. (2014). *Research Report: Teachers and Teaching of English Language in Primary Schools in Brunei Darussalam.* Department of Planning, Development and Research, Ministry of Education, Brunei Darussalam.

Suhaili, W. S. H. (2020). Brunei Darussalam – Impact of COVID-19 on Brunei's higher education teaching. In P. G. Altbach, S. Gopinathan, L. H. Yeong, & T. Balakrishnan (Eds.), *Special issue 8 higher education in Southeast Asia and beyond: How is COVID-19 impacting higher education?* (pp. 25–27). The HEAD Foundation.

Tarasat, S., Jaidi, N., & Rahman, S. K. A. (2014). *Research Report: Teachers and Teaching of Bahasa Melayu (Malay Language) in Primary Schools in Brunei Darussalam.* Department of Planning, Development and Research, Ministry of Education, Brunei Darussalam.

Tong, C. K., & Daud, K. H. M. (Eds.). (2020, October). COVID-19: Adapting to new norms. *Discover UBD, 3,* 3–16. https://ubd.edu.bn/DiscoverUBD/issue38/

Tuah, N. A. A., & Naing, L. (2020). Is online assessment in higher education institutions during COVID-19 pandemic reliable? *Siriraj Medical Journal, 73*(5) https://he02.tci-thaijo.org/index.php/sirirajmedj/article/view/246342

UBD in the COVID-19 Pandemic. (2020, July 27). Latest News: Universiti Brunei Darussalam. https://ubd.edu.bn/news-and-events/covid19.html

UNESCO. (2020). COVID-19 Educational Disruption and Response. https://en.unesco.org/covid19/educationresponse

Wong, J., Chaw, L., Koh, W. C., Alikhan, M. F., Jamaludin, S. A., Poh, W. W. P., & Naing, L. (2020a). Epidemiological investigation of the first 135 COVID-19 cases in Brunei: Implications for surveillance, control, and travel restrictions. *The American Journal of Tropical Medicine and Hygiene, 103*(4), 1608–1613.

Wong, J., Koh, W. C., Alikhan, M. F., Abdul Aziz, A. B. Z., & Naing, L. (2020b). Responding to COVID-19 in Brunei Darussalam: Lessons for small countries. *Journal of Global Health, 10*(1), 1–4. https://doi.org/10.7189/JOGH.10.010363

Ya, S. W. (2020, April 8). *Education during COVID-19*. Institute of Democracy and Economic Affairs.

CHAPTER 17

Higher Education Institutions in the New Semester: Moving Beyond 'Pandemic' Pedagogy

Najib Noorashid, Phan Le Ha, Yabit Alas, and Varissa Yabit

17.1 Introduction

We acknowledge that this chapter is further developed from an earlier article we have written for *University World News* (Noorashid et al., 2020).

As the Coronavirus Disease 2019 (COVID-19) continues to develop into unpredictable patterns, and as the rate in which it spreads differs among countries, higher education institutions (HEIs) around the world

N. Noorashid (✉) • Y. Alas • V. Yabit
Universiti Brunei Darussalam, Bandar Seri Begawan, Brunei
e-mail: najib.noorashid@ubd.edu.bn; yabit.alas@ubd.edu.bn

Phan, L. H.
Sultan Hassanal Bolkiah Institute of Education, Universiti Brunei Darussalam, Bandar Seri Begawan, Brunei

University of Hawai'i at Mānoa, Honolulu, HI, USA
e-mail: leha.phan@ubd.edu.bn; halephan@hawaii.edu

© The Author(s), under exclusive license to Springer Nature Switzerland AG 2021
Phan, L. H. et al. (eds.), *Globalisation, Education, and Reform in Brunei Darussalam*, International and Development Education,
https://doi.org/10.1007/978-3-030-77119-5_17

have taken appropriate measures to mitigate the effect of COVID-19 in their respective contexts. To date, the pandemic has affected all aspects of the sector including teaching, learning, research, finance, internationalisation, student services, community engagement, academic mobilities, access and participation, technological constraints, and teachers' and students' mental health and wellbeing (Alam & Hoon, this collection; Aristovnik et al., 2020; Schleicher, 2020; Shahrill et al., this collection; United Nations, 2020; YERUN, 2020; Ya, 2020). This is also observed in Brunei Darussalam (henceforth Brunei) and its HEIs.

Brunei reported its first case of COVID-19 on 9 March 2020. The Bruneian government immediately announced temporary closures of schools and HEIs on 11 March 2020 and imposed social distancing measures the following day. From around mid-March to the end of the last semester, the local HEIs switched completely to online teaching and learning. In the midst of these sudden actions, HEIs in the Sultanate had to find ways to implement various distance communication and online teaching and learning initiatives to quickly adapt to the new situation.

Since 7 May 2020, Brunei started to record zero cases of infection and have successfully 'flattened the curve'. The spread of the virus was contained through the commitment of the government and the people through its 'Whole of Nation Approach'. Following this, Brunei has been regarded as one of the exemplary nations in successfully managing the pandemic through its drastic actions (Bodetti, 2020; Khan, 2020; Hayat, 2020; Wong et al., 2020). As a result, on 2 June 2020, schools and HEIs were partially reopened, and since 27 July 2020, they were allowed to operate normally.

Nevertheless, at the beginning of the new semester in late July 2020, HEIs in Brunei were given delivery options that they can choose to best suit their specific conditions, their teachers and students regarding teaching, learning and pedagogical practices. Hence, these HEIs came up with different action plans and measures, ranging from fully face-to-face instructions to varied forms of blended learning (see Chap. 16 for action plans and measures undertaken by HEIs in Brunei).

The higher education sector in Brunei is rather new compared to other countries in Southeast Asia. To date, there are five public HEIs, all of which were established within the past 35 years, as seen in Table 17.1.

Upon completing this chapter, Brunei HEIs are in their final month of the new semester, and instructors have had more time to reflect on their teaching and to observe and compare their own pedagogical ideas and practices. They have also been encouraged to attend training workshops

Table 17.1 Public HEIs in Brunei Darussalam

Name in English	Name in Malay	Abbreviation	Foundation
University of Brunei Darussalam	Universiti Brunei Darussalam	UBD	1985
University of Technology Brunei	Universiti Teknologi Brunei	UTB	1986
Sultan Sharif Ali Islamic University	Universiti Islam Sultan Sharif Ali	UNISSA	2007
Seri Begawan Religious Teachers University College	Universiti Islam Sultan Sharif Ali	UNISSA	2007
Brunei Polytechnic	Politeknik Brunei	PB/BP	2012

run by institutions, organisations and colleagues nationally and internationally. Online teaching and learning as well as blended learning are no longer brand-new terms. Therefore, these instructors' reflections and observations have been informed by their experiences and continuous exposures to ideas and debates since the previous semester when the pandemic first broke out, and all the way into the new semester which started in late July when they were back on campus.

Since the start of the new semester in August 2020, the International and Comparative Education (ICE) Research Group at UBD have organised weekly ICE seminars and workshops based on the theme: 'COVID-19, Society, and Education'. Academics, administrators and students were invited to participate and share their viewpoints in these sessions between August and September 2020. The seminar series also became a platform for the staff and students to reflect on the academic situation in the previous semester during the height of the COVID-19 cases in Brunei and what is happening in the new semester today.

Moreover, various themes were raised during these sessions including societal infrastructures and technological access in education, pedagogical challenges and innovations, teachers' and students' experiences and feedback, institutional responses and support to teaching and learning, and impacts on research exercise and internationalisation. These topics and the discussions following each seminar have prompted further discussion of several key issues and questions that are of great concern and interest to many in higher education and society in general. In this chapter, we provide insights into several aspects of such discussions, with a particular focus on teaching, learning and pedagogical matters involving online delivery in the context of the pandemic. These academic stakeholders also deal with the practice of pandemic pedagogy that focuses on utilising online education where educational instruction and curriculum are designed and 'deliberately developed for the technological tools and pedagogical environment that suits distance learning' (Schwartzman, 2020, p. 502) complementary to the restricted mobility and social distancing mandate amid the pandemic.

We also further draw on our notes taken at each seminar as well as on our follow-up conversations with some seminar participants/presenters and other instructors that expressed an interest in sharing their views with us. We have obtained consent from all academics whose views we present in this chapter to include their names and affiliations.

17.2 Challenges amid Online Teaching and Social Distancing

A number of studies have discussed the efficacy and the limitations of online teaching and distance learning. For instance, Neuhauser (2002), Zhang (2005), and Castro and Tumibay (2019) identify several advantages of online teaching and learning such as the flexible practices of knowledge and accessibility of content, curriculum and place. Meanwhile, other studies include Dunlap et al. (2016), Peachey (2017) and Aljawarneh (2020) discuss the limitations of using media and technology in education, for example loss of human interactions, unequal distribution and opportunities of learning, technology-related anxiety, and security issues.

Furthermore, Lederman (2020), Moorhouse (2020) and UNESCO (2020a) further outline challenges in the sudden transition from classroom learning to online distance learning in terms of infrastructures and absence of emotional connection. Similar notions were also raised by Karalis (2020), UNESCO (2020b) and Ya (2020) who highlight the importance of the involvement of HEIs around the world to review relevant business contingency plans and policies related to national education, pedagogy and management, public health and communication infrastructures in coping with the effects of COVID-19.

Similar to other HEIs, institutions in Brunei were determined to integrate technologies and relevant online platforms to fulfil the needs of teachers and students in this challenging period (see Chap. 16 for an overview of precautionary actions and business contingency plans by HEIs). In fact, the use of technology, communication tools and online learning platforms increased during the early stages of the pandemic in the country (Suhaili, 2020). The situation was also fuelled from the mandatory social distancing practices imposed by the government to the public, HEIs and schools across the country. Hence, distance learning became a necessity, rather than an option, to all academic stakeholders during the pandemic.

Back in April, the International Association of Universities (IAU) released a Global Report Survey which includes responses from various levels of academic stakeholder in 424 HEIs in 111 countries worldwide. The Global Survey Report (IAU, 2020) summarises three major pedagogical challenges experienced by the majority of these HEIs, which are due to (1) technical infrastructure and accessibility, (2) distance learning competences and pedagogies, and (3) the field of study or subject. The report also reveals that more than 80% of research endeavours from these global HEIs were negatively impacted mainly because of the cancellation of scientific research and conferences as well as the restriction of movement and travelling. While Brunei did not participate in the survey, these occurrences were also experienced by HEIs in the Sultanate, as discussed below.

17.2.1 Slow Internet Connectivity

In the early stages, instructors at Brunei's public HEIs reported many challenges after the sudden implementation of distance learning relating to technical infrastructure and accessibility, issues of competency in distance teaching, and social mobility. In terms of technical infrastructure and accessibility, the major challenge for educators and students across all levels of education was the instability and slow internet connection. Since all HEIs in Brunei switched to online teaching and learning in March 2020 following the safety and precautionary measures and guidelines from the government, internet access and the quality of internet connection/connectivity became important issues for discussion and examination. Similar issues have also been reported in many parts of the world (Aguilera-Hermida, 2020; Bozkurt et al., 2020; Harris & Jones, 2020; Mishra et al., 2020).

In Brunei, some instructors at UNISSA normally rely on whiteboards to relay their course content. Upon the change brought about by the pandemic, they recalled the difficulties of multitasking online: teaching, attending online meetings, providing support to students and performing administrative matters. Moreover, they had to complete these tasks with an unstable internet connection. This was also raised by Kharhan Haji Jait (Director of Core Education Centre), who taught Islamic Educational Technology at *Kolej Universiti Perguruan Ugama Seri Begawan* (KUPU SB). He stated that connectivity issue and limited internet data hindered the effectiveness of teaching and learning during online classes:

> *It was a big challenge to make sure our lessons are effective and accepted by students due to the slow internet connection. There were issues of high expenditure on internet data, particularly for student learners.*

Brunei has been reported to have one of the highest consumption rate of internet and social media penetration in Southeast Asia and globally. The Bruneian Authority for Info-communications Technology Industry (2020) published the Brunei Darussalam's ICT Household Report 2019 that shows over 95% of individuals in the country use the internet daily, mainly for knowledge-seeking purposes (78.6%). Nonetheless, unstable internet connection has been an issue in Brunei, which largely affects distance education and online delivery during the pandemic. This is amid reports on the costly connectivity rate for internet speed as one of the main issues of online learning and telecommuting during the pandemic (The Scoop, 2020), as stated by Kharhan Haji Jait.

The abrupt implementation of online learning meant that a fast internet connection would be needed to maintain the quality and to enhance the attractiveness of online teaching and learning in this country. Many instructors from local HEIs claimed that a stable internet connectivity is one of the top priorities for online education. This is similar to Malaysia where the accessibility of the internet is one of the most important factors in maintaining the efficacy of online learning amid the Movement Control Order imposed in the country (Ya, 2020).

Similarly, Shahrill et al. (2020) present the results of three sets of surveys conducted with students and instructors at UBD on their experiences with online teaching and learning during the semester affected by the pandemic. According to the survey results, slow internet connection was a major setback to pedagogical interventions and to teachers' and students' satisfaction during COVID-19 at UBD. Nevertheless, the survey also shows that UBD quickly took necessary actions to improve internet connectivity where possible and to provide extra support for instructors and students so as to ensure best teaching and learning quality possible. These kinds of support have continued until this day. Similarly, UTB has continued to provide assistance and further encourage the academic stakeholders to boost the use of info-communication technology in academic and administrative affairs within the university (Suhaili, 2020).

Wasli (2020) also reports on the current multi-sectoral initiatives to help mitigate the unstable internet connection in response to the urgent and increasing demand for online teaching and learning at all levels. The sectors involved are the Ministry of Transport and Info-communications, the Ministry of Education and the Authority for Info-communication, and Technology Industry of Brunei Darussalam. These initiatives are aimed at serving the education sector and all those involved including teachers, students, administration and parents. The implementation of these initiatives exhibits a better prospect for more sustainable and effective online delivery and a digital future. Besides, the private sector in the country also collaborated with the government in supporting the initiative and further providing assistance for the government and academic stakeholders to ease the issues, including sponsoring electronic devices for learning purposes (Borneo Bulletin, 2020).

17.2.2   *Accessibility and Social Mobility on Research*

The instructors also raised issues of accessibility and social mobility affecting academic and research endeavours, which also affects other HEIs (Aristovnik et al., 2020; IAU, 2020; Schleicher, 2020; UNESCO-IESALC, 2020; YERUN, 2020).

Dr. Masitah Shahrill (Senior Assistant Professor and a Teacher Educator at the Sultan Hassanal Bolkiah Institute of Education, UBD) recalled that it was a challenge for her MTeach (Master of Teaching) students to capture their own secondary school students' attention during online learning. These MTeach students were apprentice teachers, and they were required to do school placement and record themselves teaching for assessment purposes—in an effort to maximise the evaluation process amid restriction of movement. Dr. Masitah expressed a strong sense of sympathy with the students while also questioning the effectiveness of online assessment of their school placement sessions. At the same time, the instructor also observed that the abrupt changes to the education system and the restriction of movement imposed by the government disrupted their research endeavours and social mobility:

> There are graduate students who struggled to collect data as schools were closed. They had to negotiate with schools to get access to these data. Everything was halted. I can foresee several of them will be seeking for extensions on research activities and perhaps candidature. When the schools reopen, they will be able to gain access to these data, but still they have a lot of catching up to do.

Similarly, an early observation involving 11 educators at UBD and their concerns during the pandemic reveals that the COVID-19 transmission have severely affected their working process with their students, the students' teaching practice opportunities and schools' research (Noorashid, 2020). These educators further stated that the restriction of movement and accessibility during the critical period also meant that some research projects and fieldwork by both academics were either delayed or cancelled. This includes the postponement of visits by outside academics, or in other cases, these had to be moved online. Some educators also described the situation as *constricted* as they were unable to enter faculty buildings and use facilities at the university outside of normal working hours. This caused more difficulties for research, publishing and preparing teaching materials. The pandemic had indeed caused disruption to research endeavours for most of the academics in UBD.

17.2.3 Mental Health and Emotional Wellbeing

Quite often, instructors found themselves struggling to learn and adapt to online teaching while accommodating students' learning and circumstances. This includes taking care of students' emotional health and wellbeing during the pandemic. The effects of COVID-19 on emotional health and wellbeing have been highlighted in many recent scholarships. Hughes (2020), Karalis (2020), and Karalis and Raikou (2020) have discussed the occurrence of psychological and social effects among academic stakeholders in HEIs due to the pandemic. However, this has yet to be discussed at large in the context of HEIs in Brunei until now.

Dr. Malai Zeiti Sheikh Abdul Hamid (Assistant Professor, UTB) reflected on her experience dealing with challenges in pedagogy and providing timely emotional support to her students:

> Lectures and tutorials were conducted online, and it had slowed down teaching effectiveness. My students were not able to interact with each other, and there were no practical activities due to social distancing policy. My students also felt

as if they lack emotional support during COVID-19. It was difficult to get students motivated and to stay online as the experience lacked the 'human touch' and experience.

As the leader of the UTB Wellness Research Thrust, Dr. Malai Zeiti also raised the importance of maintaining a good state of mental health and emotional wellbeing among academic stakeholders across HEIs in Brunei, and the intention is further bolstered due to the effects of the pandemic on the education system in the Sultanate. She recalled that it is *significant to ensure pedagogical functionality* in the university and beyond as the state of wellbeing for individual and academic community is as imperative as pedagogical affairs in HE. In a more creative approach and as a way to raise awareness on mental health issues, the university also organised an art contest to invite their students to express their mental health and wellbeing amid COVID-19 through artistic expression of arts and narrative accounts (UTB, 2020). This is one approach taken by UTB to show and mobilise support of mental health among the students and the academic stakeholders.

Keasberry et al. (2020) also mentioned that the pandemic has brought more mental health issues to surface, even among UBD students, due to the absence of human-to-human interactions, expressions, cultural cues and gestures during online learning. In the article, the authors highlighted the importance of humour and empathy between university instructors and the students in order to lessen anxiety and apprehension in utilising online learning. In this case, the role of instructors also expands to understanding the wellbeing of their students beyond the curriculum they teach but also the humanistic approach of understanding academic community.

Whilst further raising the case of emotional absence from conducting online learning, Dr. James McLellan (Associate Professor at the English Studies Programme in the Faculty of Arts and Social Sciences) also voiced his concerns on the disrupted connection between educators and students, where he claimed that the 'the loss of face-to-face contact with students has had a distancing effect: we no longer have the same rapport with our students'. Mayyer Ling Mohammad Tony Ling (Assistant Lecturer, UBD) also claimed that 'it was a lonely time. I think I still preferred to have students to interact with from time to time because some of the interactions online was just via voice, and not video.'

The declining motivation due to the loss of 'human touch and experience' should be addressed and acted upon, considering the issue has also been confirmed by student panellists during the ICE All Panel Student Discussion of 'COVID-19, Society and Education' held on 29 September 2020 at UBD. During the discussion, several students of different races, nationalities, socioeconomic background and field of studies voiced their concerns on their relationship with academics and peers caused by the pandemic and self-mental health as well as their emotional wellbeing (see Chap. 18 for further discussion on the implication of COVID-19 on students' emotional wellbeing in UBD). In his prediction of abrupt adjustment to online learning and social distancing, Moorhouse (2020) also raises his major concern on the relationship between students and educators in post-COVID-19 society, thus validating the significance of discussing the issue further.

Furthermore, an early report by Noorashid (2020) on the impact of COVID-19 in UBD showed that there are concerns involving mental health and emotional wellbeing as more than half of the research participants also divulge on issues regarding their relationship with students, their own personal lives and identity. Some educators add that the stress and emotional disruption can also be caused by the work-from-home mandate while managing home affairs, particularly for those who are working parents. Meanwhile, a few participants among the expatriates also report their concerns of not being able to travel to their home countries. In his report, Noorashid also observes the discourse of mental disturbance in the participants' narratives, such as 'stressful', 'exhausting', 'not conducive', 'distancing' and 'frustrated', among others. This suggests the existence of mental health concerns from the effects of COVID-19 among the academic stakeholders at the university.

17.2.4 Field of Study

Some instructors also raised issues involving teaching and learning in relation to certain fields of study and subjects. For instance, Atteyia Salleh (Assistant Lecturer at KUPU SB) shared her experiences in trying to assist students while having to keep up with the demands of the university administration. As a language educator, she found that it was a challenge to deliver knowledge of language proficiency to the students through remote learning, especially when she was used to practising interactive learning activities with her students to enhance their communicative skills in English. She also found assessing language competency among students can be challenging using online platform. Furthermore, instructors at

KUPU SB were instructed to record their students' *online* attendance, especially during online teaching and learning as part of the university's efforts in understanding the functionality of the system during the pandemic. She described the experience as exhausting:

> *The main concern during COVID-19 was to make sure all the teaching materials were delivered and learned by the students. We have to make sure the students attended the online classes and get them to participate in every session. These required extra work and were time-consuming. Lectures and tutorials needed to be adjusted and recorded for administrative evidence. Therefore, their attendance had to be taken at the beginning and at the end of every online class.*

Dr. Muhammad Zaki Haji Zaini (Lecturer of Business Statistics and Mathematics, UNISSA) shared the same sentiment and stated that it was more challenging for him in terms of pedagogy since the majority of his course contents deals with numbers and is heavily reliant on using the whiteboard to demonstrate the technical steps of solving problems:

> *During a face-to-face lecture, I would walk around to ensure students were able to capture what was explained during lessons, and this was not possible in online platforms. Students were also reluctant to admit that they were not able to capture what was taught in the class. But I had to adapt anyway. Thus, I had to closely monitor my students and incorporate relevant coursework that would be able to capture the objectives of my courses.*

Even though the other instructors did not emphasise much on issues pertaining to the field of study, it should still be further investigated in HEIs in Brunei. Studies including Allen et al. (2020), Daniel (2020) and United Nations (2020) have mentioned the necessity to understand the needs of teaching and learning related to specific field of education or/and subjects and students during the pandemic. This involves in mulling over aspects of constructing flexible curriculum, pedagogical approaches and assessment. This leads to another important issue as several instructors who facilitated language studies, teacher training, and new media and technology also raised their concerns on pedagogical approaches and assessment of their modules and courses during the sudden transition from face-to-face learning to online learning.

17.3 Embracing Opportunity in Pedagogy amid COVID-19

Azorín (2020), Moorhouse (2020), UNESCO (2020a), United Nations (2020) and Zhao (2020) predicted a number of changes and innovations regarding teaching and learning approaches and recruitment in education as a result of COVID-19. While Dennis (2020) observes the expansion of the use of technologies and online learning platforms as an obvious direction for higher education, Murphy (2020) urges all levels of education to reflect on the positive and negative effects of transitioning to more digital initiatives from this unavoidable situation. In other words, HEIs can no longer afford to stay disconnected with this new reality, seeing it as an opportunity would be a realistic approach.

Reflecting on her teaching experience during the height of the pandemic, Dr. Malai Zeiti confirmed the importance of ensuring 'social interaction', albeit virtually, between her and her students. She also believed open communication with her students had helped diversify her online pedagogical approaches. She also extended her working hours to overcome any shortcomings created by online delivery and her new exposure to online pedagogy:

> *During COVID-19 restrictions, I turned on my video conferencing platforms and allowed my students to 'see' me online to give them emotional support, and to give them the best possible 'real' experiences. I communicated regularly offline and online with my students all the time, and I placed more emphasis to ensure they get emotional support during the pandemic. I have an open door policy and if my students needed more time online to meet me, even after my non-teaching schedule, including after usual office hours or weekends, I was prepared to make the time to meet them online.*

Meanwhile, Dr. Norashikin Yusof (Assistant Professor, UNISSA) adapted her approaches and utilised virtual classrooms so as to create more sessions to ensure all 140 of her students had an equal opportunity for learning:

> *During the pandemic, I used Zoom quite a lot. However, Zoom does not allow more than 100 participants in a session, so I decided to conduct three separate lecture sessions to accommodate all my students. Good planning is the key here as there were scheduling issues in managing all these students. Some students could not make it on certain days or at certain times as other lectures were run*

at the same times too. Despite all the challenges, everything worked out well nonetheless.

Interestingly, the pandemic has encouraged many instructors to become proactive in diversifying teaching approaches in their online and face-to-face deliveries. For example, the two instructors from UNISSA stated that the situation has transformed many instructors and students. For example, these instructors have observed that students are more active in class participation as they have started to appreciate face-to-face learning after months under social distancing and online learning. At the same time, even though their university allows 100% physical lectures and tutorials, these educators still find ways to utilise online platforms to help with teaching and learning, alongside their physical classrooms:

Any replacement class can be now done online. I use more online platforms to communicate with my students nowadays, especially in terms of sharing resources and assessment. (Dr. Muhammad Zaki Haji Zaini, UNISSA)

During the onset of the first COVID-19 case, I had the chance to explore various online learning platforms and tools. With the current de-escalation phase, I find that I am still using them to further enhance my face-to-face teaching. (Dr. Norashikin Yusof, UNISSA)

In a similar situation, Kharhan Haji Jait from KUPU SB also noticed positive responses from his students as he is now implementing blended learning in class. He sees more opportunities to conduct online learning as it is gradually embraced by the students:

The students now prefer face-to-face learning for practical activities, and doing mixed-approach in mass lecture, while continuing with the 'new norm' pedagogy for everything else after COVID-19. In fact, 90% of my students who are taking the Multimedia module prefer to do it online.

Despite being able to operate normally since the beginning of the new semester, Dr. Malai Zeiti observed that UTB instructors have also adapted to the changes in teaching and learning, and become more open to online options. Likewise, it is more acceptable now to record online attendance in university meetings:

> Using online platforms have now become 'the new normal', and they will continue to be used in times when some are available to attend physical meetings. Also teaching remotely and online conferences are commonly done with people outside Brunei such as international students. My teaching pedagogy remains the same, but I am now more open to online platforms compared to before the pandemic.

While the other HEIs in Brunei have resumed face-to-face delivery, UBD has opted for blended learning this semester. Many instructors have continued to diversify their teaching methods and experiment with various approaches and platforms, not just to ensure the efficacy of their pedagogical approaches, but also to maximise any potentials in their pedagogical deliverance.

For instance, Dr. Chester Keasberry (Lecturer in the Design and Creative Industries, UBD) presented a seminar at the ICE Seminar Series on 1 September 2020. He reflected on how his own expertise in educational technology and his own experience using technologies for teaching and learning for the past decade in the United States and Brunei may have shaped his attitude and approach to online delivery. He sees the bright side of the pandemic in that it has forced instructors like him to transfer their interests and knowledge about technologies into effective educational purposes. He acknowledged that he is passionate about technologies, and so he usually invests in technologies, tools and applications to give himself an optimal experience. Online teaching was not new to him, and so when the university switched completely to online delivery in March, it did not take him long to master various applications and platforms. In so doing, he became to like Zoom and has been using it as the main teaching platform since then.

Dr. Chester Keasberry also recognised that many instructors acknowledge that online teaching cannot replace face-to-face delivery, particularly the 'human touch' aspect. At the same time, he is confident that when instructors are aware of both strengths and drawbacks of online teaching, they could transform it. Specifically, he stressed how important it is for teachers to actively ensure that online learning can be as effective as possible. He has identified several strengths in using Zoom to teach based on his own experience:

> I try to bridge the gap of the physical classroom and online learning. As an educator, we need to point out the tasks, so students can contribute and do not sit in silence. In fact, the platform can create a conducive learning environ-

ment where the more outgoing students who actively use the microphone and chat function are able to entice the usual quieter students to join. I've also found that a large class of 70 students is now easier to manage online (using Zoom) rather than finding a room to fit all of them physically.

On a similar note, Mayyer Ling, who deals with the teaching of new media and communication in UBD, also stated the necessity of understanding online learning platform vis-à-vis face-to-face pedagogy, in terms of suitability to knowledge, curriculum and space, as well as convenience for both educator and student:

The key is to understand the relative or obvious difference between online and offline learning, and to know your preferred outcomes. I mean, the affordances of online learning are potentially vast—from having the a/synchronous teaching/learning opportunities to multimodality. So, having an awareness of what you can, cannot, should, should not do in an online environment helps you make decisions. Also, with rest to the affordances, of course, you have to also be realistic. What is your intended goal, and how do you achieve this with the online platform? Try to not do everything, and use everything, even when they are available to you—only when they are relevant to your teaching and learning goals.

Throughout their shared experiences, it can be observed that although COVID-19 disrupted the teaching and learning in Brunei, HEI instructors were able to quickly adapt in order to respond to specific and additional needs of their students (pedagogically and emotionally), and to also meet the demands of their university administration. Having had to experience such sudden, unprecedented changes in education, these instructors still see the prospect in their teaching and the learning of their students.

17.4 Institutional Support During the Pandemic and into the New Semester

It is clear that by providing institutional support during the time of the pandemic is crucial in maintaining the functionality of HEIs (UNESCO, 2020a; UNESCO-IESALC, 2020; United Nations, 2020; YERUN, 2020). In the case of Brunei, instructors have reported to receive much support and commitment from their respective institutions to help ensure the efficacy and the functionality of their teaching and learning activities.

In UNISSA, the support from the university's administration and fellow academics sustained the academic community activities. For instance, the university conducted a refresher training session on Learning Management System and the initiative to increase the internet bandwidth to overcome connectivity issues for the convenience of educators and students. Moreover, the academics shared virtual teaching and learning ideas in WhatsApp groups, which contributed positively to building a friendly environment for sustaining virtual learning activities. This environment also serves as a platform for instructors and administrators to provide support and inform one another of educational ideas and solutions as they proceed to a new semester.

This support system was also observed in KUPU SB. When educators had to work from home, virtual workshops were conducted to introduce them to various online platforms they could use to conduct classes, including Zoom and Microsoft Teams. The university also provided solutions for faster internet connection, while offering user friendly software, as well as financial support to students who did not have the necessary means to access online learning platforms. Instructors and students enjoy better internet connection on campus now as they are back to face-to-face learning in the new semester.

UTB instructors also received continuous infrastructural support to enable them to conduct high-quality online teaching, while being regularly updated on initiatives to mitigate pedagogical challenges during the pandemic. As UTB is now back to 100% on-campus instruction, the experiences learnt during the previous semester are important for instructors to draw on as they prepare students for unexpected changes. Health and safety measures are also in place to keep the campus safe for all.

Meanwhile, UBD will continue its teaching and learning through distance mode, as in accordance with government directives on mass gatherings and social distancing. The university management also ensured in providing assistance to boost online and blended learning by organising online workshops about the various technologies and strategies for online delivery of module content. This also includes changes of technological advances where seminars and workshop as far as recreational activities were accomplished online via Zoom and other various media platforms. Aside from the use of Canvas that has been implemented even before the pandemic, the university management further provided university-wide subscription to Microsoft-powered platforms for those who need embedded teaching and learning applications.

Furthermore, Mayyer Ling highlighted the university's support and praised the university's effort in attending to staff's and students' wellbeing through effective and regular communication:

UBD prioritises communication with staff and students—even went as far as to send a humbling "we're in this together" message to the university community. There was a letter of support from the Vice Chancellor at the beginning of the university closure, when the university partially reopens, at the beginning of the semester—every new turn of events, really. I find that quite sensitive, and necessary at times during the pandemic.

17.5 Conclusion

Throughout the educators' experiences in dealing with pedagogical challenges during the height of the COVID-19 pandemic in the last semester, it is observed that the resilience of these instructors has made teaching and learning less difficult for them and their students. The restrictions caused by the pandemic have also encouraged them to explore opportunities in teaching and learning to maintain and further maximise their teaching capacity. The sudden transitioning to distance learning was seen as alarming at first, and it brought about many challenges for the instructors, but they accepted the reality and 'made a virtue of necessity' with the whole situation.

While Brunei has managed to 'flatten the curve' (the country is only recording imported cases of COVID-19 at the moment), there are still concerns on the possibilities of a second wave of the pandemic. This concern has also become a cause for caution as well as for proactive actions in society, including HEIs and those involved. From the experiential narratives of these instructors, this chapter has opened more conversations and raised more opportunities to further investigate the impacts of COVID-19 on educational policy, HEIs, schools, teachers, students, parents and society at large. The pandemic has raised certain issues in pedagogy in the country, for instance the provision of internet and info-communication technology, emotional wellbeing and community supports. Probing into these matters and finding solutions for them can be seen as proactive efforts to inform the public and policy, while supporting the university and the government in disseminating research findings for the betterment of education locally and globally—today and tomorrow.

The effect of COVID-19 to education in Brunei and the sudden disruption to transitioning to online learning have raised the prospect of online learning in HEIs to be more explorative. This is in line with the royal decree of His Majesty the Sultan of Brunei at the 32nd UBD Convocation on 2 November 2020 that calls upon UBD and other local HEIs to boost digital and info-communication technology initiatives as a response to the pandemic. The action plan is also aimed to increase and explore the sustainability of academic and working environment across HEIs in the Sultanate.

Furthermore, there is a need for the integration of technologies and online learning platforms in the education system for HEIs in Brunei, as proved by the recent changes due to the pandemic. This is not only the integral part of safety measures during COVID-19, but it also fulfils the country's aspiration to embrace the Fourth Industrial Revolution as part of Brunei's nation-building endeavours. Moreover, it is in sync with the reformation of previous education system to the National Education System for the 21st Century (SPN21) in the Sultanate that also emphasises on the incorporation of media and info-technology advancement.

References

Aguilera-Hermida, A. P. (2020). College students' use and acceptance of emergency online learning due to COVID-19. *International Journal of Educational Research Open*, 1–8. https://doi.org/10.1016/j.ijedro.2020.100011

Aljawarneh, S. A. (2020). Reviewing and exploring innovative ubiquitous learning tools in higher education. *Journal of Computing in Higher Education, 32*(1), 1–17. https://doi.org/10.1007/s12528-019-09207-0

Allen, J., Rowan, L., & Singh, P. (2020). Teaching and teacher education the time of COVID-19. *Asia-Pacific Journal of Teacher Education, 48*(3), 233–236. https://doi.org/10.1080/1359866X.2020.1752051

Aristovnik, A., Kerzic, D., Ravselj, D., Tomazevic, N., & Umek, L. (2020). Impacts of the COVID-19 pandemic on life of higher education students: A global perspective. *Sustainability, 12*, 1–34.

Authority for Info-communications Technology Industry. (2020). *Brunei Darussalam Information Communications Technology (ICT) household report 2019.* https://www.aiti.gov.bn/Shared%20Documents/Final%20-%20ICT%20HOUSEHOLD%20REPORT.PDF

Azorín, C. (2020). Beyond COVID-19 supernova. Is another education coming? *Journal of Professional Capital and Community, 5*(3), 1–10. https://www.emerald.com/insight/content/doi/10.1108/JPCC-05-2020-0019/full/pdf?title=beyond-covid-19-supernova-is-another-education-coming

Bodetti, A. (2020, June 22). How Brunei beat COVID-19. *The Diplomat.* https://thediplomat.com/2020/06/how-brunei-beat-covid-19/

Borneo Bulletin. (2020, April 12). Donate ICT devices, support online learning. https://borneobulletin.com.bn/2020/04/donate-ict-devices-support-online-learning/

Bozkurt, A., et al. (2020). A global outlook to the interruption of education due to COVID-19 pandemic: Navigating in a time of uncertainty and crisis. *Asian Journal of Distance Education, 15*(1), 1–126. https://discovery.ucl.ac.uk/id/eprint/10101679/1/Bozkurt%20et%20al%202020.pdf

Castro, M. D. B., & Tumibay, G. M. (2019). A literature review: Efficacy of online learning courses for higher education institution using meta-analysis. *Education and Information Technologies.* https://doi.org/10.1007/s10639-019-10027-z

Daniel, S. J. (2020). Education and the COVID-19 pandemic. *PROSPECTS, 49*, 91–96. https://doi.org/10.1007/s11125-020-09464-3

Dennis, M. (2020, May 9). Higher education opportunities after COVID-19. *University World News.* https://www.universityworldnews.com/post.php?story=20200507152524762

Dunlap, J., Verma, G., & Johnson, H. (2016). Presence + experience: A framework for the purposeful design of presence in online courses. *TechTrends, 60*(2), 145–151. https://doi.org/10.1007/s11528-016-0029-4

Harris, A., & Jones, M. (2020). COVID-19—School leadership in disruptive times. *School Leadership and Management, 40*(4), 243–247. https://doi.org/10.1080/13632434.2020.1811479

Hayat, M. (2020, July 15). Brunei Darussalam: An unexpected COVID-19 success story. *Australian Outlook.* https://www.internationalaffairs.org.au/australianoutlook/brunei-darussalam-an-unexpected-covid-19-success-story/

Hughes, C. (2020). Some implications of COVID-19 for remote learning and the future of schooling. https://unesdoc.unesco.org/ark:/48223/pf0000373229

IAU. (2020). *Covid-19: Higher Education challenges and responses.* https://www.iau-aiu.net/Covid-19-Higher-Education-challenges-and-responses

Karalis, T. (2020). Planning and evaluation during educational disruption: Lessons learned from COVID-19 pandemic for treatment of emergencies in education. *European Journal of Education Studies, 7*(4), 125–142. https://doi.org/10.5281/zenodo.3789022

Karalis, T., & Raikou, N. (2020). Teaching at the times of COVID-19: Inferences and implications for higher education pedagogy. *International Journal of Academic Research in Business and Social Sciences, 10*(5), 479–493. https://doi.org/10.6007/IJARBSS/v10-i5/7219

Keasberry, C. (2020). *Zoom in: Perceptions and perspectives of pandemic pedagogy.* Seminar presented at International and Comparative Education (ICE) Seminar Series, Universiti Brunei Darussalam, Tungku Link, September 1.

Keasberry, C., Phan, L. H., Hoon, C. Y., Alam, M., Alas, Y., & Noorashid, N. (2020). Facing the mental health challenges of COVID-19 in HE.

University World News. https://www.universityworldnews.com/post.php?story=20201201133134894

Khan, A. U. (2020, April 18). Brunei's response to COVID-19. *The ASEAN Post.* https://theaseanpost.com/article/bruneis-response-covid-19

Lederman, D. (2020, April 22). How teaching changed in the (forced) shift to remote learning. *Inside Higher Ed.* https://www.insidehighered.com/digital-learning/article/2020/04/22/how-professors-changed-their-teaching-springs-shift-remote

Mishra, L., Gupta, T., & Shree, A. (2020). Online teaching-learning in higher education during lockdown period of COVID-19 pandemic. *International Journal of Educational Research Open*, 1–8. https://doi.org/10.1016/j.ijedro.2020.100012

Moorhouse, B. L. (2020). Adaptations to a face-to-face initial teacher education course 'forced' online due to the COVID-19 pandemic. *Journal of Education for Teaching*, 1–3. https://doi.org/10.1080/02607476.2020.1755205

Murphy, M. P. A. (2020). COVID-19 and emergency eLearning: Consequences of the securitization of higher education for post-pandemic pedagogy. *Contemporary Security Policy, 41*(3), 492–505. https://doi.org/10.1080/13523260.2020.1761749

Neuhauser, C. (2002). Learning style and effectiveness of online and face-to-face instruction. *American Journal of Distance Education, 16*(2), 99–113. https://doi.org/10.1207/S15389286AJDE1602_4

Noorashid, N. (2020). *COVID-19 and responses from university teachers and students in Brunei: An initial overview and implications for research and pedagogy.* Seminar presented at International and Comparative Education (ICE) Seminar Series, Universiti Brunei Darussalam, Tungku Link, August 11.

Noorashid, N., Phan, L. H., Alas, Y., & Yabit, V. M. (2020, October 10). Beyond the pandemic, integrating online learning. *University World News.* https://www.universityworldnews.com/post.php?story=20201009150047136

Peachey, N. (2017). Synchronous online teaching. In M. Carrier, R. M. Damerow, & K. M. Bailey (Eds.), *Digital language learning and teaching* (pp. 143–155). Routledge.

Schleicher, A. (2020). The impacts of COVID-19 on education: Insights from education at a glance. OECD. https://www.oecd.org/education/the-impact-of-covid-19-on-education-insights-education-at-a-glance-2020.pdf

Schwartzman, R. (2020). Performing pandemic pedagogy. *Communication Education, 69*(2), 502–517.

Shahrill, M., Abdul Aziz, A. B. Z., Naing, L., Petra, M. I., Yacob, J., & Santos, J. H. (2020). *The developments and findings of online learning in UBD during the COVID-19 pandemic.* Seminar presented at International and Comparative Education (ICE) Seminar Series, Universiti Brunei Darussalam, Tungku Link, September 15.

Suhaili, W. S. H. (2020). Brunei Darussalam—Impact of COVID-19 on Brunei's higher education teaching. In P. G. Altbach, S. Gopinathan, L. H. Yeong, & T. Balakrishnan (Eds.), *Special issue 8 higher education in Southeast Asia and beyond: How is COVID-19 impacting higher education?* (pp. 25–27). The HEAD Foundation.

The Scoop. (2020, April 27). Internet speed, costs cited as top issues in e-learning and telecommuting. https://thescoop.co/2020/04/27/bruneians-cite-internet-speed-costs-as-top-issues-in-e-learning-and-telecommuting/

UNESCO. (2020a). COVID-19 educational disruption and response. https://en.unesco.org/covid19/educationresponse

UNESCO. (2020b, March 4). *290 million students out of school due to COVID-19: UNESCO releases first global numbers and mobilizes response* [Press release]. https://en.unesco.org/news/290-million-students-out-school-due-covid-19-unesco-releases-first-global-numbers-and-mobilizes

UNESCO-IESALC. (2020). COVID-19 and higher education: Today and tomorrow. https://www.iesalc.unesco.org/en/wp-content/uploads/2020/05/COVID-19-EN-130520.pdf

United Nations. (2020). Policy brief: Education during COVID-19 and beyond. https://www.un.org/development/desa/dspd/wp-content/uploads/sites/22/2020/08/sg_policy_brief_covid-19_and_education_august_2020.pdf

UTB. (2020, October 10). Raising mental health awareness through art. https://www.utb.edu.bn/raising-mental-health-awareness-through-art/

Wasli, W. (2020, May 18). 95% of the population use the internet daily, says ICT report. *The Bruneian News*. https://www.thebruneian.news/95-of-the-population-use-the-internet-daily-says-ict-report/

Wong, J., Koh, W. C., Alikhan, M. F., Abdul Aziz, A. B. Z., & Naing, L. (2020). Responding to COVID-19 in Brunei Darussalam: Lessons for small countries. *Journal of Global Health, 10*(1). https://doi.org/10.7189/jogh.10.010363

Ya, S. W. (2020). *Education during COVID-19*. Institute of Democracy and Economic Affairs.

YERUN. (2020). The world of higher education after COVID-19. https://www.yerun.eu/wp-content/uploads/2020/07/YERUN-Covid-VFinal-OnlineSpread.pdf

Zhang, D. (2005). Interactive multimedia-based e-learning: A study of effectiveness. *American Journal of Distance Education, 19*, 149–162. https://doi.org/10.1207/s15389286ajde1903_3

Zhao, Y. (2020). COVID-19 as a catalyst for educational change. *PROSPECTS, 49*, 29–33. https://doi.org/10.1007/s11125-020-09477-y

CHAPTER 18

Digidemic and Students' Hysteresis During Online Learning

Meredian Alam and Chang-Yau Hoon

18.1 Introduction

Since December 2019, the world has been affected by the COVID-19 outbreak from Wuhan, China, which has since halted the economic, social and international relations sectors. The pandemic has also severely impacted human interactions on a global scale since its emergence (World Health Organization, 2020). With its debilitating physical impacts on infected individuals (such as weakened lungs and other respiratory organs, severe septic conditions and mortality) (Muniyappa & Gubbi, 2020; Tison et al., 2020), COVID-19 has left much of the world's populations in graveyards or attending the funerals of innocent loved ones. This pandemic is particularly serious as it has spread across all continents and affects people of all nationalities (Sudharsanan et al., 2020). The world's educational sector has been significantly impacted by policies imposed to address the COVID-19 situation. Driven to thrive in its goal of developing the

M. Alam (✉) • C.-Y. Hoon
Universiti Brunei Darussalam, Bandar Seri Begawan, Brunei
e-mail: meredian.alam@ubd.edu.bn; changyau.hoon@ubd.edu.bn

© The Author(s), under exclusive license to Springer Nature Switzerland AG 2021
Phan, L. H. et al. (eds.), *Globalisation, Education, and Reform in Brunei Darussalam*, International and Development Education, https://doi.org/10.1007/978-3-030-77119-5_18

future of humanity, the educational sector has proven resilient during the pandemic, but learners and teachers across the world have been put under intense new pressures (Khalil et al., 2020).

The global transition from face-to-face classrooms to online learning systems has had many implications, not all of them positive, and has shown the effects of socioeconomic inequality. We have termed this phenomenon 'digidemic'. Digidemic is a portmanteau of 'digital pandemic' (Alam, 2020) and refers to the deconstructive implications for students and teachers on whom online learning is imposed as a solution to sustain education during the COVID-19 outbreak. The spread of digidemic throughout the world is marked by sociocultural and mental breakdowns due to technological structures that are unable to support their users' everyday needs (Bartram, 2020).

Additionally, the application of technology in private spaces can change individuals' social interactions with those physically closest to them. The phenomenon of socially compartmentalised space due to the intense use of gadgets or computers, such as in the case of remote or online learning, leads to individuals experiencing spatial disjuncture or spatial disorientation. This spatial disjuncture can lead to decreased learning productivity, disengagement from reality and from peer group, boredom with learning and inability to absorb subject matter and degraded motivation in the learning process (Appadurai, 1990). In sociology, such spatial disjuncture, a mismatch between objective structures and expectations, is considered a type of hysteresis—'the ways in which habitus may outlive the conditions of its genesis and come out with the demands of present conditions' (Bourdieu, 2000, p. 159). With these issues in mind, through selected interviews and encounters with students, this chapter examines how the learners coped with this hysteresis during their experiences of online learning at Universiti Brunei Darussalam (UBD). The trajectories of digidemic in higher education will be further reviewed in the following sections.

18.2 The Impact of Digidemic on Education

Higher education is still coming to terms with the crisis brought about by the SARS-2 COVID-19 pandemic. While many industries have ground to a halt or seen severe cutbacks due to the pandemic, governments have prioritised to keep students in school. The Bourdieusian sociological perspective considers education as a vital path to cultural reproduction and upward social mobility (Bourdieu, 1977), and for centuries, educational institutions at all levels are seen as vehicles to future prosperity since they embody institutionalised and objectified cultural capital. In addition, policymakers see tertiary education as a reliable staircase for vertical mobility for both students and their families (Stephens et al., 2019). Such institutions are now tasked with the huge responsibility of preserving and offering intellectually fertile ground in the COVID-19 pandemic era, thus facing new challenges for teaching and learning.

Moreover, tertiary education is a field of practice in which learners and teachers are the agents (Tsai et al., 2020). In the daily learning process, this field of practices relies on a synergy between technological equipment, the formal curriculum and the dispositions of the agents (the teachers and learners) to succeed. This synergy, of course, operated before the pandemic without any significant constraints. The global calamity of COVID-19, however, has destroyed and crippled the micro-structure of our society such as social fabrics and their mental wellbeing. As a precaution against the spread of the virus, teaching and learning activities were stopped temporarily in the early months of the pandemic. Afterwards, education began to be facilitated through online learning, which requires students to study at home to limit social interactions, instead communicating with teachers in virtual spaces using web-conferencing applications.

Before the pandemic, computing and information technology had long intervened in the world of education through the introduction of synchronous remote learning applications such as Moodle, Skype, EduMondo, Google Duo and Zoom. The use of such software further strengthens the presence of technology as a post-modernity product in the contemporary society. The excessive use of online learning technology is proven to disengage people from actual human-to-human touch and everyday interactions. In light of this impact, Burke and Larmar (2020) claim that virtual learning can 'have a deleterious impact on a student's sense of connection, leading to experiences of isolation and disempowerment' (p. 1). This will lead to an alarming situation unless social scholars are able to shed more light on this issue, and online learning and remote teaching can lead to increased individualisation.

Many higher education institutions around the world have found it necessary to impose online (or virtual remote) learning to maintain knowledge transfer during the pandemic. However, online remote learning as a product of mass technology can meet with resistance or lack of acceptance from learners because this kind of technology integration depends on the cultural, technical and social context of the recipient. Despite this, in a matter of months, online learning is now considered an essential element of the learning process, especially in higher education. The recent rapid implementation of online learning has established new structures in the field of education.

During the COVID-19 pandemic, the epistemological principle of education for nurturing future generations has been temporarily challenged. Now, the educational process depends on geographical and affirmative structural policies applied in regions with significant variations in internet access. As a result, many individuals have seen their access to education reduced. Focusing on the global South, this chapter critically examines the negative effects that 'pushed' remote learning has had on individuals in academic settings. Developing countries have been disproportionately impacted by the implementation of remote learning. It may be argued that this impact is greater than that of the prolonged drought and warming temperatures of climate change. Unquestionably, both phenomena are taking an immense human toll. Some contend that the imposition of web-conferencing learning in the era of a pandemic has evoked another pandemic layer, and in regions with unequal access to technology, the 'digidemic' has had debilitating impacts. The global South includes restrictive structures that can amplify these impacts, such as adverse economic conditions, widespread unemployment, and the lack of collective social and governmental support. In addition, such detrimental conditions often escalate students' existing mental disorders during digital learning.

The transition to socially distanced online learning has given rise to various structural consequences at the tertiary level, ranging from the mandatory use of web-conferencing tools which consume large amounts of Internet data to the restructuring of curriculum to changes in national education policies. All of these changes have led to anxiety and discomfort among both students and teachers due to the limitations of distance and time. Following Guermazi and Beschorner (2019), particularly in South and Southeast Asia, Internet coverage is unevenly available; on average, less than 60% of people in South and Southeast Asian countries have access to broadband. Indonesia has an Internet penetration rate of only 56% (i.e. only 150 million people out of a population of 268 million have reliable Internet access) (Guermazi & Beschorner, 2019). Furthermore, Guermazi and Beschorner (2019) assert coverage amounts to 56% in Thailand, 39% in Myanmar and 38% in Vietnam. Tragically, these percentages are heavily skewed by the urban population; almost no one living in a rural area can access the Internet.

The lower the Internet availability, the higher the impact of digidemic as the global South lacks the technological capital for coping with the switch to remote learning. Since Indonesia implemented online distance learning, upper-secondary students in remote villages, such as Kenalan village in Central Java, must travel every day to village and city borders in order to obtain roadside Internet coverage (Paddock & Sijabat, 2020). This is a daily challenge as roads are steep and rocky.

Limited Internet signals and poor reception are the most visible signs of digidemic in developing countries, but in addition to juggling poverty and technical difficulties in accessing learning materials online, children are still required to interact with teachers and continue their heavy homework responsibilities together with siblings. This pandemic requires remote learning policies, and during this time, increasing suicide rates have been reported. Indonesia recorded its first student suicide case in October 2020, involving a primary schooler who was apparently suffering from acute stress due to an excessive weekly homework load (Makdori, 2020). Another burden for Indonesian students is that they must often help their parents in the cultivation of rice fields.

Digidemic has also taken its toll in India. In Kerala, an upper-secondary school student committed suicide due to exorbitant anxiety. In their study, Lathabhavan and Griffiths (2020) revealed that a combination of structural pressures and the student's pressing worries concerning declining academic achievements had exacerbated her mental stress. Dysfunctional Internet access had negatively impacted her academic work. Moreover, the student's parents had been unable to find work for months, which also directly contributed to her anxiety. Other researchers have claimed that there is an increasing suicide trend among 13-to-17-year-olds in India due to forced online learning that involves high screen time and more assignments that must be done at home. At the tertiary level, students are experiencing an increase in anxiety and depression syndrome. A recent five-month study (Islam et al., 2020) conducted by university students in Bangladesh reported an increase in anxiety, depression rates and anxious mental states from online lecture delays and unreliable Internet reception.

The above analytical arguments reveal that digidemic is a new constraining and restricting structure for the developing countries of the global South that suffer from unequal Internet access distribution. This phenomenon reflects the boomerang effects of technological modernity (Beck, 1992). As a cosmopolitanised emergency, digidemic in education has led to new dimensions of mental stress not only for students but also for teachers and parents. The technological advancement of online learning has clearly created a new layer of miseries for those living and learning in geographically and socially disadvantaged locations, particularly in South and Southeast Asian countries as described above. According to Latour (2011), digidemic has perpetuated 'hegemonic extension' (p. 11)—the imposed remote learning technology has quickly gained dominance over pre-existing technologies (television, Internet, tele/smartphone, etc.). This phenomenon has required government and educational stakeholders to establish more flexible learning and teaching processes that do not compromise the mental and social wellbeing of teachers and learners.

The mismatch between the expected realities experienced by learners in the learning process and online learning has led to the formation of the hysteresis phenomenon. Hysteresis and its conceptual process will be scrutinised in the following section.

18.3 Students' Experiences

As a preventive measure against the transmission of the COVID-19 infection, Universiti Brunei Darussalam implemented online learning between March and September 2020. When lectures moved online in March, lecturers were allowed to use existing web-conferencing platforms such as BigBlueButton (integrated in the Canvas learning platform). This allowed lectures to be conducted via live webinar as well as recorded video. Until June 2020, students were required to access online learning and semester final exams at home. This was the first time that students and lecturers had experienced online learning at the university. The unexpected switch from physical classes to remote learning took place at Universiti Brunei Darussalam (UBD) on 12 March 2020, a mere three days after the first COVID-19 case was recorded in Brunei. While the swift announcement by the university to suspend all face-to-face classes was commendable, the abrupt transition left everyone in limbo. Although the primary focus during the COVID-19 pandemic has been on physical hygiene, emotional hygiene must not be overlooked. Due to the difficulties in administering and supervising online exams, the university allowed most modules to be converted to 100% coursework. However, this unwittingly led to an increase in workload for the students because they now needed to complete extra homework in lieu of exams. Some students reported that they enjoyed online learning, whereas others bitterly hated the experience.

Those who expressed the former mostly appreciated the fact that they did not have to dress up and drive to the campus early in the morning. For example, one third-year male student remarked:

> Online classes were less intense than physical classes because the pressure of judgement [from peers and lecturers] was not there. Personally, online classes did not really affect me. In fact, I enjoyed them because time management was no longer an issue. For instance, I could wake up and immediately open my laptop and go back to sleep after the lecture ends and honestly, it improves my mood.

As students undertook home-based online learning, disruption was unavoidable; many students found themselves developing new habits that made the learning process challenging. Although studying at home provides flexibility since the students are not required to commute to the university to attend lectures, some learners' experiences reveal that studying at home blurs the boundary between private and public space. Before online learning was compulsory, students participated in lectures, tutorials and peer discussions on campus and spent time relaxing and enjoying themselves at home. Since the emergence of online learning, learners must perform all academic activities at home throughout the day. If other family members were also learning online, they must share their home space, and it can quickly become noisy and chaotic. Internet access must also be considered. This is an issue not only of broadband quota but also of location accessibility. For example, if the access point can only be reached in the living room and is limited to one floor, then several family members must share the living room to use the Internet. Therefore, each home's implementation of online learning affects students' spatial disjuncture differently. This spatial disjuncture occurs as a form of asynchronous adaptation of students to new normalised circumstances that are beyond their control. Here, our discussion emphasises the ways in which students cope with spatial disjuncture while learning at home. Several case studies are used to illustrate how the trajectory of technology can affect every day learning practices.

In the first case study, a student reported that he experienced difficulty in concentrating and understanding the course material during online learning from June to August 2020. Before the pandemic, this student was accustomed to face-to-face coursework and regularly participated in group discussions for his module assignments and all academic activities on campus. Although he experienced no significant problems with Internet signal at home, he faced several challenges as a result of home-based online learning. The student reported that he felt more isolated from his family due to the amount of time (approximately six hours per day) he had to spend in front of the computer alone in his room. Additionally, online presentation activities and discussions with lecturers and friends on the web-conferencing platform worsened his relationship with his mother. This deterioration occurred because whenever he conducted online presentations or participated in discussions online, his mother loudly admonished him to be quieter as he could be heard downstairs. Additionally, when it was time to have dinner but he still had to participate in online discussions, his mother kept knocking on his door and sometimes opened it without telling him. When this happened, he was forced to sign off to follow his mother's orders. During dinner, he would become increasingly uncomfortable as he thought of the online learning activities he was missing. Incidents like this demonstrate that online learning leaves a kind of social confusion and ambivalence in the family space of the students. This case also shows how imposed online learning serves as a restraining objective structure in the family, leading to social conflicts.

In the second case, sharing the Internet connection with siblings presented certain issues in relation to the space used. One student conveyed that he had to work on assignments and participate in online lectures while he was in the living room, together with his four siblings. Before the implementation of the online learning policy, he preferred to conduct his coursework on campus and used the house to relax with his family. They usually used the Internet at home to watch movies on YouTube in the living room. In March 2020, this harmony in the home was drastically transformed. From 8:00 a.m. to 5:00 p.m., the student had to muster his patience to access online lectures in the living room with his siblings. The living room, which was usually enlivened with laughter, turned into a catastrophic space. Each of the five siblings used a headset to minimise background noise; however, when the lecturer required the student to speak in front of his class, he disturbed the concentration of his siblings. This did not only occur once or twice in the semester but many times, leading to arguments between the siblings. Both parents were overwhelmed by the disturbance. Fortunately, no fighting resulted, but none of the siblings wanted to give up the opportunity to be involved in a class discussion. These repeated incidents show that spatial disjuncture occurred when the learning interests of all five siblings conflicted and they could not enjoy their own learning space.

The third case study shows an example of conflicting emotions and interests, when students were compelled to participate in online learning at home and at the same time wanted to spend time helping their siblings and other family members. This student felt that his home situation with three younger siblings led to him compromising his study time. When online learning was implemented, the three younger siblings were still in primary school and were required to access learning materials via mobile phones. The student had to teach them how to download attachments on the platforms and help them complete their homework since both parents work full time at an office and do not return home until 3:00 p.m. Given this situation, the student had no choice but to be absent from several modules and did not have the opportunity to participate in the several web-conferencing lectures.

For other students, the compound effect of all the disruptive changes caused by the pandemic was emotional distress. The most commonly reported challenge of online learning among these participants is the lack of a conducive space for studying at home. As one student attests, 'Not everyone lives in a pleasant and harmonic, financially stable family. Not every family understands the concept of privacy. Some of my friends were struggling with online learning because the family kept on asking her to do chores even during online classes' (fourth-year female student, email communication, 23 November 2020). This student also revealed that she shares a room with her sister and lives with an extended family of ten people. She was expected to babysit her niece while listening to lectures online, which made it impossible for her to concentrate. She also wanted to help out with household chores, so she felt ambivalent about prioritising study. Another fourth-year female student who also struggled with juggling chores and studying at home argues that drawing boundaries with a family and establishing a schedule enabled her to face such challenges. All these students experienced spatial disjuncture when it was no longer feasible to balance family and learning objectives at home.

The fourth case study reveals the potential of online learning to lead to mental issues. While most students can find ways to cope with the mental distress caused by the pandemic, those with existing psychological issues experienced a decline in their mental health. One final-year female student revealed that she experienced increased anxiety, paranoia and depression during the pandemic. Due to the fear of possible infection, this student refused to leave her home until July although there had been no new infections in Brunei since early May. Her mental condition led to insomnia and panic attacks as she was consumed by the thought that 'the world is ending' and 'I am going to die', to an extent that she 'was feeling helpless and hopeless, almost no will to live'. She was one of the few students who were actually relieved that physical classes were still discouraged and most lectures remained online when the new semester started in August 2020. When she had to attend classes at the university, she would come to campus wearing a face mask and disinfect her chair and desk with antiseptic spray. She confessed, 'I was living in fear while attending the class. I could not concentrate at all, especially when there were people coughing and sneezing in the class which I immediately would rub hand sanitizer on my hands.' To cope with her worsening condition, she started practicing yoga for relaxation and sought therapy from the university counsellor. A final-year male student recounted similar struggles with depression during the pandemic; as he articulates,

> It felt as if I was being entrapped in my own room ... I was left alone with my thoughts. A subtle form of depression had eaten my mind up from thinking of every bad thing that had happened before and the calamity to come in the future. It had also worsened my social anxiety, for I had become somewhat accustomed to being alone for weeks, even months.

The effects of student and lecturer disengagement are presented in the fifth case. The dynamics of online classes are notably different from physical classes in terms of teacher-student interaction, as well as the potential for nonverbal communication. Some students struggled with online classes due to the inability to see the lecturers' body gestures, facial expressions and physical appearance, which are powerful tools in addition to verbal communication. A final-year female student states the following:

> I felt like I was intimidated to speak my opinions during online lectures because I am aware of the possibility that it might be recorded and my brain tends to overthink what goes on behind the monitor, unlike in physical classes where I get to see my friends' facial expression to be able to grasp their reaction.

Students have also described feeling loneliness and social isolation due to remote learning. For instance, one final-year male student asserts:

With little to no social contact with my other classmates, I felt a sense of loneliness, even to the point where I missed going to the campus physically—something I had never thought I would feel before. Group work was quite difficult as well; although some of us were able to come and meet physically, other members may not have had the permission to do so.

Based on the five cases above, we can see that digidemic, taking the form of spatial disjuncture, also leads to some learners losing their way in the process of online learning activities at home. Online learning ultimately fails to fully achieve its goal of enabling students to continue to enjoy and absorb knowledge. As shown above, many students come to feel ambivalence and a lack of control over their situation.

18.4 Hysteresis and Digidemic

The students' experiences above have briefly demonstrated the implications of online learning as a digidemic (digital pandemic), where remote learning tends to generate excessive deconstruction in learners at higher education institutions. As seen in the above cases, digidemic manifests in personal experiences that occur at home while participating in online learning such as the feeling of loneliness, social isolation, depression and mild stress, panic incidents and disruptions. The house becomes a place where students experience spatial disjuncture as they lose the right to maintain their private space and perform various disruptive adaptations in the shared space. This kind of phenomenon leads to a crisis, and digidemic has clearly changed the structure of social interactions at home and undermined the cognition of the learners. Digidemic has presented students with objective structures they had never encountered before, and this unpreparedness gives rise to various 'multi-temporal dynamics' (Strand & Lizardo, 2017, p. 169), characterised by unexpected distress and a sense of mental disconnection. So far, students around the world have been unable to handle this phenomenon, and they still present the maladaptive habitus as a result of the drastic changes brought about by online learning. As in the case above, this maladaptive habitus occurs during a crisis and conflict with others who use online learning technology at home. At this point, hysteresis occurs, in which the learning process 'undergoes a major crisis and [...] are profoundly changed' (Bourdieu, 2000, p. 160). Hysteresis can be described as a clash between social dispositions in a persistent society with challenging opportunities such that there is 'a structural lag between opportunities and the disposition' (Bourdieu, 1977, p. 83) amongst the students. Collective mentality impacts the individual, who must cope with witnessing disparities between the present conditions and the original conditions. Throughout history, disruptions in peasant societies have erupted in riots, protests and contentious struggles. For populations who have not been prepared with sufficient capital to move forward with a brand-new economic habitus, the introduction of a more capitalistic economy causes major disruptions to everyday life (Bourdieu, 1966). The present case is aligned to what Bourdieu examined, in which he recognised that the collision between the permeating structure of economic and social disposition has increased the level of disruptions or hysteresis (Bourdieu, 2000).

Critical reflection on this emerging phenomenon reveals that it will inevitably bring disruption to the learning and teaching process in higher education. The students' experiences as examined above unfold that face-to-face learning before the pandemic brought deep engagement as they could build relationships by engaging in conversations as well as feel the authenticity of the gestures and expressions of the lectures. This phenomenon highlights that invested feeling and belief integrated in past experiences still co-exist in the midst of rapidly changing times. In line with these temporalities, the suffering and uncertainties of people also add to the effect of hysteresis, namely the separation from broader social groups. The people's experiences often result in hysteresis effect due to a separation from social interaction with group members in their milieu (Barlösius, 2014). Supporting Bourdieu's argument on hysteresis, Barlösius (2014, p. 7) claims by recounting the individual causes of the crisis into the categories of praxis-cognitions, 'meaning the inability to process and evaluate historical, but also individual, crises according to previously formed categories of perception, appreciation and comprehension that are linked to one's social origins'. Temporalities determine the severity of the hysteresis and after-effects. And the possible solution is highly dependent on the types of externalities, stimuli, incidents and individual resources.

18.5 The Way Forward

The sociological concept of hysteresis enables us to look more closely at the implications of online learning or 'digidemic' for learners—university students in this case. The stories they share with the authors are not representative of the experiences of the general population of university students at Universiti Brunei Darussalam or those of global university-based learners. However, these are preliminary snapshots in our everyday teaching practices, and what we learn from them can encourage us to explore more stories from our students. Students in our present study exemplify the situation of hysteresis described by Pierre Bourdieu; they encounter a 'mismatch' between objective realities (online learning) and pre-existing circumstances in their homes and in relation to the reliability of Internet connections in their country. At home, they undergo continued adjustments and compromises to the inconveniences of sharing physical space with siblings and other family members. In addition, they have to face chaotic conditions in their homes as social stressors to the online learning process. In terms of mental wellbeing, they experience anxiety as intermittent coping feedback, but this also distracts their learning process. The visceral effect they perceive as a result of this digidemic is that there is no unification between body and mind in learning; instead, mild depression causes them to lose focus and develop a sense of helplessness. Thus, we emphasise that digidemic has an impact on mental state, physical conditions and deconstruction of physical space use at home.

Rather than providing prescriptive suggestions for the best policy to re-normalise the above conditions, we prefer to stand on the argument that universities as educational institutions must carry out more in-depth evaluations of the wider implications of online learning and map out the scale of impacts that imposed online learning has on the collective mental wellbeing of students. Once the shape and scale of impacts have been evaluated, it will be necessary to create alternatives to online learning that are least harmful for students. Expectedly, it enriches lecturers' understandings of the further actions they must take to prevent more mental damage. It is also worthwhile to further explore social and cultural coping strategies that students can employ in times of online learning.

REFERENCES

Alam, M. (2020). *Embracing the 'digidemic' as a time for improvisation in HE*. University World News. https://www.universityworldnews.com/post.php?story=20201113115210253

Appadurai, A. (1990). Disjuncture and difference in the global cultural economy. *Theory, Culture & Society*, 7(2–3), 295–310. https://doi.org/10.1177/026327690007002017

Barlösius, E. (2014). Pierre Bourdieu: Transformation societies and the middle class. *Middle East—Topics & Arguments, 2*(2014), 37–44. https://doi.org/10.17192/meta.2014.2.1312

Bartram, R. (2020). The infidelity of place: Medical simulation labs and disjunctures in pedagogical places. *Sociology of Health & Illness, 42*(2), 293–306. https://doi.org/10.1111/1467-9566.13002

Beck, U. (1992). *Risk society—Towards a new modernity.* Sage.

Bourdieu, P. (1966). L'école conservatrice: Les inégalités devant l'école et devant la culture. *Revue Française de Sociologie, 7*(3), 325–347. https://www.jstor.org/stable/3319132

Bourdieu, P. (1977). *Outline of a theory of practice* (Vol. 16). Cambridge University Press.

Bourdieu, P. (2000). Making the economic habitus: Algerian workers revisited. *Ethnography, 1*(1), 17–41. https://doi.org/10.1177/14661380022230624

Burke, K., & Larmar, S. (2020). Acknowledging another face in the virtual crowd: Reimagining the online experience in higher education through an online pedagogy of care. *Journal of Further and Higher Education, 1*(1), 1–15. https://doi.org/10.1080/0309877X.2020.1804536

Guermazi, B., & Beschorner, N. (2019). Southeast Asia can build stronger digital economy for all its citizen. https://blogs.worldbank.org/eastasiapacific/southeast-asia-can-build-stronger-digital-economy-all-its-citizens

Islam, N., Sharp, S. J., Chowell, G., Shabnam, S., Kawachi, I., Lacey, B., & White, M. (2020). Physical distancing interventions and incidence of coronavirus disease 2019: Natural experiment in 149 countries. *BMJ, 1*(1), 370–374. https://doi.org/10.1136/bmj.m2743

Khalil, R., Mansour, A. E., Fadda, W. A., Almisnid, K., Aldamegh, M., Al-Nafeesah, A., & Al-Wutayd, O. (2020). The sudden transition to synchronized online learning during the COVID-19 pandemic in Saudi Arabia: A qualitative study exploring medical students' perspectives. *BMC Medical Education, 20*(1), 1–10. https://doi.org/10.1186/s12909-020-02208-z

Lathabhavan, R., & Griffiths, M. (2020). First case of student suicide in India due to the COVID-19 education crisis: A brief report and preventive measures. *Asian Journal of Psychiatry, 53.* https://doi.org/10.1016/j.ajp.2020.102202

Latour, B. (2011). Network theory| networks, societies, spheres: Reflections of an actor-network theorist. *International Journal of Communication, 5*(15), 798–810. https://ijoc.org/index.php/ijoc/article/view/1094

Makdori, Y. (2020, October 20). *Siswa Bunuh Diri karena Tugas Daring, Belajar Jarak Jauh Dinilai Perlu Evaluasi* (A student committing suicide from undertaking online assignments calls for evaluation). Liputan6. https://www.liputan6.com/news/read/4388386/siswa-bunuh-diri-karena-tugas-daring-belajar-jarak-jauh-dinilai-perlu-evaluasi

Muniyappa, R., & Gubbi, S. (2020). COVID-19 pandemic, coronaviruses, and diabetes mellitus. *American Journal of Physiology-Endocrinology and Metabolism, 318*(5), 736–741. https://doi.org/10.1152/ajpendo.00124.2020

Paddock, R. C., & Sijabat, D. M. (2020, September 5). *When learning is really remote: Students climb trees and travel miles for a cell signal.* https://www.nytimes.com/2020/09/05/world/asia/coronavirus-indonesia-school-remote-learning.html

Stephens, N. M., Townsend, S. S., & Dittmann, A. G. (2019). Social-class disparities in higher education and professional workplaces: The role of cultural mismatch. *Current Directions in Psychological Science, 28*(1), 67–73. https://doi.org/10.1177/0963721418806506

Strand, M., & Lizardo, O. (2017). The hysteresis effect: Theorizing mismatch in action. *Journal for the Theory of Social Behaviour, 47*(2), 164–194. https://doi.org/10.1111/jtsb.12117

Sudharsanan, N., Didzun, O., Bärnighausen, T., & Geldsetzer, P. (2020). The contribution of the age distribution of cases to COVID-19 case fatality across countries: A 9-country demographic study. *Annals of Internal Medicine, 174*(9), 714–720. https://doi.org/10.7326/M20-2973

Tison, G. H., Avram, R., Kuhar, P., Abreau, S., Marcus, G. M., Pletcher, M. J., & Olgin, J. E. (2020). Worldwide effect of COVID-19 on physical activity: A descriptive study. *Annals of Internal Medicine, 173*(9), 767–770. https://doi.org/10.7326/M20-2665

Tsai, Y. S., Perrotta, C., & Gašević, D. (2020). Empowering learners with personalised learning approaches? Agency, equity and transparency in the context of learning analytics. *Assessment & Evaluation in Higher Education, 45*(4), 554–567. https://doi.org/10.1080/02602938.2019.1676396

World Health Organization. (2020). *Coronavirus disease (COVID-2019) situation reports.* World Health Organization. Retrieved November 21, 2020, from https://www.who.int/emergencies/diseases/novel-coronavirus-2019/situation-reports/

CHAPTER 19

Student Experiences During COVID-19: Towards Humanistic Internationalisation

Chester Keasberry, Phan Le Ha,
Mohammod Moninoor Roshid, and Muhammad Adil Iqbal

19.1　A Vignette: From *The Wonderful Wizard of Oz* to COVID-19

Looking out over the Kansas prairies, the little girl had no inkling of the challenges that she would soon face. Indeed, all she had ever known was her current circumstances, living at home with her aunt and uncle, and had perhaps never considered very much what lay beyond the Kansas horizon. Little did she know there was a coming storm she was woefully

---

C. Keasberry (✉) • M. A. Iqbal
Universiti Brunei Darussalam, Bandar Seri Begawan, Brunei
e-mail: chester.keasberry@ubd.edu.bn

Phan, L. H.
Sultan Hassanal Bolkiah Institute of Education, Universiti Brunei Darussalam, Bandar Seri Begawan, Brunei

University of Hawai'i at Mānoa, Honolulu, HI, USA
e-mail: leha.phan@ubd.edu.bn; halephan@hawaii.edu

© The Author(s), under exclusive license to Springer Nature Switzerland AG 2021
Phan, L. H. et al. (eds.), *Globalisation, Education, and Reform in Brunei Darussalam*, International and Development Education, https://doi.org/10.1007/978-3-030-77119-5_19

unprepared for, and she could not stop it from changing her life forever. When later she was caught up in the storm-fuelled cyclone, her fear of being dashed to pieces upon landing was well warranted, though she ultimately ended up none the worse for wear once the cyclone had dissipated. However, she found herself in a beautiful yet unfamiliar land that was surrounded by a great desert on all sides, with no clear way of crossing it. There was naught to be done but to saunter down the road of yellow brick in search of aid. The land was populated with a carousel of interesting characters, some benevolent and others quite sinister. One such encounter was an ostensibly powerful wizard who she would quickly discover was not exactly as she expected, yet would still help her in his own way. All in all, her companions and those she met on her journey would fill her sojourn there with adventure and meaning, and would help her understand that she would be quite alright in the end.

Published in 1900, L. Frank Baum's beloved children's novel *The Wonderful Wizard of Oz* has been a mainstay in the annals of great American literature. The U.S. Library of Congress has called it 'America's greatest and best-loved homegrown fairytale' (The Library of Congress, n.d.), and it continues to draw in new generations around the world more than a century later. In his foreword to the book, L. Frank Baum expressed that he meant for the tale to be purely wondrous entertainment without the weight of the stereotypical darker incidents and sombre moral lessons one might find in other children's literature, such as the stories from the Brothers Grimm.

Although Baum did not intend for us to make allegorical interpretations of the material, one need not delve very far to discover ourselves in the story, or indeed, the story in ourselves. How often have people related to Dorothy and her adventures—finding herself in a foreign land, meeting new people both nice and not-so-nice, being thrust into unusual circumstances and having to navigate unexpected situations? Thus, when we consider what it must have been like for Dorothy to traipse across the *Land of Oz* in search of help, we can easily draw parallels with real-life experiences

---

M. M. Roshid
University of Dhaka, Dhaka, Bangladesh
e-mail: moninoor@du.ac.bd

of people today in the present pandemic. In the context of the internationalisation of higher education (IHE), how many people, through a whirlwind of different conditions, are now in a land that is not their own, surrounded by peoples and cultures they may not know or fully understand? How many of them have found themselves stranded where they are because of the desert of COVID-19, unable to see a way home? And how have they dealt with these challenges while sheltering in place in their current country?

This chapter considers the experiences of a number of international students pursuing their degrees at a Bruneian university when the pandemic broke out, and how they have navigated the challenges they have faced due to pandemic effects and restrictions. In doing so, it surfaces a number of lessons that all those involved have learned along the way. Via the experiences, reflections and voices from these students and their accounts of what Brunei has been doing to engage them in a community of care and support, the chapter places at the central stage some core values associated with internationalisation and student mobility that have been overshadowed by the aggressive promotion of competition, commercialisation and neoliberal practices in many higher education systems. The chapter then argues for humanistic internationalisation and internationalisation at home (IaH) as core conceptualisation, policy and practice for global higher education.

19.2 The Cyclone of Circumstances

Over the past several decades, against the backdrop of globalisation, the knowledge economy, technological advancement and the increasing massification of IHE, the global mobility of international students has evolved in myriad ways and shows no signs of slowing down. Around 2.1 million students were enrolled in foreign universities in 2001, compared to 5.3 million in 2019 (International Institute of Education (IIE), 2019). The Organisation for Economic Co-operation and Development (OECD) forecasts that the number of international students had skyrocketed from two million in 1999 to five million in 2016, with doctoral and master's students making up the bulk of international mobility (Myklebust, 2019). The OECD further calculated that in 2017 the total international student population was 5.3 million (Mulvey, 2020; OECD, 2019; UNESCO, 2019), in 2018 5.6 million (OECD, 2020), and it will reach more than 8 million by 2025 as per a projection of OECD elsewhere (Dennis, 2018;

ICEF Monitor, 2017). Nevertheless, Australian experts estimate 15 million students will study abroad by 2025 (Altbach & Knight, 2007).

Though the academic levels and degree types pursued by international students vary by destination, the United States, the United Kingdom, China, Canada, Australia and France were reported to be the top host destinations accommodating two-thirds of all international students (IIE, 2019) (see Fig. 19.1). According to UNESCO (2016), though East Asia and Pacific region hosted 19% of the world's international students, the top destinations for international students remain Anglophone and/or European countries namely the United States, the United Kingdom, Australia and Canada (UNESCO, 2013) for varied reasons including considering the English language as a tool of opportunity of academic success and future career goals (Marginson, 2012).

It is evident in the literature that students tend to move to countries that offer better opportunities for education, work and migration. Host nations and universities also have strong competition among themselves to attract more mobile students as a mark of institutional prestige, a means of magnifying global influence and a source talent hunt and national revenues (Marginson, 2012). Accordingly, tertiary education institutions and their countries have made constant efforts to build an increasing academic reputation in the global context (OECD, 2007). Until now more than half of the world's tertiary international students hail from Asia (Marginson, 2012; Yang, 2018). In particular, the highest number of outbound international student mobility is from the East Asia Pacific region (around 1,500,000), followed by South and West Asia (over 500,000), while the least outbound international student mobility is found from North

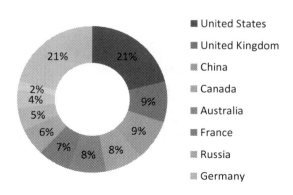

Fig. 19.1 Top host destination, 2019. (Source: A quick look at global mobility trends: Project Atlas, 2019, UNESCO, 2019)

America (IIE, 2019). As a single nation, China (662,100) and India (300,000) are the two largest countries in the market of exporting/sending international students (Marginson, 2012), while simultaneously China is emerging as the largest destination country amongst the developing countries (De Wit, 2018). The fastest-growing economies, populations and growing middle classes in Asia are greatly contributing to the outbound mobility of international students. Based on the statistics it can be anticipated that the number of middle-class populations in Asia will increase to three billion by 2030. This figure will represent 60% of the total middle-class population in the world (Dennis, 2018), and this may greatly influence future cross-border student mobility.

It is thus evident that swirling around international students is a cyclone of different circumstances and a multitude of actors that can influence their decisions of where to go and what to pursue. These factors are varied and can include geography, politics, culture, language, and so on. These influences can also be either intrinsic and more personal to the individual, or more extrinsic and determined by the juxtaposition of their existing environment and circumstances and that of the country they seek to go to, or even just the idea that a degree from a 'world-class' institution is 'better' than one from a place that is lesser known (Findlay et al., 2012). Historically, there has been a desire for Western-style and Western-based education, and this neo-colonial idea has influenced the flow of global mobility quite a bit over the years (Phan, 2018). Adding to an international student's decision to head overseas is the desire to be part of the global mobility and the idea that mobility today has great value in one's both professional and organisational life, and can be both a personal aspiration and a broader demand of society (Collins et al., 2014). The concept of international movement conjures up notions of fluidity in learning and openness to change, as opposed to stability which can be seen as negative or problematic. Beyond just gaining an international degree, there is also the socio-cultural draw; being able to travel to new places, experience new cultures and expand one's horizons are all seen as valuable parts of the educational experience and can ripple out into students' post-study lives (Collins et al., 2014, 2017). Also, as international students engage with these new places, peoples and pedagogies, their desires and motivations can often become part of a co-construction process and lead to new narratives of desires and possibilities in IHE (Phan, 2018).

Yet, the landscape has shifted in 2020; COVID-19 has caused a new storm to brew and peculiarly frightening winds to blow. The virus has adversely affected every aspect of human life on a global scale including daily life, economy, travel, political decisions, health and education. The extensity and severity of COVID-19 is on an unprecedented scale unseen since the Second World War, and it has been labelled a global pandemic by the World Health Organization (WHO). At the time of writing this chapter in December 2020, the world has observed nearly 73,000,000 infected cases and over 1,600,000 death tolls (Worldometers, 2020). Regardless of more positive news associated with several approved vaccines, there is no clear timeframe for this pandemic to end and this has caused a high level of anxiety, tension and uncertainty for people around the globe including international students, higher education institutions and education leaders.

The impact and continuation of education in natural emergencies including tsunami, economic recessions, bushfires, floods or civil war has been discussed in previous research literature (Bull, 2012; De Vreyer et al., 2015; Frankenberg et al., 2013; Postiglione, 2011; Rush, 2018). Nonetheless, the effects of the deadly coronavirus on IHE and student mobility are now being documented across disciplines, though not necessarily systematically. Recently published papers have focused in a segregated way on varied areas of higher education in different country contexts. For instance, Sahu (2020) highlights the potential education and mental health of students and academic staff in general; Jacob et al. (2020) analyse how COVID-19 impacted higher education in Nigeria; Toquero (2020) addresses how the virus brought about challenges and opportunities for higher education in the Philippines; Jena (2020) highlights major ramifications of the pandemic on higher education in India; and Aucejo et al. (2020), following their survey on 1500 students at a large public institution in the United States, show academic, economic and health-related shocks induced by COVID-19 in the United States. In Europe, the pandemic is already deterring potential future international enrolment around the world and is causing significant increases in tuition fees for international students nearly everywhere. The appeal of studying in Europe or the United States appears to have lost its lustre somewhat and is on the decline primarily due to online classes; according to a recent survey, 52% of international students are likely to cancel their studies in Europe if they have to take classes online (Schengen Visa Info, 2020).

One effect of this drop in global international enrolment is the increase in 'Internationalisation at Home' (IaH), which was first coined by Crowther et al. (2000) and defined as 'any internationally related activity apart from outbound student and staff mobility' (p. 6). This definition would later be clarified by Beelen and Jones (2015) who explained that IaH is 'the purposeful integration of international and intercultural dimensions into the formal and informal curriculum for all students, within domestic learning environments'. Over the years, institutions mulled over how best to incorporate IaH and improve and adapt their curricula and learning environments. But none was prepared for the sheer amount of unintended IaH that would begin to occur in 2020 when the pandemic arrived. Suddenly, students who had been waiting to pursue an overseas education could no longer leave, and droves of international students had to return to their home countries with no clear prospect of returning overseas to continue their degree programmes. Countries like Vietnam, for example, are now wondering what is the best recourse to increase and optimise IaH for a local student population that has found itself 'stuck at home', and student care and student wellbeing have become watchwords for the more conscientious nations and institutions during this period (Phùng & Phan, 2021).

As COVID-19 emerged as a global scourge and found its way to our shores in March 2020, many things happened in quick succession here in Brunei Darussalam (henceforth Brunei). Educational institutions across the country almost immediately shut their doors, and there was a brief respite from the daily grind of school while everyone sheltered at home. During mid-March, educational tasks moved online and everyone had to continue the academic year while getting used to the new online environments and all their quirks and foibles (see Chap. 16 for more detailed discussion of changes in educational policies and practices in Brunei). However, prior to all these happenings, other occurrences had already taken place beyond the educational and national sphere. As the virus spread across the world and the threat of international contagion loomed, borders around the world began to shut and Brunei was no exception when it came to implementing these preventative measures. On 30 January 2020, Brunei banned the entry of visitors with a travel history to China's Hubei province, the capital of which is Wuhan where the virus was first reported (Rasidah Hj Abu Bakar, 2020a). This was later extended to include Jiangsu and Zhejiang provinces. On 6 March, Brunei banned the entry of visitors from Iran and Italy after both nations experienced surges in new COVID-19 cases (Rasidah Hj Abu Bakar, 2020b). The Brunei Ministry of Health began to warn the populace against non-essential travels and urged them not to go abroad during the upcoming school holidays in mid-March. Three days later, on 9 March, Brunei reported its first case of the virus (Rasidah Hj Abu Bakar, 2020c). By 12 March, the number of cases had risen to 11 (Bandial, 2020). People began to fear what would happen next and whether things would spiral out of control. Brunei moved quickly to activate quarantine centres and measures, but by 23 March the number of new cases has reached 91 (The Scoop, 2020). The following day, in an effort to reduce the number of imported cases, the Brunei Ministry of Home Affairs made the decision to shut borders to all foreign visitors. This also included halting the issuance of visitor visas, student visas and dependent visas, and all such applications received before this suspension would not be processed.

It was within this milieu that the new educational policies were being put into place and the novel online pedagogies were being pushed and implemented. Without warning, local institutions had to undergo a massive digital shift; educators and students had to acclimatise to the abrupt changes, and many experienced mental fatigue as they sat through hours and hours of online teaching and learning (Keasberry et al., 2020). Meanwhile, there was a subset of the student population for whom the new travel restrictions brought new predicaments beyond assignment deadlines, project grades and novel online pedagogies. Universiti Brunei Darussalam (UBD), as one of the main higher education institutions in Brunei, has been fortunate enough to be able to welcome international students from various regions, including other Association of Southeast Asian Nations (ASEAN) and Asian nations, Africa, Europe and the Middle East. However, when COVID-19 hit and the borders began to close, these students who had arrived chasing the potential of international education now faced a tough dilemma—should they stay and attempt to continue their education or go back home to be with family (provided they could even afford the travel fees)? If they left, what if they were not allowed to return? That might jeopardise all the study they had put in thus far. On the other hand, if they chose to stay, when would they be able to return home? And in staying, would they be able to persevere in the face of all these unknowns, not just educationally but also emotionally and financially?

19.3 Travelling the Yellow Brick Road

One might meet many different characters while travelling down the road in an unfamiliar land. Some might be helpful and hospitable, while others might regard you with indifference, and there might even be those who treat you with hostility. This experience can be all too common for international students who arrive in a country with no relationships or prior connections. These students already face the tricky task of building a temporary home in the country of their chosen education. COVID-19 has brought with it new trials, not the least of which are the shift towards online pedagogies that have their own complications (Bettinger & Loeb, 2017; Keasberry et al., 2020); the financial struggles of covering basic living costs while the pandemic is damaging the local economy, particularly for students from disadvantaged socio-economic backgrounds (Montacute, 2020); the aforementioned travel restrictions and visa uncertainties; and even possible xenophobia and backlash against foreigners (Mittelmeier & Cockayne, 2020).

As students venture down this difficult road, the people they encounter can make or break their experience. At Griffith University in Australia, for example, international students experienced stress and disillusionment and were at times faced with racism, shortage of food and the fear that they might not be able to continue paying their school fees and living expenses (Gallagher et al., 2020). All this led to a stigma of shame that meant they did not readily ask for help, which in turn made things worse for them and led to higher emotional stress and mental pressure. Moreover, international students in Australia were initially excluded from government relief and income support. Responding to these needs, educators had to work to discover the extent of the challenges that international students faced and how to bridge the gap to support them in their time of need, whether professionally, financially, mentally or emotionally. It is support networks such as these that help international students in general deal with the sudden loss of the physical campus experience and community, as well as all the formal and informal support that went with it (Norberg, 2011; Raaper & Brown, 2020). There have been many similar stories shared by both local and international students in different countries who have had to deal with the effects of COVID-19 and how it has affected their lives (Beckstein, 2020; Fazackerley, 2020; Hallenbeck, 2020).

As previously mentioned, UBD has its own population of international students, and the university recognised that they were facing certain burdens during the pandemic period. Students from various nations chose to return to their countries, and the Brunei Prime Minister's Office issued a directive to aid this transition. However, there were those that opted to remain in the country for various reasons, despite any advice or calls to return home. Thus, UBD endeavoured to help these students by providing 'full administrative and academic support', offering medical care to any who needed it, and has continued to provide accommodation for them in the university dorms during the COVID-19 period (Iqbal & Phan, 2020). Given the wealth of experience that these remaining students had garnered in the months since the borders closed and their decision to stay, it would be worth giving them an avenue through which to share their experiences so that all might learn from one another. Thus, on 29 September 2020, the International and Comparative Education (ICE) Research Group at UBD conducted a special all-student panel discussion as part of an ongoing seminar series on 'COVID-19, Society, and Education'. At this two-hour panel discussion, ten students of various majors and degrees across faculties at the university were invited to share their experiences regarding study-work-life issues. The panel included both local and international students who reflected on how a strong sense of community had been nurtured and evolved at all levels of policy, management, communication, service and practice. All the panellists commented on the importance of reflection, sharing and caring for themselves and others during this difficult period. Apart from the ten panellists, many more students from the university were in the audience.

All the student participants expressed a strong awareness of building a support network for everyone in the current time of the pandemic. The student participants recognised that many other students lived away from home, while others might come from a lower socioeconomic background and might need more help in terms of access to the Internet and devices. They also appreciated the support and facilitation they had received from the university administration, lecturers and other staff members when they were faced with challenges, difficulties and emotional stress compounded by the pandemic. It led to quite a positive atmosphere as the students praised lecturers' efforts in trying to improve students' online learning experiences and how everyone was sympathetic, caring and accommodating. Some students confessed that the shared difficulties had made them more grateful and less demanding; even though the pandemic had affected their lifestyles, emotions and priorities, it had also changed their mentality and perceptions in that they had become more compassionate, understanding and less selfish. The pandemic had also spurred them towards helping more people while fostering a better relationship with the community.

Being homesick and worried about families back home while also feeling lonely on campus because of the strict social distancing mandate was a sentiment held by all the international students participating in the student panel. One of them was a postgraduate student from South Korea, and he shared a particularly inspiring story. Being away from home, he experienced anxiety as he saw repeated reports of the increasing number of COVID-19 cases in his home country. However, in spite of his fears, he opted to volunteer as a front-liner to help people in Brunei. During the volunteering period, he learned new meanings of respect and solidarity from witnessing collaborative efforts among many local Bruneians in containing the pandemic. These new meanings made him feel at home in the Sultanate and also made Brunei a home to him.

On campus there were a number of projects started by different people in the UBD support network. One such project was the '*Free Meal for International Students*' initiative, which became a bonding thread for many of the students. One panel participant, a PhD student from the Maldives, recalled how she and other international students staying at the UBD dorms would eagerly wait for the time they could walk down to the meal area to get food, knowing that they would see one another's faces and smiles, hear each other's voices, exchange greetings and simply be seen. It was not necessarily the generous offer of food alone that lifted their spirits; they valued and cherished the sense of a community and being there for each other.

Also active in the community, a student participant from Bangladesh opened up about her experiences of pursuing her PhD while also raising a young child. During this time, she was determined to stay hopeful and busy so that she would not be mentally and emotionally burdened with worry and fear. As a creative writer, she wrote many poems about her feelings and all the ups and downs that came her way. She was also active in giving seminars and online teaching on creative writing to various international groups. Like the Maldivian student, she spent time brushing up on her research skills and learning how to conduct academic research at a distance, since travelling to collect data was no longer an option. Both these PhD students also acknowledged that having the opportunity to talk about what they had been through was an empowering experience, as their fear, joy, happiness, homesickness, loss, doubt and anxiety were all emotional conditions that needed to be recognised, respected and validated.

'The pandemic has changed my life' was perhaps the strongest message during the panel, and it came from the personal reflections of a student participant from Nigeria who arrived in Brunei not long before the pandemic started in March. He soon found himself required to stay in the dorm and observe strict social distancing practices before he had even had the time or opportunity to build any friendships or discover much about the campus and what was around it. His Bruneian experience solely revolved around pandemic restrictions before he could even fully comprehend what was happening. This experience was not easy to accept, and he would later admit that a strong panic quickly developed inside him as more active cases in Brunei were reported. He feared the pandemic would spread all over the small nation. He worried about death and wondered if his family would be able to see him again. However, the university community was there for him. In the end, the whole COVID-19 experience had made him reflect on many issues—internally and externally—from different perspectives. Not only did he feel the essence of humanity and empathy from the local and international communities in Brunei, he also experienced first-hand a significant amount of social support during the hardship. He praised the Sultanate for its strong leadership, robust public health system, effective administration and the strong solidarity of the people.

One of us (Muhammad Adil Iqbal) also participated in the student panel and provided his own remarks. As an international student from Pakistan and the President of the International Students Club at UBD, he echoed the sentiments expressed by the others, adding that international students needed strong support to feel safe and welcomed, and so policy makers everywhere needed to remain sympathetic and empathetic to the international students in their country. Reflecting on Brunei and UBD, Adil expressed his gratitude for the unrestrained support, help, cooperation, supervision, patience and kindness the international students had received thus far from the UBD administration, particularly from campus entities that were directly involved with international affairs such as the Office of the Assistant Vice-Chancellor for Global Affairs, the Students Affairs Section and the International Student Office. Some of the aid Adil noted included how UBD still accommodated many international students who had completed their studies but were unable to return to their home countries due to travel restrictions. In addition, visa extensions had been given to such students to stay in Brunei. To lessen their financial burdens, UBD also waived their on-campus accommodation fees, and medical and health services were provided to those who needed it. On the administrative side, admissions were given to international students for the August 2020 intake and many were given scholarships as well. As UBD prioritised protections for all international students' health, safety and welfare, the students were able to experience care, attention and concern, which has led to a sense of hope and empowerment.

For a number of years, Brunei has attempted to practise the '*Whole of Nation*' approach, an initiative focused on cooperation between the Brunei government, non-governmental organisations (NGOs), the private sector, communities, individuals and the public in order to promote and support progress in various aspects of nation-building. Adil discussed how this approach also worked well for the care of UBD international students and enabled UBD to ensure that their international students were not ignored and left to fend for themselves. The impact of UBD's provision and care would not go unnoticed, however; Adil articulated that he himself, in his capacity as the President of the International Students Club at UBD, would 'remain a living testimony of this' and that what UBD had done for them would 'remain a great inspiration for the ideals of higher education in times to come, and was among the initial successes of *Wawasan Brunei 2035* (the national vision of Brunei Darussalam)' (see Chap. 1 for more information on *Wawasan Brunei 2035*). Adil was not the only student with this sentiment; other international students were determined to contribute and 'give back' in their own way, and the '*Whole of Nation*' approach brought opportunities for them to participate in Brunei's combined efforts to prevent the further spread of the COVID-19 in the country.

For example, a few of the students actively contributed in community service and volunteer work in Brunei. As previously mentioned, the Korean student—who was also the Deputy Vice President of the UBD International Students Club—had volunteered since 22 March for Brunei's Ministry of Culture, Youth and Sports in its campaign to fight COVID-19, and worked in various isolation centres, hotels, school dormitories and other places designated by the government. In addition, he assisted medical officers from the Ministry of Health and acted as a standby during the emergency situation. A PhD student from China helped in the UBD canteen at one of the campus hostels during staff shortages, as they were preparing meals for international students. Like her Korean peer, she also volunteered with Brunei's Ministry of Culture, Youth and Sports in its COVID-19 campaign. And one Indonesian Masters student took the time to impart religious education to international and local students in UBD in order to provide spiritual connection and advice to those who sought it. Adil shone the spotlight on these three international students at UBD as sources of inspiration for other international students around the world, and reiterated that it is important for international students to stand and contribute in whatever way they can to assist and help their host countries during these times of the COVID-19 pandemic. In closing, Adil affirmed how 'COVID-19 unites us in healing ways as it has united everybody to become one big family and has fostered humanity and connections between people'. He added that the 'COVID-19 experience in Brunei [also] shows the stories of human excellence'.

19.4　There Is No Place Like Home

Dorothy meets a number of friends in need during her journey. As she helps them solve their problems, face their challenges and realise their dreams, they are able to help her in return, and she discovers they provide the valuable companionship and counsel she sorely needed. Along the way, one of her companions says he cannot understand why she would want to leave beautiful Oz and go back to Kansas. She simply responds: 'No matter how dreary and grey our homes are, we people of flesh and blood would rather live there than in any other country, be it ever so beautiful. There is no place like home.'

Indeed, it is not difficult to imagine the heartache that many international students feel as they live away from their home countries and pursue their futures during an uncertain pandemic. But while they are in the land of their choice (as difficult as that choice to stay might have been), many have opted to engage, participate and contribute in many ways. Just as Dorothy changed the lives of the companions she encountered by helping them despite her own sense of being lost, international students at UBD have left their mark here in Brunei, not the least of which is how they have added new dimensions to the IaH at UBD.

In 2009, when UBD introduced the GenNEXT Programme for its undergraduate students, it was promoted as a framework meant to allow students to pursue their education based on their individual learning styles. Designed to be broad-based and transdisciplinary, GenNEXT was meant to ensure that students graduate with a personalised high-quality education that would allow them to meet the needs of a constantly changing world environment (Universiti Brunei Darussalam, 2016). These definitions of GenNEXT lend themselves to comparisons with IaH; indeed, it seems as if the programme was designed to implement IaH and improve UBD's academic content and structure. Whether or not it has adequately done so is another matter, but what is clear is the desire to prepare students to be adaptable and flexible, to realise that they live in a world where IHE is the norm and IaH is becoming increasingly viable in order to uplift and upskill the local student populace. It is also noticed that outbound mobility is a strong focus of the GenNEXT Programme, a very common element and conceptualisation of IHE found in many existing curricula introduced in institutions around the world (see Phùng & Phan, 2021 for more detailed discussion). Nonetheless, the pandemic and its unprecedented impacts on all forms of travels and mobilities including academic mobilities have forced us to rethink 'home', 'mobility' and IHE as a whole.

That international students are on university campuses, bringing their lives, knowledge, labour and compassion to make contribution to multiple *at home* communities here in Brunei has sent a strong message that the 'home' in IaH ought to be inclusive, nurtured, built and sustained by all hands and owned by all, not just by any single local community. The pandemic has offered us a powerful lens to see and reflect on the GenNEXT Programme, especially in proactively co-creating *at home* spaces for local and international students and those in the broader community to come together to make Brunei a home which is meaningful, personalised, humanistic and inclusive for all. This way, local Bruneian students could also help transform and enjoy IaH, seeing themselves as being responsible for enriching this sense of home from within alongside their wanting to reach out for international experience validation. This could help create a fine balance between IaH and outbound-mobility-induced policies and practices predominantly promoted by institutions around the world.

During this pandemic, one of the unexpected benefits of IaH-oriented implementation has been a wider and deeper understanding of one's place in the world and one's responsibility to others, whether or not they are from our own nation. Hearing the stories of the international students whose accounts are presented above has given us a different perspective and an appreciation for what each of them has had to go through in this tough season. As educators work towards IaH and the internationalisation of multiple aspects of education in our own spheres of influence, including pedagogy, curricula, delivery and research, these international students' personal accounts and anecdotes colour our understanding of their world as it collides with ours, and we are better able to see the struggles they face and how they are able to join together to rise above them. Gallagher et al. (2020) note:

> There was a deeper understanding of the needs of international students and the barriers excluding international students from accessing an equitable educational experience and necessary services. Staff had new insights into the need to find better ways to internationalise access to tertiary education, as well as a huge appreciation of the strength and resilience of the international cohort. (p. 817)

Both around the world and at UBD, international students contribute greatly to academic research and university finances, and enrich the overall campus experience with their own unique perspectives and cultures that they bring with them. While they do experience new things and return home as changed individuals, they often also touch the local lives of those they encounter, and this seems truer now more than ever in this current climate. This pandemic has shown us that the whole phenomenon of IHE is not just numbers, statistics, academic models, political shifts or procedural changes. At the ground level, IHE centres around people first and foremost, and this very humanistic internationalisation is what we uphold, build and work towards.

That said, we are well aware of dominant-deemed problematic practices in global higher education, whereby international students are a core part of any institution's internationalisation strategy and are categorised as non-citizens and temporary migrants, and cross-border students are traditionally imagined as aliens with little rights. Evidence is ample, as can be seen in academic literature (Chowdhury & Phan, 2014; Sawir et al., 2009; Marginson & Sawir, 2011) and in more recent media coverage on higher education in the time of COVID-19 (Batty, 2020; Mittelmeier & Cockayne, 2020; Yu, 2020). To many critics of higher education, what global universities and their governments do for/with IHE is treating it as a means of generating revenues to make up for reduced public funding from local and national governments (Stein et al., 2019). However, we would like to echo Kahane (2009) who has argued that 'for many educators, though, a key reason for internationalisation is ethical: it helps students to examine their implicit and explicit beliefs about whose wellbeing matters, and to develop a more globalised sense of responsibility and citizenship' (p. 49). We call for all those involved in IHE and IaH, not just educators, to cultivate and put in practice this 'internationalisation is ethical' principle. We, as well, reiterate our argument for humanistic internationalisation.

We are able to sympathise with fictional characters like Dorothy because we might relate to their experiences or because it allows us to feel for the plight of others who might go through similar situations. Thus, if we can humanise a story by connecting with its characters, should we not also humanise IHE by connecting and relating to those that are in the midst of it and navigating its many challenges, particularly now in this difficult time? It is important we do so, lest we forget that at the heart of all the theories, policies and academic rhetoric lies the human experience—real people who are facing real challenges, and from whom we can learn a great deal if we just pause, listen and lend a helping hand.

References

Altbach, P. G., & Knight, J. (2007). The internationalization of higher education: Motivations and realities. *Journal of Studies in International Education, 11*(3–4), 290–305. https://doi.org/10.1177/1028315307303542

Aucejo, E. M., French, J., Araya, M. P. U., & Zafar, B. (2020). The impact of COVID-19 on student experiences and expectations: Evidence from a survey. *Journal of Public Economics, 191.* https://doi.org/10.1016/j.jpubeco.2020.104271

Bandial, A. (2020, March 12). Coronavirus fear grips Brunei, as number of cases rise to 11 within days. *The Scoop.* https://thescoop.co/2020/03/09/brunei-reports-first-covid-19-case/

Batty, D. (2020, March 18). Cambridge colleges criticised for asking students to leave over coronavirus. *The Guardian.* https://www.theguardian.com/education/2020/mar/18/cambridge-colleges-criticised-for-asking-students-to-leave-over-coronavirus

Beckstein, A. (2020, July 24). How are international students coping with the Covid-19 pandemic? *Times Higher Education.* https://www.timeshighereducation.com/student/blogs/how-are-international-students-coping-covid-19-pandemic

Beelen, J., & Jones, E. (2015, December 4). Defining 'internationalisation at home'. *University World News.* https://www.universityworldnews.com/post.php?story=20151202144353164

Bettinger, E., & Loeb, S. (2017). Promises and pitfalls of online education. *Evidence Speaks Reports, 2*(15), 1–4.

Bull, D. D. (2012). From ripple to tsunami: The possible impact of MOOCs on higher education. *DEQuarterly, 12,* 10–11.

Chowdhury, R., & Phan, L. H. (2014). *Desiring TESOL and international education: Market abuse and exploitation.* Multilingual Matters.

Collins, F. L., Ho, K. C., Ishikawa, M., & Ma, A.-H. S. (2017). International student mobility and after-study lives: The portability and prospects of overseas education in Asia. *Population, Space and Place, 23*(4), e2029. https://doi.org/10.1002/psp.2029

Collins, F. L., Sidhu, R., Lewis, N., & Yeoh, B. S. A. (2014). Mobility and desire: International students and Asian regionalism in aspirational Singapore. *Discourse: Studies in the Cultural Politics of Education, 35*(5), 661–676. https://doi.org/10.1080/01596306.2014.921996

Crowther, P., Joris, M., Otten, M., Nilsson, B., Teekens, H., & Wächter, B. (2000). *Internationalisation at home: A position paper*. European Association for International Education.

De Vreyer, P., Guilbert, N., & Mesple-Somps, S. (2015). Impact of natural disasters on education outcomes: Evidence from the 1987–89 locust plague in Mali. *Journal of African Economies, 24*(1), 57–100. https://doi.org/10.1093/jae/eju018

De Wit, H. (2018). The new dynamics in international student circulation. *University World News*. https://www.universityworldnews.com/post.php?story=20180704143553337

Dennis, M. J. (2018). A new age in international student mobility. *University World News*. https://www.universityworldnews.com/post.php?story=20180605103256399

Fazackerley, A. (2020, December 5). 'I only see someone if I do my laundry': Students stuck on campus for a Covid Christmas. *The Guardian*. https://www.theguardian.com/education/2020/dec/05/students-stuck-on-campus-for-a-covid-christmas

Findlay, A. M., King, R., Smith, F. M., Geddes, A., & Skeldon, R. (2012). World class? An investigation of globalisation, difference and international student mobility: World class? *Transactions of the Institute of British Geographers, 37*(1), 118–131. https://doi.org/10.1111/j.1475-5661.2011.00454.x

Frankenberg, E., Sikoki, B., Sumantri, C., Suriastini, W., & Thomas, D. (2013). Education, vulnerability, and resilience after a natural disaster. *Ecology and Society: A Journal of Integrative Science for Resilience and Sustainability, 18*(2), 16. https://doi.org/10.5751/ES-05377-180216

Gallagher, H. L., Doherty, A. Z., & Obonyo, M. (2020). International student experiences in Queensland during COVID-19. *International Social Work, 63*(6), 815–819. https://doi.org/10.1177/0020872820949621

Hallenbeck, B. (2020, May 7). A floor to herself: UVM international student remains on campus. *Burlington Free Press*. https://www.burlingtonfreepress.com/story/life/2020/05/07/kenya-student-few-international-students-uvm/5176580002/

ICEF Monitor. (2017). OECD charts a slowing of international mobility growth. https://monitor.icef.com/2017/09/oecd-charts-slowing-international-mobility-growth/

International Institute of Education (IIE). (2019). A quick look at global mobility. *Project Atlas*. International Institute of Education. www.iie.org/ProjectAltas

Iqbal, M. A., & Phan, L. H. (2020, April 18). Care for international students brings greater commitment. *University World News*. https://www.universityworldnews.com/post.php?story=20200417113236746

Jacob, O. N., Abigeal, I., & Lydia, A. E. (2020). Impact of COVID-19 on the higher institutions development in Nigeria. *Electronic Research Journal of Social Sciences and Humanities, 2*(2), 126–135.

Jena, P. K. (2020). Impact of Covid-19 on higher education in India. *International Journal of Advanced Education and Research (IJAER), 5*, 77–81.

Kahane, D. (2009). Learning about obligation, compassion, and global justice: The place of contemplative pedagogy. *New Directions for Teaching and Learning, 118*, 49–60.

Keasberry, C., Phan, L. H., Hoon, C. Y., Alam, M., Alas, Y., & Noorashid, N. (2020, December 5). Facing the mental health challenges of COVID-19 in HE. *University World News*. https://www.universityworldnews.com/post.php?story=20201201133134894

Marginson, S. (2012). Including the other: Regulation of the human rights of mobile students in a nation-bound world. *Higher Education, 63*, 497–512. https://doi.org/10.1007/s10734-011-9454-7

Marginson, S., & Sawir, E. (2011). Student security in the global education market. In C. Holden, M. Kilkey, & G. Raima (Eds.), *Social policy review 23: Analysis and debate in social policy, 2011* (pp. 281–302), Policy Press.

Mittelmeier, J., & Cockayne, H. (2020, October 10). Combating discrimination against international students. *University World News*. https://www.universityworldnews.com/post.php?story=20201009142439903

Montacute, R. (2020). *Social mobility and COVID-19: Implications of the COVID-19 crisis for educational inequality*. The Sutton Trust. https://www.suttontrust.com/wp-content/uploads/2020/04/COVID-19-and-Social-Mobility-1.pdf

Mulvey, B. (2020). Conceptualizing the discourse of student mobility between "periphery" and "semi-periphery": The case of Africa and China. *Higher Education*. https://doi.org/10.1007/s10734-020-00549-8

Myklebust, J. P. (2019, July 13). Young degree holders set to double to 300 million by 2030. *University World News*. https://www.universityworldnews.com/post.php?story=20190711110157794

Norberg, J. (2011). Arendt in crisis: Political thought in between past and future. *College Literature, 38*(1), 131–149.

OECD. (2007). *Education at a glance, 2007: OECD indicators*. OECD Publishing. https://doi.org/10.1787/eag-2007-en

OECD. (2019). *Education at a glance 2019: OECD indicators*. OECD Publishing. https://doi.org/10.1787/f8d7880d-en

OECD. (2020). *Education at a glance 2020: OECD indicators*. OECD Publishing. https://doi.org/10.1787/69096873-en

Phan, L. H. (2018). Higher education, English, and the idea of 'the West': Globalizing and encountering a global south regional university. *Discourse: Studies in the Cultural Politics of Education, 39*(5), 782–797. https://doi.org/10.1080/01596306.2018.1448704

Phùng, T., & Phan, L. H. (2021). Higher education in Vietnam and a new vision for internationalization at home post COVID-19. In J. Gillen, L. C. Kelley, & L. H. Phan (Eds.), *Vietnam at the vanguard: New perspectives across time, space, and community*. Springer International.

Postiglione, G. A. (2011). Global recession and higher education in eastern Asia: China, Mongolia and Vietnam. *Higher Education, 62*(6), 789–814. https://doi.org/10.1007/s10734-011-9420-4

Raaper, R., & Brown, C. (2020). The COVID-19 pandemic and the dissolution of the university campus: Implications for student support practice. *Journal of Professional Capital and Community, 5*(3/4), 343–349. https://doi.org/10.1108/JPCC-06-2020-0032

Rasidah Hj Abu Bakar. (2020a, January 30). Brunei bans entry of visitors with recent Hubei travel history. *The Scoop*. https://thescoop.co/2020/01/30/brunei-bans-entry-of-visitors-with-recent-hubei-travel-history/

Rasidah Hj Abu Bakar. (2020b, March 6). Brunei bans entry of visitors from Iran, Italy over COVID-19 fears. *The Scoop*. https://thescoop.co/2020/03/06/brunei-bans-entry-of-visitors-from-iran-italy-over-covid-19-fears/

Rasidah Hj Abu Bakar. (2020c, March 9). Brunei reports first COVID-19 case. *The Scoop*. https://thescoop.co/2020/03/09/brunei-reports-first-covid-19-case/

Rush, J. V. (2018). The impact of natural disasters on education in Indonesia. *Economics of Disasters and Climate Change, 2*(2), 137–158. https://doi.org/10.1007/s41885-017-0022-1

Sahu, P. (2020). Closure of universities due to Coronavirus Disease 2019 (COVID-19): Impact on education and mental health of students and academic staff. *Cureus, 12*(4). https://doi.org/10.7759/cureus.7541

Sawir, E., Marginson, S., Nyland, C., Ramia, G., & Rawlings-Sanaei, F. (2009). The social and economic security of international students: A New Zealand study. *Higher Education Policy, 22*(4), 461–482. https://doi.org/10.1057/hep.2009.4

Schengen Visa Info. (2020). *52% of international students very likely to cancel studies in Europe if they have to take classes online*. https://www.schengenvisainfo.com/news/52percent-of-international-students-very-likely-to-cancel-studies-in-europe-if-they-have-to-take-classes-online/

Stein, S., Andreotti, V., & Suša, R. (2019). Pluralizing frameworks for global ethics in the internationalization of higher education in Canada. *Canadian Journal of Higher Education/Revue canadienne d'enseignement supérieur, 49*(1), 22–46.

The Library of Congress. (n.d.). *The wizard of Oz: An American fairy tale.* https://www.loc.gov/exhibits/oz/

The Scoop. (2020, March 23). Brunei shuts borders to all foreigners from March 24. *The Scoop.* https://thescoop.co/2020/03/13/covid-19-live-updates/2/#23-apr-brunei-shuts-borders

Toquero, C. M. (2020). Challenges and opportunities for higher education amid the COVID-19 pandemic: The Philippine context. *Pedagogical Research, 5*(4). https://doi.org/10.29333/pr/7947

UNESCO. (2013). *The international mobility of students in Asia and the Pacific.* UNESCO.

UNESCO. (2016). Global flow of tertiary-level students. http://www.uis.unesco.org/Education/Pages/international-student-flow-viz.aspx

UNESCO. (2019). Global flow of tertiary-level students. Retrieved July 31, 2020, from http://uis.unesco.org/en/uis-student-flow

Universiti Brunei Darussalam. (2016). *History.* https://ubd.edu.bn/about/organisation/ubd-history.html

Worldometers. (2020). Coronavirus. Retrieved December 15, 2020, from https://www.worldometers.info/coronavirus/

Yang, P. (2018). Understanding youth educational mobilities in Asia: A comparison of Chinese 'Foreign Talent' students in Singapore and Indian MBBS Students in China. *Journal of Intercultural Studies, 39*(6), 722–738. https://doi.org/10.1080/07256868.2018.1533534

Yu, A. (2020, March 17). 'It's a nightmare': International students forced to leave campus due to coronavirus. *WHYY.* https://whyy.org/articles/its-a-nightmare-international-students-forced-to-leave-campus-due-to-coronavirus/

CHAPTER 20

Wrap Up to Move Forward

Phan Le Ha, Asiyah Kumpoh, and Keith Wood

20.1 Globalisation, Education and Reform in Brunei Darussalam: Concluding Remarks and Further Thoughts

We would like to reiterate what we stated at the beginning of the book that writing about a single country's education is never easy, as you may wonder why there is a need to do so, particularly when such a country is so small like Brunei Darussalam (henceforth Brunei)—an Islamic monarchy located on the island of Borneo and with a population of less than half a million people. We hope also that we have been able to prove you wrong. As we are

---

Phan, L. H. (✉)
Sultan Hassanal Bolkiah Institute of Education, Universiti Brunei Darussalam, Bandar Seri Begawan, Brunei

University of Hawai'i at Mānoa, Honolulu, HI, USA
e-mail: leha.phan@ubd.edu.bn; halephan@hawaii.edu

A. Kumpoh
Faculty of Arts and Social Sciences, Universiti Brunei Darussalam, Bandar Seri Begawan, Brunei
e-mail: asiyah.kumpoh@ubd.edu.bn

© The Author(s), under exclusive license to Springer Nature Switzerland AG 2021
Phan, L. H. et al. (eds.), *Globalisation, Education, and Reform in Brunei Darussalam*, International and Development Education, https://doi.org/10.1007/978-3-030-77119-5_20

writing this final chapter, we are still surprised by the depth, breadth, range and complexity of the issues, topics and questions explored, examined and discussed in the book. In the coming paragraphs, we recap the main points and arguments put forth in each part of the book as well as in the individual chapters. As we do so, we also offer further thoughts and reflections.

20.2 Wawasan 2035, SPN21, MIB and Education in Brunei: A Further Look

Following Chap. 1 which contextualises Brunei and its education system and national philosophy, Chap. 2 by Muhammad and Petra provides a comprehensive overview of the history and development of Brunei education system. From a rudimentary system of vernacular education introduced in 1912 under the British Residency, the opening of religious schools in 1953, together with the formulation of several national education policies throughout the twentieth century, the chapter demonstrates the substantial changes made to the national education in order to produce an efficient education system which not only prioritised student quality but also ensured that the foundational principles of MIB were readily applied and upheld. Another transformative milestone in the education curriculum took place in 2009 with the introduction of *Sistem Pendidikan Negara Abad ke-21* (SPN21) or Brunei's National Education System for the 21st century. The launching of this enriched curriculum was intimately related to the announcement of *Wawasan* Brunei 2035 (Brunei Vision 2035) by His Majesty the Sultan and Yang Di-Pertuan of Brunei Darussalam in 2007 which, among others, aims to produce a quality population who are well-educated and highly skilled. The chapter further discusses the adoption of the SPN21 Curriculum and Assessment Framework which aligns to Brunei's Ministry of Education's strategic plan initiatives on quality education. Similar to any modern education system elsewhere in the world, SPN21 has restructured the learning curricula in order to inculcate the twenty-first-century learning skills through student-centred learning approaches. At the same time, SPN21 curriculum continues to give an equal emphasis on the delivery of religious education through the incorporation of the *Jawi* writing and the Arabic language components

---

K. Wood
Sultan Hassanal Bolkiah Institute of Education, Universiti Brunei Darussalam, Bandar Seri Begawan, Brunei
e-mail: keith.wood@ubd.edu.bn

while aiming at entrenching and instilling the tripartite parts of *Melayu Islam Beraja* (MIB). This is the distinctive and unique character of Brunei's education system which has a committed outlook towards creating a more structured, modern and competitive education system while paying a great deal of attention to bolstering and consolidating the national ideology.

Then, in Chap. 3, Sharbawi and Mabud's theoretical discussion on the tripartite parts of MIB (Malay, Islam and Monarchy) and how it shapes Brunei's philosophy of knowledge and education reasserts further the notion of uniqueness and individuality of Brunei's environment. To define the national philosophy in the broadest sense of its meaning, MIB is driven and strengthened by the Islamic principles and values based on the teaching of the Quran and the *Sunnah* as well as the *hadith* of Prophet Muhammad (Peace Be Upon Him). The Malay component of the national philosophy maintains the Malay identity of the country which establishes the preservation of distinctive cultural and traditional values of the Malays. It is worthwhile to mention that, according to the 1959 Constitution and 1961 Nationality Act of Brunei, the definition of 'Malay' encompasses the seven ethnic groups namely Brunei Malay, Kedayan, Tutong, Belait, Dusun, Bisaya and Murut. Hence, the authors argue that the Malay arm of MIB provides the fundamental condition for social cohesion and stability. The monarchy, which constitutes the head of state and government, holds the highest executive authority, as defined by the Brunei 1959 Constitution. The Constitution also outlines the main responsibility of the Monarch in ensuring the people's welfare, wellbeing and general societal progress. This generates a relationship of mutual respect, trust and loyalty between the ruler and the ruled. As argued by Ibrahim (2003), Tuah (2011) and Duraman (2016), the peace and prosperity that Brunei has been known for is primarily due to the implementation of MIB, illustrating the fact that MIB has indeed been carried out successfully as the country's national adhesive and a key source for social stability.

The national ideology is also the basis for the Monarch's transformative vision and aspiration. Marsidi's chapter examines the ways in which His Majesty's *Titahs* or the royal decrees illustrate a strong commitment to MIB as a value system which not only preserves Brunei's traditions and culture but also mitigates the effects of globalisation considered to be undesirable and harmful to the society. His Majesty skilfully connects MIB to the policies and agendas of the country, namely Brunei Vision 2035, *Negara Zikir* (Zikr Nation) and the implementation of the Syariah Penal Code Order 2013. His Majesty also demonstrates his evolving vision in pushing higher education institutions to interact innovatively with the rapid proliferation of new reforms and strategies in the educational world while consistently reminding of the need to uphold the value system of MIB. What this shows us is not only the continued relevance of MIB, as shown by His Majesty's *Titahs*, in shaping and giving meaning to the current national strategies and agenda, but it also effectively leads to the preservation and strengthening of the national ideology in the modern times.

Extending Marsidi's examination of the value system of MIB, we can identify the practice of virtue, morality and manners that constitute this value system. This practice, or the values of *akhlak* (moral), essentially derives from three components of the national ideology. Ibrahim (2003, p. 21) specifically outlines the core components of Malay *akhlak*, which include, among others, positive roles and responsibility towards oneself, family, community and country, having the courage to take risks, and striving to be innovative and knowledgeable. The Islamic *akhlak* promotes steadfastness (*istiqamah*), trustworthiness, being hardworking, promise-keeping, generosity and sincerity (Aziz, 1993, p. 16). In addition, Islam also prohibits the initiation of development plans and strategies which are deviant and do not bring benefits to the people, country and religion (Ibrahim, 2003, p. 24). The Monarchy *akhlak* reinforces these values by ensuring that all decisions, measures and actions made by the monarchical institution and government should not lead to detrimental consequences to the population and the state religion (Ibrahim, 2003, p. 23). Moreover, the Monarch's call should be listened to and acted upon, given his authority as the head of state who acts based on the Monarchy *akhlak*. The people would respond to this as Malay *akhlak* requires that they be responsible and show respect to the Monarch.

The value system of MIB is incorporated in the country's religious education, as discussed in the chapter by Muhammad and Baihaqy. Taking it further from the earlier chapter on the education system of Brunei, this chapter discusses the inclusion of MIB and religious subjects in the education system which are comprehensively delivered from primary and secondary schools to higher education institutions, in both exclusively religious schools and the non-religious (public) school system. The chapter also discusses the attempt to establish a unitary school system with the implementation of the Integrated Education Scheme in 2004. Nonetheless, the reported failure of the scheme in 2005 led to the return of the dual school systems under the Bilingual Educational System for another four years until the introduction of the SPN21 in 2009. As a matter of fact, SPN21 continues with the practices of the existing dual school systems. The authors (Muhammad and Baihaqy) have identified several challenges in the practice of dual school systems, for instance the overlapped contents in religious knowledge taught in public and religious schools and the inadequate coverage of current (modern) issues in the religious curriculum. Although the authors do not put forward specific suggestions to bridge the gaps between the dual systems, they emphasise on the critical role that needs to be taken up by the Ministry of Education (MoE) and Ministry of Religious Affairs so as to achieve and maintain an adequate education system for the nation.

As extensively discussed throughout the book, the centrality of Brunei's national philosophy, *Melayu Islam Beraja* (MIB), to the country's development and planning is evident in policies and strategies that have been implemented by the government since the 90s. The most recent and pivotal of these policies and strategies are *Wawasan* Brunei 2035 and SPN21, both of which pursue excellence in knowledge and moral character based on the teaching of MIB.

As also seen in several chapters in the book, the internalisation and preservation of MIB philosophy are strengthened throughout the teacher education programmes in both KUPU SB and in SHBIE at UBD. MIB values and skills are weaved and integrated in the innovative pedagogical content implemented in these teacher education programs, among which are twenty-first-century skills in teaching and learning, digital learning and assessment. In this sense, teacher education supports the adoption of the SPN21 Curriculum and Assessment Framework which aligns with Brunei's Ministry of Education's strategic plan initiatives on quality education which was discussed in the chapter by Muhammad and Petra. Teacher education encompasses well-established moral values and characters, those that are of high importance in teacher quality. Aisah (2006, p. 28) specifically outlines that the most important thing is the goal of education itself which is to form human beings who have the capability to create prosperity and happiness of life for self and others. This echoes Marsidi's chapter on the practice and values of *akhlak* deriving from the components of the national ideology which needs to be reflected in the teaching profession. In short, the teacher training programs in Brunei, particularly the one at SHBIE-UBD, aim to produce teachers that are reflective, innovative, research-informed, global citizens and role models imbued with MIB values (Jaidin et al., 2015).

20.3 Curriculum and Pedagogical Issues: Key Points and Further Thoughts

Three of the chapters in Part II refer to developments in the MTeach programme—considered to be a milestone innovation in teacher training in Brunei—a move that has set Brunei apart in the Asian region when it comes to teacher education. First, Salleh et al. in Chap. 6 provide an account of a study of the impact on new teachers' pedagogical beliefs about the integration of technology in the curriculum to enhance learners' twenty-first-century skills development of participation in a teacher education module entitled *Technology, Pedagogy and Content Knowledge* (TPACK). It reveals how teacher candidates' beliefs can be shaped through their collaboration in designing and planning technology-integrated lessons using a declarative, procedural, schematic and strategic framework. The authors explain how the TPACK framework provides a template to guide the teachers' collaborative, interdisciplinary planning, teaching and review of lessons leading to the development of their pedagogical content knowledge.

Then, Said in Chap. 7 reports on the use of a teaching approach designed to help students understand science concepts through engagement in classroom discussion. Beginning teachers planned, taught and reviewed lessons enacted during their school-based professional practice module in the Master of Teaching programme. Their students were required to complete a worksheet in a sequence of three stages: working individually, working in a group, and contributing to whole class discussion of the answers required by the worksheet. Designing an effective worksheet proved challenging for the teachers. Implementation of the three-stage lesson also posed problems of timing. However, the students' discussions provided the teachers with invaluable insights into what the students needed to learn to achieve the intended understanding of the science concepts; in itself an important step towards developing pedagogical content knowledge.

Next, Latif et al. in Chap. 8 describe the development of inclusive education in Brunei Darussalam from the establishment of a Special Education Unit in 1994 to the introduction of the MOE Strategic Objective 02 in 2018 'to improve system-wide inclusion by ensuring access to quality learning and educational attainment opportunities for all learners of diverse needs; to develop them to their full potential'. To achieve this objective, a Master of Teaching programme in Inclusive Special Education was designed to prepare teachers to both co-teach with subject teachers in regular classrooms and support students with moderate and profound support needs in alternative inclusive settings. *Education For All* in Brunei has further resource implications including the need for infrastructure to ensure physical accessibility, capacity building to provide Special Educational Needs Assistants, investment in specialist expertise, curriculum change and increased public awareness of inclusive education.

The other two chapters in Part II focus on other pedagogical and educational issues beyond teacher education and the MTeach programme. Specifically, Chap. 9 by Yusof and Alas reports on a study of the effectiveness of using role play in an elective course at UBD's Language Centre to teach the language of the Dusun ethnic group living in Brunei, Sabah, Sarawak and Kalimantan. In groups, students developed a performance from a scenario provided by their teacher to present to the class. The authors found this approach to be successful. The study employed a quasi-experimental design. Students in the experimental group were found to improve in oral proficiency, confidence, memorisation and use of vocabulary.

Finally, Latif in Chap. 10 explores the trade-off between academic performance and students' well-being. Standardised assessment can be used to evaluate the quality of an educational system. An example is the OECD Programme for International Student Assessment (PISA). The outcome may be seen as a measure of national competitiveness and prestige, and may influence national education reform. Brunei Darussalam participated in PISA in 2018 and was ranked third amongst the participating ASEAN countries. However, the PISA snapshot report on Brunei students' well-being raised questions about the quality of their lives. Acknowledging that both academic achievement and well-being are desirable outcomes for students, the author explored what can be done to design a valid and reliable instrument to assess Bruneian students' wellbeing. Her study examined whether using the Youth Self-Report in the Malay culture of Brunei would produce similar recognition of problems identified within Western culture. She reports that support for this is mixed.

All the chapters mentioned above point to varied innovations and reforms in support of the mission of the MoE, which is to provide a holistic education system through a meaningful and coherent curriculum introduced in relevant educational programmes that put students at the heart of attention. We, nonetheless, are well aware of the many challenges and limitations that are still in place, as the education system is going through transformations in response to local needs and to international, regional and global forces. Not least is the challenge inherent in a competence-based education system to avoid placing limitations on teaching and learning through its definition of performance and the steps taken to appraise it.

20.4 MIB in Teacher Training, Curriculum, Classroom Practice and Society: Key Points and Further Thoughts

The incorporation of MIB in Brunei's formal education system is a major theme that is examined throughout the book. Relatedly, the roles of MIB teachers in classroom teaching and in the educational and moral growth of their students are also examined. As a matter of fact, the efforts to incorporate MIB in teacher training have been met with various issues and challenges, as some authors have demonstrated. For instance, Chap. 11 by Ahad and Baihaqy examines and evaluates the incorporation of the MIB courses into the national teacher training program. Drawing on the findings of a study conducted with student teachers in KUPU SB, the chapter reveals these students' experiences with the program. The importance of educational visits to sites of interest referred to in the lectures was stressed. The students highlighted the importance of providing opportunities for the exploration of examples of *Negara Zikir* to develop their understanding. The primary aim for the inclusion of MIB in the training program is to equip student teachers with better knowledge in, and understanding of, the national ideology. Nonetheless, in their study the authors have found that many student teachers do not possess an adequate understanding of the value components of MIB. This problem makes it difficult for the primary aim to be achieved. Hence, the authors recommend that this inadequacy needs to be addressed before the student teachers can work on their teaching competency. Indeed, the teacher training program at KUPU SB should also aim to enhance student teachers' learning competency alongside its current purpose. The findings of Ahad and Baihaqy's study point out the need to revise the curriculum content of the existing MIB courses. As discussed in Part I of the book, MIB encompasses a myriad of values pertaining to the three integral components of the national ideology.

Teachers' competency becomes much more critical in light of Madin et al.'s study that explores the internalisation strategies of MIB values and principles as embedded in the curriculum designed for Year 7 (Chap. 12). The chapter discusses the incorporation of MIB in the Year 7 curriculum as part of the government's intervention efforts directed towards the reported and observed decline of morality and social values in recent times among local youths. A textbook is available for Year 7 teachers and their students which addresses the themes of living a healthy life, showing goodwill towards others, and protecting the environment, in submission to the monarch. Madin et al. provide a content analysis of the textbook while emphasising the importance of the teacher in creating learning activities for their students drawing on the contents of this resource. The MIB subject in the Year 7 curriculum is essentially about character education which aims to nurture and promote the development of character values and virtues and to foster Bruneian values in everyday life. They explain that four internalisation strategies—modelling, integration, multimodality and reinforcement—are used to develop students' moral and social values. These four main strategies are aimed at helping students internalise the knowledge, practice, sense of morality and social attitudes pertaining to the national ideology. The textbook consists of three main themes with a total of 12 units including a mixture of pictures of real scenarios and people as well as inclusion of His Majesty's *Titah* and Quranic verses. The real pictures provide modelling and reinforcement for Year 7 students. Furthermore, the inclusion of Quranic verses is aligned with the need for the Islamisation of knowledge which is elaborated in Chap. 14 by Baihaqy.

As shown by Madin et al., through students' engagement with the exercises and activities provided by the Year 7 MIB textbook, teachers have the opportunity to design learning situations which lead students to incorporate the social and moral values enshrined in the MIB curriculum within themselves as guiding principles. In *Learning and Awareness*, Marton and Booth (1997) address the question: How do we gain knowledge about the world? They explain why, for example, constructivism (individual *and* social) is not helpful in answering this question because, in both its forms, it creates a borderline between action and behaviour (the 'outer') and mental acts (the 'inner')—a dualism between what is within the learner and what surrounds him/her. They reformulated the question to become: How do people experience the world and, if one way of experiencing the world can be judged better than another, how can they come to experience it in a better way? The thesis of their book is that 'by learning about how the world appears to others, we will learn what the world is like, and what the world could be like' (Marton & Booth, 1997, p. 13).

What could be the theory of learning that underpins the design of the learning situations referred to by Madin et al.? It would need to be a theory that focuses on the qualitatively different ways in which individuals experience phenomena in the world (non-dualistic) and the variation that implies. A theory of learning that specifies designs for teaching which juxtapose different ways of experiencing phenomena such as moral values, opening dimensions of variation in relation to critical aspects of the object of learning, such that learners can come to experience the phenomenon in more powerful ways. In their description of learning activities for Year 7 MIB, Madin et al. refer to the following:

- The inclusion of varied illustrations to assist students' understanding and appreciation towards moral values, by enlightening them with real-life knowledge and surroundings outside of the curriculum.
- The infusion of contexts involving adolescents or secondary school students.
- Activities that encourage a communicative approach, self-reflection and critical thinking while providing opportunities for peer-learning.

But what are the views of teacher educators at SHBIE about the Year 7 textbook? Madin et al. carried out some interviews to find out. In Chap. 13, the authors present their findings which they claim amount to necessary guidelines for student- and practising-teachers on the potential of the MIB curriculum. The insights from these educators who are recognised for their expertise in Malay language and MIB highlight the need to take both subjects, Malay Language and MIB, into account as these have overlapping sentiments and materials that could help emphasise the elements of noble values and morality. Having a good command of Malay language is seen to be essential for strengthening MIB teachers' comprehension of the MIB curriculum and its aims of internalising and refining moral and social values.

Madin et al. in Chap. 12 argue that the success of the internalisation strategies is largely dependent upon the capacity and competency of MIB educators to effectively implement the strategies and the overall MIB curriculum. This finding speaks strongly to the findings of Ahad and Baihaqy's study on the critical need for teachers to acquire both learning and teaching competency. As further discussed in Chap. 13, Madin et al. equally emphasise on the need for teacher educators to be well equipped with, and internalise, the knowledge on MIB as well as develop a strong familiarity with the overall curriculum outlook. One could argue that such competency is similarly required for all subjects taught at school. However, as MIB provides character education, students are more likely to perceive adults in their environment as role models and the former are more likely to pick up the behaviours, attitudes, language use and manners of the latter. Absence, or lack, of immediate role models could easily sway students to resort to other role models instead (for instance, social media influencers, see Chap. 15 for more details), hence limiting the internalisation process. Thus, it is vital for teacher educators to be acquainted with the character values of MIB particularly those they find personally relevant and relatable. Teacher educators also need to recognise their misconception towards MIB and undertake sense-making exercises from which they can transform into personal narratives which are useful to enhance their learning and teaching expertise.

It is essential for these teachers to possess the core values of MIB as stated by the CDD (see Fig. 13.1, Chap. 13) in order to portray an impactful teacher's character and identity of MIB. An overlapping insight as in Chap. 14 is discussed in this chapter on the need for the inclusion of Islamisation knowledge both in the curriculum and textbook of MIB, which can be extended to early childhood and care education.

In Chap. 13, Madin et al. also highlight the importance for MIB educators to possess linguistic competency in Malay language to support the internalisation strategies specified in the curriculum. As a mode of delivery and a means of expression, Malay language, which is also the home language for most students, supports students' learning and understanding of MIB. Likewise, the authors show how appreciation of the sound of the language could lead to positive literacy development among students. Language, in the form of the Quranic verses, also plays an important role in the integration of the Islamic knowledge in the country's science education curriculum, as discussed in Chap. 14 by Baihaqy. The Quran, which essentially provides the ground for the nature of the universe, is an ideal foundation of education for Muslim children. Indeed, there is a dualism between revealed and acquired knowledge. Muhammad and Bakar (2013) have argued that quoting verses from the Holy Quran that refer to a particular scientific element is not enough to solve this problem. Rather they claim that 'humans should use their intellect to develop harmony between faith and reason'.

In Chap. 14, Baihaqy returns to the earlier solution to the problem that involves quoting verses from the Holy Quran that refer to a particular scientific element. Here he takes great measure to improve the existing textbook. The author discusses the need for the Islamisation of Science to be included in the school curriculum in order to integrate Quranic spiritual knowledge. Baihaqy examines the Year 7 Science curriculum textbook and explores how each chapter in the curriculum includes verses from the Quran. The observation made by the author is that three out of eight verses were not aligned with the content of the topics in the science textbook. The author calls for appropriate training for curriculum developers so as to address this shortcoming in the Year 7 Science curriculum. In the same vein, Baihaqy recommends that training or re-training should also be provided for teachers, specifically to enable them to have a deeper appreciation of and alertness towards the core messages in the Quranic verses as they explain scientific concepts and knowledge to students. In other words, teacher educators should possess not only sufficient knowledge to help them convey clearly the messages behind the verses (*tafseer*) but also proficiency in the language and in correct pronunciation (*tajweed*) of the Quranic verses. Only when science teachers acquire such solid understanding of the Quranic knowledge that they would be able to successfully nurture an appreciation of the Quranic verses among science students.

Although the MIB subject is a main pillar in the school curriculum and is central to any school's vision and direction, and is present in every aspect of life in Brunei, how far MIB is being implemented, perceived and practiced by individuals beyond schools remains more or less unexplored, as we have argued earlier in the book. Hence, what is discussed in Chap. 15 by Ahad regarding social media influencers and MIB is indeed refreshing and sheds light on the overall scholarship on MIB and its relevance to the current world. Specifically, in this chapter, informed by a study on social media influencers and their impacts on the public understanding of MIB, Ahad seeks to find out whether these influencers can extend the MIB-based character education beyond the four walls of classrooms.

Ahad also discusses the presentation of MIB on the internet through social media. He observes that those who would seek to influence others must uphold the highest values of MIB in themselves whilst there is a need to maintain its relevance in today's world. The results of his interviews with a number of social influencers reveal that they are aware of this responsibility. The sample includes a preacher, a comedian and a DJ who revealed their approaches in adopting and adapting their online presence to conform with MIB. The findings of the study demonstrate that, while religious and educational online contents are likely to enhance the representation of religious images of the influencers, they may not necessarily complement well the MIB education inside classrooms. These influencers feel pressured to ensure their dress code, behaviour, language as well as the values and attitudes they have portrayed online are aligned with the national ideology. They also commented on instances where certain provoking acts had caused unnecessary cultural and religious insensitivity. While social media influencers are not considered to be conventional sources of education, due to their close connection to young people and the fact that there are young individuals who also aspire to become online influencers, social media influencers have indeed become increasingly powerful sources of influence in the personal life of many young people these days. Thus, the findings of Ahad's study demonstrates the need for the incorporation of social media education and awareness into the internalisation strategies of MIB knowledge. Such incorporation will not only teach young people about the real-world situations and widen their knowledge context, but also help guide them and deepen their understanding of morality, ethics and values.

20.5 COVID-19, Society and Education: Little-Known Long-Lasting Impacts

The COVID-19 pandemic has led to massive investments in technologies and innovations so as to help enhance the teaching, learning and research experiences of all those participating in education, from students, teachers and professional staff to those in support and leadership positions. The pandemic has also witnessed a switch and push for blended learning in Brunei. While schools and higher education institutions have had two semesters to respond to the sudden changes and to accommodate and try out certain technological and pedagogical interventions, what lies ahead in terms of effectiveness, compatibility and satisfaction remains open for further investigation (see Shahrill et al. in Chap. 16; and Noorashid et al. in Chap. 17).

The pandemic has also instilled new discourses and vocabularies in the sphere of education, notably *mental health* and *emotional wellbeing* (Alam & Hoon in Chap. 18), those terms that are now dominant and appear rather frequently in writings on COVID-19 and education. Intense online learning during and beyond the pandemic has already led to tremendous health-related problems, causing consequences that may not be amendable in the short term. Indeed, the pandemic has led to a *digidemic* in education, a term that Alam and Hoon conceptualise and treat with care in their chapter.

And on a bright note, the pandemic has also brought back to the central stage core values of education in general and of the internationalisation of education in particular, whereby care, support, compassion and hospitality are embraced and put in practice by all members of education communities, regardless of race, language, ethnicity, religion, belief and nationality (see Keasberry et al. in Chap. 19). The dominant commercialisation mentality and the neoliberal mindsets driving education and the internationalisation of education over the past several decades are being questioned and even shunned, as humanity and ethical conduct of internationalisation are taking over in educational settings around the world including Brunei. In addition, Keasberry et al. engage with the new meanings associated with the *internationalisation at home* that Phùng and Phan (2021) discuss and theorise in their examination of the pandemic situation and its impact on Vietnam's higher education.

To take the conversation even further, the pandemic has also invited us to think about how Brunei's national philosophy MIB and the Sultan's leadership have enabled Brunei to set an excellent example for the world in terms of containing the pandemic while allowing the economy and education to operate under safe conditions. Importantly, the current success does not mean that Brunei would allow itself to lose sight of the potential challenges brought about by the pandemic and its long-term consequences. Indeed, with regard to education and its relations with globalisation and reform, MIB does require and expect continuous reflection on the part of policy, educational leadership, planning, curriculum, teaching, learning and internationalisation. We would like to close this book with the many inspirations from Brunei and its national philosophy for education, the inspirations that have been demonstrated throughout the book as well as shall arise as readers engage with this collection.

References

Aisah, binti Haji Mohd. Yusof, Hajah. (2006). Program Pendidikan Awal Kanak-Kanak dalam Institusi Pendidikan Perguruan. In *Fifty years of teacher education in Brunei Darussalam, a special commerative publication 1956–2006*. Universiti Brunei Darussalam, Sultan Hassanal Bolkiah Institute of Education.

Aziz, H. A. A. (1993). Melayu Islam Beraja Negara Brunei Darussalam. In *Akademi Pengajian Brunei: Melayu Islam Beraja*. Universiti Brunei Darussalam.

Duraman, H. S. (2016). *Melayu Islam Beraja: Satu Interpretasi*. Dewan Bahasa dan Pustaka Brunei.

Ibrahim, H. A. L. (2003). *Melayu Islam Beraja: Pengantar Huraian*. Universiti Brunei Darussalam.

Jaidin, J. H., Shahrill, M., & Jawawi, R. (2015). Institut Pendidikan Sultan Hassanal Bolkiah (IPSHB): 'Nurturing our legacy' Memupuk Warisan Kitani. In B. Tengah & N. R. Mokhtar (Eds.), *Tradisi dan Reformasi Pendidikan – Merista Jasa Sultan Omar' Ali Saifuddien Sa'adul Khairi Waddien sempena 100 years (1914–2014) formal education* (Vol. 2, pp. 271–279). Brunei Darussalam.

Marton, F., & Booth, S. (1997). *Learning and awareness*. Routledge.

Muhammad, N., & Bakar, O. (2013). Implementation of the "Integrated education system" in Brunei Darussalam: Issues and challenges. *Journal of Middle Eastern and Islamic Studies (in Asia)*, 7(4), 97–120.

Phùng, T., & Phan, L. H. (2021). Higher education in Vietnam and a new vision for internationalization at home post COVID-19. In J. Gillen, L. C. Kelley, & L. H. Phan (Eds.), *Vietnam at the vanguard: New perspectives across time, space, and community*. Springer International.

Tuah, H. D. (2011). *The implementation of Melayu Islam Beraja in Brunei Darussalam's public administration*. Brunei Government Printing Department.

Glossary

adab Courtesy
adat Customs
adhan Call to prayer
ahkam Obedience to the commands
Akademi Pengajian Brunei Academy of Brunei Studies
'*akhlāq* (also *akhlak*) Moral
al-Din A way of life
Alhamdulillah Praises to Allah
al-manhaj al-'ilmī Scientific method
amanah Trust
aqidah Creed
Assalamualaikum Warahmatullahi Wabarakatuh Peace be upon you with God's mercy and blessings
'*Aqly* Acquired knowledge
Awar galat Respectful humility
Bābu Al- Nikāḥ Marriage
Bahasa Jiwa Bangsa Language is the Soul of the Nation
Bahasa Melayu Malay Language
balai Community hall
Baldatun Tayyibatun wa Rabbun Ghafur A peaceful country worthy of God's mercy

Belia Berkualiti The quality youth
Belia Shumul The complete youth
Beraja Monarchy
Calak Brunei The Bruneian mould
catip An Arabic preacher also known in Brunei as an official of a mosque who is a rank below an Imam
deva God
devaraja Divine kingship
Dewan Bahasa dan Pustaka Language and Literature Bureau
Dukhan Smoke
Fara'iḍ Inheritance
Fiqh Jurisprudence
funduq A place of temporary residence or hotel
fuqaha Jurists
Generasi Berwawasan The visionary generation
hadrah Traditional/folk-music instrument
halaqah Tutorial
haram Proscribed by Islamic law
hijab Headscarf
hijabi Women who wear the *hijab*
Hijrah Muslim calendar
ḥuffāẓ Person who memorises the Quran
'ibādat Worship
Imam Leader of Muslim prayers
InsyaAllah If God Wills
Istiadat Traditions
Istiqamah Steadfastness
Jawatankuasa Konsep MIB The MIB Concept Committee
Junjung Ziarah Meet-and-greet
kātib Elite scholars
Ke Arah Kesempurnaan Insan Towards Human Excellence
Ketua Ugama Rasmi Official Head of Religion
mahram A member of one's family with whom marriage would be considered *haram* or proscribed by Islamic law
Majlis Ilmu Knowledge Convention
Majlis Tertinggi Kebangsaan MIB MIB Supreme Council
Majlis Tertinggi Melayu Islam Beraja The Supreme Council of Malay Islamic Monarchy
Mawlid Birthday anniversary of Prophet Muhammad

Melayu Malay
Menteri Besar Chief Minister
Nafs spirit
Naqly Religious knowledge
Negara Zikir God-conscious nation
Pelajaran Al-Quran dan Pengetahuan Agama Islam Learning Al-Qur'ān and Islamic Revealed Knowledge
Pengetahuan Ugama Islam Islamic Religious Knowledge
Perintah Pendidikan Ugama Wajib 2012 Order 2012 of Compulsory Religious Education
pondok (1) a small hut temporary home; (2) institution of Islamic learning in the form of traditional and orthodox
Program Perantis Apprentice Programme
Program Rancangan Pembelajaran Di Rumah Home-Based Learning Television Programme
Puak Jati Indigenous ethnic tribes
Pusat Ilmu Teras The Centre for Core Knowledge
Pusat Pengajian dan Penyebaran Al-Quran MABIMS Centre for MABIMS Al-Quran Studies and Dissemination
Quran Holy Book in Islam
raja Monarch/king
Rātib Saman Reading of the Quran
Ruh Soul
sahsiah Identity
Salam Giving greetings
s*alawāt* Praise towards the Prophet Muhammad
Shar'iyyat Legitimacy
Sistem Pendidikan Dwi Bahasa Bilingual Education System
Sistem Pendidikan Negara Abad ke-21 National Educational System for the 21st Century
Skim Rintis Pendidikan Sepadu Pilot Scheme on Integrated Education
solat Pray
Sunnah Prophetic way of life
Surau Prayer hall
tafsīr 'ilmī Scientific exegesis
tafsīr **also** *tafseer* Quranic Exegesis
tajweed Correct pronunciation of the Quranic verses
Tarbiyah Islamiah Islamic Education
Taṣawwuf Sufism

tawhid Monotheism/The Oneness of God
Titah Royal decree or command
Ugama Religion
ulama Scholar
Ulil Amri Minkum The supreme leader of the government and the nation and in the context of Brunei
ulil amri Those in authority who manage and administer
Ummah Community
'Uṣūluddīn Principles of Religion
Utamakan Bahasa Melayu Prioritise the Malay language
Wawasan Brunei 2035 Brunei Vision 2035/the national vision of Brunei Darussalam
Zakat Annual alms tax
Zikir Brunei A traditional Islamic *dhikr*
Zikr Remembrance of Allah

Index

A
Adolescents, 198, 201–212, 236, 238, 239, 247, 424
Ah as-Sunnah Wa al-Jama'ah, 32, 39, 41, 46, 57, 74, 77, 220, 225, 306, 310, 317
al-Tawhid, 60, 93, 94, 288

B
British Protectorate, 21, 22, 24–28, 74, 92–96, 221
Brunei, 1, 21, 45, 67–83, 88, 148, 152, 177, 198, 219–232, 236, 261, 289, 306, 325, 356, 382, 395, 415
Bruneian children, 31, 34, 93, 154, 202
Bruneian identity, 5, 47, 49, 52, 54, 63, 72, 79, 99, 227, 277, 318

Bruneian national identity, 5, 31, 60–62, 77, 82, 83, 100
Bruneianness, 49, 53, 78
Bruneian tribes, 230, 231
Brunei Darussalam, 1–16, 21, 22, 28–30, 32, 37, 39–41, 45–63, 85–101, 108, 151–173, 177, 198, 219–222, 235–257, 261, 285–303, 306, 307, 310–312, 315, 325–349, 356, 357, 360, 361, 399, 405, 415–416, 420, 421
Brunei Darussalam education system, 2, 3, 7, 8, 13, 15, 21–41, 80, 151, 154–156, 220, 249, 277, 326–328, 363, 372, 416, 422
Brunei education, 2, 4–7, 24, 30–32, 34, 89, 93, 99, 100, 158–160, 173, 236–239, 256, 278, 326, 349, 372, 416–419

436 INDEX

Brunei ethnic languages, 178, 179
Brunei Vision 2035, 3, 5, 49, 68, 158, 246, 416, 417

C

Celebrification, 15, 308, 316
Challenges, 3, 11, 13, 14, 27, 35, 41, 46, 76, 81, 83, 98–100, 114, 115, 118, 134, 138, 140–142, 144–147, 161, 171, 179–181, 200, 225, 229, 231, 237, 238, 277, 278, 326, 339, 340, 342, 343, 345–349, 357–365, 370, 371, 379, 381, 384, 385, 393, 395, 398, 401, 402, 406, 409, 418, 421, 422, 428
Class activities, 189
Collaborative learning, 138, 275
Community, 24, 25, 28, 30, 38, 48, 50, 51, 53, 55, 59, 61, 70, 77, 79, 82, 87, 90, 95, 98, 135, 158, 169, 170, 200, 211, 225, 227, 238, 246, 247, 249–251, 254, 265, 267, 269, 270, 288, 306, 311, 312, 319, 326, 331, 333, 335, 336, 346, 348, 349, 356, 363, 370, 371, 395, 401–405, 407, 418, 428
Conceptual understanding procedure (CUP), 133–138, 140–148
Constructivist, 133–148
Continuity of tradition, 69–72
Coronavirus disease 2019 (COVID-2019), 2, 15–16, 212, 325–349, 355–358, 360, 362–369, 371, 372, 377–380, 382, 393–409, 427–428
Curriculum, 2, 7–15, 22, 24, 27, 31, 33–37, 40, 41, 46, 77, 86–89, 91, 92, 94, 95, 97, 99–101, 111, 146, 153, 166, 171, 173, 222–223, 225–232, 235–257, 261–280, 285–303, 315, 327, 344, 358, 363, 365, 369, 379, 380, 399, 416, 419–428

D

Digital pandemic (digidemic), 377–389, 428
Dusun language, 177–179, 185, 190–193

E

Eastern, 201, 211
Education, 1–16, 21, 46, 75, 76 , 78, 87–90, 107, 134, 151–173, 179, 197, 220–222, 236, 262, 285–303, 311, 326, 357, 378–382, 396, 415–419
Educational practices, 325–349
Education policy, 25, 29–31, 152, 198, 326–331, 380, 416
Education system, 2–8, 11–13, 15, 21–41, 46, 78, 80, 97, 107, 108, 111, 125, 151–154, 156, 160, 198, 200, 220, 221, 223, 239, 249, 277, 286, 326–328, 361, 363, 372, 395, 416–419, 421, 422
Educator, 3, 6, 13–15, 47, 108, 111, 118–125, 128, 135, 142, 198, 200, 220, 222, 224, 225, 238, 250, 252–256, 261–280, 326, 343–349, 359, 362–364, 367–371, 400, 401, 407, 408, 424–426
Emotional wellbeing, 362–364, 371, 427
Evolving education, 69, 75–79
Externalising, 202, 203, 206

F

Facebook, 272, 275, 277, 307, 316

G

Global, 3, 4, 7, 14, 16, 21, 71, 72, 77, 82, 97, 107, 154, 156, 158, 167, 170, 197–212, 235, 269, 270, 302, 306, 313, 326, 348, 359, 377–381, 389, 395–399, 408, 419, 422

Globalisation, 1–16, 79–82, 197, 235, 236, 277, 311, 314, 395, 415–417, 428

Globalisation and youth, 69, 79–82

Governance, 46, 47, 49, 50, 56, 60, 63, 68, 73, 82, 336

Government, 3, 5, 7, 24–32, 40, 47, 49, 52, 54, 56–60, 62, 68, 72–74, 78, 82, 87–89, 91, 93, 95, 96, 99, 152, 168–172, 198, 199, 205, 220, 222, 251, 271, 310, 314, 317, 318, 326–331, 333–337, 341, 342, 348, 349, 356, 359, 361, 370, 371, 378, 382, 401, 405, 408, 417–419, 423

H

Higher education disruption, 388

Higher education institution (HIE), 75, 98, 326, 328, 336–338, 347, 348, 355–372, 379, 387, 398, 400, 417, 418, 427

Holistic education, 12, 41, 99, 421

Home, 78, 92, 115, 117, 249, 270, 332, 333, 341, 343, 344, 364, 370, 379, 381–387, 389, 393, 395, 399–404, 406–409, 425, 428

Humanistic internationalisation, 393–409

Hysteresis, 377–389

I

Identity, 3, 5, 7, 14, 22, 27, 31, 40, 41, 45–63, 68, 72, 76, 77, 79, 80, 83, 95, 99–101, 183, 220, 227, 266, 272, 306, 311, 313, 316, 364, 417

Impacts, 2, 3, 15, 16, 34, 46, 73, 76, 80, 82, 127, 154–155, 172, 181, 191–193, 197, 203, 210, 221, 232, 266, 271, 273, 305–319, 326, 331, 335, 338, 347–349, 357, 364, 371, 377–382, 388, 389, 398, 405, 407, 420, 426–428

Inclusive, 2, 51, 151–173, 407, 420, 421

Inclusive Special Education (ISE), 168–169, 420

Independence, 5, 10, 22, 30, 32, 35–40, 45, 46, 69, 73, 96–98, 152–153, 238, 250, 265, 327

Initial teacher preparation (ITP), 7, 167, 339

Integration of knowledge, 13, 14, 35, 285–303, 425

Internalisation, 235–257, 261, 262, 269, 272, 278, 419, 422–425, 427

Internalising, 201–203, 206, 237, 246, 255, 256, 424

International student care, 405

International student experiences, 393–409

International students, 39, 98, 368, 395–408

Internet, 41, 80, 81, 114, 115, 118, 120, 121, 272, 307, 311, 315, 332, 343, 344, 359–361, 370, 371, 380–384, 389, 402, 426
Islamic education, 7, 23–25, 31, 33, 34, 39, 74, 85–101, 248, 249

J

Jawi, 33, 37, 41, 49, 53, 54, 57, 77, 88–91, 100, 230, 231, 416

M

Malay Hindu Buddhist Kingdom, 22
Malay Islamic Monarchy, *see Melayu Islam Beraja* (MIB, Malay Islamic Monarchy)
Malay Islamic Monarchy state, 22, 46, 219
Malay language, 31–33, 48, 51–54, 77, 79, 87–89, 91, 152, 178, 183, 220, 221, 236, 261–280, 312, 330, 424, 425
Malayness, 55, 56, 80
Master of Teaching (MTeach), 2, 6, 12, 108, 109, 134, 135, 148, 167–169, 222, 263, 339–343, 361, 420, 421
Melayu Islam Beraja (MIB, Malay Islamic Monarchy), 2, 32, 33, 37, 45, 52, 68, 82, 85, 98, 99, 158, 219, 220, 236, 262, 305, 335, 416
MIB identity, 48, 220
Micro-celebrity, 308, 312, 313, 316, 319
Ministry of Education (MoE), 6, 8, 11, 12, 22, 27, 30, 32–37, 40, 48, 53, 85, 86, 88, 89, 96, 97, 99, 100, 148, 151–154, 157–161, 165, 167–169, 171, 173, 237, 267, 270, 278, 279, 289, 326–328, 331–333, 336, 340, 341, 349, 361, 416, 419, 421
Misconceptions, 34, 97, 134, 135, 140, 143, 144, 146, 147, 425
Model Inclusive Schools (MIS), 159, 170
Moral education, 76, 239, 246, 250, 254–257, 262, 265, 266, 269, 270, 272, 275, 279

N

National curriculum, 2, 8, 22, 24, 46, 99–101, 153, 237, 256, 265, 278, 327
National philosophy, 2, 5, 6, 14, 33, 45, 47, 49, 68–71, 78, 80, 82, 88, 158, 219, 222, 225, 236, 248, 257, 264, 269, 270, 279, 288–289, 302, 335, 416, 417, 419, 428
Negara Zikir, 49, 73, 224, 225, 230, 231, 317, 417, 422

O

Online learning, 333, 338, 341, 343, 346, 359–361, 363–370, 372, 377–389, 402, 427
Online learning pandemic, 360

P

Pandemic, 2, 15, 16, 325, 326, 336–339, 341, 343–349, 356–360, 362–372, 377–383, 385, 386, 388, 395, 398, 399, 401–404, 406–408, 427, 428

Pandemic pedagogy, 355–372
Pedagogical beliefs, 107–128, 420
Pedagogy, 107–128, 165, 220, 255, 263, 264, 269, 273, 275, 276, 344, 346–348, 358, 359, 362, 365–369, 371, 397, 400, 401, 407
Pedagogy opportunities, 366–369
Perception, 35, 71, 79, 115, 178, 182, 183, 188–190, 193, 203, 204, 226, 227, 261–280, 317–319, 388, 402
Personalised learning, 111, 116, 117
Preservation and promotion of religion, 54, 69, 73–75
Preservice teachers, 107–128, 166
Primary, 6, 13, 26, 27, 30, 32, 33, 35, 36, 39, 48, 57, 62, 70, 75, 78, 85, 88, 89, 93, 95, 96, 99, 100, 108, 114, 153, 154, 156, 159, 161, 168, 171, 172, 223, 226, 237, 239, 256, 264, 326–336, 342, 344, 345, 381, 382, 385, 418, 422
Programme for International Student Assessment (PISA), 2, 3, 198–200, 209, 210, 421

Q

Quran, 14, 33, 34, 40, 41, 49, 53, 59, 70, 71, 88, 91, 94, 96, 157, 170, 247, 249, 287, 289–291, 293, 297, 299, 302, 303, 312, 329, 417, 425, 426

R

Reflective teachers, 419
Reformation, 237, 255, 268, 274, 279, 372
Religiosity, 313, 314
Role-play, 177–193

S

Sahsiah, 222
Science education, 7, 134, 135, 147, 148, 285–303, 425
Science teaching and learning, 134, 147
Secondary and tertiary levels, 326
Secular, 62, 70, 81, 221, 289, 290
Sistem Pendidikan Negara Abad ke-21 (National Education System for the 21st Century, SPN21), 2, 5–8, 36, 37, 40, 41, 68, 85, 86, 89, 97, 99, 108, 109, 111, 157, 237, 253, 255, 262, 268, 273–275, 278, 327, 328, 330, 336, 416–419
Social media influencer (SMIs), 15, 307–309, 312–315, 319, 425–427
Social values, 236–239, 246–249, 251–254, 256, 262, 265, 267–269, 272, 273, 276, 278, 423, 424
Special education, 153, 154, 156, 161, 165–168, 173
Special Education Needs Assistant (SENA), 153, 156, 159, 161, 165–169, 171, 172
Special Education Unit (SEU), 152, 156, 157, 159–162, 166, 168, 170–173, 420
Spiritual, 14, 35, 36, 56, 62, 63, 72, 236, 246–250, 253, 255, 262, 265, 268, 269, 272, 273, 285–303, 405, 426
Standardised testing, 197–212
Student-centred learning, 36, 41, 107–128, 138, 416
Students, 3, 25, 48, 70, 86, 108, 133, 151, 178, 197, 220, 236, 262, 296, 326, 356, 378, 395, 416
Students active discussion, 228
Sultan Haji Hassanal Bolkiah, 22, 32, 33, 67, 68

T

Teacher education, 2, 3, 5–7, 12, 108, 128, 152, 220, 221, 419–421
Teacher-training, 6, 12–15, 135, 166, 220–223, 274, 303, 342, 365, 419, 420, 422–427
Teachers training education (TTE), 224–232
Teaching, 2, 23, 47, 71, 88, 107, 133–148, 157, 177, 220, 246, 262, 289, 313, 329, 356, 358–365, 379, 400, 417
Teaching and learning, 8, 10, 25, 40, 76, 89, 107–109, 111–115, 117–125, 128, 134, 147, 148, 165, 184–187, 223, 250, 251, 253–256, 262–268, 271–278, 329, 333, 336, 338, 340, 346, 347, 356–361, 364–371, 379, 400, 419, 422
Technology, pedagogy and content knowledge (TPACK), 107–128, 420
Textbook, 14, 27, 40, 47, 86, 89, 91, 95, 100, 237–256, 261–265, 267–278, 290–302, 423–426
Transformative vision and aspirations, 67–83, 417
21st century skills, 8, 11, 12, 40, 41, 75–77, 99–101, 108, 109, 111, 116, 119–121, 123, 125, 419, 420

W

Wawasan Brunei 2035, 3, 5–7, 36, 73, 158, 159, 173, 405, 416–419
Wellbeing, 60, 72, 157, 197–212, 331, 333–337, 346, 347, 356, 362–364, 371, 379, 382, 389, 399, 408, 417, 421, 427
Written reflection, 135, 139, 141, 142

Y

Year 7 Brunei Darussalam textbook curriculum, 14, 253, 291–302
Youth Self Report (YSR), 199, 201, 204–212, 421